THE HISTORY OF
US NAVAL
AIR POWER

The Authors

Robert L. Lawson retired as a senior chief photographer's mate (aircrewman) in 1977 after 26 years of naval service. During his association with the US Navy, he served as ship's company in four different aircraft-carriers and in 12 others on temporary photographic assignments. He considers himself fortunate in being able to work in the field of aviation for most of his career, which has enabled him to log nearly 4,500 hours flight time as a pilot and aerial photographer. During the course of his assignments he has flown in 77 different types of military aircraft. Following his retirement, Bob conceived and has edited *The Hook* magazine for the Tailhook Association, a non-profit organization for carrier aviation personnel and enthusiasts. Bob and his wife Sally reside in Bonita, California.

Ray Wagner is the author of many articles and books on aviation history, including *American Combat Planes, North American Sabre* and *German Combat Planes*. He edited the English language edition of the *Soviet Air Force in World War II*, and is a member and past Vice President of the American Aviation Historical Society. Ray has been teaching history in San Diego, California, since 1957, and earned his Master's degree at the University of Pennsylvania in 1955. Ray, a life-long aviation enthusiast, resides in San Diego with his wife Mary and their two children.

Barrett Tillman is an award-winning historian specializing in naval aviation. Born in Oregon in 1948, he learned to fly as a teenager and has over two dozen aircraft types recorded in his logbook, from vintage biplanes to military jets. His six operational histories of US naval aircraft earned him early recognition as perhaps the youngest commentator on military aviation in the United States. Barrett, an available bachelor, now works at the Champlin Fighter Museum in Mesa, Arizona, as historian and publisher, where he also serves as Executive Secretary of the American Fighter Aces Association. His outside writing includes such notable periodicals as *Soldier of Fortune* and *The Hook*, where he has been associate editor since 1981.

Commander David P. Erickson, USN, a veteran of 15 years in the US Navy, is presently Executive Officer of VT-21, an advanced training squadron at NAS Kingsville, Texas. He has accumulated over 3,500 flight hours, many of which were in the F-14A Tomcat. During the Vietnam war, Dave flew over 200 combat missions in the F-4J with Fighter Squadron 96, many of those missions over North Vietnam.

   In his current assignment he flies the TA-4J Skyhawk, training student pilots in all phases of flight, from instruments through air combat maneuvering and carrier qualifications. Dave has been selected for squadron command in 1985.

Captain William E. Scarborough, USN(Ret), was a career Naval Aviator who served 29 years in the Navy before his retirement in 1964. Bill, who started his naval career as an enlisted man in 1935, was selected for and completed flight training as an enlisted pilot (NAP) in 1939. He advanced to chief petty officer before being commissioned Lieutenant (JG) in 1942. During World War II, he flew PBY Catalinas and PV Venturas in the South Pacific. He was selected for a regular Navy commission in 1946 and subsequently served in a variety of sea- and shore-based assignments including command of Patrol Squadron Ten.

   Following retirement, Bill accepted a safety engineering position with Grumman Aircraft. After retiring from Grumman in 1977, he and his wife Sarah moved to Hilton Head Island, South Carolina, and have resided there since that time. Bill's writings are well known to aviation readers in the US.

THE HISTORY OF
US NAVAL
AIR POWER

Editor: Robert L. Lawson

The Military Press
New York

The Military Press
First English edition published by Temple Press
an imprint of Newnes Books 1985

All rights reserved.
This 1987 edition published by The Military Press
and distributed by Crown Publishers, Inc.
225 Park Avenue South
New York, New York 10003
hgfedcb

Printed and bound in Italy

Created and produced by Stan Morse
Aerospace Publishing Ltd
179 Dalling Road
London W6
England

© Copyright Aerospace Publishing Ltd 1985

Colour profiles © Pilot Press Ltd

All correspondence concerning the content of this volume
should be addressed to Aerospace Publishing Ltd. Trade
enquiries should be addressed to The Military Press,
225 Park Avenue South, New York, New York 10003.

ISBN: 0-517-414813

Editorial production
David Donald
Bob A. Munro
Trisha Palmer

Reprinted 1987

Acknowledgements

The authors are indebted to the following people for their co-operation, and especially for information and material which was frequently provided on short notice. Requests for interviews with Navy executives and offices were invariably arranged with minimum delay and were, without exception, conducted in a friendly and co-operative atmosphere, which assured maximum results with minimum interference of standard routine.

To these we are deeply indebted:
Vice Admiral R.F. Schoultz, USN, DCNO for Air Warfare
Rear Admiral W.E. Ramsey, USN, Director, Navy Space Systems
Mr Hal Andrews and Captain Dave Cowles, USN, NavAirSysCom Research and Advanced Technology
Mr Bob Thompson, (OP-50W)
Mr Roy Grossnick, Naval Aviation Historian
Mrs Gwen Smith, Naval Aviation History Office
Dr Wm J. Armstrong, Naval Air Systems Command Historian
Mr Domingo Cruz and JO1 David Kronenberger, CHINFO Still Photo Branch
personnel of the staff of the Navy Chief of information
personnel of the NavAirSysCom Public Affairs Office

Additionally, the editor would like to give special recognition and thanks to the following people for the generous giving of their time and technical knowledge in the preparation of this book:
Rear Admiral James D. 'Jig Dog' Ramage, USN(Ret), a product of the 'Fightin' Navy'
Captain Stephen T. Millikin, USN, a mentor without peer
Lieutenant Commander I.B. 'Pete' Clayton, USN, a 'blackshoe' friend with unsurpassable knowledge of aircraft-carriers
and the incomparable Robert A. Carlisle, Head Navy Department Still Photo Branch, whose help was there this time, as it has been so many times before.
Last, but certainly not least, a warm tribute to my wife Sally, whose long hours at the word processor are really what made this all happen.

Foreword

The history of US Naval Aviation is to some the most fascinating subject of military power. From the most humble of beginnings in 1911, the pioneer aviators of the Navy struggled with their balky wood-and-wire flying machines to develop within the next 30 years one of the most potent fighting forces in the history of the world. The new breed of naval officer with wings of gold upon his chest faced challenges with his superiors that were sometimes even more difficult than keeping his airplane flying.

Visionary men with such names as Ellyson, Whiting, Cunningham, Bellinger, Rodgers and Towers, sparked the flame and carried the torch that allowed the embryonic aviation branch of the Navy to grow by 1921 into the Bureau of Aeronautics. From its first Director of Naval Aviation, Captain Washington I. Chambers, to BuAer's first Chief, Rear Admiral William A. Moffett, Naval Aviation struggled for recognition and acceptance by its surface navy peers.

The greatest achievement by the early naval aviators was the development of the aircraft-carrier, the epitome of naval air power. In slightly more than 10 years from 'Spuds' Ellyson's first flight, the US Navy had its first carrier, the USS *Langley* (CV-1). The torch burned even more brightly borne by such pioneers of carrier aviation as Chevalier, Griffin, Mitscher and Pride, to name only a few. They lighted the way for the development of the USS *Lexington* and USS *Saratoga* in 1927, followed by an armada of carriers unlike anything ever imagined in their wildest dreams.

By mid-1942, Naval Aviation had firmly established itself as the Navy's dominant agency. The course was firmly set that has maintained the air arm's pre-eminence in the naval service as the manifest force for power projection and control of the seas.

It is with great humility that my associates and I attempt to bring the story of Naval Aviation to you. Our history is restricted by size limitations and therefore some subjects are necessarily treated lightly. Although mentioned, the stories of Marine Corps and Coast Guard Aviation are not told here. These are books unto their own. It is duly recognized that all facets of Naval Aviation have contributed to make naval air power the majestic force it is today.

Robert L. Lawson
Bonita, California
February 1984

This book is dedicated to that special breed of Naval Aviator, the carrier pilots and aircrew who have taken 'The Last Cut'. A special dedication is given to all of the POWs, the MIAs and KIAs of Vietnam. May God grant them peace.

CONTENTS

Foreword   5

Birth of a Fledgling   9
Ray Wagner

 1 Learning to Fly: 1911-17   10
 2 Hunting the U-boat   13
 3 Aircraft-carriers   16
 4 Navy Attack Planes   21
 5 Catapult Observation and Scout Planes   24
 6 Navy Fighters   26
 7 Patrol Planes   30
 8 Naval Aviation on the Eve of War   35

Naval Aviation in the Atlantic   39
Barrett Tillman

 9 The Not-so-neutral 'Neutrality Patrol'   40
10 Malta, 'Torch', 'Leader' and 'Dragoon'   41
11 The Hunter-Killers   47
12 Land-based Naval Aviation   49
13 The Coast Guard Contribution   53
14 Zebra Peter – the Blimps   55

'Go West, Young Man' The War in the Pacific   59
Barrett Tillman

15 "'Cause a PBY Don't Fly That High"   60
16 Year of Decision   61
17 Naval Aviation Training   71
18 The VP War   76
19 VOS; The Scouts   84
20 New Ships, New Planes   85
21 The Marianas and Beyond   89

Post-war to Vietnam – Time of Turbulence, Time of Progress

103

Robert L. Lawson

22 Peace and Demobilization	104
23 Korea – Another Carrier War	110
24 The New Planes	118
25 Research and Development, New Weapons	138
26 Post-World War	143

Vietnam – All for Naught

153

David P. Erickson, USN

27 Tonkin Gulf	154
28 The MiG Threat	155
29 Support Missions and Continuing Action	172
30 Bombing Halts and Politics	186
31 Tet and a New Year	195
32 Rumors of Peace	199

Contemporary Situations and Plans

203

Captain William E. Scarborough, USN(Ret.)

33 South-East Asia and after	204
34 Ship-based Aircraft Development	210
35 Shore-based Aircraft Development	228
36 Naval Air Power's Contribution to the Future	240

Index
251

Glossary & Designations Key
256

The early Naval Aviators were pioneers of the art, pushing the waterborne aircraft into prominence in the military spectrum. These two intrepid men sit upon a Curtiss AH-12 hydroplane, delivered in 1914.

Birth of a Fledgling

The story of Naval Air Power begins with the task of learning to fly in the frail aircraft of 1911-17. Next, World War I became a demanding school in which to learn the skills necessary to overcome the technical difficulties of developing the aircraft, powerplants, armament and equipment to fulfil the airmen's mission of anti-submarine warfare.

From 1919 to 1941, the US Navy was able to perfect the aircraft-carrier and airplanes required to meet its next greatest challenge, World War II. It was during this period that planes designed to attack their enemy's ships with bombs and torpedoes emerged. Fighter planes and tactics were developed that would lay the groundwork for the great task ahead. By 1941, Naval Aviation had just emerged from its cocoon and begun to spread its wings as the nation faced the danger of global war

1
Learning to Fly: 1911-17

The pilot of the Navy's first airplane sat in front, totally unprotected and clutching a steering wheel. Below him were the quiet waters of Lake Keuka in New York and that warm July of 1911 ushered in the beginning of American naval air operations.

Behind the pilot was the Curtiss biplane's power-plant, a 75-hp (56-kW) eight-cylinder engine, cooled by a water radiator and fueled from a 20-US gal (76-litre) tank. The 8-ft (2.44-in) propeller, also behind the pilot, pushed the machine some 45 mph (72 km/h).

This first Navy plane bore little resemblance to today's heavy, streamlined and very expensive aircraft. Its wings, built up on a spruce framework, were covered with linen fabric and tied together with six pairs of struts, metal wires and glue. The wings were 5 ft (1.52 m) wide and 5 ft (1.52 m) apart, and spanned 28 ft 8 in (8.74 m). This span became 37 ft (11.28 m) when the ailerons attached between the wings were included. These controls were attached to the back of the outer wing struts and controlled by a cable attached to the pilot's shoulders. Bamboo outriggers held the rudder and elevators, extending the length of the flimsy craft to 27 ft 8 in (8.43 m).

The whole machine was calculated to weigh 1,065 lb (483 kg) empty and about 1,575 lb (714 kg) when pilot, passenger, gas and oil were added. It floated on a pontoon measuring 16 ft (4.88 m) by 2 ft (0.61 m), and had small floats to keep the wingtips out of the water. For land take-offs, a pair of wheels was provided, and these could be lifted above the pontoon for water landings.

Glenn Curtiss had provided the Navy's first plane, finally overcoming official apathy with a series of practical demonstrations. Long before his first flight, the Navy had considered the possibility of fleet aviation, but had been awaiting the kind of progress Curtiss could show before investing its money.

Assistant Secretary of the Navy Theodore Roosevelt had, as early as 25 March 1898, suggested that Navy officers meet jointly with Army experts to examine Professor Langley's flying machine. At that time only a model existed, but the joint board reported on 29 April 1898 that flying machines could be used in wartime as a means of reconnaissance, communication between isolated stations, or as an engine of offense, dropping explosives into a camp or fortification.

All this interest had been stimulated by the Spanish-American War, but as soon as that brief adventure was over, the Navy decided to sit back and wait for aircraft to reach a practical level. No Navy money would be invested until the airplane

was proven to work.

Navy representatives did watch official demonstrations of the Army's first Wright biplane. However, Secretary of the Navy Victor A. Metcalf commented that 'this fragile and unreliable invention held no promise for the Navy'.

On 26 September 1909, nevertheless, Captain Washington Irving Chambers was delegated to handle all Navy correspondence on aviation, and although he lacked staff, funds or any authority but persuasion, Chambers was helped by the Navy's General Board (headed by the famous Admiral George Dewey) recommendation that the Navy consider using aircraft on its scouting vessels. Chambers got together with the salesmanship of Glenn Curtiss and a platform was built on the bow of light cruiser USS *Birmingham* (CL 2), anchored in Hampton Roads, Virginia. Curtiss had his demonstration pilot. Eugene Ely, fly his pusher biplane from the cruiser to the shore on 14 November 1919.

Encouraged by the world's first take-off from a ship, Curtiss wrote the Secretary of the Navy offering to train a pilot without charge. The officer chosen was 26-year-old Lieutenant Theodore G. 'Spuds' Ellyson who, on 23 December, was ordered to report to the camp Curtiss planned to open in San Diego, California. There, on North Island, then barren except for jackrabbits and sagebrush, the first American military aviation school would teach Ellyson, three Army officers and two civilians how to assemble, maintain and fly airplanes.

Chambers had arranged to have the armored cruiser USS *Pennsylvania* (ACR 4) provided with a 120-ft (36.6-m) wooden platform on the stern for a landing demonstration in San Francisco Bay. Stopping the plane after it hit the deck was a problem solved by Ellyson's suggestion: a series of 20 ropes strung athwartships weighted at the ends with sandbags. This primitive arresting gear worked fine when Eugene Ely landed his Curtiss on 18 January 1911; within the hour he took off from

Above: The A-1, the US Navy's first airplane on Lake Keuka in July 1911. Glenn Curtiss holds the control wheel, with Lieutenant T. G. Ellyson beside him.

Bottom left: Eugene Ely's Curtiss biplane on the scout cruiser *Birmingham*'s bow platform just before demonstrating the world's first take-off from a ship.

Below: A moment after take-off, on 14 November 1910, Ely dipped down into a wave but his Curtiss pusher regained altitude and made it to the Virginia shore.

Right: In the area of pilot training the US Navy realized the importance of having an adequate fleet of aircraft to process the large numbers of Navy aviators, hence an order for 50 Aeromarine Model 39-As and 150 Model 39-B (illustrated) two-bay trainers which could be configured for wheeled or floatplane operations.

Above: Naval Aviator Number One, Lieutenant 'Spuds' Ellyson, grips the wheel of a Curtiss pusher. The shoulder control by his right arm operated the ailerons.

Above right: Ropes weighted with sandbags served as arresting gear when Ely landed on *Pennsylvania*'s aft platform on 18 January 1911, the world's first landing on a ship. Ely was killed less than a year later while stunt flying.

Bottom right: Glenn Curtiss and his biplane are hoisted aboard the *Pennsylvania* by the ship's boat crane, proving that aircraft could be taken aboard ships.

Below: The Curtiss aviation camp on North Island, by San Diego Bay in 1911. Two imported Antoinette monoplanes and three Curtiss biplanes were available to train student aviators.

the *Pennsylvania* and flew back to shore.

Curtiss took another step forward on 26 January when, after overcoming difficulties in finding the right shape for his floats, he made the first successful flight from water in the United States. A Frenchman had made such a take-off in the previous year, but the Curtiss take-off from San Diego began a line of steady progress in naval seaplanes. On 17 February Curtiss taxied another of his hydroplanes over to *Pennsylvania*, now anchored in San Diego Bay, was hoisted aboard with his plane by the ship's boat crane, had tea with the captain, was hoisted back on the water, and went back to shore.

By now the Navy could see that airplanes could indeed operate from ships and on 4 March 1911 Congress granted $25,000 for Naval Aviation. By 8 May a contract for two Curtiss biplanes was begun, and eventually these were designated the A-1 and A-2. Ellyson, now Naval Aviator No. 1, went to Hammondsport, New York, where the Curtiss planes were being custom-built, one at a time.

Air and land developments

On 1 July 1911 the $5,500 A-1 made its first four flights from Lake Keuka, Glenn Curtiss piloting the first two and Ellyson the others. By that time, two more officers had begun flight training; Lieutenant John Rodgers reported to the Wright brothers in Dayton, Ohio, on 17 March and Lieutenant John H. Towers came to Hammondsport on 27 June. The Navy's second aircraft, the Curtiss A-2 trainer, with a 50-hp (37-kW) engine, was flown on 13 July. The third aircraft, the Wright B-1 biplane, was originally a landplane, but was modified to hydroplane configuration.

The Navy's first three planes and pilots were stationed at Annapolis, except for a few months at

San Diego in 1912, until a proper naval air station could be prepared. Experiments and training exercises proceeded, as catapults and wireless sets were tested, and more airplanes were purchased. The Navy's first flying-boat, the Curtiss C-1, was tested on 30 November 1912. In 1913, the aviation section participated in fleet maneuvers at Guantanamo, Cuba, and on 13 June, the Navy's first aviation fatality occured when Ensign William Billingsley was thrown from his Wright pusher 1,600 ft (490 m) above Chesapeake Bay; after that, safety belts were required.

The Navy got its first permanent air station when the Annapolis camp was broken up and all aviation personnel and equipment went aboard the battleship USS *Mississippi* (BB 23) which was ordered to Pensacola, Florida. The aviation unit arrived there on 20 January 1914 with seven aircraft and nine officers, and opened the naval air station that is still the Navy's largest aviation training station.

Birth of a Fledgling

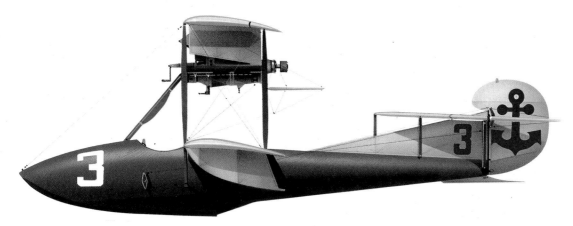

Left: The large '3' identifies this as the Curtiss AB-3 (formerly C-3); the 'A' designates Curtiss as the first manufacturer of aircraft for the Navy, and the 'B' identifies the aircraft as a flying-boat. This was the first US military aircraft to be used in operations against another country when Lieutenant (JG) P.N.L. Bellinger flew from *Mississippi* to look for mines in Vera Cruz harbour, Mexico, on 25 April 1914.

On 21 April 1914 *Mississippi*, carrying the Curtiss AH-3 hydroplane and AB-3 flying-boat, sailed for Vera Cruz, Mexico, to support the American intervention there. Lieutenant Patrick Bellinger flew these planes in the first Navy missions in support of a military operation, beginning 25 April, with the AB-3. On 6 May, after flying the AH-3, he discovered bullet holes in his rudder – the first combat damage to an American plane. At the same time *Birmingham* operated near Tampico, carrying three aircraft commanded by Lieutenant Towers, but this detachment saw no action.

The brief intervention over, the detachment returned to Pensacola to resume training. The old *Mississippi* was sold to Greece and replaced as naval aviation ship by the armored cruiser USS *North Carolina* (ACR 12). This was fitted with an aircraft catapult, used for the first time on 5 November 1915.

The most important aircraft development of this period was replacement of the pusher biplane with safer tractor hydroplanes with the crew in enclosed fuselages. Two of the last pushers built were the interesting swept-wing Burgess-Dunne biplanes. The most successful of the new tractor seaplanes was the Curtiss N-9, provided with a 100-hp (75-kW) engine and single pontoon under the fuselage. When 30 were ordered in August, 1916, for delivery between November 1916 and February 1917, it became the first Navy plane ordered into quantity production and became the standard training seaplane of World War I. Not until 8 January 1917 was a machine gun, a Benet-Mercie, tested on a Navy plane, the Burgess-Dunne AH-10.

Above: The first catapult launch from a warship was made by Lieutenant Commander H. C. Mustin from *North Carolina* with the Curtiss AB-2 flying-boat. The date was 5 November 1915, and the armored cruiser was in Pensacola Bay.

Above left: Lieutenant Ellyson flies a Curtiss pusher by the old armored cruiser *West Virginia* in San Diego Bay during 1911.

Left: A Curtiss N-9H trainer with a Hispano-Suiza engine on 24 November 1918. This type was the first US Navy plane in mass production.

Under the designation NC-TA, three Curtiss NC flying boats gathered at Trepassy Bay, Newfoundland for their transatlantic flight. NC-1 and NC-3 were both forced down in the sea with NC-1 sinking, but this aircraft, NC-4, completed the journey to the Azores. It then flew on to Lisbon and Plymouth.

Above: Firepower for the air Navy in 1918 is represented by this 0.3-in (7.7-mm) Lewis gun on a Scarff mount. The drum magazine held 97 rounds.

Right: Developed from the Curtiss *America,* this H-12 prototype, with 100-hp (75-kW) Curtiss engines, was the only twin-engine aircraft in the US Navy when the USA entered the war. Sisters with Rolls-Royce engines in British service had their first combat successes in May 1917.

Far right: Curtiss HS-2L flying boats with Liberty engines were the most widely used Navy aircraft during 1918. Three-seaters, they were armed with a Lewis gun and two 230-lb (104-kg) depth bombs.

2
Hunting the U-boat

Only three years after the A-1, Curtiss was completing the largest plane, so far attempted in the United States. His Model H *America* was the first twin-engine American plane, a flying-boat ordered by the wealthy merchant Rodman Wanamaker.

What Wanamaker wanted was a machine that could make the first transatlantic flight to win a handsome prize offered by a London newspaper. Two such flying-boats were ordered August 1913, and the first was ceremoniously launched on 22 June 1914. The crew proposed for the flight was to be Lieutenant John C. Porte, Royal Navy as pilot and Lieutenant John Towers, USN, as copilot. Two 90-hp (67-kW) Curtiss engines, a 74 ft (22.56 m) wing span, an enclosed crew compartment and 300 US gal (1136 litres) of fuel for an 1,100-mile (1770-

km) flight were planned.

The outbreak of World War I cancelled the expected flight, but on his return to the UK Porte persuaded his government to purchase both *America* prototypes, which were shipped abroad on 30 September 1914. The Royal Naval Air Service bought a few more as the Curtiss H-4, but installed British engines. A contract for 50 H-4s placed in March 1915 by the UK began the first American quantity production of a twin-engine plane. Along with British orders for 200 JN and R-2 landplanes, this caused Curtiss to move aircraft production from little Hammondsport to Buffalo, New York.

The H-4s proved useful for training and limited patrol work, and another order for a larger boat with 92 ft (28.04 m) wing span was placed. When the first arrived in England in July 1916, the 160-hp (119-kW) Curtiss engines proved inadequate and 275-hp (205-kW) Rolls-Royce Eagles were installed. These Curtiss H-12s began operations over the North Sea and became the first American-built

Right: Twin-engine H-16 flying boats carried five guns and four depth bombs. Number 836 (foreground) was built by Curtiss, while No. 3479 came from the Naval Aircraft Factory.

Birth of a Fledgling

planes used in combat.

A crew of four, a wireless set, two 230-lb (104-kg) depth charges and four Lewis guns were carried by each H-12, which had a 6-hour endurance and an 85 mph (137 km/h) top speed. On 14 May 1917 an H-12 sortied from Yarmouth to intercept a Zeppelin. It swept down below and alongside the cigar-shaped airship and with short bursts from the twin Lewis guns sent the Germans down into the sea in flames, the first victory by an American plane.

The most important task of the Curtiss boats, however, was to fight the submarine menace that by April 1917, when the USA entered the war, had reached unprecedented intensity. Indeed, so threatening was the U-boats' sinking of Allied ships, that the UK was left with only a three-week supply of grain on hand. The first American admiral sent to London, William S. Sims, was told that the Germans 'will win unless we can stop these losses . . .'

Curtiss H-12s, with British-built Felixstowe F.2s, did their best on anti-submarine patrols over the North Sea and the Channel. Beginning on 20 May 1917 several U-boats were attacked. However, post-war analysis confirms only one actual sinking by an H-12, the *UB-32* on 28 September 1917, the first U-boat sunk by an American, or any other, flying-boat.

US Navy participation in the war centred on fighting submarines, and American destroyers joined Allied operations less than a month after war was declared. It took months, however, before any Navy airplanes could actually operate overseas.

When the USA declared war on 6 April 1917, there was only one naval air station, Pensacola, and 54 Navy airplanes, all unarmed trainers. Not even a squadron organization for combat operations existed. In May, a joint Army-Navy Technical Board on aircraft was established, and on 25 May this board recommended an initial Navy production program: 300 school planes, 200 service seaplanes, 100 large seaplanes (flying-boats) and 100 'speed scouts', a type whose mission remained to be defined.

Curtiss flying-boats

For the training mission, the Navy already had in production the Curtiss N-9, and 560 would be delivered as the Navy's standard seaplane trainer of the war. For the service seaplane, Curtiss offered the R-6 two-seater with a 200-hp (149-kW) Curtiss engine and twin floats; 76 were on order. Only one large twin-engine flying-boat was on hand, an H-12, with the 200-hp (149-kW) Curtiss powerplant, delivered in March, 1917. The same engine was used on a single-engine prototype, the HS-1 flying-boat.

It was immediately apparent that a better power-plant would be needed for serious combat missions, and the Navy shared sponsorship of the United States Standard Aircraft Engine, the famous Liberty. The first of the 12-cylinder 360-hp (268-kW) model was installed on the HS-1. After successful flight tests, which began 21 October 1917, over 1,200 HS flying-boats were ordered, Curtiss to build 675 and the rest shared by five other firms. Deliveries of the HS-1L (L for Liberty engine) to the service began in March 1918 and the first

US Navy

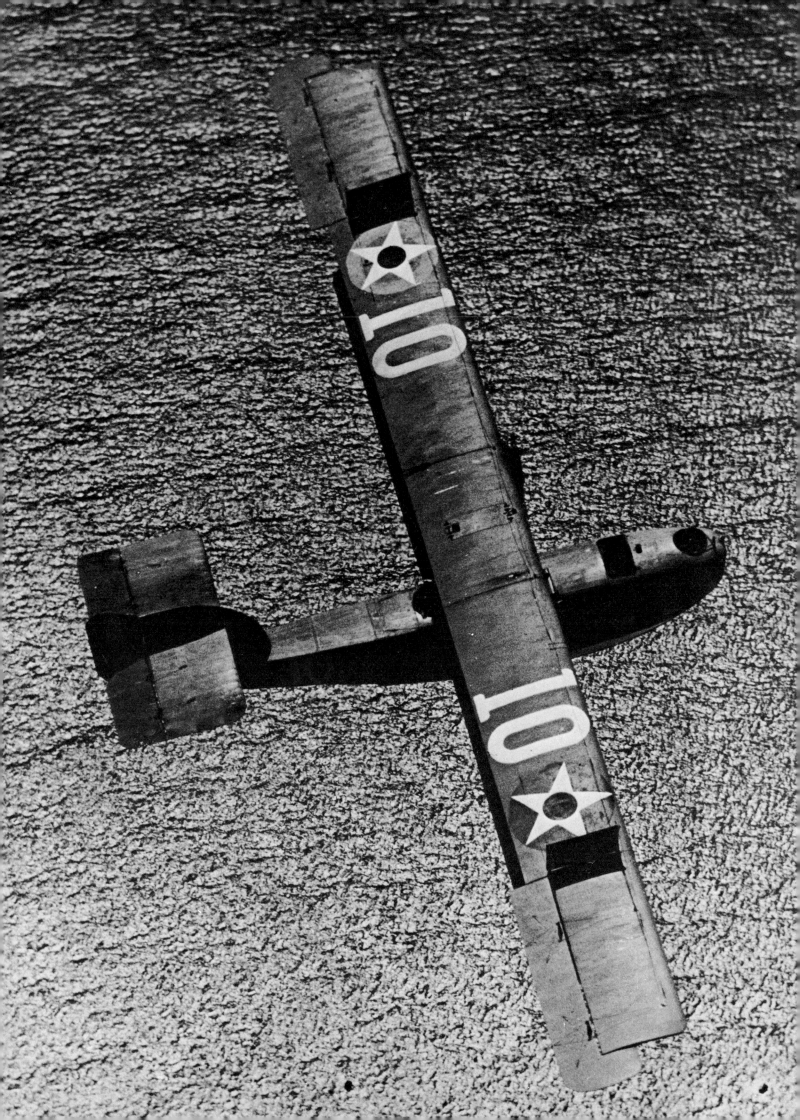

eight arrived in France on 24 May. Until then Navy pilots at air stations in France had had to use French flying-boats; their French instructors spoke no English and the students no French, so progress was uneven. Since the two depth charges carried by the HS-1 weighed only 180 lb (82 kg), larger wings were installed on the HS-2 so that two 230-lb (104-kg) weapons could be used.

Twin-engine flying-boats were needed and Curtiss began delivery in January 1918 of 19 H-12s with Liberty engines. More effective was the larger H-16, carrying four 230-lb (104-kg) depth charges and five Lewis guns. Curtiss built 124 H-16s and 150 more were made at the Naval Aircraft Factory in Philadelphia. A larger British design, the F-5L, followed the H-16.

Navy anti-submarine patrols made some 30 attacks against German submarines in 1918, but post-war studies have not confirmed that any were sunk by Navy aircraft alone. However, the 22,000 flights over submarine-infested waters did contribute to the safe arrival of every American convoy to Europe, and destroyers alerted by the airmen got the credit for several successful attacks.

By the war's end, the Navy had 2,107 airplanes on hand, along with 15 small airships and 212 balloons. Overseas air stations had grown to 27 in Western Europe, one in the Azores, two in Canada, and on the Panama Canal Zone, with 570 aircraft sent to overseas stations. Perhaps the most important result of the anti-submarine campaign was the rich heritage of technical experience, especially visible with the big multi-engine Navy/Curtiss NC boats, whose transatlantic crossing in 1919 became the Navy's first post-war spectacular.

3
Aircraft-carriers

Since the aircraft carrier joined the Navy after World War I, the Americans could profit from British experience. Americans thus avoided the wrong directions which earlier efforts had taken.

The first ship-based air attack came on Christmas Day 1914, when three British steamers lowered nine Short seaplanes into the water about 80 miles (130 km) off the German coast. Two of the twin-float, two-place biplanes were unable to lift off the

Above: The first American carrier, *Langley*, carried 34 planes, and taught the US Navy how to operate planes from a flight deck. Here she is seen in the Pacific in June 1927.

water, but the others dropped small bombs on Cuxhaven harbor and three returned to be hoisted aboard the seaplane carriers. Three other crews were recovered by a submarine and the last crew was interned. While no British airmen were lost, there was little damage to the Germans.

Rough waters limited more North Sea operations, but the calmer Aegean Sea brought the appearance of seaplane carriers in August 1915. Short seaplanes made the first successful torpedo plane attacks in history against Turkish supply vessels. Ship-based aircraft sank their first ships with 14-in (356-mm) torpedoes, and also hit land targets with 112-lb (51-kg) bombs.

Seaplane carriers were adopted by the Japanese and other foreign navies, but not by the United States. Not only did the carrier have to stop and hoist its seaplanes in and out of the water, but rough water often prevented take-offs, and the Royal Navy had not yet acquired catapults.

Possibly the most important disadvantage of the seaplane was the performance handicap imposed by the drag and weight of the floats. To take advantage of the better performance of wheeled aircraft, flying-off platforms were built over the bows of some 22 British light cruisers. On 21 August 1917 a Sopwith Pup from HMS *Yarmouth* flew off and shot down a Zeppelin for the world's first victory by a fighter launched from a ship's deck. Afterward, since there was no landing deck, the Pup made a controlled crash on the water so the pilot could be picked up.

The first true aircraft carrier was HMS *Furious*, converted from a battle-cruiser of peculiar design. It had only a bow fly-off deck when commissioned in

Left: This Aeromarine 39-B trainer made the first landing aboard *Langley* on 26 October 1922, after many tests on a wooden dummy deck ashore developed an elaborate system of axle hooks and a trailing hook. First US carrier landing was made by Lieutenant (JG) Guy de C. Chevalier.

Right: The call to US manufacturers to produce new designs for the war program was answered by the Lewis & Vought Corporation in the form of the VE-7, an advanced trainer which quickly gathered large orders. Wartime production did not materialize due to economies, but post-war production was on a large scale for the time; one hundred and twenty eight naval aircraft were produced. The aircraft's good performance enabled it to be used in several roles, such as this VE-7 standard two-seat trainer.

Above: This crowded hangar deck suggests why *Langley* was called the 'Covered Wagon'. Vought VE-7SFs of VF-2 and a DT-2 fuselage can be seen.

structure amidships, *Furious* looked strange, but could carry 12 Sopwith 2F.1 Camel fighters and eight Short seaplanes at cruiser speeds.

Seven Sopwith Camels from *Furious*, each armed with two 50-lb (23-kg) bombs, on 19 July 1918 attacked a German airship base and destroyed two Zeppelins. But since a safe way of landing aboard ship had not been perfected, the only way for the pilots to be recovered was to land on the water alongside *Furious* and be picked up. Two Camel pilots did come down alongside after the raid, but others found it more feasible to head for neutral Denmark.

The first really practical carrier was HMS *Argus*, converted from a liner and provided with a full-length flush deck that allowed safe take-offs and landings. Provided with a squadron of single-seat torpedo planes, it joined the fleet in October 1918, too late for action, but in time to demonstrate practical carrier operations.

All this experience was available to the United States when Congress, on 11 July 1919, appropriated funds to convert the collier *Jupiter* into the first American aircraft carrier. With the Navy turning to oil for its fuel, coal ships were less necessary and *Jupiter*'s plentiful storage space, electric-drive engines (the first in a Navy vessel when installed in

July 1917, for 10 aircraft carried in the hangar. In an effort to provide a safer way of recovering aircraft, the ship was sent back to the yards to get a landing platform and another hangar in the rear. By March 1918, with a deck on both ends and super-

Right: When commissioned in 1927, *Lexington* (CV 2) and her sistership, the *Saratoga* (CV 3), were the world's longest warships and had more speed and guns than most cruisers. Here the 33,000-ton *Lexington* moves thru the Panama Canal.

US Navy

1913) and its adaptability to a full-length wooden flight deck, made this ship a logical choice.

The ship was commissioned as the USS *Langley* (CV 1) on 20 March 1922 at Norfolk, Virginia, with a 11,050-ton displacement and capacity for 12 single-seat fighter spotter, 12 two-seat spotter and 10 torpedo planes. A single aircraft elevator raised the planes from the hangar to the 534 ft (162.75-m) flight deck.

Lieutenant Virgil C. Griffin became the first American to take off from a carrier, when on 17 October 1922 he flew off *Langley* in a Vought VE-7SF single-seater. After a series of successful experiments, *Langley* moved through the Panama Canal to join the Battle Fleet in the Pacific Ocean. With only 7,000 hp (5220 kW) *Langley* could manage only 15 kts, not enough to keep up with the battleships, and she had no anti-aircraft artillery at

first, with only four 5-in (127-mm) guns mounted for surface protection. The *Langley* was essentially an interim ship, necessary for test and training, but to be replaced in time by a true combat carrier. As the Flagship, Aircraft Squadrons, Battle Fleet, *Langley* operated out of San Diego for a dozen years beginning in December 1924. In 1937 CV 1 was converted to a seaplane tender and part of her flight deck was removed.

As *Langley* was being prepared for work, several events shaped the Navy's future. The Bureau of Aeronautics was begun 1 September 1921, with Rear Admiral William A. Moffett as Chief, giving Naval Aviation the sustained leadership it needed. During the previous July, a German battleship, cruiser and destroyer had been sunk by Army bombers in a series of tests to determine the vulnerability of ships to air attack. Army Air Service General William Mitchell asserted that air power's superiority over sea power meant that American coasts could be better defended by bomber squadrons than warships.

During the hot debate that followed, Navy aviation leaders were able to focus on the need for a strong Naval Aviation force and proposed conversion of two forthcoming battle cruisers into aircraft carriers. The new national administration that came into office with President Harding in 1921 was conservative, opposing President Wilson's international policies and horrified by the cost of the 'Navy Second to None' then being built. Secretary of State Charles E. Hughes called the Washington Conference on the Limitation of Armaments, which met just three years after the Armistice that ended World War I.

Aircraft carriers and air groups

These negotiations resulted in the 5:5:3 ratio of the United States, British and Japanese naval strength, limiting the size and the number of battleships. This first strategic armament limitation treaty allowed the UK and USA each 135,000 tons of aircraft-carriers, or enough for five 27,000-ton ships, while Japan could have 81,000 tons, or enough for three 27,000-ton carriers. The 27,000-

Right: Ninety planes could be carried on *Lexington* (CV-2) shown in 1927 with a Martin T3M torpedo plane leading the take-off.

Left: Boeing F2B-1 fighters and Martin T3M-1 torpedo planes, the latter with folding wings, fill *Saratoga*'s flight deck in about 1929.

US Navy

Left: Less than half the cost and size of her predecessors, *Ranger* (CV 4) was the first American ship designed entirely as an aircraft-carrier.

Birth of a Fledgling

ton size limit could be exceeded by two ships of 33,000 tons each; this clause had been inserted by the Americans to cover their conversion of the 'Lexington' class. While the total tonnage could not be exceeded, smaller vessels could be built to spread the tonnage quota over as many separate hulls as desired. Signing of the Washington Treaty on 6 February 1922 brought the huge capital-ship program to a halt. The battle-cruisers *Lexington* (CC-1) and *Saratoga* (CC 3), about one-third completed when the treaty was signed, were redesigned to replace their eight 16-in (406-mm) guns with a flight deck and hangar that could easily accommodate 90 aircraft. They were redesignated CV 2 and CV 3 respectively.

Commissioned on 16 November (CV 3) and 14 December 1927 (CV 2), these were the longest (888 ft/270.66 m) and most powerful (180,000 hp/134226 kW) warships in the world. Their speed of over 34 kts has not been surpassed by other conventional carriers since. Eight 8-in (203-mm) guns provided defense against hostile surface ships and a dozen 5-in (127-mm) anti-aircraft guns were carried.

Carrying a three-place torpedo plane squadron, a two-place scouting plane squadron, two single-seat fighter squadrons and a utility unit, and under men like Rear Admiral Joseph M. Reeves, Commander, Aircraft Squadrons, Battle Fleet, who developed new tactics to fit the ships, these vessels added a novel dimension to warfare at sea. Instead of hanging behind the line of battle with the supply ships, as *Langley* had to do, the new carriers could race ahead for a sudden strike at the target.

In January 1929, during the naval exercise called Fleet Problem IX, Admiral Reeves had *Saratoga* swing around to the south of the Panama Canal and launch 83 planes in a dawn strike that, in theory, 'destroyed' the locks and air bases in the Canal Zone. Army fighters completely failed to block the attack, but the carrier's vulnerability was also revealed when both big ships were theoretically sunk by both counterattacking aircraft and encounters with 'enemy' battleships.

Based at San Pedro, California, until 1940, the carriers gave many more demonstrations of carrier air power; one that should have taught a lesson was the surprise attack made during fleet maneuvers one Sunday morning. Rear Admiral Harry Yarnell brought his two big carriers north-east of Oahu and launched a predawn attack with 152 planes that caught the defenders completely unprepared; the date was 7 February 1932. However, the Navy was controlled by 'battleship admirals' who did not fully comprehend the true value of this new naval weapon, and the carriers were treated more as ships of the train than of the line. Along with the tenders

US Navy

and other logistic ships, the carriers were stationed at a respectful distance to the rear of the formation.

The most important difference between the fourth US carrier and her predecessors was the price; CV 2 had cost nearly $46 million and CV 3 nearly $44 million, but CV 4 was to cost not more than $19 million when authorized by the Congress in the last weeks of Mr Coolidge's presidency on 13 February 1929. President Hoover was in no hurry to begin construction, which did not start until 26 September 1931. As the first American ship designed from the keel up as an aircraft-carrier, the USS *Ranger* (CV 4) was a 14,500-ton vessel which could handle 86 planes, but had no provision for larger torpedo planes.

Ranger tested the choice of using a smaller carrier, which could give the Navy a larger number of the ships for the same tonnage. In a repeat of history, this same question became a source of controversy 40 years later. *Ranger* carried eight 5-in (127-mm) guns, and 53,500 hp (39895 kW) allowed the 769 ft (234.4 m) vessel to reach 29½ kts. Commissioned on 21 June 1934, *Ranger* went to San Diego in April 1935 and remained with the Pacific Fleet for nearly four years. In April 1939 she began more than five years of service in the Atlantic.

Franklin Roosevelt's interest in the Navy enabled the start of CV 5 and CV 6, the USS *Yorktown* and *Enterprise*, in 1934. These 19,900-ton sisters were of more efficient design, having three elevators to move their 90 planes. With 120,000 hp

Above: Grumman F3F-1 fighters of VF-4 on *Ranger*'s flight deck in 1938, as she follows the *Lexington* and *Saratoga* in the Pacific.

US Navy

Left: Last of the Washington Treaty carriers was *Wasp* (CV 7), whose size exactly met tonnage limits. When commissioned in April 1940, her air group included SBU-1 and SB2U-2 scouts, BG-1 dive-bombers and F3F-1 fighters.

Right: The red tail surfaces of this Curtiss SBC-3 of VS-5 signify assignment to *Yorktown* (CV 5), whilst the blue cowling and fuselage band denote that the aircraft is assigned to the leader of the third section of this squadron. Such markings were commonplace in the mid-to-late 1930s.

Above: Twin-engine Martin MT-1s, developed from a US Army bomber, were delivered in 1920 and served ashore with a US Marine squadron.

Above right: The first American torpedo plane was the Curtiss R-6L with a Liberty engine, shown testing its lightweight Mk VI torpedo in 1919. Top speed was 104 mph (167 km/h) and range 368 miles (592 km).

(89485 kW) the 809 ft (246.6 m) ships had a 34 kt speed and were armed with light 5-in (127-mm) guns. CV 5 was commissioned on 30 September 1937 and CV 6 on 12 May 1938, and by April 1939 both were with the Pacific Fleet.

Of 135,000 tons alloted by the Washington Treaty for carriers, CV 2 to CV 6 had used 120,300 tons, so the next, CV 7, was laid down as the 14,700-ton USS *Wasp* on 1 April 1936. She could handle as many aircraft as *Ranger*, but had a starboard-side island structure (similar to that of *Yorktown*) on her 741 ft (225.9 m) length, while 75,000-hp (55925-kW) turbines limited top speed to 29½ kts.

Up to this time Japanese aircraft-carrier construction had kept the same pace as American, although their six carriers were smaller than their American counterparts. On 21 December 1936, after militarists had gained control of its government, Japan abrogated the Washington Treaty. The invasion of China in July 1937 made the

decision for war manifest. Two 25,675-ton carriers were laid down, IJN *Shokaku* in December 1937 and *Zuikaku* in May 1938. Their completion in 1941 would provide the Japanese navy with the task force needed for the Hawaii operation.

In the United States, CV 8 was laid down 25 September 1939, during the first month of the war in Europe. The 20,000-ton USS *Hornet* was nearly identical to the 'Yorktown' class units. When the *Wasp* was commissioned 25 April 1940 and *Hornet* on 20 October 1941, the seven carriers that would fight the Navy's first year of World War II were on hand.

4
Navy Attack Planes

If Rear Admiral Bradley A. Fiske had had his way, the United States Navy would have been the first with attack planes. As early as July 1912 he had patented a system for carrying and releasing a torpedo from an aircraft. He proposed that 50 torpedo planes at each of the 10 principal naval districts would be important for defense, and that the problem of defending the most vulnerable American possession, the Philippines, should be handled by shore-based torpedo planes.

Admiral Fiske also suggested that New York could be defended by 100 'battleplanes' armed with guns of up to 3-in (76-mm) caliber, presumably the Davis recoilless weapon then being tested for aircraft use. Unfortunately, the progressive Fiske was replaced in 1915 by Rear Admiral William S.

Right: Husky Douglas DT-2 torpedo planes served at five US Navy shore stations in 1924. The familiar 420-hp (313-kW) Liberty engine allowed only 99.5 mph (160 km/h) with a 1,835-lb (832-kg) torpedo between the floats.

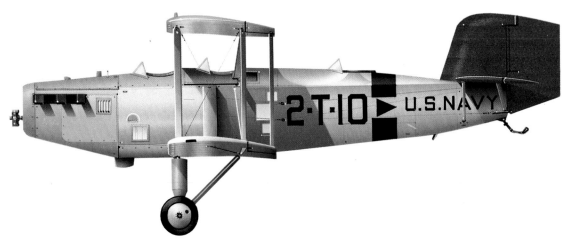

Left: One of 100 Martin T3M-2 aircraft which saw service with the US Navy between 1926 and 1932, this particular example displays the 1928 insignia of Torpedo Squadron VT-2. The basically similar T4M featured a radial engine in place of the T3M's inline unit.

Benson, the Navy's first chief of Naval Operations. A conservative approach would now characterize US Naval Aviation development during World War I, for Admiral Benson abolished the Office of the Director of Naval Aviation, leaving the fliers without strong leadership during the war. No aircraft available in 1917 could carry a torpedo large enough to damage a big warship, and no suitable aircraft was developed. As for the Davis gun-carrier, only two prototypes of the N-1 were ordered and they were not especially good.

Torpedo-plane attacks were begun by British pilots based on seaplane carriers in August 1915. They had two-place, twin-float Short biplanes carrying a torpedo or four 112-lb (51-kg) bombs, the weight of the former sometimes proving too much for the seaplanes to lift off the water. Nevertheless successful attacks were made against Turkish supply ships. Germany had shore-based torpedo squadrons, with no need to limit aircraft size, so twin-engine machines of higher performance could be used. When the carrier HMS *Argus* became available, the British could use the Sopwith Cuckoo, a single-seat torpedo plane with wheels and folding wings for flight deck operations.

US Navy use of the aerial torpedo was delayed until May 1919, when a 1,036-lb (470-kg) light-weight version of the Mk VI torpedo was tested with the Curtiss R-6L. This version was the old R-6 biplane re-engined with a 360-hp (268-kW) Liberty. With its pilot in the rear seat and no guns, it could carry this torpedo 368 miles (592 km).

The first Navy contract for new torpedo planes was placed on 30 September 1919, for 10 twin-engine Martin TM-1s, an Army bomber design modified to carry a 1,618-lb (734-kg) torpedo and four Lewis guns. Endurance was 5½ hours, and top speed 105 mph (169 km/h). Further use of such twin-engine airplanes with wheeled landing gear was discouraged by legislation giving the Army responsibility for all aircraft operating from land bases. The Martins were then turned over to the Marines.

With single-engine seaplanes needed as torpedo carriers, the Naval Aircraft Factory combined R-6 fuselages, HS-2 wings and Liberty engines to complete 33 PT-1 and PT-2 planes. Torpedo and Bombing Squadron One used them for the first large-scale torpedo practice on a live target. On 27 September 1922, 18 PTs attacked the battleship USS *Arkansas* (BB 33), which was running at full speed, and scored eight hits with dummy warheads.

New aircraft for new tasks

The first new Navy plane designed entirely for torpedo work was the Curtiss CT-1 of March 1921, a three-place, twin-float low-wing monoplane. Another twin-engine monoplane, the Stout ST-1, was flown in April 1922 with wheeled landing gear

US Navy

Left: Three-place torpedo biplanes were the pattern through 1924-35, including 100 of these Martin T3M-2s with a 710-hp (529-kW) water-cooled Packard engine. This VT-9 seaplane in 1928 launched its torpedo less than 50 ft (15 m) above the water.

and all-metal construction, but only one each of the CT-1 and ST-1 had been completed when the rest of the contracts were cancelled. The Navy even imported test examples of a single-seat biplane, the British Blackburn Swift, and the Dutch two-seat Fokker FT-1 monoplane.

The plane chosen for service operations was the first naval product of Douglas, the sturdy DT-2 biplane with a Liberty engine. Although the prototype was a single-seater delivered on 20 November 1921, 77 others were acquired as two-seaters with landing gear interchangeable from twin float to wheels as needed and folding wings for storage aboard ship. For the most part, the DT-2s served at shore stations with squadrons at Hampton Roads; San Diego; Cavite, Philippines; Coco Solo, Canal Zone and Pearl Harbor.

The next standard type was designed by the Navy itself as a three-place biplane for scouting, torpedo or bombing missions. The first prototypes were completed by Curtiss in November 1923 as the CS-1 with Wright inline engines. They had a 1,618-lb (734-kg) torpedo, a Lewis gun for defense, folding wings and interchangeable landing gear. Martin won the production order for 75 SC-1/2s and 124 T3M-1/2s.

When the *Lexington* appeared, the T3M-2s of VT-1B (Hampton Roads) were the first squadron

The Great Lakes BG-1 dive-bomber served Navy and Marine squadrons from 1934 to 1940.

Robert L. Lawson Collection

Above: The first scout-bombers, with a 500-lb (227-kg) bombload, joined the fleet in 1935. This Vought SBU-1 operated with VS-42 on the *Ranger* in 1940 during the Neutrality Patrol.

Above right: The first monoplane aboard American carriers was the Douglas TBD-1 torpedo-bomber. This VT-6 aircraft flew from *Enterprise* in November 1939.

aircraft aboard in December 1927, while VT-2B, from San Diego, went to the *Saratoga* in 1928. While shore-based torpedo seaplanes still operated at Hampton Roads, Coco Solo, Pearl Harbor and Cavite, they were reorganized as patrol squadrons in 1931.

The next development was the use of air-cooled Pratt & Whitney Hornets to power the Martin T4M-1 and Great Lakes TG-1 (1928-1930). Last of the torpedo biplanes was the TG-2 that served aboard the *Saratoga* from 1931 to 1937.

The next evolutionary step was the dive-bomber. This technique is generally credited to have originated with US Marines attacking guerrillas in Nicaragua. Navy fighter pilots were then trained to dive on ships with 116-lb (53-kg) bombs under the wings, and the success of this tactic led the Navy to develop a two-seat dive-bomber that could handle a 1,000-lb (454-kg) bomb. Martin built 33 BM-1/2s, which went into service with *Lexington* in October 1932. Great Lakes then built the BG-1, which went aboard *Ranger* in October 1934.

The first monoplane to go aboard the carriers was the Douglas TBD-1, with three seats under a sliding canopy and wheels retracting backwards into the folding wings. A 15-in (381-mm) 2,167-lb (983-kg) Mk XIII torpedo was carried, but the 'B' in the designation indicates provision for a Norden bomb sight when horizontal bombing with one 1,000-lb (454-kg) or two 500-lb (227-kg) bombs was desired. One 0.3-in (7.62-mm) fixed gun and one 0.3-in trainable gun were provided. The TBD-1 began to replace the TG-2 biplanes in October 1937, and equipped all four Pacific Fleet torpedo squadrons by 1939.

Top speed on torpedo planes had risen from 96 mph (154 km/h) on the PT-1 to 206 mph (332 km/h) on the TBD-1, but the attack mode remained the same: the torpedo had to be delivered at 80-ft (24-m) altitude at no more than 80 kt (92 mph/ 148 km/h) and released not more than 1,000 yards (915 m) from the target.

The scout-bomber classification had come aboard during November 1934, when the Vought SBU-1 biplanes, the last carrier planes with fixed landing gear, began to re-equip the three carrier scouting squadrons. They were joined in June 1937 by the Curtiss SBC-3 biplane, which also had a 500-lb (227-kg) bombload but had retractable wheels and, in December 1937, by the Vought SB2U-1 monoplane, carrying a 1,000-lb (454-kg) bomb. In April 1938 the new *Yorktown* got Northrop BT-1 monoplanes.

In 1939 the Navy and Marines had 16 squadrons

Right: The Northrop BT-1 dive-bomber, here flown from *Enterprise* by VB-6, was the predecessor of the SBD Dauntless.

of two-seat dive-bombers with six types of aircraft. The classic dive-bomber of the war, however, also existed in prototype form as the XBT-2. On 8 April 1939, Douglas got its first production contract for the SBD Dauntless, which by 1942 would replace all previous dive-bombers in squadron service. Carrying a 1,000-lb (454-kg) bomb and three machineguns, the SBD-1 was first flown 1 May 1940 and was soon serving with both Marine and Navy squadrons. It would become, for future historians, the most decisive single air weapon used in 1942.

Above: In May 1940, the first SBD-1 scout-bombers began rolling out of the Douglas factory, and by 1942 would replace all the older dive-bomber types in US Navy squadron service. Marine Bombing Squadron Two was first to get the new plane.

5
Catapult Observation and Scout Planes

Even before World War I the Navy wanted shipboard seaplanes to scout ahead of cruisers and spot gunfire for battleships. Catapults were developed to launch seaplanes, which were recovered by the ship's crane after landing on the water.

A fixed catapult had been installed on the stern of armored cruisers USS *North Carolina* (ACR 12) and *Huntington* (ACR 5). When the war began, *Huntington* did carry two R-6 floatplanes when it escorted a convoy to England. But the planes were not used and during October 1917, the catapult and all aviation gear were removed from both cruisers so that their normal operations would be unimpeded. This happened despite the fact that not a single US cruiser fired a shot during the war.

By 1921, Navy engineers had compressed-air turntable catapults which made it possible for warships to launch their seaplanes without changing course. Recovery, of course, still required slowing down to pick up the aircraft. Navy gunners now could count on aircraft to direct firing at over-the-horizon targets.

The first US battleship with 16-in (406-mm) guns, which had a 35,000-yards (32000 m) reach, was the USS *Maryland* (BB 46). For such weapons, fire-spotting aircraft were a necessity, so a catapult was installed on the quarterdeck. One floatplane sat on the catapult and another waited on a cradle nearby to be hoisted up by the stern crane. Later, a second catapult, with a third aircraft, was placed atop the third gun turret.

Routine shipboard catapult operations began 24 May 1922, when *Maryland* launched a Vought VE-7 biplane. Before long, every US battleship had catapults. Ten new 'Omaha' class light cruisers were commissioned in 1923-5, the first US Navy cruisers since 1908. Designed as fast scout ships, with a dozen 6-in (152-mm) guns, they had two catapults amidships, with a seaplane on each.

The first planes used aboard these ships were two-seat Vought VE-7H trainers fitted with a 150-hp (112-kW) water-cooled Wright-Hispano, large central pontoon and wingtip floats. A 200-hp (149-kW) air-cooled Wright radial powered the first Vought actually designed for shipboard use, the UO-1 two-seater without armament. Beginning in 1924, two or three of the UO-1s were carried on every battleship and light cruiser. Wheels could replace the wooden central float when needed.

At the same time, the Navy had purchased some shore-based observation types whose weight and power were not limited by catapult launch weights. Some were monoplanes, like the high-performance Loening two-seater on wheels, and the all-metal Martin MO-1 three-seater on twin floats. but with the decision to reserve land-based aircraft mainly for the Army, that line of development was discontinued. More successful were the Loening OL amphibian three-seaters used aboard battleships and shore stations. Eventully these were considered more as utility than as observation aircraft.

The Navy was quick to take advantage of the light weight and high power of the air-cooled radial engine and had sponsored development of the Pratt & Whitney Wasp engine. The first Navy plane designed around this powerplant, originally rated at 450 hp (336 kW) was the Vought O2U-1 two-seater biplane flown 2 November 1926. As the first Vought plane trade-named Corsair, it set new world's records for seaplane performance, and 131 were built for the Navy. They were armed with a 0.3-in (7.62-mm) gun fixed on the upper wing, another gun in the rear cockpit and underwing racks for four 116-lb (53-kg) bombs. The landing gear was interchangeable between the single central metal float and wheels.

In 1928 a Marine observation squadron, VO-7M, used O2U-1 landplanes in combat in Nicaragua, where they bombed and strafed a rebel force. One Marine pilot won the Medal of Honor for rescuing

Bottom left: A Loening OL-2 amphibian of VO-18 is launched from *California*'s turret catapult in 1927.

Below: An O2U-2 of VS-3B in August 1928 illustrates the wheeled configuration used when the Corsair operated from an aircraft-carrier.

Right: The first US Navy aircraft to be built around the famous Pratt & Whitney Wasp engine was the Vought O2U observation biplane, the first aircraft to carry the famous Corsair appellation. Service aircraft in the form of 130 O2U-1s began reaching the Navy in 1927 and could operate with a wheel chassis, or in the floatplane configuration with a single central float and wingtip stabilizers. By mid-1928 the O2U-1 was standard observation squadron equipment, as illustrated by this VO-4B aircraft.

Above: The most widely used floatplane was the Curtiss SOC, seen here on *West Virginia*'s catapult. This scoutplane would serve through World War II.

wounded marines from an isolated unit. The dive-bombing potential of these aircraft led to the use of Curtiss OC and O2C two-seaters as Marine aircraft, but Navy observation units continued with the improved Vought O3U-1 seaplane series.

In 1932, the S (for scouting) designation was revived and applied to wheeled two-seaters operated by carrier-based scouting or Marine observation squadrons. Most of these were also Vought Corsairs, but with heavier engines than the catapult models. This line of development led directly to the scout-bombers that entered service in 1935.

Catapult planes on cruisers

New heavy cruisers entering service in 1930 had two catapults on silos amidships as well as a hangar large enough to enclose four seaplanes with their wings folded. After much experimentation, the Curtiss SOC Seagull was chosen as the standard type; the original intention was to use an amphibian, but the weight limit imposed by the catapult launch discouraged that. Although catapults used gunpowder now, the SOC's weight was held to about 5,300 lb (2404 kg), limiting engine size and fuel capacity. An attempt to develop a more advanced seaplane, the Bellanca XSOE-1, failed because of excessive weight.

Easily convertible to landplanes, the 307 Seagulls built by 1939 carried two gun racks for two bombs or a depth charge. Slots and flaps reduced stalling speed to 57 mph (92 km/h) endurance was about 7 hours and top speed was 164 mph (264 km/h).

New cruisers finished after 1937 had their SOCs in a stern hangar with an elevator and crane to lift them on to a pair of quarterdeck catapults. How much the seaplanes increased the vision of a fleet commander was shown by this example from a contemporary source. When visibility was 5 miles (8 km), a single cruiser at 25 kts speed could cover an area 10 nautical miles (18.5 km) wide and 250 nautical miles (463 km) long in 10 hours; if four airplanes flying at 120 kts (138 mph/222 km/h) speed were added, an area 50 nautical miles (93 km) wide and 780 nautical miles (1445 km) was covered, increasing the search area from 2,500 to 39,000 square miles (6475 to 101000 km^2).

The SOC pilots were briefed by their ship's navigator before he climbed up to his catapult-mounted plane. A 5-in (127-mm) gunpowder charge shot the airplane down the 60-ft (18.3-m) track, accelerating it to 60 mph (97 km/h). After scouting about 200 miles (320 km) ahead of the cruiser, the seaplane landed in a slick made as the ship swung in a turn, taxied up to a rope net in the water and was then hoisted back on the ship's crane.

The last catapult plane to enter service before Pearl Harbor was the Vought OS2U-1 Kingfisher. Its observation-scout specification required a two-seat aircraft small enough, without the use of folding wings, to operate from battleships. With the same 36-ft (10.97-m) wing span limit seen on the SOC, O2U and O3U types, the OS2U-1 was an all-metal monoplane with a 450-hp (336-kW) Wasp and

Right: As the first monoplane to work from US Navy catapults, the Vought Kingfisher operated from battleships, but this OS2U-2 was attached to VS-5D4 at Cape May in December 1940, for inshore patrols.

improved performance. Even after protection for fuel tanks and crewmen was added to the OS2U-2 model, gross weight remained slightly less than that of the SOC. Going aboard battleships for the first time in August 1940, the Vought Kingfisher became the most famous American seaplane of the war.

Curtiss had designed an XSO3C-1 monoplane to replace the SOCs on cruisers. Using a new Ranger engine and with wings folding for hangar storage, this type was faster than the Kingfisher, but it turned out to be a failure after entering service in 1942. Fortunately, both the SOC and OS2U types performed splendid service during the war.

6
Navy Fighters

Naval fighters must do the same thing as fighters of any other service: they must destroy enemy aircraft. The big difference is that naval fighters are based on aircraft carriers, which means that certain difficult requirements must be met. The requirements include size limits, short take-off and landing runs, and arresting gear.

There were no Navy fighter squadrons in World War I, but a good two-seater triplane prototype was built by Curtiss in 1918 as a shore-based fighter, and pilot David Ingalls became the first Navy ace by flying with a Royal Air Force Sopwith Camel squadron.

After the war, a few Camel, Nieuport 28 and Hanriot single-seat biplanes were purchased by the Navy. Following a British example, wooden flying-off platforms were built on turrets of eight battleships. With the platforms pointed into the wind, the little fighters of that time could lift off the ship, attack enemy aircraft and then land at the nearest shore base, if one was handy. Otherwise, a forced landing at sea was necessary. On 9 March 1919, a Camel made the first such flight from the USS *Texas* (BB 35), but by the end of 1920 this technique was abandoned.

Two Navy fighter squadrons organized to prepare for the *Langley* had, for interim equipment, a single-seat version of the Vought VE-7 trainer. One of these, a VE-7SF, made the Navy's first carrier take-off on 17 October 1922.

In the meantime, a Navy fighter design called the TS (tractor single-seater) was prepared by the Bureau of Aeronautics in 1921, and Curtiss got the small production contract. Powered by a 200-hp

(149-kW) radial, the TS-1 weighed only 1,920 lb (871 kg) and did 125 mph (201 km/h) and its landing gear was interchangeable from wheels to twin floats. TS-1s were use by VF-1 and VF-2, both squadrons being stationed at NAS San Diego, to support the Battle Fleet.

Rivalry between two private companies for Navy fighter business began in 1925 with delivery of the Boeing FB-1 and Curtiss F6C-1 single-seaters with water-cooled Curtiss D-12 engines. These fighters and their improved models equipped five Navy and three Marine Corps squadrons in 1927.

These fighters could carry two machine-guns and add two 116-lb (53-kg) bombs below the wings. On 26 October 1926, VF-2 made the first fleet demonstration of dive-bombing. As battleships sailed out from San Pedro, Curtiss fighters dived almost vertically from 12,000 ft (3660 m) in a simulated attack. So successful was this tactic that the second single-seat squadron that went aboard the *Saratoga* and the second in the *Lexington* in 1928 were redesignated as bomber units. Later, two-seaters developed to carry larger bombs assumed the dive-bomber role.

The first Navy fighter with a supercharged engine was the Vought FU-1 single-seater, a version of the UO-1 observation plane. Fitted with a large central pontoon and wingtip floats, it was used by VF-2B in 1927 when that squadron operated from the fleet's battleship catapults.

Pratt & Whitney's Wasp radial engine, the

Above: The first way fighters went to sea with the US Navy was on platforms built on battleship turrets. This Hanriot HD-1 is aboard *Mississippi* in 1919. Once launched, there was no way the fighter could be recovered by the ships.

Left: The first fighter to operate from *Langley* (CV 1) was the Vought VE-7SF. The landing gear extension was provided to reduce damage from noseovers.

Above: Vought FU-1 seaplanes were operated by VF-2 from battleship catapults in 1927-8. Supercharged 220-hp (164-kW) engines gave them a 147-mph (237-km/h) speed.

Above right: Curtiss F6C-3 single-seaters were so good at dive-bombing with small bombs that this *Lexington* squadron was redesignated VB-1B.

R-1340, was this period's finest technical achievement and was tried in several fighter designs. It had its greatest success on Boeing single-seaters, which progressed from the F2B1-1 of 1927 through the F3B and F4B types and culminated in the F4B-4 of 1932. Popular with pilots and model builders, the colorful Boeing did 188 mph (303 km/h) with a 550-hp (410-kW) Wasp, had two 0.3-in (7.62-mm) guns and handled two 116-lb (53-kg) bombs or a 55-US gal (208-litre) drop tank.

One carrier fighter squadron had two-seaters when VF-1B got Curtiss F8C-4 Helldivers in 1930, carrying three guns and four 116-lb (53-kg) bombs. These were replaced in 1932, however, by single-seaters, so that there were then five Navy and two Marine fighter squadrons equipped with Boeings.

Retractable wheels and enclosed cockpits first reached Navy squadrons in 1933 when *Lexington*'s VF-5B was equipped with the first Grumman fighter, the two-place FF-1. At the same time, *Saratoga* got the Curtiss BFC-2 (originally F11C-2), single-seat bomber-fighters which could handle a 474-lb (215-kg) bomb under the fuselage. Another model, the BF2C-1, with retractable wheels, was the first fighter aboard *Ranger*. Export versions of this model were used in combat by the Chinese air force.

From biplanes to monoplanes

Navy fighter squadrons of the 1935-9 period were re-equipped entirely with Grumman single-seaters, all compact and deep-bodied biplanes. The first to enter service, in February 1935, was the 231-mph (372-km/h) F2F-1, which had survived competitive tests with experimental monoplanes by Boeing, Curtiss and Northrop. Although the Army Air Corps had shifted to monoplanes in 1934, the Navy continued getting biplanes until the last F3F-3 was delivered in May 1939.

The first monoplane fighter purchased in quantity for the Navy was the Brewster F2A-1. After 11 had been delivered by December 1939, the

Right: A 'razzle-dazzle' formation by a Grumman F2F-1 flight from *Lexington*'s VF-2B about 1939. This was the famed 'Flying Chiefs' squadron, composed mostly of enlisted pilots.

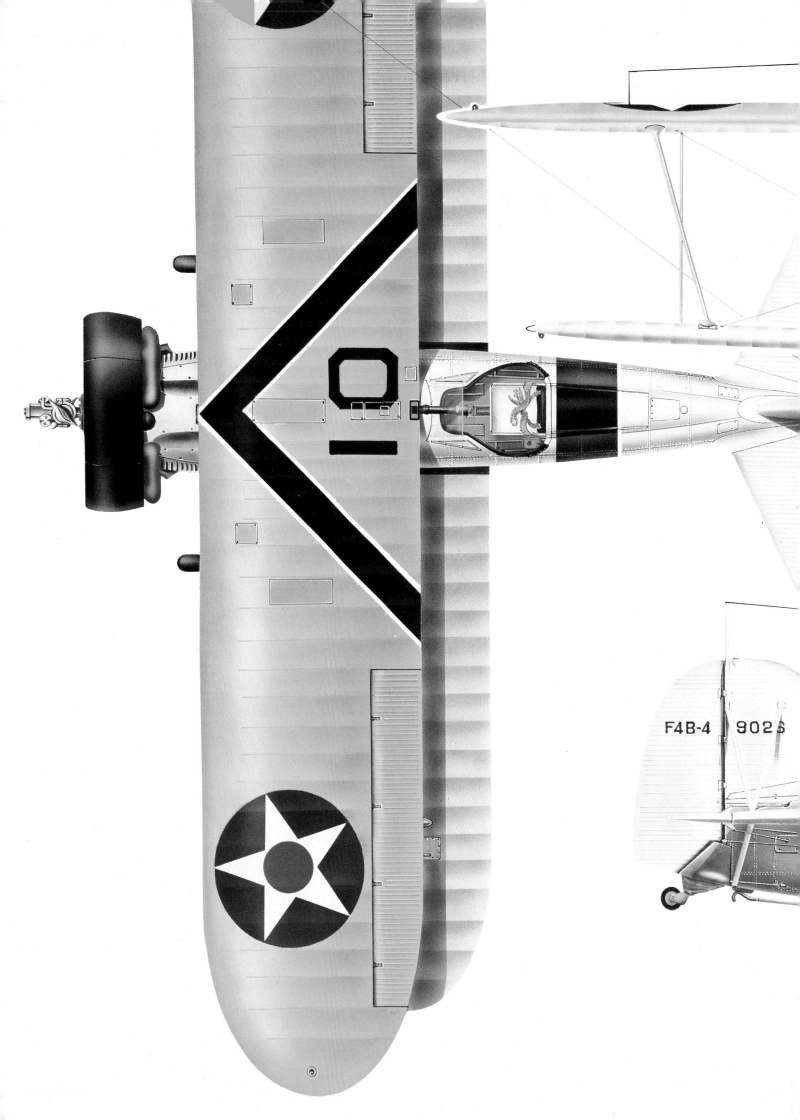

F4B-4 9025

Bearing the 'Felix the Cat' insignia of Navy Fighter Squadron VF-6B, this Boeing F4B-4 biplane was one of 200 or so which saw active service with the Navy between 1929 and 1938. Operating from *Saratoga* (CV 3) during 1935, it features the black upper wing chevron, engine cowling and fuselage band of the leader of No. 4 Section within the squadron, such markings being a distinctive and colourful feature of the Navy between the wars.

First flown on 3 February 1928, Boeing's Model 77 was adopted by the Navy as the F3B-1. 74 were built, serving with VF-2B on *Langley*, VB-2B on *Saratoga*, VF-3B and VB-1B on *Lexington*. Most of the F3B-1s were later modified with a drag-reducing Townend ring around the engine.

Featuring a hand-operated retractable undercarriage, the Curtiss BF2C-1 was the redesignation in 1934 of the F11C-3. 27 were produced and these served with VB-5 aboard *Ranger*. They served only a few months before being withdrawn due to difficulties with the landing gear.

Known as the 'Fifi', the FF-1 was the first in a long line of naval fighters from Grumman's 'Iron Works'. The Navy ordered 27 of this, their first fighter with retractable undercarriage, and all served with VF-5 on *Lexington* before being passed on to reserve units.

Deliveries of the Boeing F2B-1 were made initially on 30 January 1928 to two units based on *Saratoga*, VF-1B and VB-2B. Armament consisted of one 0.30-in and one 0.50-in forward-firing machine guns and power was provided by a Pratt and Whitney R-1340B of 425-hp (317-kW).

Built as a multi-purpose fighter, the Curtiss F8C-4 was known as the Helldiver to its crews as it was often employed in the dive-bombing role. These served with VF-1B before passing to the Marine Corps and finally to the reserve units.

Below: The second production F4F-3 Wildcat is tested in summer 1940. The prop spinner and cowl guns were deleted from the remaining ships on the contract. Yellow wings and silver fuselage were standard paint schemes of the period.

Right: This dazzlingly marked Brewster F2A-2 Buffalo of VF-2 'Flying Chiefs' aboard *Lexington* (CV 2) during March 1941 was one of 43 aircraft of the type which were delivered to the US Navy at the beginning of the 1940s.

Above: Formation flying was especially stressed in the early days as these BF2C-1s of VB-5B show near San Diego. Great pride and competition existed between the carrier squadrons of the day.

degraded their performance.

An even more advanced fighter had been tested as the XF4U-1, which reached 405 mph (652 km/h) on 2,000 hp (1491 kW). On 30 June 1941 the Navy ordered Vought to begin F4U-1 production and Grumman to build two XF6F-1 prototypes. As December 1941 approached, all the carrier fighter squadrons were equipped with monoplanes and the pattern of wartime fighter developmnt had been established.

7
Patrol Planes

'The principal function' of the patrol plane, stated a 1941 commentary, 'is to protect the United States fleet against surprise attack.'

At the end of World War I, most Navy aircraft were patrol planes, with lots of experience in watching for submarines, then the major danger of surprise. In 1921, 625 flying-boats were left and production of new service types to replace them did not resume until 1929: Navy contracts concentrated on ship-based fighter, observation and torpedo aircraft in the 1920s.

Nevertheless, there were important developmental efforts in this period, primarily at the Naval Aircraft Factory in Philadelphia. There, the PN prototype series improved the F-5L formula for a twin-engine biplane with open cockpits by better powerplants and more efficient construction. The series began with the PN-7 of 1924 with new wings and engines for the traditional hull. A metal hull was introduced on the PN-8, and the PN-9 followed with Packard engines.

Navy pilots were improving their skills at long-distance flying, but the task was difficult. While the Newfoundland to the Azores transatlantic flight of

rest went to Finland, while the US Navy awaited delivery in 1940-1 of new models with protected fuel tanks and cockpits. While the barrel-shaped Brewster Buffalo was not especially popular with US Navy and US Marine pilots, it was very successful fighting for the Finns against the Soviets.

In November 1940, a *Ranger* squadron became the first to get the famous Grumman Wildcat. The F4F-3 monoplane, armed with four 0.5-in (12.7-mm) wing guns, and fitted with pilot armor and wing racks for two 116-lb (53-kg) bombs, was an enormous improvement over the TS biplanes that went aboard *Langley* in January 1925. Powered by a 1,200-hp (895-kW) Wasp, the F4F-3 had a top speed of 330 mph (531 km/h) and weighed about 7,000 lb (3175 lb). The F4F-4 model on order had six 0.5-in (12.7-mm) guns, self-sealing fuel tanks and folding wings allowing more of the planes to be fitted aboard carriers. However, heavier weight

Right: The US Navy's first post-war flying-boat was the PN-7 with two 525-hp (391-kW) Wright engines, a top speed of 104 mph (167 km/h) and a 655-mile (1054-km) range. This VS-1 boat is seen flying 7 April 1925.

the Navy/Curtiss NC-4 in May 1919 was heroic, the fact remained that two of the three four-engine flying-boats came down on the water and were unable to complete their flights. When another pair of NC boats tried to fly from San Diego to the Canal Zone in December 1920, both were lost after forced landings. But all 12 twin-engine F-5Ls on the same mission succeeded after 18 days.

In May 1925, a PN-9 flight test demonstrated an endurance of 28 hours 35 minutes, which was thought to be enough to make the Navy's most sought-after long-range flight, the 2,200-mile (3540-km) hop from California to Hawaii. Commander John Rodgers (Naval Aviator No. 2) and his four-man crew took off from San Francisco on 31 August 1925, destined for Hawaii. A companion PN-9 was forced down only 300 miles (480 km) out, but Rodgers' boat went on against headwinds until it ran out of fuel and landed about 360 miles (580 km) short of Oahu. The airmen were credited with a 1,841-mile (2963-km) distance record, and demonstrated the seaworthiness of the hull by sailing the PN-9, using fabric from the wings, towards the islands for 10 days. The Hawaiian hop, it seemed, was not yet quite within the state of the art.

Refinement of the PN series, helped by the air-cooled engine, had proceeded to the PN-12, when the Navy contracted with four private companies to produce the twin-engine patrol 'boats. The first in service, beginning in June, 1929, was the Douglas PD-1. Powered by two 525-hp (391-kW) Wright Cyclones, the PD-1 carried two trainable guns, four 230-lb (104-kg) bombs, had a 121-mph (195-km/h) top speed and 1,300-mile (2092-km) range.

By 1932, 108 twin-engine Douglas, Martin, Keystone and Hall boats had been delivered for eight Navy patrol squadrons. Four squadrons were home-based at Pearl Harbor, two at Norfolk and two at Coco Solo, while aircraft tender vessels were available to provide mobility.

Reconnaissance dirigibles

Rigid lighter-than-air airships offered another opportunity for long-range reconnaissance, and in 1919 the Navy authorized construction of the ZR-1 (*Shenandoah*) by the Naval Aircraft Factory, and the ZR-2 (R 38) from the UK. The latter contract was inspired by the first east-to-west Atlantic flight of the R 34 from Scotland to New York. The airship had been aloft for 108 hours and such endurance had obvious naval utility.

An ominous portent of the future came in August 1921, when the R 38, under test before delivery to

the Navy, broke in two and crashed with the loss of 44 men. Perhaps British construction was too light; the Navy ordered a replacement, the ZR-3, from Germany's Zeppelin company in June 1922. The American ZR-1, first rigid airship to use helium rather than the inflammable hydrogen, was first flown 4 September 1923 and began operations with the fleet in the following August. But on 2 September 1925, *Shenandoah* was torn apart in a storm over Ohio and 14 men died.

In October 1924 the ZR-3, named *Los Angeles,* flew 5,000 miles (8050 km) from Germany to the airship station at NAS Lakehurst in 81 hours, and established a considerable reputation for reliability in the next eight years. Successful flights of the German-built ZR-3 and the appearance of the larger *Graf Zeppelin* passenger airship encouraged the order, in October 1928, of two giant rigid airships from the Goodyear Zeppelin Corporation in Akron, Ohio. USS *Akron* (ZRS-4) and *Macon* (ZRS-5) were to be the largest aircraft built in the United States, with eight engines each and a hangar for four single-seat biplanes to be used to extend the airship's scouting range. *Akron* made its first flight on 23 September 1931, and soon demonstrated its endurance and lifting capacity.

There was serious doubts about the usefulness of the big airships in the day of large carriers. Three days before its sistership was to make its first flight, *Akron* crashed in a storm on 4 April 1933, with 73 deaths, including Rear Admiral Moffett, Chief of the Bureau of Aeronautics. When *Macon* was lost in a storm on 12 February 1935, the Navy's rigid airship program was over. Fortunately, new long-range flying-boats now presented a practical alternative.

The task of building a patrol plane which could

Above: Douglas PD-1s, production versions of the PN series, entered service with VP-7 in San Diego in June 1929.

Left: In 1925, the PN-9 used Packard engines and greatly enhanced fuel capacity to attempt a flight to Oahu, but the effort proved beyond its reach.

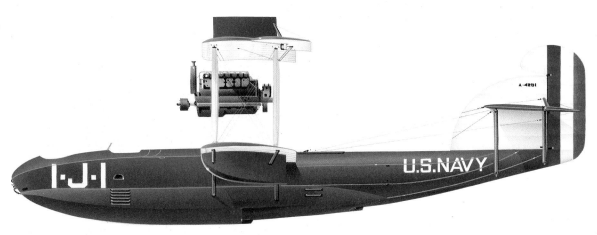

A-4291

Right: Improvements to the Curtiss H-12 and H-16 by Britain's Royal Navy led to adoption by the US Navy, which decided to manufacture the refined design. Designated F-5L, the aircraft were powered by the new Liberty engine, with this example manufactured by the Naval Aircraft Factory. The aircraft has received the post-war fitment of much larger vertical tails of new design.

Above: Patrol Squadron Ten got the first Consolidated P2Y-1 flying-boats in 1933 and flew these six from San Francisco to Pearl Harbor in January 1934 to establish new time and distance records.

safely fly nonstop to Hawaii, Alaska or the Canal Zone, or could go on across the Pacific from Hawaii to the Philippines, demanded a new technological level. An all-metal monoplane design was proposed by Navy engineers. Using the Navy's general lines, Consolidated Aircraft's I.M. Laddon designed the XPY-1, first flown 10 January 1929.

The fabric-covered metal-frame wing was erected on struts above an all-metal hull with five open cockpits. Two 450-hp (336-kW) Wasps and 1,021 US gal (3865 litres) of fuel provided a speed of 118 mph (190 km/h) and 2,620-mile (4216-km) maximum range. The Navy requested that provision be made for a third engine, above the wing, but this was later deleted.

Martin underbid Consolidated on the nine-plane production contract. These planes, known as the P3M-1 and P3M-2, went into service in 1931 with VP-10. Consolidated went ahead with an improved version, the P2Y-1, which had new engines, stream-

lined engine cowls and added a half-size lower wing supporting the outboard floats.

The first production P2Y-1 went to VP-10F in February 1933 and immediately opened new operational possibilities. The new planes were flown in formation to the Canal Zone and to San Diego, but the most important flight was by six VP-10F P2Y-1s from San Francisco to Pearl Harbor in January 1934. The 2,400-mile (3860-km) formation flight took 24 hours 35 minutes. Naval bases in Hawaii and California were now linked by patrol planes, and the Japanese were so impressed they bought a P2Y-1 of their own. Improved P2Y-2 and P2Y-3 versions soon entered service.

The most successful patrol plane of that period was the XP3Y-1 monoplane delivered in March 1935, the prototype of the famous Consolidated Catalina of World War II. Competing with a Douglas XP3D-1, the Consolidated design was the cleanest flying-boat yet built in the USA, with retractable wingtip floats and internal fuel tanks in the cantilever wing, uncluttered by external struts. An enclosed bow turret had a 0.3-in (7.62-mm) gun, while three other guns were mounted at twin waist hatches and a tunnel opening.

When Consolidated's new San Diego factory began deliveries in October 1936 to NAS San Diego on North Island across the bay, the new aircraft were designated PBY-1, the 'B' indicating provision for the Norden bomb sight in the bow and underwing racks for four bombs weighing up to 1,000 lb (454 kg) each. Another option was four depth charges or a pair of Mk XIII torpedoes. PBY-1 range was 2,115 miles (3405 km) normal and 4,042 miles (6505 km) with maximum fuel.

As soon as the new patrol bombers reached squad-

Right: The best known of all US Navy flying-boats was the Consolidated PBY-1. In June 1937, VP-3F flew these nonstop from San Diego to the Canal Zone, completing the 3,292-mile (5298-km) flight in 27 hours and 58 minutes.

Birth of a Fledgling

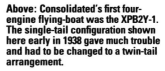

ron service, full squadron flights to the Canal Zone and Hawaii became matters of routine deployment. On 28 January 1937, for example, VP-6F's 12 new PBY-1s flew from San Diego to Pearl Harbor, covering 2,533 miles (4076 km) in 21 hours and 40 minutes. On 22 June, VP-3F flew from San Diego to Coco Solo, covering 3,292 miles (5298 km) in just under 28 hours. Patrol Wing One, with four squadrons, began making 48-plane mass flights in 1939. It was the best possible training for the future.

By June 1939 the Navy had received 208 PBYs, and one still in the factory was being completed as the XPBY-5A amphibian, a new configuration that would add enormous utility to the type. The Soviet Union had purchased the right to build the Consolidated flying-boat for its own navy. A single example was purchased by the British and, in July 1939, became the first military aircraft flight-delivered across the Atlantic. The RAF originally wanted the PBY only for tests, for a faster and more heavily-armed British twin-engine flying-boat, the Saro Lerwick, had been ordered into production. But after the war in Europe had begun, it was realized that the Lerwick had unsatisfactory flying qualities, and the RAF turned to the PBY Catalina as its standard twin-engine flying boat, while using the better-armed, four-engine Short Sunderland where enemy fighters might be encountered.

Improved performance and defensive armament were desired by the US Navy, and was obtained by doubling the power; four Wasp engines powered the Sikorky XPBS-1 flying-boat tested in 1937 with a 0.5-in (12.7-mm) tail-gun position. Consolidated's four-engine XPB2Y-1 in 1938 and Martin's twin-engine XPBM-1 of 1939 also had more advanced performance than the PBY could offer.

The disadvantage of these types was their cost and need for larger crews, and by 1939 only six PB2Y-2s and 20 PBM-1s were on order. The former cost three times more each than a PBY. The largest patrol bomber ever was the four-engine Martin XPB2M-1 ordered in 1938, with a 200-ft (60.96-m) wing span and five power-operated turrets, while Consolidated was developing a twin-engine private venture claimed to be the world's fastest flying-boat.

When war began in September 1939, the US Navy needed a lot of planes for the Neutrality Patrol, and since the primary mission was anti-submarine, early delivery and reliability of many units were more important than high performance. The largest single Navy contract since World War I was placed for 200 PBY-5s in December 1939. Consolidated received orders from the UK, Australia and Canada at about the same time, and by November 1940 was delivering PBYs to both the Navy and the Commonwealth countries.

The Navy had 224 PBY and P2Y flying-boats in its 19 patrol squadrons in 1939, serving five patrol wings. San Diego, Pearl Harbor, Coco Solo, Seattle and Norfolk were the bases for Patrol Wings 1 to 5 respectively. When World War II in Europe began, the first task was the organization of the Neutrality

Patrol to establish combined air and sea observation of the sea approaches to North America and the West Indies. Squadron redeployment began when a PBY squadron went to Guantanamo, Cuba, and another to San Juan, Puerto Rico. Another squadron, VP-21, took its PBY-4s to the Philippines as the first fleet aviation force there since 1932.

With each step that brought war closer to the United States, the work of patrol units expanded. In September 1940, a trade of 50 old 'four-piper' destroyers provided the Americans with a line of bases from Newfoundland to Jamaica. The Lend-Lease Act stimulated closer co-operation between American and British military and naval pilots, and 17 US Navy pilots experienced in PBY flying were, very quietly, assigned to help the British with their new Catalinas. Airborne radar, a British development, was first installed on a PBY in 1941 and gradually introduced aboard planes of Patrol Wing 7.

On 26 May 1941, the German battleship *Bismarck* was located by a British Catalina whose co-pilot was an American, Ensign Leonard B. Smith. The battleship was sunk on the next day, which was also the day President Roosevelt proclaimed an unlimited national emergency and ordered all defense forces to be in readiness to repel any acts of aggression directed towards the Western hemisphere. In August 1941 patrol planes operations began from Iceland.

New aircraft joined the patrol squadrons, the first being the Martin PBM-1 that came to Norfolk in September 1940. In October 1941 Consolidated delivered the first production PBY-5A amphibian and the Navy requisitioned 20 Lockheed Hudsons (PBO-1) from a British Lend-Lease contract. The long-standing policy barring the Navy from operational landplanes was ending. Few then could have predicted that someday the Navy's entire patrol force would consist entirely of Lockheed landplanes.

At this chapter's beginning, the patrol planes' principal function was to protect the fleet against surprise attack. On 7 December 1941, seven of the

Above: Consolidated's first four-engine flying-boat was the XPB2Y-1. The single-tail configuration shown here early in 1938 gave much trouble and had to be changed to a twin-tail arrangement.

Left: The first land-based US Navy patrol bombers were the Lockheed PBO-1 Hudsons obtained for VP-82 in October 1941 from a British contract. VP-82 operated these planes from Argentia, Newfoundland.

Right: Adoption of the Consolidated P2Y-1 patrol plane by the US Navy offered new operational horizons. This is one of six P2Y-1s operated by VP-10F on the unprecedented San Francisco to Pearl Harbor flight in January 1934, a distance of 2,400 miles (3860 km).

Right: Adoption of the Consolidated P2Y-1 patrol plane by the US Navy offered new operational horizons. This is one of six P2Y-1s operated by VP-10F on the unprecedented San Francisco to Pearl Harbor flight in January 1934, a distance of 2,400 miles (3860 km).

81 PBYs at Oahu were aloft and at 07.15, one pilot from VP-14 radioed he had attacked a submarine approaching Pearl Harbor. The first enemy bombs were dropped about 40 minutes later.

8
Naval Aviation on the Eve of War

Thirty years after Glenn Curtiss taught the first Naval Aviator to fly, the same San Diego Bay was used for regular take-offs by VP-13's four-engine Consolidated PB2Y-2s. Instead of 75 hp (50 kW) and 20 US gal (76 litres) of fuel, the 30-ton flying-boats had 4,800 hp (3579 kW) and a 4,400 US gal (16656 litres) of fuel while six 0.5-in (12.7-mm) guns and 12,000 lb (5443 kg) of bombs could also be carried.

Seldom had one generation seen such an advance in technical performance and power as that demonstrated by airplanes from 1911 to 1941. Herein are aircraft different from ships. Many ships 10 and even 20 years old fought well in 1942, but very seldom was an aircraft more than two years old of any combat value. Even the PB2Y-2 mentioned above lacked the armor and fuel tank protection essential for bombers.

The Two-Ocean Navy Act of July 1940 provided an enormous amount of money and authorized raising the Navy's aircraft strength from the 1,741 on hand to a 15,000-plane level. Now time, not money or technology, was the enemy. In Japan, the militarists recognized that they could never match such an American naval expansion and decided that if they were to attack at all, it must be before the new ships and aircraft were built. Only a surprise attack could be successful, it was realized, and

it must be made before the end of 1941.

The United States Pacific Fleet, so named on 1 February 1941, when Admiral Husband E. Kimmel became commander, had been based at Pearl Harbor since May 1940. Its 12 battleships were supported by the four big carriers: *Lexington*, *Saratoga*, *Enterprise* and *Yorktown*. These ships had among them four squadrons each of fighter and torpedo planes and eight squadrons of scout-bombers.

The United States Atlantic Fleet, commanded by Admiral Ernest J. King, was based at Norfolk, Virginia, and had the three oldest battleships and the two smallest carriers, *Ranger* and *Wasp*. Four fighter and four scout-bomber squadrons were aboard. The Atlantic Fleet also looked forward to the commissioning of the first escort carrier, the *Long Island* (AVG 1), whose VS-201 squadron would have 12 Curtiss SOC-3A two-seater biplanes and seven Brewster F2A-3 single-seat fighters.

The battleship was still considered the most important element of naval power, and few suspected that big-ship firepower was about to be replaced by the combined punch of carrier-based dive-bombers and torpedo planes. When the Atlantic Fleet needed strengthening, three battleships were shifted through the Canal, along with *Yorktown*, which left Pearl Harbor 20 April 1941 and arrived in Bermuda on 4 May.

Supplying aircraft to these ships was the Bureau of Aeronautics, whose chief since 1 June 1939, was Rear Admiral John H. Towers (Naval Aviator No. 3). There were 3,437 aircraft (1,774 combat) on hand on 1 July 1941 and enough contracts placed to double this total by July 1942, with plans to double it again by 1943. Expansion of the training organization and shore base establishment had to lead the way. On 1 October 1941, the popular names so familiar in press releases were officially established for all Navy aircraft.

US Navy

Right: In December 1940, the US Navy received its first Consolidated PB2Y-2, the most heavily-armed patrol bomber of that time. Here it sits in San Diego, with 1,000-lb (454-kg) bombs under the wings.

Birth of a Fledgling

Of the nine Navy and four Marine fighter squadrons in place by December 1941, all had Grumman F4F-3 Wildcats but two with F2A-3 Buffaloes (VF-2 in *Lexington* and VMF-221 at San Diego). The Marine fighter squadron was VMF-211 at MCAS Ewa on Oahu and on Wake Island.

Naval Aviation Organization status

Navy Wildcat squadrons in the Pacific were VF-3 and VF-6 on CV 3 and CV 6; note that squadron numbers followed the *Saratoga* and *Enterprise* hull numbers. On the Atlantic coast the fighter units were VF-41, -42, -5, -71 and -72 for *Ranger*, *Yorktown* and *Wasp*, while VF-8 was waiting for the newly-commissioned *Hornet*. The December inventory of the most recent fighter type was 344: 107 F2A-3, 176 F4F-3, 61 F4F-3A and five six-gun F4F-4 fighters were added by the year's end.

The largest (and slowest) carrier monoplanes on hand were 99 Douglas TBD-1 Devastators, most of them equipping five torpedo-bomber squadrons: VT-2, -3, -5, -6 and the *Hornet's* new VT-8. The weaknesses of the TBD type were becoming apparent, but a more powerful replacement, the Grumman TBF, was on order. Dive-bombers were the Navy's main punch, with 14 Navy and five Marine squadrons using scout-bomber equipment. Although the scouting (VS) and bombing (VB) squadrons were separately designated, both were being equipped with the new Douglas SBD Dauntless, so the distinction became unnecessary as their operations became virtually identical.

Paired with the hull numbers of their host carriers, the SBD-2 or SBD-3 units were VB-2 and VS-2, VB-3 and VS-3, VB-5 and VS-5, and VB-6 and VS-6. Vought SB2U-1 and SB2U-2 Vindicators served VS-41 and -42 in *Ranger*, as well as VS-71 and VS-72 in *Wasp*. *Hornet's* VB-8 and VS-8 at NAS Norfolk were working up with Curtiss SBC-4 biplanes.

Dive-bombers were also operated by the Marine shore-based establishment. Marine Air Group Eleven at MCAS Quantico, Virginia, had VMSB-131, VMSB-132 and VMO-151 with SBD-1, SB2U-3 and SBC-4 types respectively. Marine Air Group Twenty-One at Ewa had VMSB-231 with the SB2U-3 and VMSB-232 with SBD-1.

Carrier-based dive-bomber aircraft would include 290 SBDs by the year's end, while older types available included 146 SB2Us and 117 SBC-4 biplanes; fortunately, the older machines would seldom be needed in combat. Shipboard aircraft also included some 250 SOC/SON biplanes and 290 O2U monoplanes, most of these fitted as floatplanes under the command of their host battleships and cruisers. While these aircraft were organized into squadrons for administrative purposes, they operated as individual ship planes.

Navy patrol bombers were deployed among 25

squadrons in December 1941. Hawaii had Patrol Wing One at NAS Kaneohe, with 36 PBY-5s in VP-11, -12 and -14, while Patrol Wing Two on Ford Island at Pearl Harbor had 27 PBY-3s in VP-21 and -22, and 18 PBY-5s in VP-23 and -24. Commanding these flying-boats was Rear Admiral P. (Pat) Bellinger, the pilot who had been shot at while over Vera Cruz in 1914.

At Cavite in the Philippines, 28 PBY-4s of Patrol Wing Ten served VP-101 and -102. The West Coast was covered by Patrol Wing Four at Seattle, controlling 24 PBY-5s of VP-41, -42, -43 and -44, while in San Diego the transitional training squadron, VP-13, had four PB2Y-2s and five PBYs and was awaiting new PBY-5A amphibians.

Patrol Wing Three, from Coco Solo, covered the Canal with 11 PBY-5 and 13 PBY-3 boats of VP-31 and -32. The Atlantic coast had Patrol Wing Five at Norfolk with 26 PBY-5s in VP-51 and -52, and a transitional training squadron. Patrol Wing Seven operated from advanced bases in Newfoundland, Iceland and Bermuda with 36 PBY-5s of VP-71, -72 and -73 and the 13 PBM-1s of VP-74. The newest organization was Patrol Wing Eight, which had one squadron each of PBYs (VP-81), PBO-1 Hudson landplanes (VP-82) and the first new PBY-5A amphibians (VP-83). The latter type was also scheduled for VP-91 commissioned 1 December 1941.

Even more impressive than the aircraft deployed among the 67 carrier-based patrol and Marine tactical squadrons was the mass of aircraft on order for delivery in the next two years. The Vought F4U-1 fighters, Curtiss SB2C-1 dive-bombers, Grumman TBF-1 torpedo planes, and the Martin PBM-3 and Consolidated PB2Y-3 patrol bombers on order promised an air power beyond that ever sent to sea by any nation.

Thirty years after the beginning of American Naval Aviation, it had become the world's strongest naval air force. The shock of enemy attack would soon show weaknesses, as well as strengths, but the pioneers of the air navy could take a justified pride in their accomplishments.

William E. Scarborough

Above: Eleven of the 13 US Navy and US Marine fighter squadrons in 1941 used Grumman F4F-3 Wildcats like this one from *Wasp's* VF-71 at Norfolk.

Right: Vought OS2U-1 Kingfishers from *Mississippi* flying, for the time being, without their floats.

Left: Last of the biplane scout-bombers was the Curtiss SBC-4. Production was completed in May 1941, and this one was flown by Naval Reserve Air Base New York.

Bombing Squadron 4 SBD-5s aboard *Ranger*. Operating with the British Home Fleet, *Ranger* launched Dauntlesses, Avengers and Wildcats against Axis shipping near Bodo, Norway in Operation 'Leader'.

Naval Aviation
in the Atlantic

Naval Aviation has fought two Battles of the Atlantic: 1917-8 and 1941-5. In those 28 years, enormous growth and technical advancement were achieved, but some patterns were repeated. In 1917, US Naval Aviation consisted of one air station, four dozen pilots and perhaps 50 aircraft. Under press of wartime demand, planes and aircrews were increased by orders of magnitude; extensive new bases were built (Europe, the Azores and Central America) and combat operations were directed primarily against the U-boat.

Beginning in 1941, well before Pearl Harbor, history repeated itself; extensive new bases were constructed in Europe, Africa and Latin America. Once again, combat operations were directed primarily against the U-boat. The main difference the second time around was the tiny escort carrier and her hunter-killer teams of Wildcats and Avengers. These carriers, teamed with their land-based patrol bomber brethren and the plodding, silvery blimps, reversed the U-boat threat, so keeping the sea-lanes open and enabling the unintercepted flow of materials and men that were necessary to bring ultimate victory in Europe.

9
The Not-so-Neutral 'Neutrality Patrol'

World War II began in Europe with Germany's invasion of Poland on 1 September 1939. Four days later President Roosevelt issued a declaration affirming US neutrality and the nation's intent to enforce that stance. It was both inaccurate and optimistic, for the president was strongly pro-British and American military strength was ill-prepared for war, but such a policy was required for political reasons.

The Navy was ordered to establish the Neutrality Patrol to 300 nautical miles (345 statute miles/ 556 km) off the US east coast, running southwards along the boundary of the Caribbean. Any foreign warships entering the zone were to be reported immediately.

On paper, a reasonably imposing force was available to 'enforce' the patrol: four battleships, five cruisers, 40-odd destroyers and two aircraft-carriers (the USS *Ranger* and *Wasp*) were active in the region. However, the bulk of actual patrol work would be conducted by five flying-boat squadrons supported by four tenders. In all, 36 Consolidated PBYs and 18 older Consolidated P2Ys were based at Newport, Rhode Island; Norfolk, Virginia; and in Cuba and Puerto Rico. Detachments were also sent to Charleston, South Carolina, and Key West, Florida.

In 1940 two patrol squadrons were commissioned at Norfolk, and before the year's end Admiral Ernest J. King became Commander Patrol Force. King later figured prominently in America's wartime hierarchy as Chief of Naval Operations.

A contingency organization, the Support Force Atlantic Fleet, was established in March 1941 with destroyers and a five-squadron patrol wing. Directed to prepare for operations in northern waters, the patrol crews practised convoy escort and anti-submarine warfare. The intent was to prevent German commerce raiders and U-boats from interrupting USA-UK shipping routes.

Elements of VP-52 arrived at Argentia, Newfoundland, in mid-May 1941 with the tender USS *Albemarle* (AV 5). The conditions were wretched: horrible weather, poor communications and few facilities. On 24 May, just six days after the PBYs arrived, came news that the German battleship *Bismarck* had sunk HMS *Hood* in the Denmark Strait between Iceland and Greenland. Eleven of

VP-52's PBYs took off to search for the raider but became lost and scattered. It was days before they all returned to Argentia.

Bismarck had turned south east after her victory over the British battle-cruiser but could not elude detection much longer. And Americans were actively involved in finding her.

Co-operation with the RAF

Seventeen PBY pilots had been sent to the UK in April to instruct Royal Air Force Coastal Command in Catalina operations. The effectiveness of some 'instructors' was openly doubted by the fliers themselves, as some were fresh-caught ensigns with only 30 hours in type.

Nevertheless, the Navy pilots began flying search missions with Coastal Command squadrons. One such was Ensign Leonard B. Smith, assigned to No. 209 Squadron at Lough Erne, Northern Ireland. Upon news of *Hood*'s loss, Smith found himself airborne on his second mission with the RAF, flying with the crew of Pilot Officer Briggs.

Arriving in the search area eight hours after take-off, 'Tuck' Smith looked ahead and slightly to starboard. He hardly believed his eyes: there, perhaps 5 miles (8 km) away, was a battleship. Slipping in closer for visual confirmation at 2,800 ft (855 m) the Catalina was spotted and all doubt as to the battleship's identity was removed when she opened accurate fire at the flying-boat. Smith stood the PBY on a wingtip, scooting back for the safety of nearby clouds.

Smith and Briggs' crew tracked *Bismarck* for the next four hours, awaiting relief. Each of the next two Catalinas to arrive on station also had a US Navy pilot aboard. When the British battleship/ cruiser force caught and destroyed *Bismarck* at virtually the last moment, naval airpower received a big boost. Flying-boat patrol planes had found the

Above: Much of the Neutrality Patrol was conducted by PBY-5s such as this flying boat from Patrol Squadron 44. The official intent was to watch for hostile action in American waters before the US entry into World War II, but in fact was as much a guise for US aid to Britain.

Left: America was ill-prepared even for the passive role of coastal watchdog in 1940-1. Several Neutrality Patrol squadrons flew obsolete aircraft such as this Consolidated P2Y-2 of VP-52 at Charleston, North Carolina.

courtesy Bruce van Alstine

Above: The Navy's first F4F-3 fighters joined the fleet with VF-4 in November 1940. Similarly identified with the neutrality star, Wasp's VF-72 Wildcats rest at Bourne Field, Virgin Islands.

raider and carrier-based torpedo bombers had slowed her down.

Anglo-American co-operation continued that summer as six new Martin PBM Mariners of VP-74 and six PBY-5s of VP-73 moved to Skerja Fjord in Iceland during August. Though supported by the tender USS Goldsborough (APD 32), the patrol 'boats also used RAF moorings. Spartan accommodation and facilities rendered Iceland a difficult duty post, but the patrol range was considerably extended. In October four Catalinas also deployed to Greenland for three weeks.

Three aircraft-carriers participated in the Neutrality Patrol, operating from Norfolk, Virginia, most of the time. Ranger, Wasp and Yorktown made periodic sorties into the Atlantic and Caribbean, but in truth these were more training exercises for various squadrons than anything else. In

fact, Wasp was at sea on 7 December with Yorktown's fighter squadron VF-5 aboard. Yorktown was rushed to the Pacific, and VF-5 did not catch up with its parent air group for over six months. It was just one of many long-term effects of the Neutrality Patrol.

But now the USA was no longer neutral.

10
Malta, 'Torch,' 'Leader' and 'Dragoon'

The Pacific war naturally captured the public's attention for aircraft-carrier operations. But American 'flat tops' were active in the European-African theater from an early date, and not solely on anti-submarine patrol.

First into the European war was Wasp, which left the US east coast in late March 1942 and arrived at the Royal Navy anchorage at Scapa Flow on 4 April. Loading 47 Supermarine Spitfires to reinforce the Mediterranean island of Malta, Wasp conducted her first delivery on 20 April: she flew off a combat air patrol of Grumman F4F Wildcats, then launched the British fighters when within range of the island; Wasp returned to Scapa Flow six days later.

But Malta's garrison air force suffered high attrition, especially from continual Axis bombing. A

US Navy

Right: USS Wasp (CV 7) made two ferry runs to Malta, reinforcing the RAF fighter strength on that beleaguered island. Here Spitfires share the deck with Wildcats on 19 April 1942.

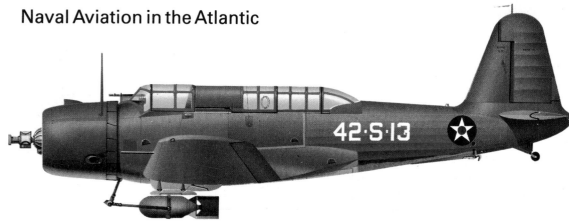

US Navy

Left: Assigned to VS-42 on *Ranger* (CV 4), this Vought SB2U-2 Vindicator features non-specular blue grey upper surfaces, these being extended to encompass the undersides of the folding wing surfaces. Note also the unusual extending bomb crutch.

US Navy

second reinforcement trip began on 2 May with 47 more Spitfires flown off on 9 May. It was this cruise which prompted Prime Minister Winston Churchill's quip, 'Who said a wasp can't sting twice?' The carrier returned to the USA almost immediately, preparing for deployment to the Pacific where she would meet her fate off Guadalcanal.

Ranger also ferried fighter aircraft to distant shores, but they were USAAF Curtiss P-40s instead of RAF Spitfires. She delivered 68 Warhawks to Africa's Gold Coast in April and made a second run in June.

Shortly thereafter, *Ranger* embarked her air group and began work-ups for the most ambitious naval operation yet conducted in the European-African theater. Simultaneous Anglo-American amphibious landings were scheduled for Morocco and Algeria in early November 1942 as Operation 'Torch'.

Supporting the American effort were four carriers operating in three task groups. Their combined strength numbered 62 bombers (Douglas SBD-3s and Grumman TBF-1s) plus 109 F4Fs. Battleship- and cruiser-based floatplanes also contributed scout-observation and rescue capability to the task force's air arm.

The US landings were centered upon Casablanca, with additional beaches to the north and south. *Ranger* and the escort carrier USS *Suwanee* (ACV 27) steamed off Casablanca while the USS *Sangamon* (ACV 26) and *Santee* (ACV 29) operated off the northern and southern areas, respectively. (Escort carriers were redesignated CVE on 15 July 1943.)

The overall aviator experience level was low; average flight time in one F4F squadron amounted to a mere 400 hours. However, VF-4 in *Ranger* had been the original Wildcat unit, and Lieutenant Commander Tommy Booth's pilots generally had 500 hours or more in F4Fs alone. But the task force

Above: Operation 'Torch' was the first Anglo-American offensive undertaking of the war. Four US carriers, including *Ranger*, supported the amphibious invasion of Morocco, held by Vichy French forces. Here a VF-9 F4F-4 prepares for launch, with tie-down rope still dangling from the port bomb rack! US Army L-4s circle overhead.

Above left: Cruiser-launched floatplanes provided numerous support missions during the three-day operation in November 1942. Here a cruiser-based SOC launches on a 'Torch' spotting mission.

US Navy

Left: SBDs and F4Fs crowd the deck of an escort carrier during 'Torch'. Note the impromptu 'signposts' painted on the deck, showing the distance to home. Other nonstandard markings include yellow rings around fuselage insignia.

Right: Embarked aboard USS *Ranger* (CV 4) in November 1942, this VS-41 Douglas SBD-3 Dauntless was employed in support of the Allied landings in North Africa. The yellow outline to the national marking was applied to all Navy aircraft engaged in operations in this theatre.

Above: USS *Chenango* (ACV 28) delivered 60 P-40 Warhawks of the US Army Air Force to Morocco; yet another employment of the versatile, hard-working little 'jeep carriers'.

had been assembled and dispatched so fast that there had been almost no opportunity to practise, and some pilots had not flown in two weeks.

The big question, however, was not the fliers' experience but enemy reaction. Morocco was garrisoned by Vichy French forces, technically guarding unoccupied French territory from invasion. Opinion was divided as to whether or not the Vichy French would oppose the American landings; there was no doubt they would fight the British.

French naval and air force squadrons amounted to almost 200 planes, including many American-built Martin and Douglas bombers and Curtiss fighters. Many of the Vichy French pilots were combat veterans of the Battle of France, now obliged to fight the very men who had come to begin the liberation of France. For further irony, one of the French fighter units traced its ancestry to the *Escadrille Lafayette*, the squadron of American volunteer aviators in World War I.

The landings began at dawn on 8 November. But in the hope of avoiding conflict, American fliers

were specifically forbidden to shoot unless fired upon. The radio call sign for French opposition was 'Batter up'. The task force would then authorize return fire by calling 'Play ball'.

The game began poorly. A flight of seven *Santee* fighters became disoriented and ran low on fuel. One ditched at sea and five crash-landed ashore. Though these six pilots turned up safe, another had disappeared and was later reported killed.

Ranger's fighter pilots of VF-4 and VF-9 learned the hard way that they could not dogfight the agile French fighters, and they learned to respect automatic weapons fire from the ground. 'Fighting Four' lost six planes in its first mission, though VF-26 from *Sangamon* claimed three bombers and a fighter without loss.

But the center of attraction in Casablanca harbor was the French battleship *Jean Bart*, adding her 15-in (381-mm) guns to the shore batteries. Eighteen *Ranger* dive-bombers attacked naval facilities in the harbor, including submarine moorings and *Jean Bart* herself. The battleship was hit, though not fatally, while one submarine was sunk.

When a French cruiser and destroyer force sortied to engage the American warships, SBDs and F4Fs dropped down to bomb and strafe. The light cruiser and two destroyers were beached to prevent their sinking.

The secondary objectives, Fedala to the north and Safi to the south, were captured during the first day. Port Lyautey was taken the following afternoon, with P-40s being flown in from the USS *Chenango* (ACV 28).

Meanwhile, SBDs and TBFs flew anti-submarine patrol and attacked enemy airfields and strong-points. But Casablanca's batteries continued to give trouble during 9 November: nine of *Ranger*'s

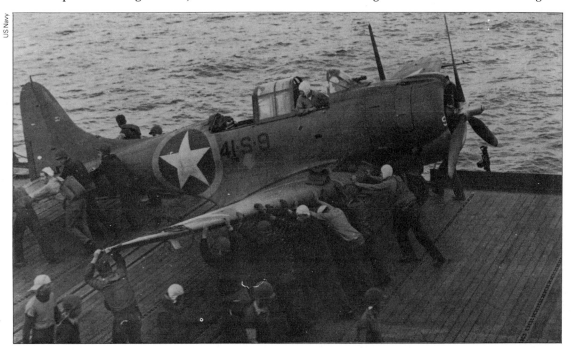

Right: A Douglas SBD-3 of VS-41 is spotted on *Ranger*'s flight deck by plane-handlers. The Dauntlesses flew repeated bombing, strafing and reconnaissance missions.

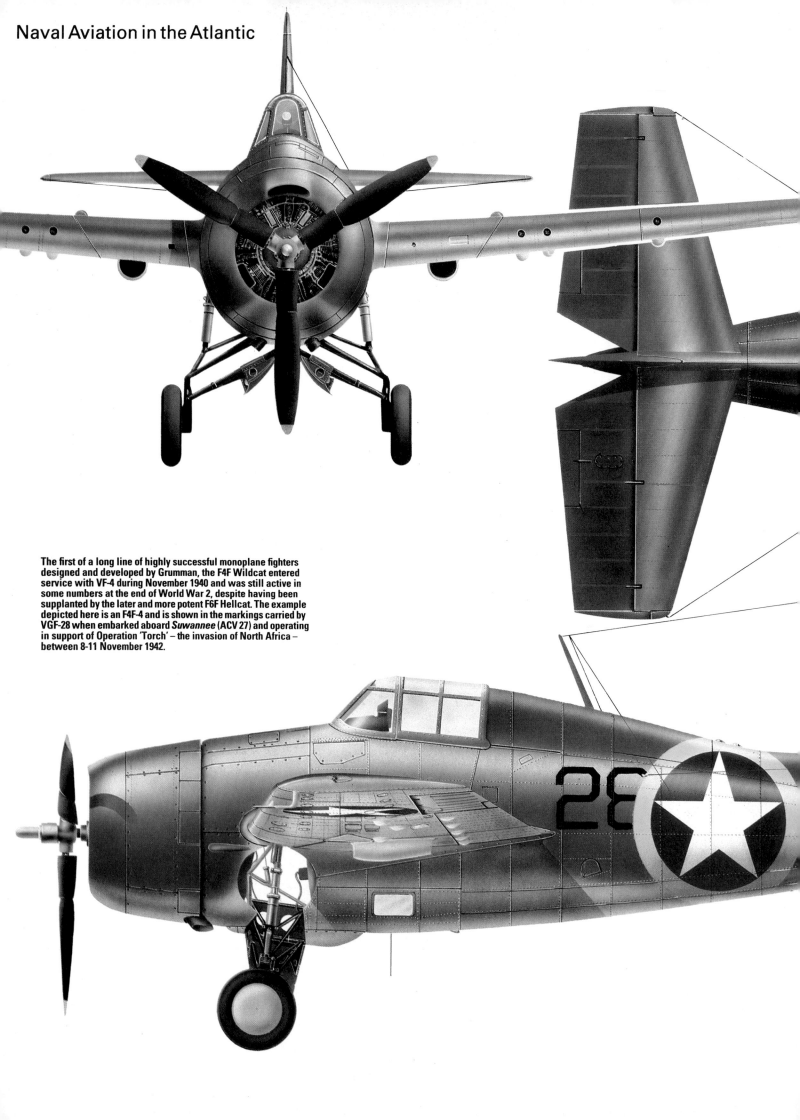

The first of a long line of highly successful monoplane fighters
designed and developed by Grumman, the F4F Wildcat entered
service with VF-4 during November 1940 and was still active in
some numbers at the end of World War 2, despite having been
supplanted by the later and more potent F6F Hellcat. The example
depicted here is an F4F-4 and is shown in the markings carried by
VGF-28 when embarked aboard *Suwannee* (ACV 27) and operating
in support of Operation 'Torch' – the invasion of North Africa –
between 8-11 November 1942.

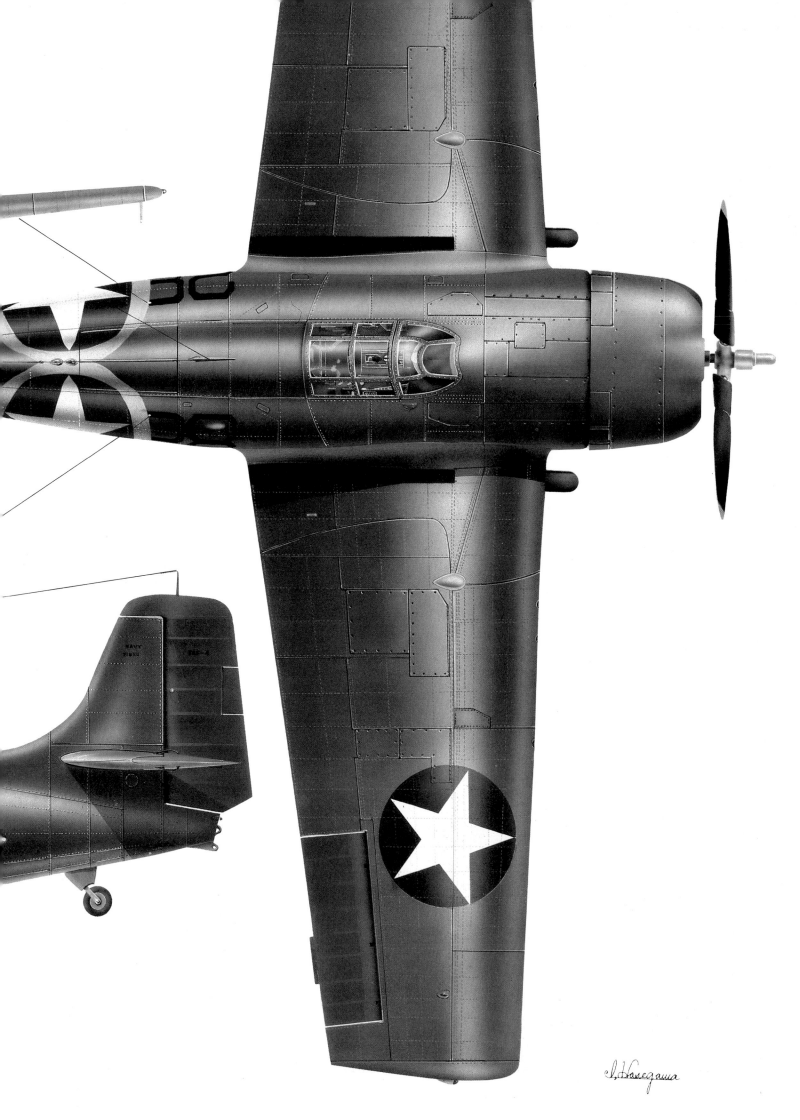

Naval Aviation in the Atlantic

Dauntlesses attacked with 1,000-lb (454-kg) bombs, scoring two direct hits which finally put the *Jean Bart* out of action. The French surrender came early on the morning of 11 November.

Aside from outflanking the Axis forces in North Africa, Operation 'Torch' provided Naval Aviators with a relatively mild introduction to combat. Air-ground support tactics had been proven, and anti-submarine techniques tested. (*Suwanee*'s TBFs sank at least one French boat at sea.) In air combat the untried F4F pilots downed about five opponents for each loss, having learned early that mutual support and the maintenance of airspeed led to success. But carrier aircraft losses to ground fire and operational causes were steep. With nearly 25 per cent aircraft attrition in three days, the task force could not have sustained operations much longer. But that, too, was a lesson learned.

From 'Torch' to 'Anvil/Dragoon'

The next power-projection mission for an American carrier in European waters occurred almost a year after 'Torch'. Again, *Ranger*'s air group was involved. Operating with the British Home Fleet, *Ranger* was alerted for an unusual mission: a strike against Axis shipping in and around Bodo harbor on the Norwegian coast.

Ranger reached launch position about dawn on 3 October 1943, closely escorted by a powerful Royal Navy force. She sent off two waves: 20 Dauntlesses followed by ten Avengers, each escorted by six to eight F4Fs. Making a low-level approach to avoid radar detection, each strike climbed to attack altitude within visible distance of the rocky shore. Then, in succession, the bombers went after coastal targets of opportunity and shipping anchored in the harbor itself.

There was no airborne opposition, though a four-plane division of Wildcats on CAP splashed two German reconnaissance aircraft near the task force during the day. Between them, VB-4 and VT-4 destroyed six ships and seriously damaged three more. Three bombers were lost, and one fighter was extensively damaged. Undeniably a success, Operation 'Leader' marked the end of *Ranger*'s combat career. She would soon report to the US west coast and serve as a training carrier for the remainder of the war.

The next and last such work by US carriers in the European theater offered a startling contrast. The scene shifted from north of the Arctic Circle to the sunny French Riviera as two escort carriers supported Operation 'Anvil/Dragoon', the invasion of southern France.

Not only were the climate and ships different, so

too were the aircraft. By August 1944, the escort carriers USS *Tulagi* (CVE 72) and *Kasaan Bay* (CVE 69) each flew a squadron of Grumman F6F-5 Hellcats. *Ranger* had requested F6F-3s for 'Leader' but none were then available because of pressing need in the Pacific. Now, however, there were plenty to go around. Each ship operated 24 of the big 2,100-hp (1566-kW) fighter-bombers.

Also unusual was the background of one Hellcat outfit. Observation-Fighting Squadron One (VOF-1) had been selected and trained as a gunnery spotting organization. Originally equipped with Vought F4U-1s, the unit was informed that Corsairs could not safely operate off carriers. That came as a surprise to Commander W.F. Bringle's pilots, who had qualified aboard ship with little difficulty. So VOF-1 went to war with Hellcats in *Tulagi* while VF-74 flew them from *Kasaan Bay*.

Operation 'Dragoon' was supported by seven British CVEs in addition to the pair of American 'flat tops'. But because of the F6F's superior range, VOF-1 and VF-74 could conduct most of the deep inshore reconnaissance flights.

On D-day (15 August) the two American squadrons flew 100 sorties, directing naval gunfire against German troop concentrations and supply routes. But in the following several days all manner of sorties were flown: bombing, strafing, rocketing and armed reconnaissance. German aircraft were first encountered on 19 August, and that evening a

Above: Hellcats arrived in the European theater in 1944. VOF-1 and VF-74 flew from escort carriers in support of Operation 'Anvil-Dragoon', the invasion of Southern France in August 1944. VOF-1 F6F-5 crashed *Tulagi*'s barrier but the pilot, Ensign William McKeever, was unharmed.

Left: The *Wildest Wildcat* was Eastern Aircraft's FM-2 version, which replaced the Grumman-built F4F-4 and Eastern's FM-1 in early 1944. This VC-36 FM-2 launches from USS *Core* (CVE 13) on 12 April 1944 in the Atlantic ASW paint scheme.

Above: By late 1943 the CVEs and their escorting destroyers had a firm grip on the German submarine threat. F4F-4s and TBF-1Cs of VC-29 prepare to launch from *Santee* in November of that year. In all, the squadron sank three U-boats.

Above right: Composite Squadron One, operating from *Card* (CVE 11), was among the early hunter-killer units, accounting for five submarines. Here the landing signal officer brings aboard a VC-1 Avenger during 1943 operations.

Below: A 1943 photograph of veteran escort carrier *Santee,* whose aircraft sank three German submarines.

section of two VOF-1 Hellcats shot down three Heinkel He 111s.

But there were losses. In two line periods totalling 13 days, the two CVE squadrons lost 11 F6Fs, including five on 20 August. But they had done their job, and more: over 800 vehicles were credited as destroyed and 84 locomotives wrecked. 'Rail-outs' and other communications cuts were also accomplished. The air-to-air score was computed at eight to nothing, for all the Hellcat's aerial victims were multi-engine aircraft.

Thus ended US carrier aviation's strikes against the western Axis powers. But the CVE war against the U-boats continued.

11
The Hunter-Killers

Despite extended coverage by land-based aircraft, Allied convoys still sailed through hundreds of miles of the Atlantic beyond air cover in early 1943. The answer was obvious: the merchantmen needed to sail with their own air umbrella.

The solution was the escort aircraft carrier (CVE) with specially-equipped planes and fliers trained for anti-submarine warfare (ASW). The first of these 'baby flat tops' were conversions from freighter hulls. And babies they were, compared with the 27,100-ton, 888-ft (270.66-m) 'Essex' class carriers. Most CVEs were barely 500 ft (152.4 m) in length, displacing less than 15,000 tons fully loaded. They operated fewer than 30 planes and steamed at a maximum 17 to 19 kts. This was not much compared with the 80-plane air groups of the upcoming 'Essex' class CVs with their top speeds of over 30 kts. But the CVEs were well suited to their specialized role. They could easily keep pace with merchant convoys, and their planes had only one task: hunting submarines and killing them.

USS *Bogue* (CVE 9) was first of the hunter-killers, putting to sea with two destroyers in February 1943. And she arrived at a crucial period. March was the third-worst month of the war for Allied merchant vessels as the wolfpacks destroyed over 600,000 tons in those 31 days. Originally equipped with Douglas SBD dive-bombers and Grumman F4F fighters, *Bogue* and her sisters shortly settled upon the Grumman TBF Avenger (and its General Motors variant, the TBM) as the ideal ASW aircraft. Bigger and longer-ranged than the Dauntless, the TBF packed more ordnance as well. Additionally, it had folding wings, an all-important factor aboard the diminutive CVEs.

Eventually TBFs and TBMs hunted subs with radar and sonobuoys and killed them with depth charges, bombs, rockets and acoustic torpedoes. Wildcats (F4F-4s and finally FM-2s) added bombs and rockets to their armament, becoming potent ASW aircraft themselves.

Naval Aviation in the Atlantic

But much of this was months in the future. *Bogue* escorted three convoys through March and April without engaging any U-boats. Not until late May did any of her aircraft get a shot at a sub.

It was an ON convoy (UK to Halifax, Nova Scotia). The skipper of *Bogue*'s Composite Squadron Nine (VC-9) was Lieutenant Commander W.M. Drane, who caught a U-boat on the surface on the evening of 21 May and inflicted significant damage with bombs. Three more sightings the next day indicated that the aerial hunters were sailing in a nautical version of the fabled happy hunting ground.

A fourth opportunity proved the value of tenacity in sub-hunting. A radio fix that afternoon established a U-boat only 20 miles (32 km) from *Bogue*, and a prowling Avenger immediately made visual contact. The capable pilot put four bombs close aboard, forcing the submarine down. Operating in relays, VC-9 kept aircraft in the vicinity, knowing that the damaged U-boat would have to surface before long. When she did, Lieutenant Howard Roberts straddled her with a spread of depth charges. The *U-569* dived once more but popped back up, fatally damaged.

ON-184 completed its voyage without a single loss. No other statistic could possibly have better proven the value of carrier-based ASW.

Bogue aircraft made two more kills in June, and the next month the composite squadrons of the USS *Core* (CVE 13) and *Santee* (CVE 29) scored their first successes. In all, the three hunter-killer teams deprived Admiral Karl Doenitz of six U-boats in July. But that same month carrier aviators began encountering terrific amounts of flak from German submarines. Multiple-mount 20- and 37-mm anti-aircraft guns made surfaced U-boats formidable opponents, and Doenitz's fight-back orders were widely obeyed.

What this meant to US airmen was demonstrated on 13 July. An Avenger and Wildcat of VC-13 caught the tanker *U-487* and, according to doctrine, split to divide the defenses. But the German gunners shot down the fighter and kept the TBF at bay. Finally, three more *Core* aircraft were called in

before another Avenger was able to finish the job.

Obviously, the battle was heating up. But *Santee* aircraft destroyed two U-boats without difficulty during the next two days When the U-boats submerged, TBFs were on hand with the new Fido homing torpedoes which faithfully followed their targets' engine noise.

With six kills during July and six more in August, the U-boat war had taken a decided turn for the better from the carrier airmens' viewpoint, to say nothing of the merchant sailors. Things thinned out during the fall months, but by the end of the year, the CVEs had destroyed 23 U-boats since May. Composite Squadron Nine, flying first from *Bogue* and then from the USS *Card* (CVE 11), was responsible for eight kills.

By the spring of 1944, some of the excitement had abated. Contacts were less frequent, and aircrews flew hours and hours along the convoy routes without a sighting. In fact, the hunter-killers bagged only nine U-boats in the Atlantic throughout the year. But the reduced pace of combat by no means eliminated all the excitement, or casualties. On two occasions TBFs pressed their attacks so close that they were destroyed by the explosion of their own bombs.

Nor were the losses limited to airplanes and flight crews. On 29 May 1944 a U-boat torpedoed the USS *Block Island* (CVE 21) off the African coast. She was the only US carrier sunk in the Atlantic, and she was immediately avenged by the destroyers of her screen. In four ASW cruises her planes had sunk two U-boats and assisted in two more 'kills'. During January one of her Avengers had made the first American rocket attack on a submarine.

Avengers verus U-boats

Earlier that year the CVEs had begun experimenting with a means of harassing U-boats round the clock. Some of *Card*'s TBMs were stripped of almost every possible pound to optimize fuel load. Even armament was sacrificed in an effort to gain maximum endurance. Reduced to a two-man crew of pilot and radarman, the modified Avengers could remain airborne as long as 14 hours, more than

Below: An alert photographer caught this VC-9 TBF-1D striking the ramp of *Solomons* (CVE 67) in April 1944. Note that the Avenger is equipped with wingtip radar and rocket rails, as the LSO ducks flying wood splinters from the deck.

US Navy

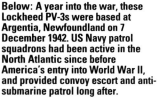

Above: *U-118* under attack by Lieutenant (JG) W. F. Chamberlain of VC-9 off USS *Bogue* (CVE 9) on 12 June 1943. Two Mk 17 depth charges have exploded close aboard. The first hunter-killer CVE, *Bogue*'s task group finished the war with 12 U-boats to its credit, but Chamberlain, who participated in three kills, was lost in May 1944.

Below: A year into the war, these Lockheed PV-3s were based at Argentia, Newfoundland on 7 December 1942. US Navy patrol squadrons had been active in the North Atlantic since before America's entry into World War II, and provided convoy escort and anti-submarine patrol long after.

made him the only U-boat hunter who added a 'tame' seawolf to his trophy collection. Ignominiously, the German submarine was towed into Bermuda on 19 June, flying the stars and stripes.

Another unusual hunt was concluded late that month in the same area when *Bogue* aircraft tracked a submarine through the night of 23 June. Expert sonobuoy use by VC-69 led to a confirmed kill of a Japanese submarine, the big *I-52*. She had been on a liaison cruise to France, but never arrived. It was the only kill of a Japanese submarine in the Atlantic.

Bogue, which had scored the first hunter-killer success, also recorded the last. That came on 20 August when several of her Avengers ganged up on *U-1229*. It was the 31st destruction of an enemy submarine by hunter-killer aircraft in the Atlantic. While British aircraft and Anglo-American ASW vessels sank several hundred U-boats during the war, the US Navy CVEs had performed services out of proportion to their number. That task was proven every time one of their convoys arrived at its destination intact.

enough to pursue a submarine contact from dusk to dawn. The aircraft would then call in destroyers to make the kill.

Card's nocturnal fliers found no U-boats, but the next month, March, brought substantial gains. Composite Squadron 58 in USS *Guadalcanal* (CVE 60) began similar experiments, but Captain D.V. Gallery wanted his 'Night Owls' to keep their talons. Once his Avenger pilots were night-qualified, Gallery's staff worked out a relay schedule intended to maintain four TBMs airborne through the night. With preliminaries settled, VC-58 began nocturnal flying in earnest on 7 April.

The results were dramatic. During a 30-day period of daylight operations, *Guadalcanal* had recorded not even a sighting. On the second and third nights of the new program, VC-58 shared one kill with destroyers and made a solo kill as well.

Gallery and the *Guadalcanal* hunter-killer group figured prominently in an even more spectacular episode in early June. On 4 June, operating near the Azores, a submerged submarine was tracked visually by airborne Wildcats. The fighters directed a destroyer-escort to the scene, which forced *U-505* to the surface. The Germans set scuttling charges and abandoned ship, but boats from the carrier and an escort destroyer put sailors aboard who disarmed the charges and kept the sub afloat. Galley had planned for such a contingency and his forethought

12
Land-based
Naval Aviation

Naval Aviation's war in the Atlantic was primarily an anti-submarine effort. For the first 18 months of America's entry into World War II anti-submarine warfare (ASW) squadrons were exclusively land-based. Though spread wide on both sides of that contested ocean, their range left wide gaps in the trade routes where U-boats could operate with little fear of air attack.

Once Germany was formally at war with the USA (11 December 1941), Admiral Karl Doenitz lost little time. In January, 1942 the U-boat master sent wolfpacks to American waters, where they found perhaps the best hunting of the war. Ill-prepared for hostilities, the Atlantic coast continued to glow with city lights and navigational beacons operating normally. The U-boat skippers could hardly believe their good fortune and sent 26 ships to the bottom off the US and Canadian coasts that month. In February, the U-boats slipped into the Gulf of Mexico, preying on oil-laden tankers and assorted

Left: The US Navy's war against the U-boat took patrol squadrons well south of home waters. This PBY-5A unloads captured German submariners at Natal, Brazil in February 1943.

merchantmen. Forty-two sinkings were recorded, as tonnage scores climbed and more Knights' Crosses were awarded by Doenitz. Student Naval Aviators flying out of Corpus Christi, Texas, found miles of beaches polluted with oil from sunken ships.

The situation did not markedly improve, as throughout 1942 Allied shipping losses continued to exceed new construction. However, measures were taken which would slowly alleviate the crisis.

Elements of the Neutrality Patrol were already positioned when the shooting war started. Patrol Wing Seven covered the northern routes from Newfoundland and Iceland. PatWing Five operated out of Norfolk, Virginia, and PatWing Three flew from the Panama Canal Zone. Natal, Brazil, had been prepared as an ASW base in December 1941, and by late 1942 three patrol squadrons were operational there. Eventually they were joined by Martin PBMs and Lockheed Venturas of Fleet Air Wing Sixteen in 1943.

Meanwhile, the German submarine force continued to enjoy fine hunting in American waters. The enemy crews termed this period the 'second happy time', for only once before had they racked up such fat scores. May was the worst month yet, with

72 sinkings. While few submarines were lost, the VP squadrons did score occasional successes. That summer a VP-73 Consolidated Catalina made a direct hit, impaling a depth charge in the wooden planking of a surfaced U-boat. A courageous, if unenlightened, crewman lifted the bomb out and pushed it overboard. The PBY crew watched incredulously as the depth charge reached its preset depth and exploded under the sub. A confirmed kill.

Gradually the ASW squadrons assimilated their experience and evolved a workable doctrine. New equipment also helped, as improved search radar, more effective weapons and more efficient aircraft arrived. The submarine war was perhaps the most technological of all, and small improvements in detection or warning equipment gave each side temporary advantages in the see-saw contest.

Perhaps best-suited for the ASW role was Consolidated's big four-engine Liberator bomber. Designed for the Army Air Corps as the B-24, the Liberator became the PB4Y-1 in Navy service, later modified to the Privateer in the single-tail PB4Y-2 model. With exceptional range and armament capacity, it made an excellent sub-hunter. But so did aircraft as different as the PBM Mariner flying boat and the slow, under-rated blimp.

Below: The US Navy adapted the US Army Air Force's B-24 Liberator to maritime patrol work. This PB4Y-1, modified with the distinctive US Navy 'bow turret', was based at NAS Norfolk, Virginia in December 1943.

Right: Long-range patrol operations over the Atlantic Ocean were accomplished by the Consolidated PB4Y-1 Liberator. Operating from Dunkeswell, England this VP-110 example was typical of the aircraft assigned to this often-monotonous and unrewarding duty.

Another innovation designed to counter the U-boat threat was the establishment, in 1942, of 15 inshore patrol squadrons in the East Coast and in the Caribbean. These squadrons guarded the US eastern coastline and navigable waterways. (German submarines had even been operating in Chesapeake Bay.) Assigned to the various Sea Frontiers, they originally carried designations relating to the Naval District in which they were based, such as VS-1D5. (Scouting Squadron One, Fifth Naval District.)

Fifteen similar squadrons were also established on the West Coast, at Coco Solo and Pearl Harbor. On 17 October 1942, the inshore patrol squadrons came under administrative control of the Pat-Wings. On 1 March 1943, they were redesignated as normal VS squadrons, the 'S' still standing for scouting. (The current VS, for anti-submarine squadron, did not come into use until 1950.)

Originally equipped with Vought OS2Us, the squadrons also acquired Douglas SBDs for their ASW mission. By mid-1944, with the U-boat threat greatly diminished, the inshore patrol squadrons began disbanding. By war's end, they would be gone.

New bases helped close the 'Atlantic Gap' where air coverage had previously never existed. Airfields in the West Indies, the Brazilian coast, then Ascension Island did much to expand convoy protection.

But new aircraft and improved gadgets could not alone defeat the aggressive U-boats. When sinkings began to trail off that fall of 1942, it was as much the result of perseverance as anything. Persistence counted for a great deal in anti-submarine warfare; the willingness to stick with a contact, cap a sub in relays if necessary until it had no choice but to surface. As Fleet Air Wing 16 noted, 'It has been a war where patience and steadiness have counted for as much as brilliance and dash in other theaters where there has been more shooting.'

Cover for the trade routes

Before that dreadful year was out, Navy patrol squadrons were operating on both sides of the Atlantic. Fleet Air Wing Fifteen's two original squadrons were flying from Casablanca and Port Lyautey within hours of the French surrender in Morocco on 11 November. And they were badly needed, as Axis submarines sank 11 Allied ships and damaged five more during Operation 'Torch'.

Ventura and Liberator squadrons added their weight to the ubiquitous PBYs during early 1943, covering the North Atlantic trade routes from Iceland to Morocco to the extent of their range. Meawhile, a permanent institution for studying aerial ASW was established at Quonset Point, Rhode Island. The Anti-Submarine Development Detachment conducted operational research into the best methods of combating the U-boat.

But the Germans had new ideas themselves. As Allied coastal air patrols increased, Luftwaffe maritime aircraft became increasingly aggressive during May, 1943. Previously Focke-Wulf Fw 200s and other long-range aircraft had been mainly content to shadow convoys, reporting their position, course and speed. Now they attacked ships more frequently in the Bay of Biscay, diverting Allied squadrons from ASW work to convoy air defense.

That summer Doenitz ordered his U-boat

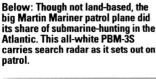

Below: Though not land-based, the big Martin Mariner patrol plane did its share of submarine-hunting in the Atlantic. This all-white PBM-3S carries search radar as it sets out on patrol.

US Navy

skippers to stand up to aircraft: they were to remain surfaced and shoot it out. This fight-back tactic resulted in casualties on both sides. For instance, FAW-15 out of Gibraltar made 16 attacks on U-boats during the first half of June, claiming five kills. But three Liberators and a PBY were badly damaged by return fire.

Bay of Biscay flights now regularly met aggressive Junkers Ju 88s, and Luftwaffe aircraft contested the Mediterranean approaches as well. On 12 June occurred perhaps the most bizarre aerial combat of the war as two Condors fought two PBYs assigned to cover a rescue ship en route to Casablanca. One Catalina stayed low to watch for reported submarines but the other PBY could not climb fast enough to prevent an attack on the ship, which resulted in a bomb hit.

But as the Condors closed for the kill, the remaining PBY met them head-on time after time. Though considerable ammunition was expended on both sides, the ship was saved by the Catalina pilot's determination to force the Germans off course during their attacks.

Meanwhile, Fleet Air Wing Seven had established itself at Dunkeswell in Devon as the resident US Navy ASW unit in the UK. In late July 1943 VP-63, a PBY squadron, joined the Liberators of VP-103 and VP-105. Equipped with Magnetic Anomaly Detection (MAD) gear, Patron 63's Catalinas became the first 'MAD-Cats' in the United Kingdom. But their tour began poorly, losing a plane to German fighters on the second day of operations. It fit the pattern, for another FAW-7 unit, VB-110, lost half its PB4Ys and one-third of its crews in the first six months. Weather and enemy aircraft were factors to be reckoned with. The first U-boat kill by a MAD-equipped aircraft was on 24 February 1944, when VP-63, two other squadrons and two ships joined forces to sink *U-76* in the Straits of Gibraltar.

However, August 1943 was a banner month, with only two merchantmen sunk in areas patrolled by US Navy aircraft. There were no submarine kills in September, but FAW-7 was busy anyway. Increasing German fighter patrols in the Bay of Biscay forced the Liberators to practise air-to-air combat tactics. The wing doctrine was primarily evasion, turning to a westerly heading at first sign of inter-

ceptors. But the situation was reminiscent of heavyweight boxing champ Joe Louis's wisdom: 'You can run but you can't hide.' The faster German twin-engine fighters could usually overtake a PB4Y and force a combat. Ju 88s and twin-engine Messerschmitts downed two Liberators that month and two more in October. Since the Liberators seldom flew anything but solo patrols, they were vastly outnumbered by enemy formations numbering six or more aircraft.

Nor were the Germans the only threat. FAW-15 planes were also harassed by Spanish fighters. On at least one occasion a PBY was attacked and narrowly escaped. The air wing staff had a remedy for that. Two speedy, well-armed Lockheed PV Venturas were deployed to Agadir, Morocco, as an advanced base and took over the PBY patrol route. The next time the 'neutral' Spaniards came up to play, they found more sport than anticipated. The potent PV foiled any subsequent mischief, without loss to either party.

Operating under the direction of RAF Coastal Command, FAW-7 played a big role in the D-Day landings in Normandy. Dawn-to-dusk patrols kept the Germans at bay and no Allied ships were lost to U-boats in the ensuing three weeks. During that period the Liberators made 17 attacks, leading to some dandy shootouts. but there were no aircraft losses.

A postscript to the Dunkeswell story involved a now-famous American name. Lieutenant Joseph P. Kennedy, Jr, was the son of the former American ambassador to the UK. As a patrol-plane commander in VB-110 he completed over 50 missions from mid-1943 to the summer of 1944. Squadron-mates recall him as 'a hell of an aviator' who sometimes exhibited 'more guts than good sense'. On one occasion when his lone PB4Y was jumped by two Messerschmitt Me 210 fighters, Kennedy ignored doctrine and turned into the attack so his gunner could open fire. The Messerschitts disengaged.

Kennedy was recruited for Project 'Aphrodite', a joint program which began in June with the Army Air Force. It involved loading war-weary bombers with tons of high-explosive and guiding them into precision targets by remote control. State-of-the-art technology did not permit the drones to take off without a pilot and ordnanceman aboard to arm the

Below: It takes teamwork to win a war, and here's teamwork personified: a PBY-5A of VP-63 with a 'K' class blimp on anti-submarine patrol over the Atlantic.

Right: An important operator of the Grumman Duck was the US Coast Guard, with 14 JF-2s in service. This aircraft, the tenth to be delivered, was based at Port Angeles, Wa. For Coast Guard operations the tail arrester hook was removed.

explosives. Once under remote control from the PV-1 lead ship, the two-man crew bailed out over the UK and the mission proceeded.

Kennedy and his co-pilot, Lieutenant Bud Willey, were assigned a PB4Y-1 named *Zoot Suit Black*. Their Liberator was loaded with 12 tons of Torpex intended for a V-1 missile site in northern France. They took off safely on 12 August and headed for the Suffolk coast when *Zoot Suit Black* exploded for no apparent reason. Both men died instantly. The effect upon history was that Joe's younger brother John became President of the United States in 1960, a position for which, many say, young Joe was being groomed.

While 'Aphrodite' drones did hit some difficult targets such as rocket sites, the overall project was a marginal success. Advancing technology would be required before such 'smart bombs' reached a degree of reliability. But dedicated aviators like Kennedy and Willey had helped show the way.

Another aspect of land-based Naval Aviation was involved in the D-Day period. Allied experience in the amphibious invasions of Sicily and Italy proved the extreme vulnerability of slow, lightly-armed floatplanes to enemy fighters. But the VOS aircraft were needed to call naval gunfire. Therefore, the British equipped five RAF squadrons and four Fleet Air Arm units with single-seat fighters flown by specially-trained pilots who could perform the spotting mission.

The US Navy followed suit. Seventeen pilots from the VOS units of the three American battleships and three cruisers assigned to Operation 'Overlord'

were pulled out for fighter training. Instruction by the Royal Navy at Lee-on-Solent, Hampshire, got the Americans qualified in Supermarine Spitfires borrowed from the US 9th Air Force. Then they learned standardized techniques which would allow them to work with any Allied ship on D-Day. Aside from the obvious benefit of greatly improved self-defense, the erstwhile floatplane pilots reveled in the thrill of flying the world's most glamorous fighter.

All 10 naval support squadrons operated from Lee-on-Solent, not only spotting naval gunfire but flying tactical reconnaissance as well. The US Navy pilots flew 10 per cent of all such sorties in the three weeks following D-Day, contributing their special skill and knowledge to the Allied effort.

From ungainly Catalinas to elegant Spitfires, Naval Aviators played an important, if unheralded, role in the European war.

13
The Coast Guard Contribution

By Act of Congress, the Coast Guard functions as part of the Navy during time of war. President Roosevelt jumped the gun a bit when he ordered the Coast Guard placed under the Navy's operational control on 1 November 1941, but the arrangement worked smoothly.

Below: Flying out of Norfolk another PBM-3S searches Atlantic Coast sealanes. The Mariner became perhaps the flying-boat most used by the US Navy in World War II as it was rugged, reasonably fast and versatile.

Naval Aviation in the Atlantic

Left: Coastal patrols were flown by USCG aviators in a variety of aircraft. Many were unarmed civilian types such as this Grumman J4F-1. However, one US Coast Guard J4F was credited with sinking *U-166* off Louisiana on 1 August 1942.

Some Navy officers expressed mild surprise at how efficiently the 'Coasties' made the transition. By definition and by tradition, the Coast Guard is dedicated to saving lives, and some in the military profession have noted an ingrained streak of pacifism in the 'revenue service'. But that very portion of the job had frequently brought Coast Guardsmen into violent conflict with seagoing outlaws, mainly liquor smugglers during the prohibition period of the 1920s.

Coast Guard aviation has always been extremely small; in 1941 it was absolutely miniscule. The service's aviation component during World War II involved nine air stations and one operational squadron, though each air base had planes assigned for patrol and liaison purposes.

The only USCG unit actively engaged in offensive operations was Patrol Bombing Squadron Six, flying Consolidated PBY-5s from Greenland and Iceland. But in concert with aircraft assigned to stateside air stations, it made its presence felt. From 1942 on, Coast Guard aviators conducted 61 attacks on hostile or unidentified submarines. But more in keeping with the service's primary mission,

its aircraft located 1,000 or more survivors of torpedoed ships and actually rescued almost 100.

The most common operational aircraft were Vought OS2U Kingfisher floatplanes and Grumman J2F Duck amphibians. However, an exceptional event occurrd on 1 August 1942 when an armed Grumman J4F Widgeon from Houma, Louisiana, sank *U-166* off the mouth of the Mississippi river.

Interestingly, the most innovative aspect of USCG aviation involved helicopters. Interest in helos dated from April 1942 with a demonstration of Igor Sikorsky's XR-4. Three Sikorsky HNS-1s (identical to the Army Air Force's R-4) were delivered to NAS Floyd Bennett Field in New York, and in December 1943 the local Coast Guard detachment prepared to conduct formal classes the following month. By that fall the station had 13 helicopters, including some British aircraft and students.

Almost forgotten is the fact that USCG aviators performed one of the world's first helicopter rescues: a Canadian transport plane had crashed 125 miles (200 km) from Goose Bay, Labrador, in April 1945,

Below: Perhaps the service's most important contribution to aviation was proof of the helicopter as a practical aircraft. US Coast Guardsmen developed procedures for employing early choppers such as the Sikorsky HNS-1s seen at Rockaway, New York in 1944.

US Navy

Almost lost in the antiquity of Naval Aviation is the origin of generic designators for aircraft types and squadrons. The 'V' prefix, still employed today, designates heavier-than-air fixed-wing aircraft; 'VF' for fighter has remained unchanged since the early 1920s. But the 'Z' prefix is unknown to a full generation of Naval Aviators, though once it stood for lighter-than-air, or LTA in the trade.

The Navy had operated both rigid and non-rigid airships well before World War II. But dirigibles had departed the scene during the 1930s, leaving only non-rigid (frameless) airships, or blimps, also known as 'poopy bags' by the irreverent.

The origin of the word 'blimp' is generally contested and widely ignored among heavier-than-air devotees. It is sometimes accredited to the sound made when one's finger is flipped against one of the inflated monsters. What is known, however, is that Congress authorized an increase in Navy blimp strength to 200 airships in June 1942.

Three types of blimps were employed by US Naval Aviation during the war. Most common was the K-ship, which largely replaced the smaller L-type. ZPKs (lighter-than-air patrol type K) were 250 ft (76.2 m) long ships with 400,000 cu ft (11327 m³) of helium capacity. Intended primarily as anti-submarine platforms, they carried radar, sonobuoys and depth charges in addition to a new gadget, the magnetic anomaly detector. MAD had the advantage of being a passive underwater detector but had to be used at very low altitudes; usually below 200 ft (61 m).

Larger M-ships were produced during the war but failed to replace the K series. Their advantages in relation to cost were too limited to warrant large-scale production.

In May 1943 the Vice Chief of Naval Operations approved 10 LTA sites on the Brazilian coast to expand convoy protection. A major base was established near Rio de Janeiro, the Santa Cruz facility with its giant shed which previously serviced

Above: Early recognition of the potential value of the helicopter came in 1944 when this US Coast Guard Sikorsky HNS-1 Hoverfly was evaluated in the air-sea rescue role at New York NAS. Subsequently, the Navy became an ardent advocate of this type of flying machine.

stranding most of the crew. The melting spring snow prevented further rescue attempts by ski-equipped aircraft, and 11 men remained marooned in the rugged, inaccessible terrain. To complicate matters, one rescue plane had been wrecked, leaving two more men at the scene.

One of the Floyd Bennett Sikorskys was dismantled, stowed in an Army Air Force Douglas C-54 and ferried 1,000 miles (1600 km) to Labrador. There the HNS-1 was reassembled and began a series of flights into the crash site where the men had been waiting for two weeks. It was slow going (the HNS cruised at 57 mph/92 km/h and had one passenger seat) but the job was completed within five days of notification of the mission. Six Coast Guardsmen received decorations for this feat, including the helo pilot, Lieutenant August Kleisch.

Helicopters did not regularly operate from ships until shortly after World War II, but the first deployment of an aircraft carrier with an assigned helo was made with a Coast Guard aircraft and pilot. The 'Coasties' had showed the way.

Right: Illustrative of the part played by the blimps in the anti-submarine campaign in the Atlantic is this surrender of *U-805* off New Hampshire. Despite their vulnerability to attack from the U-boats' heavy-calibre automatic weapons, the blimps provided effective convoy protection by stalking submerged submarines for hours at a time.

Naval Aviation in the Atlantic

Germany's showpiece, the *Graf Zeppelin*. The Santa Cruz base would prove capable of operating and maintaining a dozen airships. By September, Fleet Airship Wing Four had begun operations, conducting convoy patrol and rescue work.

The rescue role afforded by blimps caught the Coast Guard's interest in the era before practical helicopters. Experiments conducted by the USCG Air-Sea Rescue Service found that raft-to-blimp transfers were possible, thereby expanding the realm of maritime lifesaving. The Coast Guardsmen urged adoption of the technique as standard practice, and while apparently few such rescues were performed, the concept was well proven.

Meanwhile, Gulf Coast 'BlimpRons' had been commissioned. Aggressive U-boat sorties into the Gulf of Mexico required establishment of several LTA stations, each capable of handling as many as six ships. Inevitably built on marshes, these facilities featured large, hungry mosquitoes and ever-present mud.

While the mere presence of aircraft could keep submarines submerged and therefore out of range of convoys, the Germans proved willing to surface and fight on several occasions. In one of the more bizarre combats of World War II, ship *K-74* of Florida-based ZP-21 engaged *U-134* in a blimp/submarine shootout. It was not much of a contest, for blimps were intended to stalk submerged submarines. With heavy-caliber automatic weapons, a surfaced U-boat could shred a blimp's envelope in seconds.

During early 1944, 10 ASW BlimpRons were organized as Fleet Airships Atlantic under Commodore G.H. Mills. They stretched from Nova Scotia to Rio de Janeiro, providing Atlantic coast convoy protection the length of the New World. But blimps would operate on the far side of the ocean as well.

Commander E.J. Sullivan's ZP-14 was based in North Carolina when chosen to fly to Africa. The unit prepared its staging base at NAS South Weymouth, Massachussetts, and dispatched the first pair of ships, *K-123* and *K-130*, on 28 May 1944. Following the Newfoundland–Azores route, the two blimps arrived on 1 June at Port Lyautey, French Morocco, after a 58-hour transit. It was the first Atlantic crossing by non-rigid airships, but not the last. Four more had arrived in North Africa by 1 July.

Detachments were sent to bases almost the width of the Mediterranean, but the squadron's primary duty lay along the Riviera. Operation 'Anvil/Dragoon', the Allied amphibious invasion of southern France, came in late August. On 17 September two ships of ZP-14 moored at Cuers airport near Toulon, being supported by an advance party of 23 personnel which had flown in equipment by Douglas R5D transport plane.

Sullivan's crews were assigned minesweeping duty in and around Toulon Harbor. French-flown PBYs located German minefields and the blimps, because of their extreme low-altitude and low-airspeed capability, were ideal platforms for charting mines with precision. They then directed minesweepers by radio or loudspeakers.

The BlimpRon 14 ships also flew at night, using their radar to search for enemy submarines or small craft trying to enter Toulon Harbour to torpedo the Allied shipping anchored there. No such attempts were discovered, but the nocturnal patrols surely eased the port commander's mind.

However, ZP-14 didn't get off without loss. Ship *K-123*'s envelope was deflated and destroyed by a Vichy agent posing as a Free French officer at Port Lyautey, and *K-109* was lost at its mooring in violent winds. But replacements were dispatched and safely arrived, bringing to eight the number of K-ships which crossed the Atlantic. They remain the only non-rigid aircraft to perform that feat, giving ZP-14 a monopoly on the world record which lasted until blimps were retired from the Navy in 1961.

The record remains uncontested even today.

Right: Lighter-than-air formation flying is seldom accomplished, but these 10 training blimps from NAS Moffett Field managed an echelon of sorts in December 1943. Moffett trained LTA pilots for service in both the Atlantic and Pacific.

Below: Among experiments conducted with blimps were temporary mooring and refuelling aboard aircraft-carriers. This 1944 experiment helped expand liaison and anti-submarine procedures offshore.

Named for the Revolutionary War battle, *Cowpens* (CVL 25) steams off the Atlantic coast in July 1943. Light carriers originally had SBD dive-bombers assigned to their air groups but entered combat with one Hellcat and one Avenger squadron, a total of some 30 planes.

'Go West, Young Man' The War in the Pacific

Covering more than 64 million square miles, the Pacific Ocean contains nearly half of the Earth's water. It is more than twice the size of the Atlantic. The 2,100 miles (3380 km) from San Francisco to Hawaii alone is farther than the direct route from Paris to Moscow. The stretch from Hawaii to Tokyo is nearly three times farther still, establishing the Pacific as the largest combat arena in history.

The obvious gladiator to fight in this arena was air power, largely carrier-based air power. From 1942 through 1945 the US Navy commissioned some 150 aviation ships for its own use. This unprecedented building program produced 30 fast carriers, 82 escort carriers and some 40 seaplane tenders. Tens of thousands of aircraft and hundreds of thousands of fliers and technicians were trained to man and support these ships. The doctrine and strategy for effective use of all this power was mainly developed during the condensed period of 1942-4. The nature of this undertaking assumed truly gigantic proportions. Only a nation such as the United States with its resources and fundamental ideals could have developed the required effort to successfully complete this gargantuan task.

15
"'Cause a PBY
Don't Fly That High"

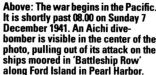

Discounting the debacle at Pearl Harbor, US Naval Aviation's initial combat experience occurred in the Philippines. Patrol Wing 10 consisted of two Consolidated PBY squadrons, VP-101 and -102, each with 14 Catalinas. Three seaplane tenders serviced the patrol squadrons while a utility squadron performed ordinary chores with an assortment of 10 floatplanes.

Heightened tension in South East Asia directly affected Patwing 10's activities. Japanese interest in Indochina and the oil-rich Dutch East Indies prompted the Asiatic Fleet to inaugurate patrols to Formosa, the Indochina coast and the island of Hainan in November 1941. Ordered to avoid detection when possible, the Catalina crews were nevertheless sometimes found by Japanese aircraft, which occasionally made practice gunnery runs. The men of PatWing 10 held no illusions about their prospects of surviving determined fighter attack in a slow-climbing Catalina. They sang, 'You can't get to heaven in a PBY, 'cause a PBY don't fly that high.'

Patrols off Luzon noted increased Japanese activity during the first week of December. Japanese search planes were encountered on three consecutive days, 5, 6 and 7 December.

Asiatic Fleet headquarters in Manila learned of the Pearl Harbor attack at 03.00 on 8 December local time. Four hours later, the tender USS *William B. Preston* (AVD 7) anchored in Davao Gulf radioed she was under air attack. Two PBYs were sunk, and the war was on.

Most Catalinas were dispersed to remote areas where some sort of support facility existed. Lakes, coves, even swamps were turned into impromptu seaplane bases while five P-boats and the tender USS *Childs* (AVD 1) remained in Manila Bay. Availability of amphibian aircraft proved a blessing, as it allowed minimal US airpower at a time when airfields ashore were quickly neutralized or captured by the rapidly-advancing enemy.

The patrol squadrons had a hectic, busy day on 9 December. Two cargo ships were attacked: a Japanese freighter which conveniently identified itself and a Norwegian vessel which declined to reply when challenged. One PBY disappeared on patrol and two more were damaged; one by Japanese fighters and the other by 'friendly' anti-aircraft gunners.

Offensive missions were planned for 10 December

but only partially carried out. Five Catalinas from Manila attacked a Japanese naval force at mid-day, dropping 20 bombs in all and claiming possible damage to a battleship. A second strike armed with aerial torpedoes was completely broken up during take-off from Olangapo: Mitsubishi A6M Zero fighters swarmed over the base at that inconvenient moment and shot up two planes which immediately force-landed. Air gunners thought that they had shot down one assailant, but PatWing 10 was being slowly whittled down.

Things only got worse. Two days later, more Zeros burned seven PBYs at their moorings as active Japanese reconnaissance located most of the dispersed bases. By now reduced to barely the strength of one squadron, the wing could do little more. On 13 December, the surviving aircraft were ordered southwards, temporarily beyond range of enemy aircraft. But the situation continued to deteriorate, and the day after Christmas, Admiral Thomas C. Hart and his Asiatic Fleet staff departed Manila by submarine.

The trauma of PatWing 10

A dawn attack on 10 January 1942 caught all five PatWing 10 planes on the water at Mariveles. Remaining personnel who were stranded without transportation formed an impromptu naval 'brigade' and prepared to fight as infantrymen.

Before the end of December, 16 PatWing 10 aircraft (10 PBYs and six utility planes) had flown to the Dutch East Indies. They were joined by two tenders, but their stay was a short one. Reinforcements were intercepted or insufficient to repulse the wide-ranging Japanese, and not even the US Navy's first aircraft-carrier could help: the USS *Langley* (AV 3), converted to a seaplane tender before the war, was on a ferry mission attempting to bring in a load of badly-needed Curtiss P-40 fighters to Java on 27 February. Caught by Japanese

Above: The war begins in the Pacific. It is shortly past 08.00 on Sunday 7 December 1941. An Aichi dive-bomber is visible in the center of the photo, pulling out of its attack on the ships moored in 'Battleship Row' along Ford Island in Pearl Harbor.

Left: Smoke and anti-aircraft bursts cloud the sky over Pearl Harbor as the Japanese surprise attack proceeds. Initially startled, US sailors and Marines recovered to fight back with their army colleagues, but too late. All eight battleships of the Pacific Fleet had been sunk or seriously damaged.

long rush to speedy conquest in those Asian waters, they might have pondered a lesson for the future.

16
Year of Decision

The Pacific War, from 1941 to 1945, involved nearly 20 surface engagements worthy of being called battles. Of these, the Japanese won more than they lost. But in nearly every crucial battle, the deciding factor was carrier airpower. Nowhere was this better illustrated than at the Battle of Midway where carrier airpower turned the tide of the war.

This almost exclusive reliance upon the aircraft-carrier as the primary weapon of both sides made 1942 a salient year in the history of naval warfare. No matter how limited the history of the submarine or the infantry landing craft, the fact remained that there did exist some degree of previous experience with each. In the 12 months following the attack on Pearl Harbor, neither the submarine nor the landing craft had a substantial effect upon the war. The US Navy's exceptionally effective use of submarines against the Japanese merchant marine from 1943 to 1945 was a major factor in winning the victory. So was the development and employment of an astonishing variety of amphibious vehicles. But emergence of the carrier as the most important warship came as a surprise to many officers in several navies.

Only three nations employed aircraft-carriers in combat: the UK, USA and Japan. The Royal Navy used flat tops in the Pacific both at the beginning and at the end of the war, and skilfully employed them in the latter period. But their numbers were never remotely similar to those of their American allies. Nor could they be, for the UK still claimed an empire, with far-flung holdings and responsibilities, and the demand for carriers and warships of all types was thus great in the Atlantic, the Arctic, the Mediterranean, the Indian and the Pacific Oceans. Many of the advances in Naval Aviation originated with the Royal Navy, but the fortunes of war dictated that no British carrier ever fought another ship of its own kind. All five of the world's aircraft-carrier battles were fought by the US and the Imperial Japanese Navies. Four of these battles occurred within a six-month period of 1942.

Above: Military airfields were prime targets for Japanese aircraft. Here a PBY burns at NAS Kaneohe while sailors attempt to minimize damage. The major Japanese error was failing to send a third strike group to destroy the American fuel depot, wide open to attack.

bombers, the old 'Covered Wagon' went down with her cargo.

The remnants of Patrol Wing 10 withdrew to Australia a few days later. In some 300 sorties they had sunk a freighter, damaged two light cruisers and a transport, and shot down perhaps eight or more Japanese aircraft. Their own aircraft losses amounted to nearly 100 per cent. Fifteen PBYs had been shot down, and while only three were lost to operational accidents, 17 other aircraft had been destroyed or damaged beyond repair at bases in the Philippines and East Indies. Seventeen commissioned pilots had been killed or disappeared on missions, plus seven enlisted pilots. Aircrew casualties were equally heavy.

PatWing 10 had practically been doomed from the first day, and surely the aviators and support personnel recognized that fact. But it is not recorded that they ever abandoned their mission or their self-respect. Had the Japanese paused in the head-

Below: Peacetime light-gray overall color schemes adorn the SBD-2s of Scouting Squadron Five from the carrier _Yorktown_. VS-5 would see considerable combat in the Pacific during 1942.

The War in the Pacific

Japan, though a small, isolated island nation, possessed two important advantages. Strategically, it benefited from unified command and the option to strike wherever it chose. The Allied forces were widely dispersed, and no central command or control, and had virtually no experience in operating together. This fact became painfully evident during the Battle of the Java Sea in February 1942: the scratch-built American-British-Dutch-Australian force was soundly defeated by the unified Japanese.

Additionally, Japan had an important tactical advantage. The Imperial Navy boasted nine aircraft-carriers in the fall of 1941. The US Pacific Fleet had only three, and the British dispatched merely one to the Indian Ocean. This latter ship was HMS *Hermes*, sunk by Japanese aircraft off Ceylon in early April 1942.

Since the respective fleets were nearly even in surface and submarine combatants, the odds should have been balanced. On paper, a traditional naval war in the Pacific should have resulted in a stalemate between the Japanese and Allied fleets in late 1941. But the Japanese ignored tradition. They opened hostilities with a brilliantly planned and boldly executed carrier-launched air strike against the heart of the US Pacific Fleet. The Pearl Harbor attack of 7 December caught all eight front-line Pacific fleet battleships immobile, helplesss to defend themselves in port. Each was either sunk or badly damaged.

But partly by fate and partly by design, the three US Pacific Fleet carriers were away from port that disastrous Sunday morning.

Sisters USS *Lexington* (CV 2) and *Saratoga* (CV 3) were battle-cruisers converted to carriers by a provision of the Washington Naval Treaty of 1921. They had been commissioned in 1927, and on 7 December the former was delivering Marine Corps aircraft to Midway while the latter was on the US west coast. The third carrier was the newer *Enterprise* (CV 6). She was within 100 miles (160 km) of Pearl Harbor, having ferried fighters to Wake Island, and narrowly escaped destruction in the raid. It was extremely fortunate for the American cause: the 'Big E' would become the greatest fighting ship in the history of the US Navy.

In late 1941 each of these carriers embarked a standard complement of 72 aircraft. The American table of organization called for an air group permanently assigned to every flat top. Each air group was composed of four squadrons: fighter, dive-bomber, scout-bomber and torpedo.

The US Navy designator for a fleet carrier was 'CV': *Lexington*, for instance, was CV 2, and each of her squadrons was numbered accordingly. *Lexington*'s fighter squadron was VF-2, her dive-bombers were VB-2, the scouts were VS-2 and her torpedo plane squadron was VT-2. Not until much later did air groups become numbered in the same fashion. Before the war, and well into it, the air groups were known by the name of their ship. Thus, the Pacific Fleet operated Lexington Air Group, Saratoga Air Group and Enterprise Air Group. The latter units flew squadrons designated three and six, respectively.

This orderly arrangement lasted until the Battle of Midway. For the rest of 1942, the few US carriers in action at any one time often had a mixture of squadrons from two or even three air groups. This grouping was an operational necessity. As carriers were sunk their squadrons were dispersed, decommissioned or held in reserve. Early in the Guadalcanal campaign, for instance, *Enterprise* had only two of her original squadrons: VF-6 and VB-6. Her scout squadron was from the sunken *Yorktown* (CV 5) and the torpedo unit was VT-3 from the damaged *Saratoga*.

The *Yorktown* arrives

At the time of Pearl Harbor, carrier squadrons generally operated three types of aircraft. Fighter squadrons flew the Grumman F4F-3 Wildcat; scout and bomber units had the Douglas SBD Dauntless; and torpedo squadrons flew the Douglas TBD-1 Devastator. Each squadron had 18 of these respective aircraft types, so a typical air group possessed 36 SBDs (the combined total of the scout and bomber squadrons), 18 F4Fs and 18 TBDs; a total of 72 airplanes.

An exception was Fighting Squadron Two in *Lexington*. This unit had not yet received F4Fs, and operated Brewster F2A-3s. However, the Brewster Buffaloes were soon relegated to shore-based Marine squadrons. Their only combat in US service occurred at Midway in June 1942, where they were shown to be dramatically inferior to Japan's Mitsubishi A6M Zero fighters.

Almost immediately after Pearl Harbor, a fourth carrier joined the Pacific Fleet. This was *Yorktown*, sister of *Enterprise*. Transferred from the Atlantic,

Below: F4F-3s flown by the US Navy's two best-known fighter pilots of the early war period. Lieutenant Commander John S. Thach, CO of VF-3, flies F-1 while his wingman is Lieutenant Edward H. O'Hare. O'Hare was credited with shooting down five Japanese bombers in defense of *Lexington* (CV 2) off Rabaul on 20 February 1942.

US Navy

Right: Extensively employed as a dive bomber during the long and bloody campaign in the Pacific, the Douglas SBD-3 Dauntless is represented here by an aircraft from *Enterprise* (CV 6) during February 1942, shortly after the USA entered the war.

Yorktown operated VB-5, VS-5 and VT-5. Her regular fighter unit, VF-5, had been replaced by VF-42. Fighting Squadron 42 was nominally part of Ranger Air Group, but would prove itself one of the most proficient VF outfits in the US Navy while flying from *Yorktown*.

There were four other pre-war American carriers. *Langley* (CV 1) had been converted from a collier in 1922 and served mainly as an experimental platform before the war. She was again converted in 1937, becoming a seaplane tender as (AV 3). Her wartime career was short: she was sunk ferrying planes to the Dutch East Indies in February 1942.

For the time being, the remaining three flat tops remained on the east coast of the United States. These were the USS *Ranger* (CV 4), *Wasp* (CV 7) and *Hornet* (CV 8). The latter pair would engage in combat in the Pacific during 1942, and both would be sunk. *Ranger* sailed to Hawaii in mid-1944, where she served briefly as a training ship for replacement air groups. She spent the remainder of the war on the west coast as a training carrier.

Contrary to what has been written elsewhere, most US Navy aviators of the early war period were reasonably experienced and well trained. Nearly all the squadron commanders were graduates of the Naval Academy, as were many of their pilots. The other fliers were mainly pre-war reservists, usually with several hundred hours of flight time. There also existed a small but highly experienced cadre of non-commissioned pilots.

US Navy fighter pilots at this time were perhaps the world's best-trained in deflection shooting. Their illuminated reflector sights enabled accurate gunnery at wide angles with high probability of lethal hits on enemy aircraft. Most other air arms stressed maneuvering for shooting position in the classic dogfight pattern. But the US Navy design philosophy required internal protection for its aircraft. The weight of armor plate and self-sealing fuel tanks, plus carrier operating equipment, put such fighters as the Grumman F4F Wildcat at a disadvantage against lighter, more maneuverable planes. US Navy fighter pilots practised deflection shooting in order to avoid the necessity of closing directly behind the target to score hits. Additionally, the F4F's rugged construction enabled it to fly home with damage which might otherwise have been fatal to lesser aircraft.

US carrier squadrons were also fortunate in having innovative leaders such as Lieutenant Commander John S. 'Jimmy' Thach, skipper of fighting Squadron Three. It was Thach, and an aggressive young fighter pilot in his squadron, who had sat at Thach's kitchen table in Coronado, California, and with matchsticks developed the basic defensive fighter tactics credited with saving untold Navy fighter pilots throughout the war. The young pilot, Lieutenant Edward H. 'Butch' O'Hare, would win Naval Aviation's first Medal of Honor of the war when he shot down five Japanese Mitsubishi G4M 'Betty' bombers on 20 February 1942 off Rabaul. O'Hare was credited with saving *Lexington* from the attacking enemy aircraft.

US Navy

Right: New warpaint is evident in this early 1942 photo of Dauntlesses and Devastators. Sea-blue upper surfaces have replaced the peacetime light gray, while red-and-white rudder stripes have been deleted.

In the Douglas SBD, the US Navy had perhaps the finest dive-bomber in the world. Though the Dauntless never won the publicity accorded Germany's Junkers Ju 87, it was superb in its intended role. With exceptional stability and light control responses, the SBD made dive-bombing part art and part science. At the time of Pearl Harbor it was considered obsolescent, and the fleet anxiously awaited delivery of the new Curtiss SB2C, which promised more range, payload and speed. But the SB2C suffered a long development period and did not reach combat until the end of 1943. Even then, it proved less accurate and not much faster than the SBD. Usually carrying a 1,000-lb (454-kg) bomb on strike missions and a 500-lb (227-kg) bomb on searches, the Dauntless would become known as 'the workhorse of the Pacific' in the year after Pearl Harbor.

Torpedo force weakness

The weak link in US carrier air groups was the Douglas TBD torpedo plane. Designed in 1934 and joining the fleet in 1937, the TBD-1 was the first all-metal monoplane carrier aircraft in the US Navy. By 1937 standards it was a good airplane, stable, easy to fly and to land aboard ship. But by 1942 the rush of aeronautical progress had left it behind. The Devastator was slow, had a poor climb rate and very short range. It was particularly vulnerable to fighters.

Even worse were the torpedoes which TBDs had to carry. The Bureau of Ordnance steadfastly refused to allow operational research on torpedoes before the war, claiming that live tests were expensive and unnecessary. As a result, US submarine and aerial torpedoes were notoriously defective through the crucial first year of the Pacific War. Not until well into 1943 did reliable torpedoes reach the fleet to encourage the brave men who had to use them. However, the Mk 13 torpedo that Naval Aviators were forced to carry into combat in the first half of the war was a stain on the record of BuOrd.

Shortly after Midway, all torpedo squadrons received a new airplane, Grumman's TBF-1. The Avenger was faster than the TBD-1, and possessed significantly greater range. Avengers were later built by General Motors Corporation under the designation TBMs. A total of nearly 10,000 TBFs and TBMs was delivered from 1942 to 1945, far more than any other carrier-based bomber in history.

Japanese carrier aviation was well matched against its American opponent. Though some of the pre-war carriers and the conversions of 1942 embarked far fewer aircraft, most Japanese carriers were comparable. They operated from 54 to 72 planes of approximately the same types as the Americans. The difference was in ratio of each type, as the Imperial Navy's air groups generally possessed more torpedo planes and fewer dive-bombers than US Navy squadrons.

Japanese aircraft were efficient designs armed with effective weapons. By far the best-known to history is the Mitsubishi A6M (Type 0) fighter, shortened to 'Zero' and later 'Zeke' by the Americans. (Allied code names came into being in late 1942.) Introduced to combat in China during 1940, the Zero was unlike any other fighter then flying. With exceptional range, amazing maneuverability and sensational rate of climb, flown by very competent aviators, the Zero was not easily defeated.

Called 'Val' by the Americans, the Aichi D3A (Type 99) dive-bomber was a fixed landing gear design with underwing dive brakes. It was bigger and heavier than the SBD, but could deliver a 900-lb (408-kg) bomb with astonishing accuracy.

Similarly, the Nakajima B5N (Type 97) bomber was one of the world's best torpedo planes. US intelligence dubbed it 'Kate', a dangerous lady. With good speed and reliable torpedoes, the 'Kate' posed a serious threat to Allied warships. Like the TBD and TBF, the Nakajima could perform as a high-altitude horizontal bomber, but this method of attack was poorly suited to naval warfare. Hitting a maneuvering ship from high level proved an almost impossible task under combat conditions.

From a tactical viewpoint, reconnaissance was probably the greatest difference between Japanese and American carrier doctrine. The Imperial Navy emphasized maximum strike capability in its air groups, leaving most of the scouting to battleship and cruiser floatplanes. This tactic freed the dive-bombers and torpedo planes for attack missions. The US Navy, as already noted, devoted one-quarter of its carrier air strength to reconnaissance. This decision required the SBDs to perform double duty: searching for the enemy as well as sinking him.

Before the Battle of the Coral Sea in May 1942, the principles of carrier warfare were understood by both sides; it would remain for actual experience to

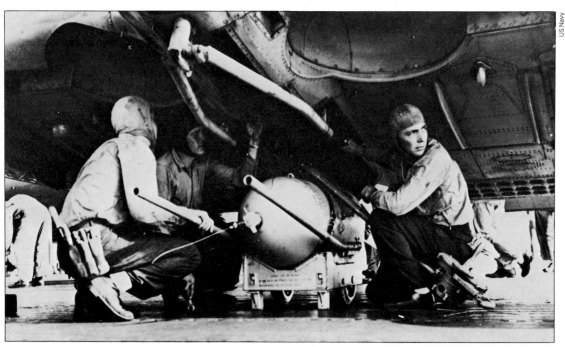

US Navy

Left: VS-6 ordnancemen load 500-lb (227-kg) bomb on the centerline rack of an SBD, during the Battle of Midway. Dauntlesses flew strike and search missions almost continuously from 4 to 7 June, and deck hands had little time for rest while servicing aircraft.

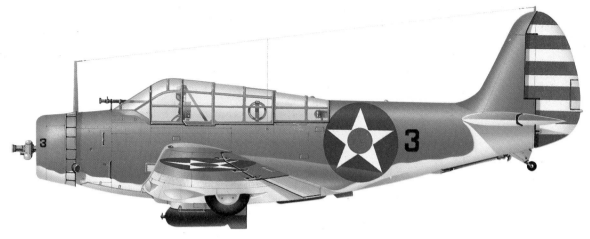

Right: Douglas TBD-1 Devastator operated by Torpedo Squadron VT-6 aboard USS *Enterprise* in February 1942. Representing an important step in the evolution of US naval air power as the service's first production-status monoplane designed specifically for carrier operations, the TBD was no match for the superior performance of newer types serving in the Pacific theatre.

draw the line between theory and practice. Though there were exceptions, the following concepts were applicable to carrier battles.

As in most forms of warfare, the first rule was to strike first. Reversing the biblical phrase, Americans said, 'Do unto others before they do unto you.' This basic dictum assumed even greater importance in carrier warfare because of the physical nature of the ship. Concentrated in one small area were exceptionally volatile materials: gasoline, bombs, torpedoes and fuel oil. Ignition of any item could spark a chain-reaction which would doom the ship. Additionally, the carrier's narrow deck could be rendered inoperable by only a few bomb hits. Torpedo damage was more likely to put a flat top out of action for a longer period if a list developed which could not be corrected. While both bomb and torpedo damage could frequently be repaired in a short time, in most forms of aerial warfare, time is often the commodity in shortest supply.

An old adage states that he who hesitates is lost, and certainly it was true in carrier war. The classic example was Vice Admiral Chuichi Nagumo's decision at Midway to delay launching his second strike of 4 June 1942 when he learned of American carriers in the vicinity. Originally armed with bombs for a second mission against Midway Island, Nagumo's planes were rearmed for an anti-shipping strike. By waiting to reorganize and rearm his bombers, he invited disaster, which was shortly visited upon him by three squadrons of SBDs from the American carriers. His aircraft were still on

deck when the American planes struck. Sometimes it is better to strike with what is available rather than wait to employ maximum force.

Communications was another factor which counted heavily in most carrier battles. Information was only valuable in relation to its timeliness. Hence the importance of long-distance radio. Both voice radio and Morse code were employed in 1942, but the state of the art left something to be desired. In the Battle of the Eastern Solomons (24 August) the US task force was plagued with poor air-to-air and surface-to-surface communications, resulting in missed opportunities and substantial confusion. Not until 1943 did reliable communications become available with VHF radio sets.

Efficient communications enabled tactical co-ordination and flexibility which could mean the difference between victory and defeat. But this applied not only to search and strike missions, for it was equally important to aerial defense of a carrier force. All US carriers had air-search radar which, linked to fighter direction networks, provided a means of intercepting enemy aircraft before they got within range. But fighter direction suffered from technical difficulty and lack of experience. This problem was best illustrated with *Hornet* in the Battle of Santa Cruz (26 October 1942) when Japanese planes got through the F4F combat air patrols as a result of poor co-ordination among task force FDOs (Fighter Director Officers). As usual, experience was the best teacher, but the lessons were sometimes costly. *Hornet* was abandoned and sunk after sustaining damage from repeated

US Navy

Right: TBD-1s of Torpedo Squadron Six aboard USS *Enterprise* (CV 6) in early 1942. Though modern for its day, when introduced to the fleet in 1937, the Devastator was well past its prime five years later.

Left: *Enterprise*'s F4Fs and SBDs, probably in May 1942 immediately before Midway. Her dive-bombers were instrumental in the decisive defeat of a greatly superior Japanese task force, though her torpedo planes suffered heavily.

Japanese air attacks.

Early experience demonstrated the need for more fighters aboard both American and Japanese carriers. Thus began a trend which continued until the end of the war, as fighters increasingly constituted larger portions of each air group. The reason was simple. A task force commander could use the bulk of his fighter strength either for defense of his ships, or as escort for dive-bombers and torpedo planes. There were seldom enough F4Fs to go around. Consequently, at Coral Sea 32 per cent of the American aircraft were Wildcats and 37 per cent of embarked Japanese planes were Zeroes. By the time of Eastern Solomons three months later, both sides had 41 per cent fighters and maintained that ratio to the end of the year.

Rather than reduce the number of torpedo planes to accommodate the extra F4Fs, most US carriers simply endured more crowded conditions. By late 1942 the average American air group contained nearly 90 aircraft, a 22 per cent increase over the pre-war complement.

Japanese air defense was complicated by the fact that Imperial Navy ships seldom had radar during the first year of the war. Therefore, the Japanese relied upon standing fighter patrols and sharp-eyed lookouts for advance warning of air attack. It was a disadvantage which US Navy pilots exploited more than once. Thanks to radar, no American carrier was surprised by an air attack in the first year of the war. But Japanese ships were likely to be pounced upon almost anytime with little or no warning. Low clouds and reduced visibility could aid a scout-bomber team in tracking an enemy force without being detected, allowing a quick attack before the defenses were aroused.

Ideally, once a hostile carrier force was located, at least one full air group would launch a co-ordinated strike with dive-bombers and torpedo planes. This procedure split the anti-aircraft guns and defending fighters, while the attack group's escorts engaged the enemy interceptors. It was a fine theory, and it worked when implemented in sufficient strength.

But in practice, the theory was seldom realized during 1942. On 7 May 1942, the first day of the Coral Sea battle, 93 planes from *Lexington* and *Yorktown* attacked the Japanese light carrier *Shoho*. The two air groups overwhelmed the defense and quickly sank the small carrier, even though she was protected by four cruisers and a destroyer. This remained the only fully co-ordinated US air strike

during the four carrier battles of 1942. The Japanese, however, mounted several well-organized attacks, but of smaller composition. The following day *Lexington* was lost to a Japanese air attack. This resulted in part to the Imperial Navy's tactic of dispersing its ships in several units well separated from one another. The Japanese believed that they stood a better chance of trapping enemy surface forces by attempting to surround them, and it afforded the opportunity of employing a small unit as a decoy. These goals were seldom accomplished, but the Japanese disposition did make the American fliers' job more difficult because they could not always concentrate their airpower at the decisive point.

Even where air attacks were effectively co-ordinated, torpedo planes on both sides frequently suffered high attrition. Nowhere was this better illustrated than at Midway, when three squadrons of Douglas TBDs were annihilated attacking the powerful Japanese force. Forty-one of the lumbering TBDs were launched and only five survived the attack. VT-8 was wiped out completely. Poor communications, a lack of timing, and simply bad luck all combined to pit the outmoded, underarmed TBDs against the might of the Imperial Navy. The six Wildcats in the area had to fight for their own lives against the greatly superior number of Zeroes. Consequently, the US torpedo planes suffered a loss rate of nearly 90 per cent.

Japanese torpedo bombers also endured heavy

Below: The saga of Torpedo Eight is well known, as USS *Hornet* (CV 8) lost all 15 of her TBDs. But a land-based detachment of six brand-new TBF-1s also sustained terrible casualties. This VT-8 Avenger, flown by Ensign Bert Earnest, was the only TBF to return to Midway, with a dead gunner and wounded radioman.

Right: *Enterprise*'s hangar deck, lined with tired maintenance and handling personnel. SBD is positioned on elevator, ready to be taken to the flight deck for another mission.

losses at the hands of defending fighters when caught without escort or the support of dive-bombers. Even the 'Kates', which could make faster and higher attacks with their superior torpedoes, were easy meat for determined F4F pilots. In the Santa Cruz battle one Wildcat pilot got among a group of Nakajimas attacking *Enterprise* and shot down five, plus two 'Vals'. Though the surviving Type 97s launched torpedoes, the violence of Lieutenant Stanley 'Swede' Vejtasa's attack disrupted the enemy concentration. On the same day another F4F pilot, Ensign George Wrenn off *Hornet*, accounted for five Japanese bombers.

One other aspect requires examination: the leadership of carrier forces in the first year of the Pacific War.

The men in charge

No senior officer on either side with overall responsibility for the conduct of a carrier battle was himself an aviator. This was partially due to the evolution of carriers within the combatant navies. Carriers had only been in existence for 20 years. Career patterns for officers with aviation backgrounds had not fully developed by 1942. As a result, the early carrier pilots were usually junior to

other flag officers.

The most experienced US carrier leader of the early war period was Rear Admiral Frank Jack Fletcher. An able officer, Fletcher was handicapped by a lack of prior association with aviation. Thus, he proceeded cautiously (some said timidly) by feeling his way as he went. Fletcher was in overall or partial command of US forces in the first three carrier duels: Coral Sea, Midway and Eastern Solomons.

At Santa Cruz in October 1942, Rear Admiral Thomas C. Kinkaid was Officer in Tactical Command. Like Fletcher, he was not an aviator and had even less practical experience. Kinkaid's handling of the battle has been widely criticized, but he bounced back to prominence as an amphibious leader.

Undeniably, the most successful American carrier commander of the first year after Pearl Harbor was Rear Admiral Raymond A. Spruance. Though he held only one such command, and for a very brief time, it was the one which counted most: Midway.

A staff officer and cruiser sailor most of his career, Spruance was acknowledged as one of the most intelligent men in the US Navy. When Vice

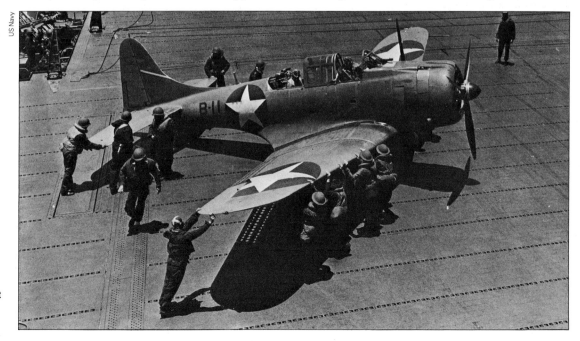

Right: A rare photo of a VB-8 SBD-3 aboard *Hornet* during the Midway battle. Hornet Air Group missed most of the action on 4 June, though her torpedo squadron was completely destroyed.

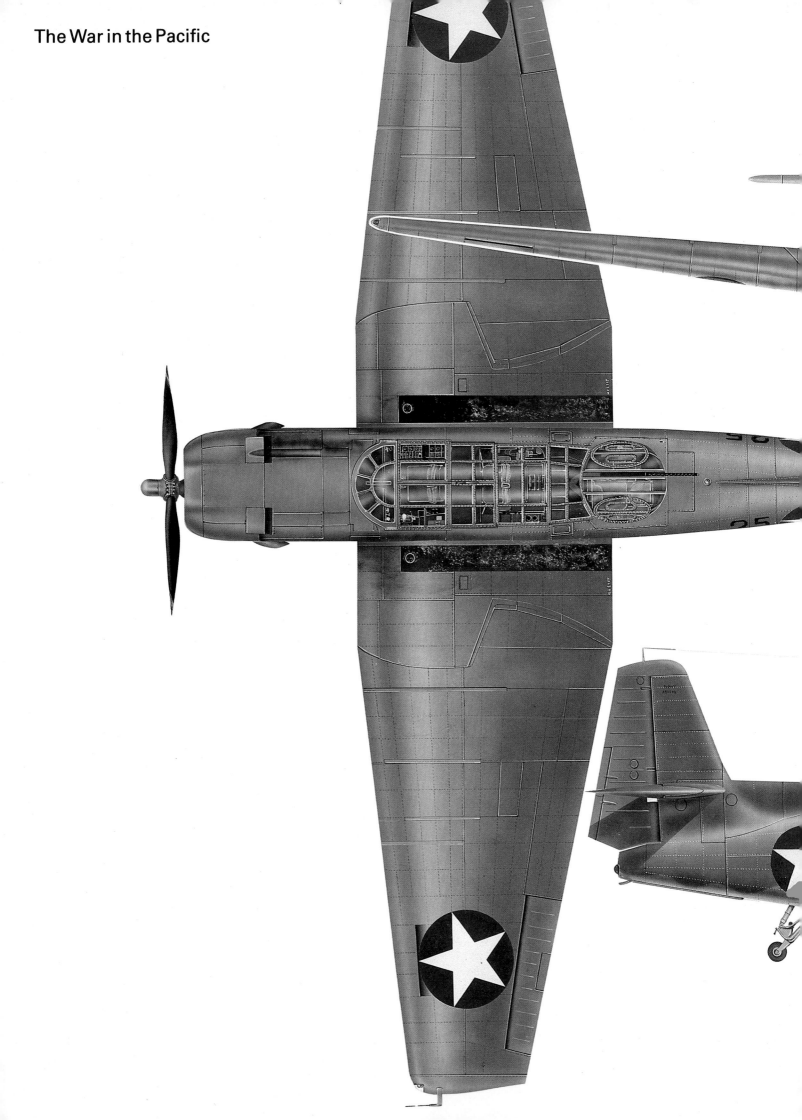

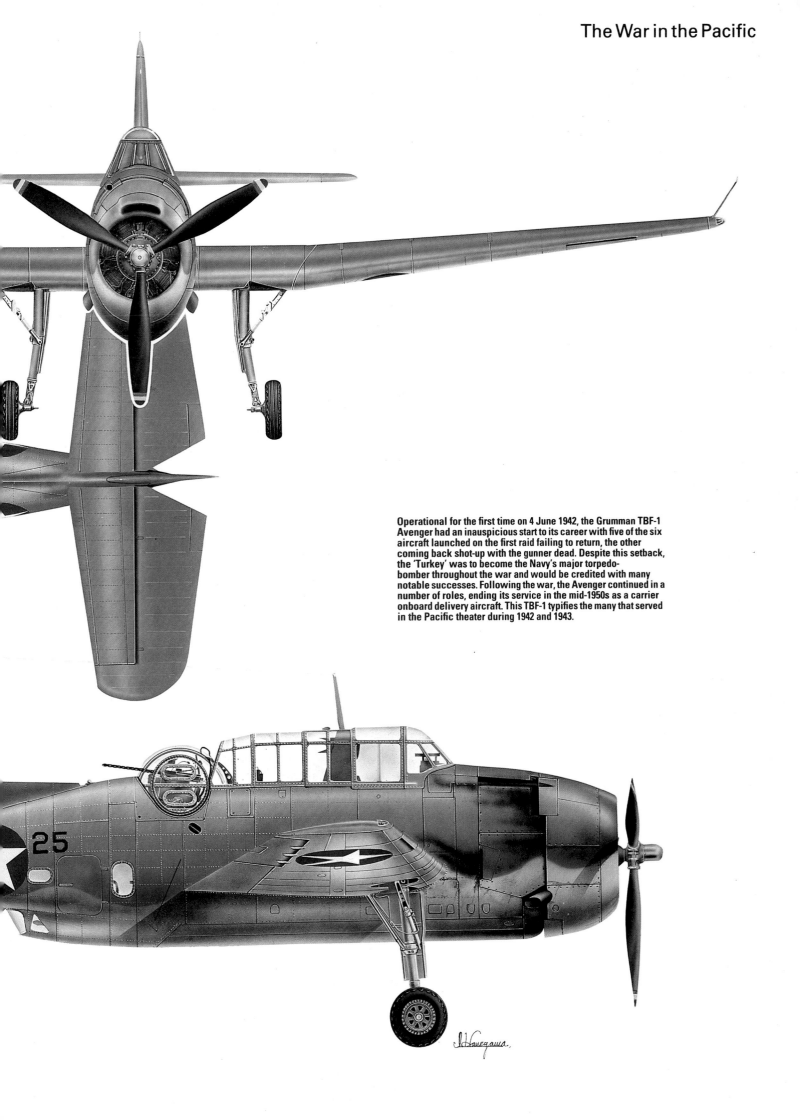

Operational for the first time on 4 June 1942, the Grumman TBF-1 Avenger had an inauspicious start to its career with five of the six aircraft launched on the first raid failing to return, the other coming back shot-up with the gunner dead. Despite this setback, the 'Turkey' was to become the Navy's major torpedo-bomber throughout the war and would be credited with many notable successes. Following the war, the Avenger continued in a number of roles, ending its service in the mid-1950s as a carrier onboard delivery aircraft. This TBF-1 typifies the many that served in the Pacific theater during 1942 and 1943.

Left: Bombing Eight crew Lieutenant Jim Riner and gunner examine battle damage following a strike against Japanese ships near the end of the Midway engagement. American carrier aircraft sank four enemy flat tops on 4 June and a heavy cruiser two days later.

Far left: Midway, six months after Pearl Harbor. Repair crews work diligently to repair bomb damage to USS *Yorktown* (CV 5). They did their job so well that the second enemy air strike launched from the only remaining carrier hit the *Yorktown* again, believing she was an undamaged target. Finally sunk by a submarine on 7 June 1942, CV 5 was instrumental in winning the battle that turned the tide of the war.

Admiral William F. Halsey became ill shortly before the Battle of Midway, he named Spruance to take command of the *Enterprise* and *Hornet* task force. Halsey was one of the more experienced carrier commanders at the time, for he had become a flier before the war. Like many of his contemporaries, he came late to aviation, filling a requirement for senior officers with minimal aviation background. He was originally a battleship officer, but learned to fly in 1934 at age 52.

Once at sea with Halsey's command, Spruance relied heavily upon his staff for technical and operational advice. But after Fletcher's flagship *Yorktown* was disabled by Japanese air attacks, Spruance assumed overall command of the crucial Midway engagement. He combined prudent caution with intelligent aggressiveness, and was rewarded with a stunning victory.

American leadership met the challenge at upper and lower levels as well. Admiral Chester Nimitz, a submarine officer commanding the Pacific Fleet, possessed the wisdom and courage to allow his task force commanders, Fletcher and Spruance, to fight the battle without interference from above. Fortuitously, the tactical leaders at air group and squadron level, particularly in *Enterprise* and *Yorktown*, were mostly dedicated professional aviators. Two standouts were classmates from the Annapolis class of 1926: Lieutenant Commanders Wade McClusky leading Enterprise Air Group and Maxwell F. Leslie commanding Bombing Squadron Three in *Yorktown*.

The Imperial Navy's Carrier Striking Force was led almost exclusively by one man, Vice Admiral Chuichi Nagumo. With a broad knowledge of destroyer and torpedo tactics, Nagumo was perhaps even more poorly placed than his American counterparts to direct a carrier battle. His immediate subordinates were only marginally more experienced in aviation, so the middle-level Japanese staff officers wielded considerable influence. His staff included veteran fliers like Commander Minoru Genda, the brilliant strategist, and Commander Mitsuo Fuchida, strike leader of the Pearl Harbor attack. He also had other combat-experienced air operations planners or tactical commanders.

Nagumo's force led an exceedingly active nine months after Pearl Harbor. Following close upon the dramatic success of the Hawaiian attack came a victorious sweep of the Indian Ocean which drove British Naval power from that region. Coral Sea was the only carrier battle in which Nagumo did not participate in 1942, as his units were in Japanese home waters during early May. But shortly after, they embarked upon the ill-fated Midway venture, calculated to draw out the remaining American flat tops and destroy them near Hawaii.

Nagumo also directed the Eastern Solomons and Santa Cruz engagements associated with the Guadalcanal campaign. Following Midway, however, he grew even more cautious than he had been previously. (At Pearl Harbor he ignored staff advice to launch a follow-up strike to destroy the US fuel supplies. His squadrons had destroyed the American battleships which were his main objective, and he withdrew, adhering to the letter of his orders.) Nagumo finished his career as a shore-based admiral and died on Guam in June 1944.

Of the four 1942 flat top battles, Midway was the only clear-cut tactical and strategic victory for either side. The USA lost *Yorktown*, but the elite of Japanese naval aviation went down with the *Kaga*, *Akagi*, *Hiryu* and *Soryu*. In the Coral Sea and Santa Cruz duels, the Americans lost more matériel than the Japanese but preserved the strategic status quo. This was especially true of Coral Sea, which cost the *Lexington* but foiled the Japanese thrust towards Port Moresby, New Guinea and thus kept Australia out of danger. The Japanese lost the light carrier *Shoho*. Eastern Solomons has often been called a draw, but the US came out ahead, blunting the first enemy riposte at Guadalcanal. The great disappointment of this battle (also called the Stewart Islands) was the number of missed opportunities.

In these four engagements the US Navy lost three carriers and the Japanese six. *Wasp* was sunk by a Japanese submarine in September, raising total American carrier losses to four. With *Saratoga* out of commission from submarine-inflicted torpedo damage, the USA had only *Enterprise* to rely upon

Below: Based on *Yorktown* (CV-5) for the Midway battle, VF-3 was forced to seek a new home when that carrier was fatally damaged. Here, VF-3's skipper LCDR 'Jimmy' Thach recovers aboard *Hornet* (CV-8) on 6 June from *Enterprise* (CV-6). Thach assumed command of the combined VF-3 and VF-8 survivors.

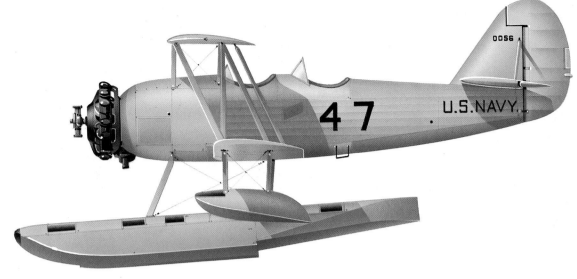

from late October when *Hornet* went down off Santa Cruz.

Experienced aviators were also in short supply during 1942. The same names repeatedly appear in the after-action reports, and it has been reliably estimated that approximately 400 Navy pilots bore the main burden of carrier warfare in the crucial period from Pearl Harbor to Guadalcanal. Not until the expanded flight training program in the USA took effect in 1943 could these few hundred fliers expect relief.

Midway and Guadalcanal determined that the Pacific War would become a prolonged conflict of attrition, the type of war Japan could not afford. This in itself is reason enough to consider the aircraft-carrier the dominant weapon of the era. Simultaneously, these battles proved that the battleship was no longer supreme in the world's navies. From 1942 to 1945 the Imperial Navy lost 10 of its 11 'battlewagons' to enemy action. Six of these were sunk by carrier-based aircraft.

In short, the aircraft-carrier in all its sizes and roles became the new capital ship of the 20th century. As such, it became the number one target for destruction by its opponents. As war correspon-

Below: Naval Air Training Command used a variety of obsolete aircraft early in the war. These Boeing F4Bs, still wearing fleet colors, were flown by advanced student pilots in 1941-2 in addition to F3Bs and SBUs.

dent Ernie Pyle observed, it was a tenuous honor, but a proud one.

17
Naval Aviation Training

It was hard enough to produce a naval air force by ordering more aircraft during the abrupt transition from peace to war. It was perhaps harder still to turn out the men to maintain and fly those planes. For, granting the immense industrial and engineering effort of producing over 60,000 combat aircraft during the war years, the Navy needed tens of thousands of highly-qualified young men and women to fly and maintain them as well.

Suddenly involved in a shooting war, with a draft system in effect, Navy airpower faced the haunting prospect of losing many of those people to Army conscription. But a method was quickly found to preserve the manpower pool. Various deferred entry schemes were enacted, the two most common being the V-1 and V-5 programs. Both involved college students who expressed an interest in Naval

Robert L. Lawson Collection

Left: A floatplane N3N-1 beached at Pensacola. Strong, stable and versatile, the N3N series remained in Training Command until well into the war.

Far left: Floyd Bennett Field was the Naval Air Station at New York. In 1941 the training base operated N3N-1s built by the Naval Aircraft Factory.

Aviation. The V-1 program guaranteed college freshmen and sophomores that they could complete their first two years of study. The majority of these young men were earmarked for flight training. V-5 was an all-aviation program which insured completion of the first year of college.

With a manpower pool assured, the Navy quickly turned to the means of providing quality training to the student fliers. Fortunately, work was already under way for such a buildup at the time of Pearl Harbor. The civilian Pilot Training Program (later called War Training Service) provided for 20,000 Navy or Marine Corps pilots per year at 92 educational institutions around the country. Contracts with local civilian flying schools enabled the prospective airmen to receive initial exposure to aviation and helped substantially reduce the number of 'washouts' at Navy training bases later on.

Naval flight training involved four stages: preflight, primary, intermediate and advanced. Preflight was just that, with no actual flying but intense preparation. This phase consisted of rigorous physical conditioning with constant emphasis upon teamwork. An effort was also made to convince the future combat pilots that they were being prepared not merely to fly, but to fight. In the words of one Navy account 'We were fighting a vicious foe; preflight was to prepare the pilot for this fact, in mind as well as in body.'

Five preflight schools were established in 1942, and they worked around the clock. It was almost impossible to cover all the pertinent subjects in the allotted time, but the job was done. Of particular importance to Naval Aviators was swimming ability, a skill lacking among over one-fourth of all

entering trainees. Those who failed to learn, failed to fly; it was literally sink or swim.

In the huge expansion program, primary flight training was moved from Pensacola, Florida, and Corpus Christi, Texas, the traditional hatcheries of Naval Aviation. Naval Reserve Air Bases were established to handle the initial training of fleet pilots: a work- and study-crammed three-month course which got the students soloed and acquainted with such techniques as aerobatics and formation flying. The aircraft were Boeing-Stearman N2S and Naval Aircraft Factory N3N biplanes; rugged, easily-maintained trainers with tandem seating. The instructor sat up front, communicating with the student via a Gosport speaking tube. Some instructors took additional means of education. A lettered notation on the goggles strap frequently read, 'Climb and glide – 65 knots'. Since the student's forward view stopped with the back of the instructor's head, the message was well learned.

Originally some 3,000 primary trainers were envisioned with 2,100 primary instructors, including 300 ground-school teachers. But these figures were eventually passed as the program grew. Ground school, while never glamorous, was essential. Mathematics, theory of flight and meteorology all had to be absorbed in addition to flight instruction.

Intermediate flight training involved 14 weeks at Pensacola or Corpus Christi. Here the student pilots transitioned to more sophisticated aircraft: North American SNJs which prepared them for combat types. All-metal monoplanes with retractable landing gear and constant-speed propellers, the 'J-Birds' were notoriously tricky to land because of their narrow landing gear. Additionally, gunnery

Left: With a vastly expanded pilot-training program, Naval Air Training Command needed hundreds of new aircraft. The N2S series filled the gap, as it could be produced faster and for less cost than the prewar N3N design. This N2S-2 was photographed at NAS Corpus Christi, Texas in 1943.

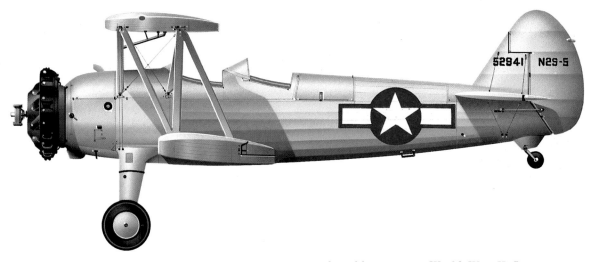

Right: Employed as a primary trainer for much of World War II, Stearman's Model 75 biplane was known in naval parlance as the N2S, several thousand being delivered to this service. The aircraft shown here is to the final N2S-5 standard.

and night navigation flights were introduced. At the conclusion of the intermediate stage, cadets were allowed to fly fleet-type aircraft: fighters, torpedo planes or patrol planes

The pilot-training program

From primary through intermediate, trainee attrition averaged about 30 per cent. In many cases, 'attrition' involved the literal interpretation as fatalities occurred. Stall-spin accidents were the most frequent killer, as they have been since the dawn of powered flight. Mid-air collisions came next among fatal accidents, though landings were by far the greatest cause of all accidents. As one training manual noted, 'Naval Aviation is *not* a sport – it is a scientific profession', and attitude had much to do with safety.

But rather than death or injury, most washed-out students failed for inability to keep up with classmates. It was not that they could not fly, for CPT eliminated most of those cases. It was simply that they failed to meet the Navy's rigorous standards in the available time. With a global war in progress, it was impractical to provide additional instruction when seven out of 10 students were progressing well.

Experience proved that some washout criteria were too severe, however. By far the most-men-

tioned problem among World War II fliers was Morse code. Failure to master the dit-dah alphabet or its efficient transmission and reception undid hundreds (perhaps thousands) of otherwise qualified individuals. In fleet service, Morse code was hardly ever used by tactical pilots. Radio specialists in attack and patrol aircraft handled that chore.

Advanced, or operational, training concluded the student Naval Aviator's studies. Here the pilot was assigned the type of aircraft he would fly in the fleet: fighter, dive-bomber, torpedo plane, observation or patrol plane. The program included more gunnery and ordnance experience than intermediate had permitted, for the aviators were now specialized.

Scout-observation pilots (VOS) went through two months of training for flying off catapults on battleships and cruisers. Patrol plane pilots (VP) experienced a similar period of 'finishing school' before they joined Consolidated PBY or Martin PBM flying-boat squadrons. Land-based patrol bombers (VPB) included Consolidated PB4Y-1 Liberators and Consolidated PB4Y-2 Privateers in addition to twin-engine Lockheed PV Venturas and North American PBJ Mitchells.

Carrier pilots had one final and dramatic phase before them. Whether assigned to fighters (VF), dive-bombers (VB) or torpedo planes (VT), they had to qualify with a minimum number of launches and

Below: Without doubt one of the most widely used trainer aircraft of all time, North American's Texan saw extensive service with the US Navy. This picture depicts SNJ-4s on the Corpus Christi flight line during World War II when the training effort was at its peak.

landings aboard an aircraft-carrier – the element that has always separated carrier aviators from other pilots. Amid the appaling shortage of flat tops early in the war, an innovative stop-gap was found. Two Great Lakes excursion vessels, flat-bottom paddle-wheelers, were hastily modified with flight decks and arresting cables. The Carrier Qualification Training Unit operated on Lake Michigan until winter drove the organization to San Diego on the west coast, where escort carriers were available. But from 1943 on, CQTU remained in the Great Lakes, teaching fledgling tailhook aviators the tricks of the trade. CQTU also provided new landing signal officers with practical experience.

Most Naval Aviators emerged from advanced training with at least 250 hours of flight time, and frequently with 300 or more. But the Navy needed more than pilots, because even with thousands of new aviators, personnel were often stretched thin. In the VP community, for instance, prewar practice called for three rated pilots per crew. The aircraft commander nearly always occupied one seat, alternating with the two junior pilots. One of the latter was designated navigator for a particular flight. Since P-boats typically flew 700-mile (1125-km) searches, navigational skill was devoutly to be desired.

However, with aviator requirements expanded by orders of magnitude, it was seldom possible to assign three pilots to a flying-boat or patrol bomber. This led to training of non-pilot navigators; individuals who sometimes lacked the physical qualifications for pilot's wings but who could master the variety of navigation techniques in the limited time available. The curriculum was a daunting one; celestial navigation by day and night, dead-reckoning, map-reading, radio navigation and related subjects. Many people can be taught to navigate but it is a rare individual who understands the subject.

Another oft-neglected aspect of Navy flight training is ship and aircraft recognition. The first consideration in any type of combat is, simply: friend or foe? As a means of helping answer that fundamental question, the Navy in January 1942 turned to the greatest source of untapped talent in America: its school children.

The Navy asked elementary and high school students, many of whom were already aviation enthusiasts, for a half-million models of US, British, Japanese and German aircraft. Each model was scaled to represent the genuine aircraft as seen from a half-mile when placed 35 ft (10.7 m) away. Working with government-supplied drawings, the youngsters met the quota in so short a time that the Navy asked for 300,000 more models before the end of the year.

Pilot trainees were also drilled in silhouettes of aircraft with exposure times ranging from $\frac{1}{10}$ to merely $\frac{1}{75}$ of a second. Eventually even ship silhouettes were mastered this way, and the aviators were also taught to recognize the characteristics of ships' wakes. While this type of training was certainly useful, it had inherent limits. Accurate intelligence on Japanese combatant and merchant vessels was often incomplete, and translation of ship names frequently erred. By way of example, when the light carrier *Shoho* was sunk in the Coral Sea, she was labled *Ryukaku*, a complete misnomer. Similarly, at 1st Philippine Sea in June 1944, Task Force 58 aviators reported seeing 'Hyataka' class carriers. No such ship type existed in the Japanese or any other navy.

By early 1944, the Navy had ample pilots on hand to meet anticipated needs for operations. Therefore, those in the training pipeline were reduced to a point marginally above that which would provide for replacement of combat and operational losses. Student Naval Aviators were reduced from 25,000 to 20,000 and eight training establishments were closed. It came as a blow to the students cut from training, as nearly all of them would have won their Wings of Gold. Few of these men opted for the chance to return to civilian status, as that inevitably meant being drafted into the army. What worse fate for a sailor? Most transferred to aircrew training, as a shortage existed there, or opted to try for commissions as deck officers on surface vessels.

However, the Navy had a cadre of experienced, professional non-commissioned aviators. Officially designated Naval Aviation Pilots, these men were rated as petty or warrant officers, but possessed significant flying experience. The NAP program originated in 1932, at a time of budgetary crisis, as a

Above: 16 North American SNJ-1s were ordered following the success of the fixed-undercarriage NJ-1. Subsequent marks of SNJ (SNJ-2 thru SNJ-6) were used in large numbers as advanced trainers. Several were fitted with arrester hooks for deck training.

Left: Operational training was conducted all over the United States in a variety of aircraft. PV-1 Venturas provided additional experience for new patrol-bomber crews at Sanford, Florida in 1943.

Right: Yankee ingenuity at work. To meet the crying demand for trained carrier pilots, two Great Lakes paddle-wheelers were hastily converted to aircraft-carriers. Here an SNJ-3C operates off one of the improvised flat tops, the *Wolverine*, on 2 November 1942.

US Navy

means of manning cockpits without the expense of commissioning all pilots. There were some 850 NAPs by 1941, and most eventually obtained commissions, if only 'for the duration'. NAPs were most frequently found in transport or patrol planes, but they also flew fighters and torpedo bombers throughout 1942.

Though the last of the 'Flying Chiefs' retired in 1971, the NAP program remains a landmark of pride and competence in Naval Aviation.

Aviation training was consolidated in 1943 under Naval Air Training Command. This arrangement streamlined the program and aided standardization, procurement and procedures to an extent that required little modification thereafter. Non-flying training continued much as before, but with closer coordination.

Aircraft maintenance was one of the areas most affected by the sudden wartime expansion. In December 1941, for example, fewer than 8,000 sailors were engaged in all phases of aviation technical training. Twelve months later there were over 31,000 in primary technical schools alone. Airframe, powerplant, ordnance and electronics specialists all had to be provided to fleet units and shore-based support facilities and bases around the globe.

Pre-war carrier squadrons had their own maintenance personnel, but those were the days when each flat top usually operated its own air group. With the reshuffling and rotation policies required in wartime, it became inefficient to try to arrange

for transfer of squadron mechanics to appropriate ships all the time. Thus, the Carrier Aircraft Service Unit came into being. Originated in early 1942, by mid-1943 it had gained wide favor. CASUs provided detachments to carriers, in effect becoming part of the ship's company. Incoming squadrons brought some of their own support personnel, but heavy maintenance was performed by detachments (CASDs) as resident specialists.

CASUs operating at forward airbases sometimes had a foot in the infantry world as well as aviation. One such unit went ashore on D+4 at Tarawa to prepare for the arrival of two fighter squadrons.

Another early wartime innovation was the Aviation Volunteer Specialist program at Quonset Point, Rhode Island. Established in February, 1942, the AV(S) rating was just one of a number in the administrative field. Regulars joked that the newcomers commissioned as reservists were 'ninety-day wonders', since they held equal rank with ensigns commissioned after four years at Annapolis.

The temporary nature of AV(S) officers' careers was explained in the slang of the period as meaning 'After Victory, Scram'. But the fact remains that the Navy could not have functioned without the thousands of professional and semi-professional men who became AV(S) officers. Lawyers, accountants, stock brokers, journalists and college instructors were all represented.

Those Quonset Point graduates slated for aviation filled a variety of duties. They became photo-

Below: Outdated or substandard aircraft remained in training squadrons well into the war. Representative of such types was this Brewster SB2A-4, flown by prospective scout-bomber pilots at Vero Beach, Florida circa 1942-3.

US Navy

Left: Learning the trade, a fledgling dive-bomber pilot practices with live ordnance at NAS Fort Lauderdale, circa 1944. The SB2C-1 was regarded as a tricky aircraft to fly well, and demanded close attention from its crew.

graphic interpreters, combat intelligence officers and engineering supervisors. But perhaps the most sought-after individuals became fighter direction officers.

With the advent of radar at sea, control of carrier-based interceptors was a natural progression. Such was the importance attached to the FDO program that at one time it ranked in Navy priority second only to that service's role in developing the atomic bomb. The Navy therefore received virtual carte-blanche on prospective FDOs and selected only highly competent candidates.

Since a fighter director is nothing if not a manager, individuals with successful business records were prime candidates. The ability to think spatially, to express oneself clearly and to remain calm under stress marked the proficient FDO. His training involved wild extremes: from riding tricycles to learn the concepts, to mastering scientific and technical data on radar performance.

Aviation training at all levels was organized and conducted with time-proven methods tailored to the urgent press of war. Yet the quality of that training remained extremely high, and even 40 years later Navy veterans of World War II, be they fliers or photographers, are still recognized as among the finest of all time.

18
The VP War

The dominant characteristic of the Pacific conflict was distance. Covering over 64 million square miles, the Pacific represents nearly half the Earth's water surface. While combat operations occurred in 'only' about half that area, it was still by far the largest arena of all time.

Consequently, aircraft operated by both sides needed amphibious or long-range capabilities, or even both. Flying-boats and land-based patrol bombers played a largely unheralded role in the Pacific War, but some operations would have been impossible without them. This, briefly, is their story.

The US Navy lumped all its multi-engine aircraft into two generic categories, designated VP (for patrol) or VB (for bombing). They were later more properly defined as VPB for patrol bomber, but their missions were approximately similar.

Among the flying-boats and amphibians, the ubiquitous Consolidated PBY has already been introduced. Aircrews called the high-wing, twin-engine airplane the '90-kt wonder', since it could

Left: Life's embarrassing moments can be many for a naval aviator. This F4U-1 pilot ended up in the catwalk of escort carrier *Guadalcanal* (CVE 60) on 4 May 1945. Over half of all Corsair losses in World War II were in training or other non-combat categories.

US Navy

Above: A typical scene on the Aleutian Islands during the course of 1943 when the USA was embroiled in the war in the Pacific. Eight examples of the Lockheed PV-1 Ventura can be seen alongside a brace of Consolidated PBY-5A Catalina amphibians. These patrol planes were assigned to VB-135 and -136.

cruise for 20 hours or more at 110 mph (177 km/h). Long-ranged and surprisingly versatile, the Catalina nonetheless had limitations. Chiefly, it was poorly equipped to defend itself and consequently did much of its good work at night.

Undoubtedly the most famous PBY operations were those conducted by the 'Black Cat' squadrons. Actually, both the units and their aircraft became known as Black Cats. Well-suited to nocturnal flying, with radar and bombs or torpedoes, they were just that, black-painted PBYs which stalked Japanese ships and raided their bases by night.

The first of the nocturnal prowlers devoted wholly to such work was VP-12, flying from Guadalcanal in December 1942. The concept proved so successful that other squadrons such as VP-54 and -81 became engaged in night search and strike missions.

As the Allied forces gained new bases further up the Solomons, more Black Cat units were trained and sent to the theater. Fleet Air Wing 17 in New Guinea sent three Black Cat squadrons against Rabaul during the latter part of 1943 into 1944, helping blockade the important naval-air base. Eventually the aerial stranglehold tightened and very few enemy ships could enter or leave the harbor by day or night.

However, to hundreds of US and Allied fliers, PBY spelled Dumbo. Nobody seems to recall just

how Catalinas became associated with the name of Walt Disney's popular cartoon elephant, but Dumbo missions were no laughing matter to downed aviators in hostile waters. PBY squadrons recorded numerous spectacular feats in the air-sea rescue business, some of which explored the boundaries of human courage.

Patrol Squadron 34 was a PBY-5A unit which flew frequent Dumbo missions. On 15 February 1944, Lieutenant Nathan Gordon was circling on standby duty while Army Air Force Douglas A-20s and North American B-25s struck Kavieng harbor in New Britain. Three of the twin-engine bombers were shot down in the harbor, and the Republic P-47 escort called in Gordon to attempt a rescue.

Despite intense anti-aircraft and small-arms fire, Gordon landed near the first raft he saw. Taxiing close, he found it was empty and took off. But shortly after this six bomber crewmen were spotted in another rubber raft and the Cat splashed down nearby. However, Gordon's crew reported that the army fliers had trouble getting aboard; the idling engine tended to blow the raft away from the aircraft. Gordon shut down to ease the transfer, all the while under fire from shore. He then restarted, turned about and took off into heavy swells.

A third landing was accomplished to rescue three more men, but the PBY had sprung serious leaks.

US Navy

Right: The rugged beauty of the Aleutians must have pleased this PBY crew, if for no other reason than the view ensured a good flying weather. Catalinas operated in Alaska from 1941 throughout the war.

Headed home with nine survivors and considerable water aboard, Gordon was notified that yet another raft had been sighted by the Thunderbolts. He wheeled around and headed back, willing to risk 19 lives (counting his own crew) to save another six.

This landing was the wildest of the day. Gordon had to fly an approach directly over the beach at low level in order to reach the army men. He landed a mere 600 yards (550 m) from shore, fully exposed to automatic weapons fire. Somehow he got the final half-dozen fliers aboard and managed an overloaded take-off with 25 people in the crowded PBY.

Nathan Gordon became only the fifth Naval Aviator awarded the Medal of Honor in World War II. No other decoration was thinkable.

Dumbo crews continued such heroics almost to war's end. Little more than a year later another Catalina found itself in similar circumstances. US 7th Air Force North American P-51s, based on newly-won Iwo Jima in the Bonins, flew frequent strikes against nearby enemy islands. A Mustang pilot had bailed out near Chichi Jima and was reported immobile in his liferaft. The duty Dumbo landed offshore and moved in close while under mortar and machine-gun fire. The army pilot remained in his raft, but rather than abandon him the PBY crew actually put a man in the raft to confirm the flier was dead. Only then did the flying-boat depart.

This episode, while resulting in no rescue, re-quired a particular brand of courage. The Catalina crew risked more than death, for Chichi Jima was occupied by fanatical Japanese under a barbarian commander, later executed for war crimes which included ceremonial beheadings and cannibalism of captured American fliers.

Coronado and Mariner

Two other flying-boats served in the Pacific, including Consolidated's follow-on, the PB2Y Coronado. This huge four-engine aircraft, with a 115-ft (35.05-m) wing span and gross weight of 68,000 lb (30845 kg), first flew in December 1937, but was built only in limited numbers. Because of the then-extravagant unit price of $300,000 (three times a PBY) only 176 PB2Y-3s were built. Coronados experienced very little combat, but with their 200-mph (322-km/h) top speed and 140-mph (225-km/h) cruise they remained in service to the end of 1945. The last 41 were built exclusively as transports in the PB2Y-3R variant, raising total production to barely 220.

Martin's gull-winged PBM Mariner was a more numerous and undoubtedly more successful flying-boat. The twin-engine, twin-tailed PBM first flew in February 1939 and joined the fleet in the fall of 1940 with VP-55. Its gross weight fell five tons below that of the Coronado and it lacked the PB2Y's speed, but its combat capability was considerable. A 2,000-lb

Above: Patrol Squadron 52 was one of the famed 'Black Cat' units which prowled the dark night in search of Japanese shipping in the South Pacific. Airborne radar greatly aided nocturnal search and attack, though number 45's black paint is wearing thin.

Left: Consolidated's follow-on to the PBY was the giant PB2Y Coronado. This PB2Y-3R transport version has arrived at NAS Honolulu.

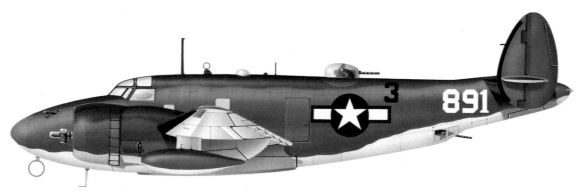

Right: Typical of the large number of Lockheed PV-1 Venturas which saw combat duty during World War II, this particular specimen was assigned to Bombing Squadron VB-135 in 1944 when this unit was in action over the Pacific Ocean.

Above: The PB2Y-5 seemed even larger than previous models, with addition of a radome aft of the flight deck. This in-flight shot graphically shows off the Coronado's 115-ft (35.05 m) wingspan.

served well. Exceptionally fast and well-armed, they toted two 0.5-in (12.7-mm) guns in the nose, another pair in a power turret, and twin 0.3-in (7.62-mm) guns in a ventral mount. Equipped with six depth charges or 500-lb (227-kg) bombs, PV-1s could find their prey in darkness or poor weather with airborne radar. In fact, a Marine Corps squadron became the naval service's first night-fighter unit in combat with PV-1s, flying in the Solomons.

The bigger PV-2 Harpoon was ordered in June 1943. With almost 10 ft (3.05 m) more wing span and a half-ton heavier, its top speed was lower than that of the PV-1 but cruise was marginally faster and range slightly greater. Some 500 Harpoons equipped 14 Navy squadrons throughout the war in all theaters. At least three VP units flew PV-2s in the Pacific, including one in the Aleutians.

PV crews saw much action in that perennially fogbound region. Warm air accompanying the Japanese Current inevitably meets cold fronts generated in Siberia, resulting in quite possibly the world's worst year-round flying weather. PatWing Four established its headquarters on Adak Island in March 1943, with two PV-1 squadrons to help support the invasion of Attu in May. One escort carrier was on hand with F4Fs, but the Grummans fared poorly: eight Wildcats and five pilots were lost in bad weather, with no enemy-inflicted casualties.

In April 1944, the PV-2s arrived and began operations against the Kuriles in what became known as the route of 'The Empire Express'. PBYs had originally accompanied Army Air Force B-25s on these

(907-kg) ordnance load of bombs or depth charges was possible, and the PBM-3C and PBM-3D variants carried radar primarily for anti-submarine work. Over 1,300 PBMs were built, and their service life of 16 years remained second only to the Douglas A-1 Skyraider in the US Navy as of 1970.

Among land-based naval aircraft, two main types dominated. Lockheed's PV series began with navalized Venturas, including 380 taken from lend-lease shipments to the UK. Some 1,600 PV-1s were delivered from late 1942 to mid-1944, and they

Right: Seaplane tender USS Tangier (AV-8) hoists a PBM-3D aboard for maintenance in November 1944. Mariners had extensive service in the Central Pacific from late 1943, usually on long-range reconnaissance missions.

The War in the Pacific

A Lockheed PV-2 Harpoon of VB-142 in the Marianas Islands at the end of World War II. It was one of the original and most common variants with a forward-firing armament of five guns, two high in the nose and three below the nose, with this number later increased to eight. Although the general configuration was similar to the PV-1 Ventura, the PV-2 incorporated larger fins and rudders, increased wing span and fuel capacity.

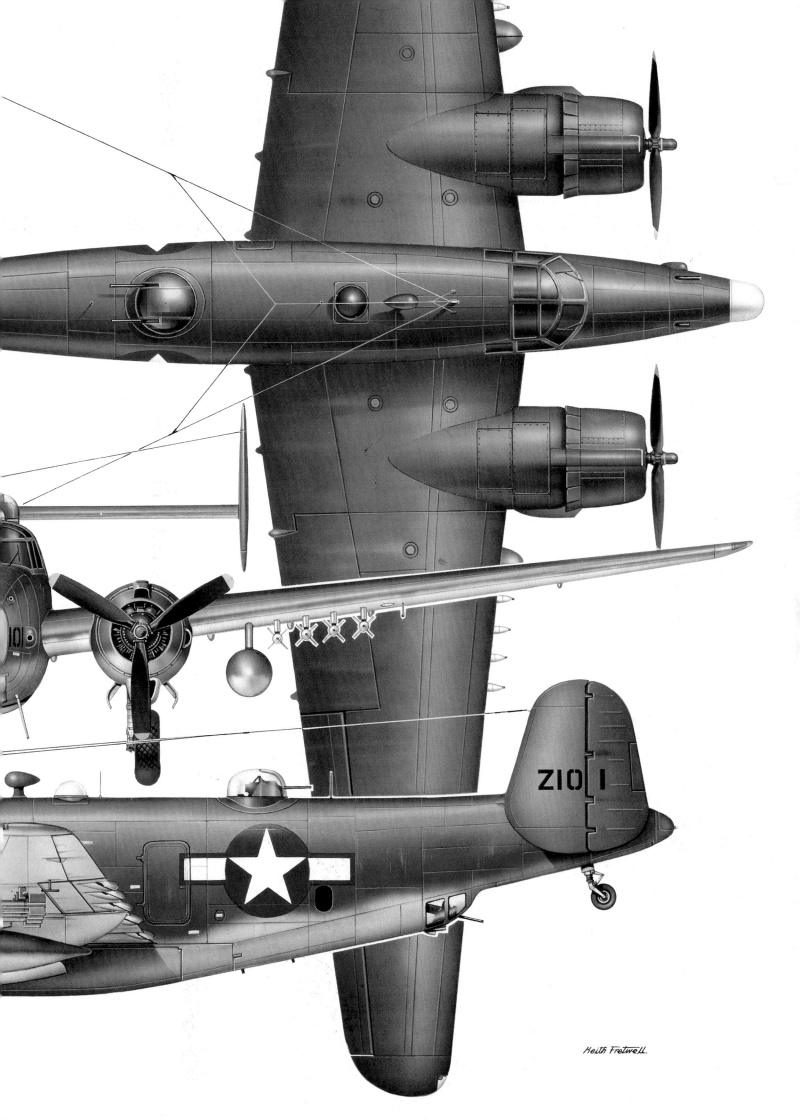

Keith Fretwell.

Left: The late-war color scheme of overall gloss blue adorns this Lockheed Ventura on Guam near the war's end in July 1945. Retention of full armament was frequently unusual in secure areas, but this PV has both nose and turret guns in place.

missions, but the Catalinas had insufficient speed or altitude to regularly perform the chore. Therefore, the Harpoons went to work and soon made their presence felt in northern Japanese waters. With five forward-firing 0.5-in (12.7-mm) guns and rails for rockets, the PV-2s were highly effective anti-shipping aircraft.

Multi-role Liberator

However, first and foremost among the VP types was the Consolidated Liberator. Like the PV, it was built in two distinct versions: first were Army Air Force B-24Ds, the initial batch of what became nearly 1,000 PB4Y-1s. That was in August 1942, when the Navy recognized the need for land-based heavy bombers capable of not only great range, but both offensive and defensive capability.

As previously related, Navy Liberators figured prominently in the anti-submarine campaign in European waters. In the Pacific it was a different story. Their primary role was not significantly different from their Army Air Force counterparts, but the means of employment was unique.

Partly owing to limited numbers and partly to doctrine, the PB4Ys usually operated singly or in pairs. The first squadron was VPB-101, which began flying in the Solomons in February 1943. These were stock B-24Ds with bombardier noses, vulnerable to frontal fighter attack. Early missions sustained relatively heavy losses, so VPB-101 switched to night-flying until July.

By then, however, the first Navy-modified Liberators had arrived. These were the planes of VPB-102 with 'bow turrets' containing two 0.5-in (12.7-mm) guns. The CO was legendary in VP circles. Lieutenant Commander Bruce Van Voorhis took his squadron into Guadalcanal in April 1943, and quickly established a reputation for unusual (some said wild) aggressiveness.

In any case, Van Voorhis got things done, at a price. He became the only patrol-bomber pilot to win the Medal of Honor when the took his PB4Y-1

into a Japanese beehive, Kapingamorangi Atoll near the Solomons, on 6 July 1943. The enemy base was home of a flock of seaplanes and a weather station, and Van Voorhis meant to destroy it. He made repeated low-level attacks in the face of alerted flak and fighters, sustaining accumulating damage. On the sixth pass his Liberator was finally shot down with loss of the entire crew. The squadron completed its first tour in the next month.

Another VPB skipper with a reputation for aggressiveness was Commander Harry Sears of VPB-104. Flying a lengthy search to the north, he found six Japanese transports southbound, undoubtedly from Truk in the Carolines. Sears swung his patrol bomber into position and proceeded to whittle down the convoy methodically. In a series of masthead attacks he sank four ships, probably a fifth and damaged the sixth. His expert low-level bombing had not lacked opposition, however, as the PB4Y limped home on only three engines.

Sears' crews flew two tours in PB4Ys, having originally been equipped with Catalinas. They hunted enemy reconnaissance aircraft and bombers as enthusiastically as Japanese ships, and shot down at least nine hostile airplanes.

An unheralded aspect of Liberator operations was the activities of five photo-reconnaissance squadrons. The first of these, VD-1, came to Guadalcanal in April 1943, the same month as Van Voorhis' VPB-102. Next came VD-3, which flew into Tarawa shortly after the Marines took that hotly-contested atoll in November. VD-4 operated

Bottom left: The 12-man crew of 'Mitzi-Bishi' flew with VB-106, one of the early PB4Y squadrons committed to combat. Inaugurated to the Solomons campaign in the fall of 1943, US Navy Liberators eventually flew to the Philippines, China and Okinawa.

Below: The heavy in the VPB line-up was Consolidated's B-24 Liberator adapted to naval use. These PB4Y-1s, with early radar under the wings, were photographed in flight during the summer of 1943.

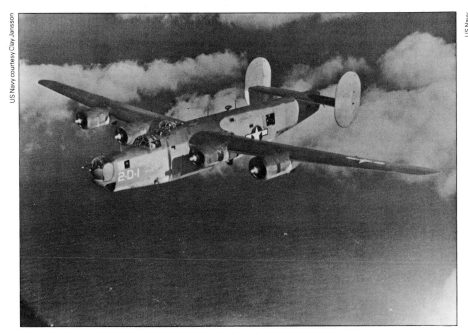

Above: The PB4Y-1P variant was a long-range photo aircraft assigned to Photographic Squadron Two in 1945. Intelligence-gathering and reconnaissance were just two of the missions assigned to naval Liberators in the Pacific.

Above right: Despite the name, this PB4Y-1P of Photo Squadron One apparently did its job, as indicated by 25 cameras painted under the cockpit, indicating the number of missions completed. Photo squadrons flew dual reconnaissance and bombing missions.

Below: A PB4Y-2 Privateer in flight, circa 1945. The first air-launched guided missiles used in combat by the United States were dropped by PB4Y-2s against Japanese shipping that year.

from Guam in the Central Pacific, eventually being relieved by VD-5.

These long-range 'photo bombers' (PB4Y-1Ps) covered thousands of miles of the vast Pacific, bringing back priceless information on Japanese bases and facilities. And just for spice, they usually carried a bombload as well. The other photo squadron was VD-2, which remained on the east coast as a training unit. The PB4Y-1P soldiered on to 1950 in a reduced peacetime structure of two squadrons: VPP-1 and -2.

The ultimate PB4Y arrived late but made a name for itself. That name was Privateer; as the PB4Y-2, it was distinguished from the PB4Y-1 by its tall, single tail. First flown in September 1943, the first of 740 Privateers was delivered in March 1944. Equipped with the most advanced airborne radar employed by the United States in World War II, the PB4Y-2 had stations for two radar-electronic warfare operators.

Entering combat in January 1945 with VPB-118, the Privateer specialized in coastal patrol and anti-shipping missions. Wide-ranging PB4Y-2s prowled up and down the China coast from Philippine bases,

covering the Malay peninsula and Indochina as well. Japanese communications were frequent targets as the patrol bombers cut rail lines, closed canals and bombed bridges.

Fleet Air Wing 10 initiated a new generation of weapons to Naval Aviation during the spring of 1945. Based on Palawan west of the Philippines, VPB-109 became the first 'Bat' squadron in combat when it attacked Japanese shipping with the new ASM-N-2 missile. The Bat was a 1,000-lb (454-kg) radar-controlled weapon, the first stand-off ordnance in the US Navy. The initial combat use occurred during a strike on Balikpapan during April, when three Bats were launched. Two small freighters were hit and sunk or damaged, and an oil-storage tank was destroyed. But bemused aircrews returned to explain that their target (a large transport) remained untouched! However, on 27 May a Bat claimed an enemy destroyer and FAW-10's two other Bat squadrons also became operational.

So ended the patrol plane war in the Pacific. In many ways it was not much different from VP activity in the Atlantic. Long, dull, uncomfortable searches or patrols (16 hours were not uncommon) were the norm. Combat, or even a sighting of enemy ships or aircraft, were relatively rare for most flights. But losses to enemy action or weather became frequent remainders that the VP crews were engaged in a lethal occupation. While flying-boats and patrol bombers never attained the glamor of carrier operations, their war was no less real.

19
VOS: The Scouts

Though carrier-based aircraft dominated Naval Aviation and received nearly all the public attention while land-based Navy planes came second, the third portion of Navy Aviation was the oldest. Float-equipped observation and scouting aircraft (VOS) ranked first in seniority in all the naval air arms of the world, and they continued to perform admirably throughout World War II.

Based on battleships and cruisers (and launched off catapults and recovered by towed sleds or cranes) the 'slingshot fliers' were almost exclusively concerned with two aircraft types. First came the Curtiss SOC Seagull, an angular but attractive biplane which entered fleet service in 1935. Only about 260 were built, but the 'Sock' (fliers said the designation stood for 'Scout on Catapult') was a popular aircraft with its crews. Armed with light ordnance, it made a surprisingly good dive-bomber.

Next came Vought's OS2U Kingfisher, an all-metal monoplane introduced in the summer of 1940. Like that of the SOC, its two-man crew was composed of a pilot and radioman-gunner. These slow, somewhat underpowered aircraft were intended for spotting naval gunfire, reconnaissance and, occasionally, search-and-rescue. But on occasion they did more.

Early proof of the VOS type's versatility occurred on the first day of the Pacific War. The commanding officer of NAS Kaneohe was eating breakfast at 08.00 on 7 December, anticipating a Sunday morning flight in his favorite Kingfisher. He never made that flight. The OS2U, actually the property of Patrol Wing One, was strafed to destruction by marauding Mitsubishi A6M Zero fighters.

However, a pair of SOC-1s made up the deficit. USS *Northampton* (CA 26) was nearing Pearl Harbor that morning after escorting *Enterprise* on her run to Wake Island. At 11.15 the cruiser launched her two scouts on a search to the north. The SOCs flew a tight low-level formation with the lead plane stepped up from the wingman. Some 15 miles (24 km) west of Kauai they were approached by a fast low-wing monoplane which the crews first thought to be a Douglas SBD. But the stranger initiated a gunnery run, removing all doubt as to his nationality and intent.

Turning to put the Zero on their port beam, the SOCs gave their gunners a better field of fire. However, the fighter's speed was such that it overshot and pulled up for another pass before the rear-seat men could shoot. The Seagulls headed for the wavetops, beginning a 20-minute combat.

The section leader, Lieutnant M.C. Reeves, turned each time to present only a quartering angle to the Zero. This effectively compounded the Japan-

US Navy

ese pilot's gunnery problem while allowing the SOCs to return fire. While the wingman's gunner expended his ammunition during the combat, RM1/C Robert P. Baxter conserved his own ammo. The Zero had made six passes when Baxter noted that the Japanese always mushed slightly in his pullouts. At that moment the Mitsubishi was vulnerable.

On the seventh pass Baxter picked his moment, placed his sights on the Zero's nose and fired. He was rewarded with a satisfying stream of black smoke as the stricken fighter limped off towards the small island of Niihau.

Each SOC had a dozen or so holes in its fabric but landed safely at Pearl Harbor. However, that was not quite the end of the tale.

The damaged Mitsubishi put down on Niihau, a privately owned and isolated island off Kauai. The Japanese pilot began a six-day reign as 'conqueror'. With no communication to other islands and largely without weapons, the Hawaiian natives tried to placate the new arrival until help could come. Eventually the enemy flier overplayed his role. He alienated the locals to such an extent that one of the village elders literally took matters into his own hands. Despite being shot three times by the pilot, Beni Kanahali picked up the Japanese and smashed the man's head against a wall. Happily, the big Hawaiian survived his wounds.

Although never officially credited for downing the Zero, SOC gunner Baxter may very well have scored the first US victory over a Japanese aircraft in the war.

Floatplane crews experienced a variety of equally bizarre combat episodes throughout the war, but perhaps the most dramatic were rescues of downed fliers under enemy fire. There were several such episodes. During the first Truk strike, on 17 February 1944, Lieutenant (JG) D.F. Baxter landed his OS2U in the atoll's lagoon to scoop up a carrier pilot. During the follow-up raid in April, Lieutenant (JG) J.A. Burns rescued seven aircrew from certain capture and possible death by torture.

Two events during July 1944 demonstrated the vast differences in VOS operations. During strikes against the Bonin Islands on 4 July an OS2U from the light cruiser *Santa Fe* (CL 60) was jumped by a Zeke. The Kingfisher pilot, Lieutenant (JG) R.W. Hendershott, employed his Vought's low-speed maneuverablity to give his back-seater a shot at the speedy fighter. ARM2/C Arthur Hickman drew a bead with his flexible-mounted 0.3-in (7.62-mm) gun and shot down the A6M5. Like *Northampton's*

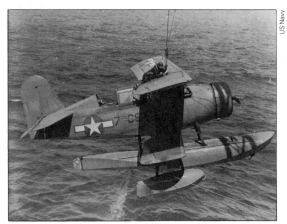

US Navy

Above: An OS2U pilot carefully taxies on to a recovery sled towed from a cruiser. This innovative method of recovery allowed warships to operate spotter planes without stopping, an important consideration in a combat zone. Once attached to the sled, the aircraft was hoisted aboard by crane while still under way.

Left: The popular Curtiss SOC was called Seagull, but floatplane pilots said SOC stood for 'Scout On Catapult'. This SOC-3 belongs to Cruiser Scouting Squadron Seven, being hoisted aboard ship. A pair of SOCs from the cruiser *Northampton* (CA 125) shot down a Zero during the Pearl Harbor attack.

single-seat configuration, the SC was unlike anything the US Navy had ever flown. It possessed twice the ceiling of previous VOS aircraft, immensely better armament, and was at least 140 mph (225 km/h) faster than the OS2U. Though over 560 SC-1s were built, the war had progressed to the point where their spectacular performance (for a floatplane) was never to be witnessed by the enemy.

However, SOCs and OS2Us – those humble floatplanes often sneered at by carrier pilots – more than paid for themselves. Whether correcting naval gunfire, rescuing precious aviators from capture or death, or even shooting down enemy fighters, they proved the old adage that 'It's not the size of the dog in the fight, it's the size of the fight in the dog.'

20
New Ships, New Planes

A new generation of aircraft and carriers entered combat in the late summer and early fall of 1943. They formed a team which proved indomitable for the remainder of the war.

Two classes of fast carriers (those capable of 30 kts) formed the striking arm of Naval Aviation in the Pacific. The 'Essex' class CVs incorporated design features such as deck-edge elevators which had been lacking in previous carriers. But *Essex* (CV 9) was only the sixth US carrier built as such from the keel up. Therefore, American naval architects were still learning how to design such men-of-war.

However, through the war the CV 9 design benefitted from early carrier combat experience and emerged as a near-perfect instrument. Indeed, because of its longevity the 'Essex' class CV has

Above: The last word in World War II floatplanes came, not surprisingly, from Curtiss. The SC-1 Seahawk entered the combat area toward the end of the war from US battleships. It was far faster and better armed than other observation-scout aircraft, but with advent of the helicopter, the 'slingshot airplane' disappeared from the US Navy in 1949.

Below: Hellcats entered combat in September 1943 during hit-and-run raids against Japanese-held island bases. Lieutenant Commander Jimmy Flatley, Jr., CAG-5, prepares to launch from the *Yorktown* (CV 10) during the Hellcat's first combat missions on 31 August 1943 against Marcus Island.

SOCs off Pearl Harbor, the OS2U should not have been able to win against a fighter, but did.

Later that month, during a strike against Yap in the Carolines, *Santa Fe*'s sister ship *Columbia* (CL 56) had an OS2U in action. Air Group 31 off the light carrier *Cabot* (CVL 28) lost a Grumman TBM to anti-aircraft fire and *Santa Fe* launched a Kingfisher to attempt a rescue close to shore. Taxiing so close to the beach that the Japanese heavy-caliber guns were unable to depress low enough, the OS2U plucked the three-man Avenger crew from the water and taxied 5 miles (8 km) to the duty lifeguard submarine.

Though SOCs and OS2Us remained in service, a wholly new type of floatplane emerged in time to see limited operational use. Curtiss first flew the high-performance SC-1 scoutplane in early 1944, and Seahawks initially were assigned to the new 'supercruiser' *Guam* (CB 2) in October. With two 0.5-in (12.7-mm) guns, fittings for airborne radar and

Left: The first Corsair squadron was VF-17, charged with preparing the gull-winged F4U for combat. This Fighting 17 aircraft rides the elevator of *Charger* (CVE 30) during carrier-suitability tests on 8 March 1943. It would be nearly two years before F4Us operated from carriers in combat.

Far left: Lieutenant John M. Clarke sends a VF-16 F6F-3 on its way during operations against the Marshall Islands in November 1943. The 'Airdales' of VF-16 became one of the hottest fighter squadrons in the Pacific, knocking down over 150 Japanese planes in nine months of flying from *Lexington* (CV 16).

been called 'the DC-3 of aircraft-carriers'.

With an 872-ft (266-m) flight deck and 27,100-ton displacement, the 'Essexes' could operate 80 to 100 aircraft. Added to the more obvious characteristics were well-planned Combat Information Centers where specially-trained officers and men monitored and controlled the air defense of a carrier force. A variety of radars provided coverage of all quadrants from nearly sea level to over 30,000 ft (9145 m).

Fourteen 'Essexes' engaged in combat operations during World War II. But the crying need for more fast carriers led to implementation of a conversion scheme for light carriers, or CVLs. Merchantmen had already been converted to escort carriers (CVEs) by the British and Americans, but these were convoy protection ships with speeds of under 20 kts. Therefore, a series of nine light cruiser hulls was marked for conversion to speedy CVLs, 11,000-ton 'middleweights' capable of 30 kts or more.

Most prominent among the new aircraft was Grumman's F6F Hellcat. Designed and flown in response to the Mitsubishi Zero threat, the F6F-3 went from first flight to combat in only 14 months. It bore a family resemblance to the Wildcat but possessed considerably more range, speed and climb. Big, rugged and easy to fly, the F6F was perhaps the epitome of the carrier aircraft designer's art, and Grumman produced over 12,000 F6F-3s and F6F-5s from 1942 through 1945.

In order to meet the nearly insatiable demand for Hellcats, Grumman arranged to have Eastern Aircraft Division of General Motors take over F4F Wildcat and TBF Avenger production. GM plants at Trenton and Linden, New Jersey, produced over 5,000 Wildcats and 7,500 Avengers under the FM and TBM designations. By mid-1944 the standard escort carrier complement was entirely GM-built, with FM-2 fighters and TBM-3 bombers.

Avengers remained the only torpedo plane on all classes of US carriers throughout the post-Midway period. Slowly the workhorse Douglas SBD series was replaced by the newer, somewhat faster Curtiss SB2C (also produced as the SBW and SBF), beginning in November 1943. Dive-bomber squadrons were ambivalent about the big Helldiver; it required more maintenance than the Dauntless yet carried an identical bomb load with no greater range. The prewar optimism for the 'beast' withered in service use, and in fact shortly before the last two SBD squadrons left *Lexington* (CV 16) and *Enterprise* (CV 6) in July 1944, plans were considered for re-equipping with Dauntlesses. However, logistics and supplies were all oriented toward the SB2C, which remained active beyond VJ-Day.

As for the Vought Corsair, this potential world-beater struggled through a lengthy evolution before gaining clearance for fleet service. Landing gear and assorted other faults rendered the early F4U-1s difficult to land aboard ship, and even after squadrons and the factory developed fixes, the Corsair remained land-based. Not until the *Kamikaze* crisis of late 1944 did Corsairs go aboard carriers on a permanent basis. When they did, they proved their worth as perhaps the most versatile fighter-bombers in the world.

Right: Landing signal officers were known for their individual modes of dress, but Lieutenant Dick Tripp, LSO of *Yorktown* (CV-10), here waving an F6F-3 aboard, surely dressed for comfort in tennis shoes and floral pattern shorts!

Left: A sister squadron of VF-17 in *Bunker Hill* was VB-17, with the first Curtiss SB2C-1 Helldivers. Nicknamed 'The Beast' by pilots and mechanics, the SB2C experienced a long, difficult gestation period before emerging as a fully operational dive-bomber.

The War in the Pacific

In the meantime, F4Us entered combat as land-based fighters in the Solomons campaign of late 1943 to mid-1944. A night-fighter squadron, VF(N)-75, took up residence in the Solomons shortly before the better-publicized VF-17 commenced daytime operations in the same arena. These units, with a few early F6F-3 squadrons, supported Allied operations against the Japanese bastion at Rabaul, New Britain and outlying bases. The success of such F4U outfits as the 'Skull and Crossbones' squadron, VF-17, showed the way toward the day when F4Us would regularly fly from carriers. Meanwhile, other Navy tactical squadrons flying Wildcats, Dauntless and Avengers also contributed to the eventual defeat of Japanese air and seapower in the Solomons.

The Fast Carrier Task Force

By the end of August 1943, the first 'Essex' and 'Independence' class carriers, as well as the Hellcat, were initiated to combat in the Central Pacific, when the *Essex* (CV 9), *Yorktown* (CV 10) and *Independence* (CVL 22) launched their air groups on strikes against Marcus Island on 31 August. The standard tactical organization was the task group; eventually two CVs and two CVLs operated with cruiser and destroyer escorts, though frequently modern battleships capable of steaming with the carriers were added for anti-aircraft gunfire. It was a curious reversal of prewar doctrine in which carriers were most often regarded as secondary to battleships.

The Fast Carrier Task Force was composed of four task groups under the overall command of a vice admiral. Depending upon the fleet commander (William F. Halsey with the 3rd Fleet or Raymond A. Spruance with the 5th Fleet) the carrier striking arm was designated Task Force 38 or Task Force 58. The designation changed whenever the fleet command alternated for planning purposes. This system allowed one team to conduct an operation while the other prepared for the next. It also acted as a ploy to confuse the Japanese.

When the Fast Carrier Task Force was instituted in January 1944, the commanding officer was Vice Admiral Marc A. Mitscher. He remained in command, alternating the TF-38/58 designation, until that fall. Thereafter he alternated with Vice Admiral John S. McCain. Mitscher was Naval Aviator number 33, a veteran flier who had earned his wings in 1916 and made the first landing aboard *Saratoga*. In contrast, 'Slew' McCain was representative of the latecomers to aviation like Admirals

Above: Reflecting new air group composition in early 1944, Air Group Two's SB2Cs and F6Fs crowd *Bunker Hill*'s flight deck headed westward. 'Essex' class carriers operated Hellcats, Avengers and Helldivers during most of 1944-5.

Ernest King (Chief of Naval Operations) and Bill Halsey. As battleship or cruiser sailors, these men possessed the seniority which carrier aviation required and were put through Pensacola in the 1930s as captains.

The task group leaders were rear admirals, nearly all of whom had spent the majority of their careers in aviation. They were the original flying admirals, men who had personally tested early carrier aircraft, designed and perfected shipboard equipment, and evolved the tactics of dive-bombing and torpedo attack. They had names like Jerry Bogan, 'Jocko' Clark, 'Raddy' Radford and 'Dave' Davison.

The escort carrier force was of necessity more dispersed than the fast carrier but was organized along similar lines. Four to six CVEs with destroyer and destroyer-escort screens supported amphibious landings and provided close-in air and anti-submarine patrol. Smaller CVE units escorted convoys and the all-important fleet train with oilers and supply ships which kept task forces at sea for weeks or months at a time. Japanese officials interrogated after the war identified this sophisticated logistical support as a key reason for the Empire's collapse; for seapower determined the result of the Pacific war and sustaining carriers on station determined who ruled the sea.

Left: Another US Army Air Force bomber accepted by the US Navy was North American's B-25 Mitchell. Designated PBJ by the US Navy, this twin-engine medium bomber packed exceptional firepower and was used in combat by the US Marines.

Right: Nine 'Independence' class light carriers were built during the war, all modified from light cruiser hulls. Displacing 11,000 tons, they could keep pace with the bigger fleet carriers capable of 30 kts or more. This is USS *Monterey* (CVL 26), fifth ship of the class.

21
The Marianas and Beyond

In the 10 months following the combat debut of the new ships and aircraft, the fast carriers worked hard to perfect equipment and techniques. Along the way they learned much, inflicting considerable damage upon the Japanese. Anti-shipping strikes at Rabaul in November 1943 and at Truk in the following February demonstrated the enhanced range and striking power of Naval Aviation. These feats, combined with carrier air support of the successful amphibious operations against Tarawa, Kwajalein and other enemy garrisons, set the stage for the most important attempt yet: the Marianas.

Located in mid-Pacific, the Marianas objectives were several island airfields on Guam, Saipan and Tinian. Marine Corps and US Army assault troops were put ashore on 15 June 1944 evoking a heavy response from the Imperial Navy. The Marianas are only some 1,500 miles (2400 km) from Tokyo; their fate was directly connected with that of the Empire.

Thus evolved the 1st Battle of the Philippine Sea. Fourteen fast carriers were aligned against nine Japanese flat tops, with the Imperial Navy employing the advantage of still-unoccupied Guam as a staging base.

It was the first carrier duel since Santa Cruz in October 1942. It would remain the largest such battle ever. But now the situation had changed; the

US Navy enjoyed both quantitative and qualitative superiority. Attrition among Japanese carriers and especially among aircrews had greatly diminished the Emperor's naval air capability.

The battle opened shortly after dawn on 19 June when a sizable portion of TF-58's 400-strong Grumman F6F Hellcat complement flew combat air patrols (CAPs) over the task force and the islands. Several combats broke out as Japanese scout planes and fighters took off, but not until mid-morning did the major engagement begin. The Japanese carriers launched the first of four air strikes at the American force, which lacked precise knowledge of the enemy's location.

In the end, it did not matter. With ample F6Fs on hand and expert fighter direction, each successive raid was intercepted and repulsed with severe loss. American fighter pilots had never enjoyed such good hunting. Of 64 enemy planes in Raid One, only 22 survived. And so it went throughout the day. When it was all over, more than 300 aircraft had been shot down. Seven Hellcat pilots had splashed five or more bandits during the day, including Lieutenant Alexander Vraciu of *Lexington*'s VF-16. Vraciu bagged six Yokosuka 'Judy' dive-bombers to become temporarily the Navy's top ace with 18 kills. The man who succeeded him in the top spot was Commander David McCampbell, leading Air Group 15 from the *Essex*: the Annapolis alumnus from the Class of '33 shot down seven planes in two sorties. He would end the war as the Navy's top fighter ace with 34 confirmed kills.

Below: SBD-5s of Scouting Squadron 51 during the work-up of *San Jacinto* (CVL 30) prior to deployment in early 1944. By the time the CVLs entered combat their dive-bombers had been replaced to increase the number of torpedo planes. The SBD's non-folding wing put too great a premium on already-invaluable space in light carriers.

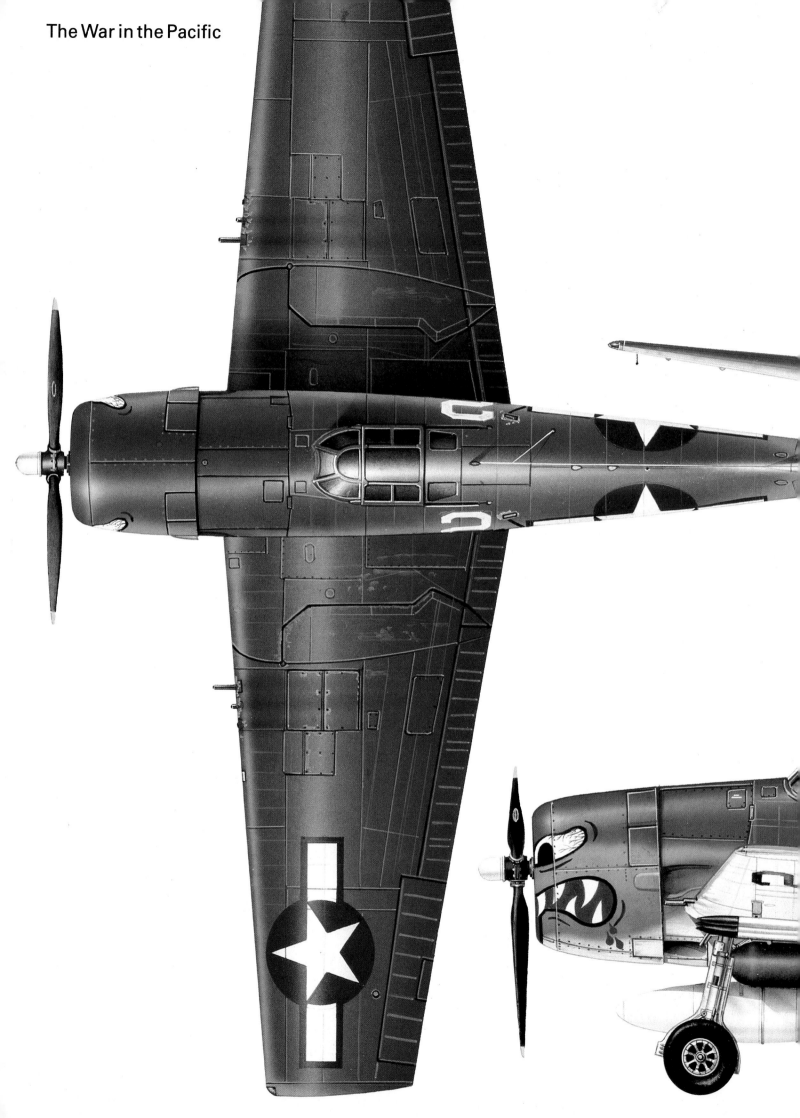

Representing the many Grumman Hellcats which saw combat duty in World War II, this specimen is an F6F-5 from VF-27 and is depicted in late war colors as applied when operating from USS *Princeton* (CVL 23). This carrier was lost to enemy action during October 1944 when participating in the battle for Leyte Gulf. Full armament complement including underwing rocket projectiles and bombs, is carried.

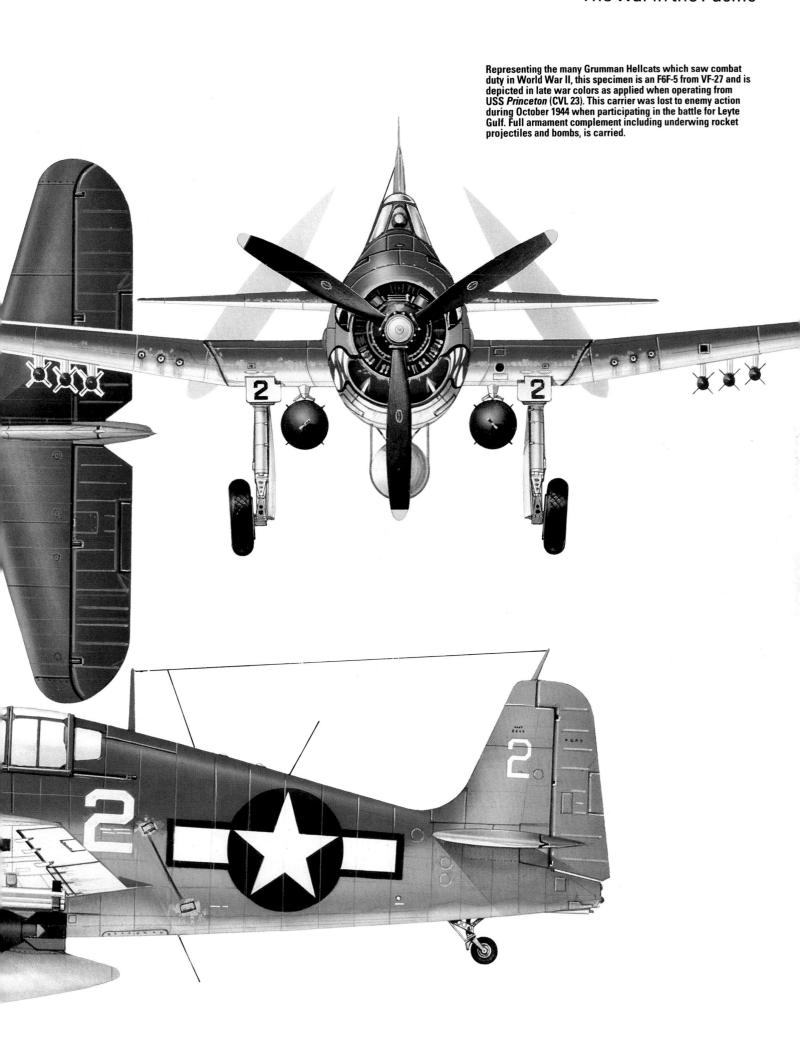

Left: *Cowpens'* LSO scrambles to get out of the way as a Hellcat pilot crowds the port side during landing in October 1943. Whatever their size, aircraft carriers are crowded, noisy and dangerous places to work, and there's always a premium on alertness.

American aircraft losses amounted to fewer than 30, of which 16 were Hellcats lost in combat. While a handful of Japanese bombers got through the efficient CAP to attack TF-58 ships, no significant damage was inflicted. The enemy, however, lost a carrier to a US submarine. On the next morning, it was the Americans who went on the offensive.

Search aircraft located the enemy force well to the west in mid-afternoon. Vice Admiral Mitscher calculated the odds of retrieving some 220 planes in darkness, for the enemy flat tops were over 300 miles (480 km) away. Also, his pilots were largely untrained in night carrier landings. After pondering the situation for a moment, he decided to go. Turning to his staff on *Lexington*'s bridge, he only said, 'Launch 'em'.

It was a long flight into the westering sun that evening, and darkness was approaching as the strike groups selected their targets and attacked. The priority targets were enemy carriers (none had been brought to battle in 20 months) but the air group commander of *Wasp* (CV 18) went after the Japanese oilers. They were the first enemy vessels sighted, and while two were sunk the other air groups tackled what *Enterprise*'s VB-10 squadron leader, 'Jig Dog' Ramage, called 'the fighting navy'.

The results were disappointing. Intense enemy flak and limited but aggressive fighter cover reduced the effectiveness of the strike and only one

Left: If one aircraft type put the US Navy in a position to bounce back from the debacle of 1941-2, it was the Douglas Dauntless. These VB-5 SBDs were past their prime when the second *Yorktown* (CV-10) joined the fleet in 1943, but they had held the line at Coral Sea and Midway and helped take the offensive at Guadalcanal. SBDs served in *Enterprise* (CV 6) and *Lexington* (CV 16) until July 1944.

Right: Several ships claimed the title "Fightin'est Ship in the Navy" but none could match this carrier – USS *Enterprise* (CV 6). Veteran of every carrier battle except Coral Sea, she qualified for 20 of 22 possible battle stars in the Pacific Theater. Here she stands out of Pearl Harbor on 2 August 1944.

Above: Air Group 30 aboard the *Monterey* (CVL 26), en route to its baptism of fire in the Gilberts and Solomons during December 1943. The initial operations brought little contact with the enemy, but VF-30 and VT-30 more than made up the deficit through May 1944, when their first tour ended. A second tour aboard *Belleau Wood* (CVL 24) lasted the first half of 1945.

carrier was sunk. Torpedo Squadron 24, off *Belleau Wood* (CVL 24), launched a four-plane division which selected *Hiyo* as its target. Three of the Grumman/Eastern TBM pilots completed runs on the carrier, and probably two hits were scored. The division leader was Lieutenant (JG) George Brown, an exceptionally courageous flier who had promised his skipper to get a flat top. And he did, but his Avenger was so badly shot up that he ordered his crewmen to bail out. They were recovered but Brown flew into the darkness and never returned.

Having sunk one carrier and damaged another the TF-58 fliers turned for home. About 20 planes

were lost to the enemy defenses, but the nearly 200 remaining now faced a bigger battle, that of finding their ships in total darkness. Many ran out of fuel and others simply became lost. When nearing the recovery point, however, the aviators were astonished to see a myriad of lights showing the way. Ignoring the submarine threat, 'Pete' Mitscher had decided to risk all for his fliers. The lights, however, proved both a blessing and a hazard. With every ship in the task force shining searchlights, or anything else they could manage, the resultant mass of lights was confusing and blinding to the exhausted pilots. In retrospect, showing only the carrier lights would have been the better course. Alex Vraciu, returning to *Lexington* after making his 19th kill, could hardly believe the sight. The depth of his gratitude was such that years later he named one of his sons after Mitscher.

When it was all over, nearly half of the 216 planes on the mission were lost. Fuel starvation was the main cause, and the Curtiss SB2C force was particularly hard-hit. Supposedly longer-ranged than the Douglas SBD it replaced, the Helldiver made a miserable showing that night. Of 50 launched on the strike, only five were back aboard the next morning. Over half had run out of fuel and the remainder had been shot down or jettisoned with battle damage. By comparison, the two Dauntless squadrons had lost one plane in combat and one in the *Enterprise* landing pattern. Later, with more

Right: *Enterprise* prepares to launch VB-20 Helldivers during an early October 1944 strike against Okinawa. Six months later 'The Big E' was back in these same waters flying a night air group.

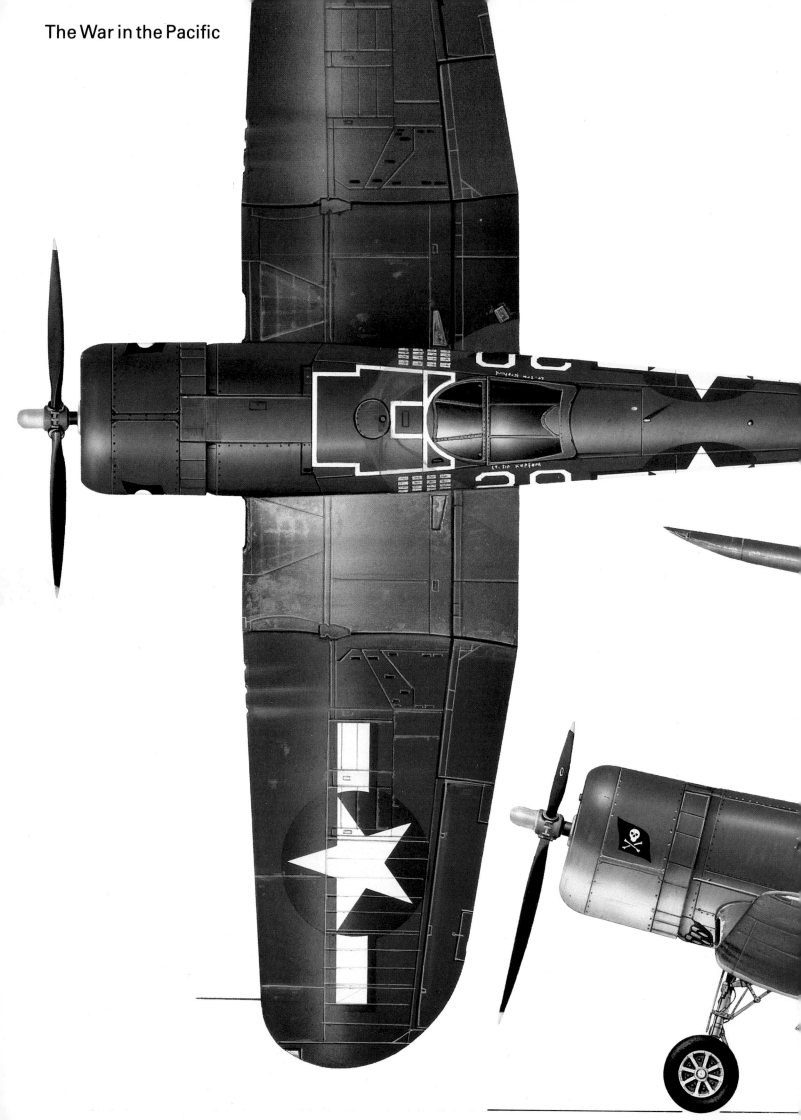

This Vought F4U-1A Corsair is depicted in the personal markings of Lieutenant Ira C. 'Ike' K. Kepford, the US Navy's leading ace in the South Pacific campaign. Assigned to Fighter Squadron VF-17 at the time (early 1944), Kepford had accounted for no less than 16 Japanese aircraft, each of these victories being represented by a miniature 'Rising Sun' emblem below and slightly forward of the cockpit on both sides of the aircraft. VF-17's unit insignia, consisting of a 'Jolly Roger' flag, is also visible on both sides of the engine cowling. Apart from these individual touches, the aircraft is typical of the many Corsairs which saw action in this long campaign.

US Navy

experience, SB2C pilots got more range from their Curtisses, but never again would Mitscher look upon the SB2C with any degree of confidence. However, one bright spot of the battle was the recovery of 77 per cent of the downed fliers in subsequent rescue operations.

Continuing operations over the Marianas and the Bonins (with Iwo Jima the main base) further enhanced American air supremacy. Large, violent dogfights continued in these arenas for a short time as the eager F6F pilots sought to emulate the 'turkey shoot' of 19 June. But following occupation of the Palaus in August, only 500 miles (800 km) from the Philippines, even greater opportunities arose.

The multi-faceted Battle of Leyte Gulf (in late October 1944) provided multiple opportunities for the fast carriers (now TF-38) to prove themselves. In the Sibuyan Sea, on the western side of the Philippines, carrier air destroyed one of the largest battleships afloat on 24 October. Multiple strikes against Vice Admiral Kurita's surface force put the 64,000-ton battleship *Musashi* under, in large part due to an Air Group 20 attack led by Lieutenant Commander Joe Lawler, executive officer of VF-20.

Kurita's powerful battleship and cruiser force was turned back, but during that night reversed

course and headed for San Bernardino Strait. The object was General MacArthur's amphibious force in Leyte Gulf which, if attacked by Kurita's big-gun ships, stood little chance of survival. A typically complex Japanese plan involved Vice Admiral Ozawa's four carriers well to the north and another surface unit to the south. Halsey was correctly assessed by the Japanese as being unable to resist the decoy flat tops and took his fast carriers north to engage Ozawa, leaving Leyte Gulf wide open.

The southern force was annihilated in a nocturnal surface engagement but Kurita emerged into the gulf shortly past dawn on 25 October. All that stood in his way was an escort carrier unit composed of six CVEs and their destroyer and destroyer-escort screen. This tiny group, code-named 'Taffy Three', took on four battleships, eight cruisers and 11 destroyers.

However, with air support from nearby 'Taffy Two', Rear Admiral Clifton Sprague fought off the overwhelming enemy force in a morning-long slugfest. The escort carrier *Gambier Bay* (CVE 73) succumbed to cruiser shellfire, as did some of the escorting destroyers. But Kurita, astonished by the ferocity of the CVEs' response and mindful of the pummelling he had sustained the day before, called it quits. Just as a decisive victory was within his

Above: Other Navy squadrons also flew in the Solomons during this period. Here a VS-64 SBD-3 overflies New Georgia on 27 December 1943. Note that the small, solid-rubber tailwheel used aboard carriers has been replaced by a larger pneumatic type.

US Air Force

Left: Meanwhile, back in the Solomons . . . the island campaign continued from late 1943 into early 1944. Fighting 17, being bounced off *Bunker Hill* owing to F4U parts problems, entered combat as a land-based squadron in October. This F4U-1A experienced a forced landing at Nissan Island in March 1944.

Right: NAS Moffett Field, California based Martin JM-1 Marauders (US Navy B-26s) flew a variety of missions in Utility Squadron One. JMs wear the standard utility squadron paint scheme of the time.

Far right: This VT-2 TBM-1C returned to *Hornet* (CV 12) with heavy battle damage on 30 April 1944 during the second strike against Truk Atoll in the Carolines.

Below: 'The Big E' and SBDs were a potent combination. Bombing 10 aircraft prepare for launch in early 1944. Enterprise Air Group's Dauntlesses flew into the war when they arrived over Pearl Harbor on the morning of 7 December 1941, and continued the contest through the Marianas campaign in June and July 1944.

grasp, he disengaged. The invasion transports were safe.

Still, 'Taffy Three' remained in peril. That afternoon *St Lô* (CVE 63) was dived upon by a Japanese aircraft which made no visible effort to pull out. Wracked by fire and explosions from the impact, the CVE went down, first victim of the *Kamikazes*. Six other escort carriers were damaged by suicide aircraft at about this same time.

Meanwhile, the fast carriers had sunk all four of Ozawa's decoys off Cape Engano. Commander Dave McCampbell, who established the Allied record by downing nine planes in one mission on 24 October, helped to direct strikes against the nearly-empty Japanese flat tops during 25 October. The USS *Lexington* (CV 16) and *Langley* (CVL 27) air groups wrote the final postscript on the Pearl Harbor episode as VT-19 and VT-44 teamed up to sink *Zuikaku*, last survivor of the six carriers which

launched the attack against Pearl Harbor on 7 December 1941.

Aside from the CVE losses, the US Navy wrote off *Princeton* (CVL 23), which was fatally bombed the morning of 24 October. She was the first fast carrier lost since the original *Hornet* at Santa Cruz, and the last such carrier of the US Navy destroyed by any cause.

In exchange, not only did the Allies have a firm foothold in the Philippines, but Japanese naval strength had been severely depleted. Carrier planes scoured the Philippine waters during 26 and 27 October to pick off a light cruiser and four destroyers, bringing total enemy losses in what became known as the 2nd Battle of the Philippine Sea to 26 combatants displacing 300,000 tons.

For the remainder of the war, the primary threat to the fast carriers was the astonishing variety of *Kamikaze* aircraft. Since Midway, American

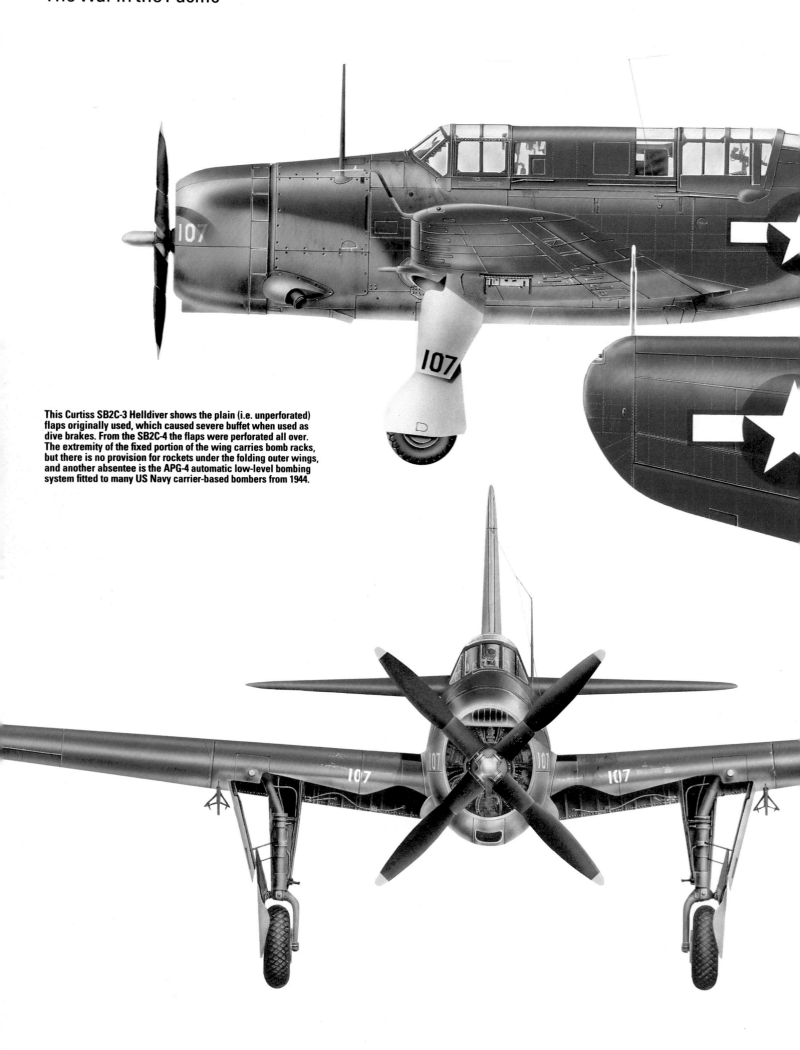

This Curtiss SB2C-3 Helldiver shows the plain (i.e. unperforated) flaps originally used, which caused severe buffet when used as dive brakes. From the SB2C-4 the flaps were perforated all over. The extremity of the fixed portion of the wing carries bomb racks, but there is no provision for rockets under the folding outer wings, and another absentee is the APG-4 automatic low-level bombing system fitted to many US Navy carrier-based bombers from 1944.

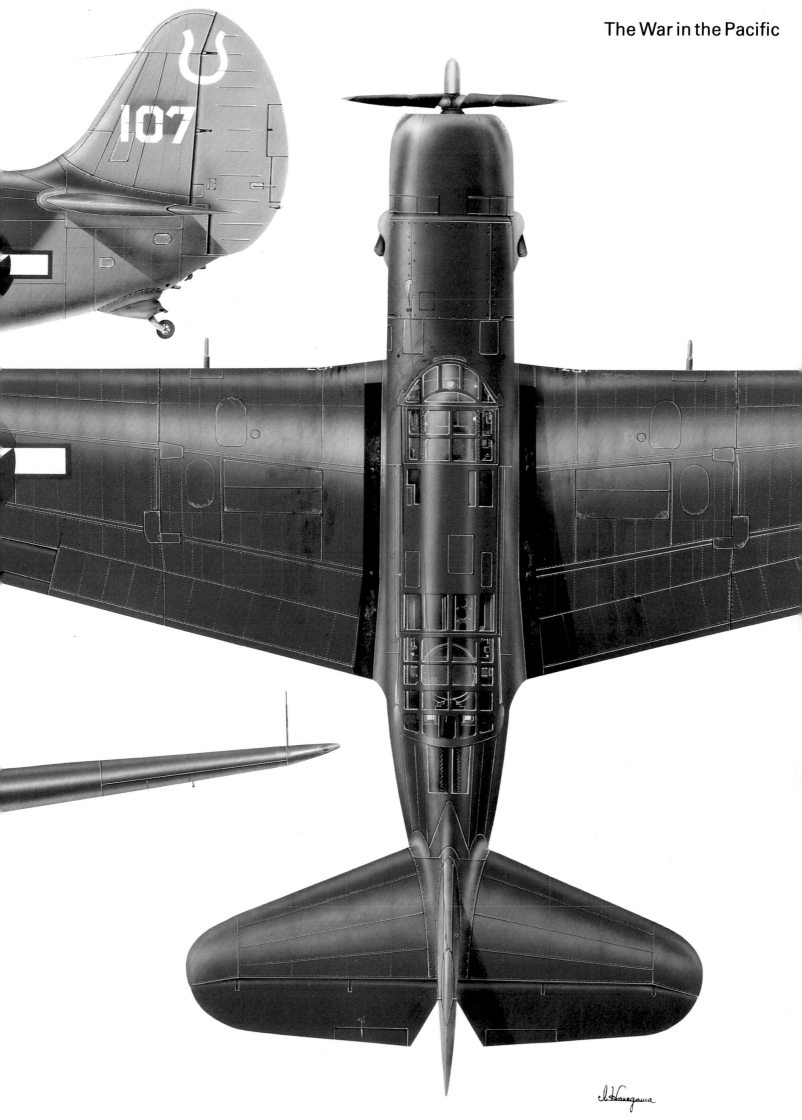

The War in the Pacific

carriers had been almost entirely safe from conventional air attack, but with the appearance of the suicide weapon, the air defense system had to be 100 per cent effective. Naturally, this was not possible and at Iwo Jima in February 1945, the aging *Saratoga* took four *Kamikazes*. Although knocked out of the war, the 'Sara' still steamed under her own power. Things only got worse off Okinawa following the invasion of 1 April.

Only a few hundred miles from southern Japan, Okinawa amounted to the Empire's doorstep. In order to support the major undertaking of occupying Okinawa, the carriers had to remain in a limited area usually no more than 100 miles (160 km) offshore. This requirement solved the enemy's main problem, locating his target. For two months the fast carriers, ably assisted by the CVEs, fought a continuous battle against conventional and suicide air raids in addition to performing the necessary role of ground-support for Marines and infantry.

Late 1944 and early 1945 brought some dramatic advancements in carrier capability. The first night air group entered combat in August, early in the Philippine campaign. Air Group 41 flew from *Independence* until January 1945. This operational experiment proved so successful that three CV air groups followed in its wake. As noted, *Saratoga* with the day- and night-flying Air Group 53 served briefly at Iwo Jima. Night Air Group 90 in *Enterprise* began combat early in the new year under the expert guidance of Commander William I. Martin. An early advocate of night CV operations, Bill Martin's unit exploited the knowledge of Commander Turner Caldwell's Air Group 41 and inaugurated the big-deck nocturnal carrier to combat. In addition to night strike, heckler and intruder missions, Martin's TBM-3Es also conducted some of the earliest electronic warfare missions in Naval Aviation history. The 'Big E', veteran of every major Pacific battle except Coral Sea, was finally hit by a suicide Mitsubishi Zero off Japan on 11 May and, badly damaged, sailed for home. The last night-flying unit in combat was Air Group 91 aboard the new 'Essex' class ship *Bon Homme Richard* (CV 31).

The fast carriers flew their last missions over Japan on 15 August 1945. On that date, with strikes already in progress, word came through that the Japanese had agreed to unconditional surrender. The attack groups were recalled and the rest of the day was spent reinforcing the CAP against enemy pilots who may not have received the word. In all, Navy carrier squadrons shot down 34 Japanese planes that day ('In a friendly sort of way,' according to Halsey's order for treatment of any Japanese fliers found airborne.) It raised the tally of Navy fighters, dive-bombers and torpedo planes to 6,826 since that long-ago Sunday morning at Oahu. It had been a long road back, but Naval Aviation had led the way.

Above: F6F-3s of VF-4 in *Bunker Hill* at the start of their tour in November 1944. The air group moved to the *Essex* in late November, relieving Air Group 15, but was soon rotated out of combat owing to heavy losses.

Below: Peace is at hand. These four Curtiss SB2C-4E Helldivers from VB-87 aboard *Ticonderoga* (CV 14) are seen returning to their parent carrier after participating in the final strike of World War II on Janpanese territory on 15 August 1945.

Fresh from his record-setting nine-victory mission of 25 October 1944, Commander David McCampbell is photographed in his Hellcat on 4 November. By month's end he had added 13 more 'meatballs' to his scoreboard, emerging as the top fighter ace of the US naval service. His Air Group 15 destroyed more Japanese planes and sank more tonnage than any other unit in the US Navy.

The swept-wing F9F-6 Cougar was developed from Grumman's successful Panther series and began appearing in the fleet with VF-32 in 1952. VF-24 'Corsairs' F9F-6s here launch from *Yorktown* (CVA 10) during CVG-2's 1953-4 deployment.

Post-war to Vietnam- Time of Turbulence, Time of Progress

At the close of World War II, the US Navy was commencing a period of technological change unprecedented in its previous history. In the 19-year period between 1945 and the official commencement of hostilities in Vietnam during the infamous summer of 1964, Naval Aviation entered the jet age, fought another carrier war in Korea and survived a life-and-death struggle with its youngest sibling, the US Air Force. It also developed the most powerful instrument of warfare in the history of man, the big-deck carriers with their nuclear weapons.

Naval Air's early experiences with jet aviation and the carriers brought near-disaster when catastrophic accident rates caused serious doubt that the new planes could be successfully operated at sea, until the Navy incorporated new landing aids into its large-deck carrier designs. Additionally, it developed a three-part conversion and modernization program for the World War II design 'Essex'-class carriers to give them the capability to operate the powerful new aircraft.

The helicopter came into its own, first joining the carriers as life-saving 'angels' rescuing downed aircrews from the sea and from behind enemy lines in Korea and then, coupled with another new innovation, the hunter-killer anti-submarine warfare aircraft, becoming a potent force protecting the carrier groups. The patrol plane community evolved from its early patrol-bombing role to a powerful ASW umbrella protecting the world's sea lanes.

However, all of the technology, dedication of personnel and superior weaponry in the world cannot overpower inept and bumbling politicians. This point would be clearly made in the 10 years following Naval Aviation's finest hours.

22
Peace and Demobilization

VJ-Day brought victory over Japan, and was the day that the US Navy and all of America had been waiting for since that fateful Sunday morning of 7 December 1941. As the document of surrender was being signed on 2 September 1945 aboard the battleship USS *Missouri* (BB 63) in Tokyo Bay, the gears that would drive the mechanics of demobilization had already been engaged. Indeed, the majority of the plans had been prepared more than a year before.

After the cessation of hostilities with Japan on 15 August, Naval Aviation was faced with the immediate problem of what to do with 431,000 Navy and Marine Corps officers and enlisted personnel who no longer had a war to fight or train for. Additionally, there were approximately 41,000 fixed-wing aircraft and blimps to be concerned with; the 27 helicopters were no problems.

The industrial might of the nation had produced an unprecedented armada of ships for the Navy. Never before in history had the oceans of the world borne such weight as these vessels imposed. Of the Navy's approximately 1,500 combatant ships, Naval Aviation had at its command 99 carriers on VJ-Day. Seventeen 'Essex' class ships were in commission, as were the three pre-war carriers *Saratoga* (CV 3), *Ranger* (CV 4) and *Enterprise* (CV 6). Eight of the cruiser-hull CVLs had survived, along with 71 escort carriers. Additionally, 39 more carriers were on order, in various stages of construction or nearly ready for commissioning.

Three new battle carriers (CVBs) were nearing completion. The USS *Midway* (CVB 41), the name-ship of the class, would hoist her commissioning pennant on 10 September, followed closely on 27 October by *Franklin D. Roosevelt* (CVB 42). The third and final ship of the new armored-deck, 45,000-ton giants of their time, *Coral Sea* (CVB 43), joined her sisters on 1 October 1947.

Two of nine 'Essex' class CVs under construction, the *Reprisal* (CV 35) and *Iwo Jima* (CV 46), had

been cancelled, and completion of the *Oriskany* (CV 34) was ordered suspended. Before the year was out, two more 'Essexes', *Princeton* (CV 37) and *Tarawa* (CV 40), were placed in commission. Of the smaller carriers, two of the all-new 'Saipan' class CVLs were building and would join the fleet in 1946 and 1947. Twenty-four CVEs had been ordered but 16 were cancelled. Orders for new aircraft were drastically cut back, cancellations actually beginning in 1944!

Immediate post-war plans called for the reduction of the Navy's air stations and major aviation facilities from a wartime high of 168 to 94. Before the end of the year 234 smaller facilities, such as outlying fields and bases, were scheduled for deactivation. Many more air stations would face closure in the next years of military budget reductions.

Above: Demobilization quickly brought a drastic reduction of the US Navy's 99 active World War II carriers to 15 by June 1950. Seen from front to rear are the *Essex* (CV 9), *Ticonderoga* (CV 14), *Yorktown* (CV 10), *Lexington* (CV 16), *Bunker Hill* (CV 17) and *Bon Homme Richard* (CV 31), all mothballed in Puget Sound's Reserve Fleet in 1950.

Left: At the end of World War II the US Navy had approximately 41,000 fixed-wing and lighter-than-air aircraft in its inventory. By the outbreak of the Korean War this number would be reduced to 14,000.

Right: Grumman's F7F Tigercat appeared with US Marine Corps night-fighter squadrons in 1945. They served in only two US Navy fleet squadrons, VC(N)-1 at Barbers Point, Hawaii, and VC(N)-2 at Key West, Florida. Some were converted to drone controllers as F7F-2Ds and flew with utility squadrons. Here a VU-4 F7F-2D pilot checks the engines before a flight.

Balogh/Menard Collection

However, there was still the immediate job at hand of occupying the newly-gained territory of Japan as well as establishing a stabilizing presence throughout Asia and Europe. Many of the carriers assumed a new and unfamiliar role, that of ferrying troops back to the USA from the forward areas. With the exception of recently arrived USS *Antietam* (CV 36) and *Boxer* (CV 21) in the Western Pacific, most of the larger and some of the smaller carriers returned to the west coast to be converted into temporary troop transports. On the east coast, *Lake Champlain* (CV 39), commissioned 3 June, assumed a similar role in the Atlantic. Although all were commissioned before the end of the war, none of these three 'Essex' class carriers entered service in time for combat.

During the maelstrom of activity surrounding the immediate post-war days, an event passed with little notice in the Navy Department that would have far-reaching implications on events in the next two decades. On 3 October, the Bureau of Aeronautics established a committee to study the feasibility of placing a satellite in orbit around the earth by means of a rocket. As the committee seated itself for its first meeting, no one in the room dreamed that 15 years later the first American into space would be a Naval Aviator, or that the first to orbit the Earth would also be a Naval Aviator, albeit of Marine Corps persuasion.

Consolidation and reorganization of commands became virtually a way of life for aviation units over the next few years. Air groups and fleet air wings were decommissioned faster than the notices could be posted. Manpower in Naval Aviation was reduced by mid-1946 to one-fourth its wartime high peak. In November 1945, reorganization of the Naval Air Training Command was begun. The Naval Air Operational Training Command that had provided the combat pilots for the Navy ceased to exist on 1 November, along with Naval Air

US Navy

Right: Operation 'Crossroads' tested the effectiveness of the atomic bomb against naval vessels at Bikini in July 1946. Joint Task Group One F6F-5K Hellcat drones were flown through cloud formation to test radioactivity. Colored tails on drones seen here indicate different radio frequencies.

Left: USS *Franklin D. Roosevelt* at anchor bay at Piraeses, Greece, 9 September 1946. *FDR* initiated 'show the flag' and good-will visits to the Mediterranean on this cruise, which established a US Navy carrier presence that remains to this day.

Intermediate Training Command. The new NATC was located at NAS Pensacola with three subordinate commands: Naval Air Basic Training, Naval Air Advanced Training and Naval Air Reserve Training.

Reduction of the Navy's carrier force proceeded rapidly. By 1 April 1947, 13 of the 'Essex' class carriers had joined *Enterprise* and seven of the surviving World War II CVLs in mothball fleets on both coasts. Additionally, only nine CVEs were still active. The grand old veteran *Saratoga* had been sunk at Bikini in July of the previous year during Operation 'Crossroads' atomic bomb tests. *Independence* (CVL 22), although a survivor of the same tests, was a burnt-out, radioactive hulk. Good only for future weapons tests, *Independence* finally succumbed to the waves off the coast of California on 29 January 1951. *Ranger*, America's first carrier designed and built from the keel up, had been sold for scrap in January 1947. After a short post-war tour at Pensacola as the training carrier, she had been decommissioned on 18 October 1946.

A similar fate befell the air groups and CVEs. By 1 April, there were 13 air groups still operating from the 13 larger carriers in service, along with two small groups in the USS *Sicily* (CVE 118) and *Badoeng Strait* (CVE 116). Six Marine fighter squadrons manned the same number of CVEs. By the end of 1947, a total of 16 CVs, 7 CVLs and 59 CVEs had been deactivated and placed in reserve fleets.

The 'big boat' Navy fared well compared with its carrier brethren. Seven seaplane tenders remained active on the east coast in the spring of 1947. Out west, nine tenders were still available to mother their broods.

Events in early and mid-1946 had occurred that would have far-reaching effects on the foreign policy of the United States. These events also provided the foundation of US carrier employment in the Mediterranean to this day. Following Soviet pressure on Turkey for control of the Dardanelles and the USSR's support of an attempt by the communists in Greece to take over that country, the *Missouri* was ordered in April to Istanbul as a demonstration of support for Turkey. This 'show of force' was intended as a warning to the Soviets of the limits the Allies would accept on their sphere of influence. Since the invasion of southern France in mid-1944, the US naval presence in the Mediterranean had been limited, with no ship larger than a light cruiser deployed there.

Carrier presence

A follow-up deployment to the eastern Mediterranean was made by *Roosevelt* and CVBG-75 from 8 August 1946. Calling upon several ports, including Athens, the big carrier and her air group represented a power greater than that of the air force of any Mediterranean nation of the time. During *Roosevelt*'s 'good-will tour', Secretary of the Navy James V. Forrestal announced that Navy would maintain a carrier presence in the Mediterranean on a permanent basis. *Roosevelt*'s deployment thus instituted a policy which has continued for 39 years. Since 1946, with only a few short-term exceptions, the US Navy has kept at least one and generally two carriers in the Mediterranean in support of NATO's southern flank.

A series of redesignations of naval aircraft and aviation units came into effect following the war. On 11 March 1946, 'B' and 'T' mission-identifying designations for Bombing and Torpedo aircraft

Left: Reversing the trend of cutbacks, new-type carrier squadrons VW-1 and VW-2 were established 6 July 1948 to be the first carrier AEW squadrons. VX-1 at Key West was responsible for development of TBM-3W for fleet use.

Right: Almost the last Grumman F8F-1 Bearcat to be built, this aircraft was the mount of US Navy Commander C.E. Clarke, CO of fighter squadron VF-72 embarked during 1949-50 aboard the carrier USS *Leyte*.

Right: Almost the last Grumman F8F-1 Bearcat to be built, this aircraft was the mount of US Navy Commander C.E. Clarke, CO of fighter squadron VF-72 embarked during 1949-50 aboard the carrier USS *Leyte*.

were dropped in favor of the all-inclusive 'A' for Attack. However, this change applied only to new aircraft (thus the Martin BTM-1 became AM-1), the Grumman/General Motors TBM and Curtiss SB2C retaining their original designations until they were phased out of service. Patrol bombing (VPB) squadrons reverted, on 15 May, to the pre-war VP designation. On 15 November, in an attempt to make some semblance of order of the hodge-podge of designations caused by demobilization, the entire numbering system was reconstructed. Carrier air groups were redesignated according to the type of ship to which they were assigned. Battle carriers each had an air group designated CVBG, attack carriers a CVAG, light carriers a CVLG and escort carriers a CVEG. All carrier squadrons became VF or VA, eliminating the VB, VBF and VT series. Suffix letters A, B, L and E indicated their carrier type assignment (for example, VF-1A and VA-1E for Fighter Squadron One Attack and Attack Squadron One Escort). VP squadrons assumed, with their new numbers, a letter code indicating their aircraft (for example, VP-MS-1 for Patrol Squadron One Medium Seaplane). VO squadrons assumed their parent ship division numbers while adding 'B' or 'C' indicating battleship or cruiser assignment (for example, VO-1B and VO-2C).

Below: F8F-1 Bearcats began relieving Hellcats as the Navy's main fighter in 1945, but never made it to combat. VF-15A and VF-16A F8F-1s prepare for launch from USS *Tarawa* (CV 40) in 1948.

Utility squadrons traded their VJ for VU and VPP replaced the enigmatic VD designation for photo squadrons. Meteorology squadrons became VPM instead of VPW. The new, complicated scheme lasted less than two years and was scrapped for an entirely new system in September 1948.

In late May 1948, a merger of the Naval Air Transport Service (NATS) and the Air Force Air Transport Command (ATC) was initiated with the establishment of two support wings under the Commander, Fleet Logistic Support Wings. On 1 June, NATS and ATC were consolidated to form the Military Air Transport Service (MATS) under the direction of the Air Force. On 1 July NATS, which had remained in service to assist with the formation of MATS, was formally decommissioned after 6½ years of supporting the Navy's airborne logistics requirements.

Reversing the trend of cutbacks, a new form of carrier squadron was formally established 6 July, when Carrier Airborne Early Warning Squadrons One (VW-1) and Two (VW-2) were commissioned on the east and west coasts. These were the first squadrons to be established specifically for the carrier AEW mission.

In 1948 BuAer, realizing that the 1946 aviation unit designation system made little sense and was

confusing to use, revamped the entire program once again. Effective from 1 September, the former system was replaced with a new one of logic and simplicity. All carrier air groups became CVGs, dropping the type identifier. The attack and fighter squadrons assumed two- or three-digit numbers without suffix letters. The first one or two digits of the squadron number corresponded with the assigned air group number. Thus, Air Group One (CVG-1) for example, was comprised of VF-11, VF-12, VF-13, VA-14 and VA-15. CVG-19 had VF-191, VF-192, etc. At the same time, the term 'Fighting Squadron' was dropped in favor of 'Fighter Squadron'. All patrol and transport squadrons became VP and VR. VC squadrons changed to VAW, VFN or VAN depending upon their mission of early warning, night fighter or night attack. This same system is basically in effect today. However, decommissioning and transfer of squadrons from one air group/wing to another has once again left the system in a shambles.

The end of World War II had brought with it a refreshing air of optimism and hope for peace in the world. The warmth of this hope, unfortunately, was soon chilled by events in Eastern Europe that ushered in a new era dubbed the 'Cold War'. The pre-war suspicions and paranoia that had existed between the USSR and what became the Western Allies had only been partially set aside during the war for the sake of mutual self interest. It returned once again in full force by 1948.

Following months of harassment of Allied occupation forces in the western sectors of Berlin, on 24 June 1948 the Soviets blockaded all ground and waterborne traffic in and out of the former German capital. In response to this attempt to starve the West out of the partitioned city, an airlift was established under the direction of the US Air Force to defeat the communist tactic. Under Operation 'Vittles', MATS squadrons VR-6 and VR-8 were ordered to Germany in October from their Pacific bases to assist with the airlift. US Navy participation in this successful humanitarian effort continued until 31 July 1949. In the intervening months, the Navy Douglas R5D squadrons had flown a total of 45,990 hours, carrying 129,989 tons of life-sustaining necessities into Berlin's Tempelhof field. The two squadrons had averaged 10 hours per plane each day on the run from Rhein-Main to Berlin while battling the worst European weather conditions of the year. The Soviets, realizing that their inept tactic had been defeated by the airlift, on 12 May 1949 cancelled their blockade.

New developments continued for Naval Aviation and the military in general during the latter part of the post-war decade. An interesting program was initiated in 1949 that would prove to be most successful over the succeeding years, and continues to this day. On 1 October, an exchange program began between the Air Force and Navy to indoctrinate selected pilots in the operational and training requirements of each other's service. Eighteen

pilots from the Air Force reported to Navy squadrons as eighteen Navy and Marine pilots joined Air Force units to begin one-year tours of duty. The exchange program would grow to include 25 Naval Aviators and Naval Flight Officers and a similar number of Air Force members each year. Under current regulations, it has also expanded to include six months of training and a two-year tour of duty.

Conflict of interests

Despite this one program of co-operation, the post-war struggle for annual funding intensified interservice rivalries between the Navy, Army and the newly-established Air Force. The apex of this rivalry, centered upon roles and missions, was reached during 1948-49 and was epitomized by the 'B-36 vs aircraft-carrier' controversy.

Under the National Security Act signed by President Truman on 18 July 1947, a National Military Establishment was formed under a Secretary of Defense. It also established the Air Force as a separate service on 18 September. This new organizational plan, however, did not clearly define strategic roles or wartime missions of the individual services. The lack of a clearly defined mission precipitated one of the greatest crises ever faced by Naval Aviation.

At the Joint Chiefs of Staff level, the Army and its Air Force progeny agreed to support each other in mutual efforts to limit the size of the Marine Corps and strategic missions for Naval Aviation. They concluded that there was no need for the Navy to have a strategic capability which newly designed carriers could provide. They reasoned the country's future military needs should be centered around strategic bombing carried out by the Air Force under a unified military command system. Addi-

Above: Naval Air Transport Service (NATS) was abolished in 1948 and placed under Air Force control in the Military Air Transport Service (MATS). This MATS R5D-3 Skymaster of VR-3 is over NAS Moffett Field home station on 12 March 1951.

Below left: Flown for the first time in November 1946, the Lockheed R60-1 Constitution was conceived in response to a Pan American requirement, but never served with that company. Two were built, and both found their way to the Navy, with which they remained active until 1955.

Below: During 1949 congressional investigation of the US Air Force's B-36 procurement, Admiral Arthur W. Radford, CinCPacFlt, termed the airplane a 'billion-dollar blunder'. VMJ-3 F9F-5Ps escort an RB-36H demonstrating the 'big and little' of photo reconnaissance.

Above: Two all-new, built-from-the-keel-up CVLs joined the fleet in 1946 and 1947. The *Saipan* (CVL 48) and sistership *Wright* (CVL 49) were larger and heavier than their World War II predecessors.

tionally, under the unification plan, the size of the Marine Corps would be reduced and its assets transferred to the Army. The Navy, likewise reduced, would serve in a support role to the Air Force. Army and Air Force leaders argued that the Navy had no requirement for a long-range nuclear strike mission, as this would duplicate the Convair B-36's strategic bombing role.

Through political wangling, Chief of Naval Operations Admiral Louis E. Denfeld and Secretary of the Navy John L. Sullivan were able to strike a compromise for the FY 1949 budget in the spring of 1948 which provided the Navy appropriations for a new 'super-carrier', USS *United States* (CVA 58).

However, the fiscal and unification battles continued into the following year. Supported by a sympathetic Truman administration, the Army and Air Force arguments and astute political maneuvering carried the day. On 23 April 1949 Secretary of Defense Louis A. Johnson, who had taken office only on 28 March, halted construction of *United States*. Building of the giant flushdeck carrier, designed to stretch 1,090 ft (332.2 m) in length and displace 65,000 tons, had begun only five days previously. The decision by the anti-Navy Johnson to cancel the new ship was made without the knowledge of Admiral Denfield or consultation with Secretary of the Navy Sullivan. This breach of respect prompted Sullivan's immediate resignation. The leadership of Naval Aviation launched an immediate but unsuccessful counterattack on the B-36, which was termed by the outspoken Admiral Arthur W. Radford, Commander-in-Chief Pacific Fleet, in testimony before the House Naval Affairs committee as a 'billion-dollar blunder' by the Air

Force.

Admiral Radford's remarks formed the vanguard of testimony by several more senior naval officers, including Admiral Denfeld, which protested the unfair treatment given Naval Aviation by the Secretary of Defense and the Joint Chiefs of Staff. This testimony became known as the 'admirals' revolt' and cost several of Naval Aviation's World War II leaders their careers. The candid testimony also brought attempted reprisals against others by Johnson and the ineffective new Secretary of the Navy, Francis P. Matthews. Denfeld, a submariner by trade, was denied a second term as CNO and retired in 1950. He later authored a stinging attack on Air Force leaders in an article in *Colliers* magazine entitled 'The Only Carrier the Air Force Ever Sank'.

In addition to cancelling the Navy's super-carrier program, Johnson also restricted expansion of Naval Aviation by cutting Navy and Marine Corps aviation funds, which he then transferred to the Air Force. He ordered the reduction of Marine Corps Aviation by one-half, limited the Fleet Marine Force to four-fifths its size and emasculated the Navy's aircraft research and development budget. Reduction of the Navy's patrol squadrons from 30 to 20 was also proposed. The future of Naval Aviation and its capability to be a viable force in the defense of the nation was in serious jeopardy.

FY 1950 proposals called for a reduction of 29,500 Navy personnel and for the mothballing of 24 more ships. Another 418 aircraft were to join the thousands that had preceded them to storage depots around the country or to the smelters at North Island and Norfolk. Nine more air stations were to be closed; three others were to be reduced to standby status. USS *Princeton* (CV 37), *Tarawa* and *Antietam*, none more than four years old, joined 15 other 'Essex' class carriers in the mothball fleet during the summer of 1949. The latest cut of the attack carriers left only the three CVBs operating in the Atlantic Fleet with *Kearsarge* (CV 33), *Leyte* (CV 32) and *Philippine Sea* (CV 47). On the west coast, the vast reaches of the Pacific were the responsibility of *Boxer* and *Valley Forge* (CV 45). *Philippine Sea* joined her west coast sisters in January of the following year. Events in the Far East would soon prove the fallacy of the Secretary of Defense's policies toward Naval Aviation as well as the importance of the mobility and flexibility of aircraft-carriers.

Right: The US Navy's aerial flight demonstration team 'Blue Angels' was formed in June 1946, flying F6F-5 Hellcats. They quickly shifted to the higher-performance Bearcat in the same year.

23
Korea - Another Carrier War

They called it the 'Land of the Morning Calm', but this peaceful appelation is at odds with Korea's turbulent history. Following centuries of political turmoil and instability, characterized by fighting between various warring factions, the Korean peninsula was annexed and subjugated in 1910 by Japan. At the end of World War II it was divided at the 38th parallel to facilitate the surrender of Japanese troops to Soviet occupation forces in the north and American forces in the south.

The communists soon established the Korean People's Republic in their sector and, in the south, the pro-western Republic of Korea was formed. After nearly five years of abortive attempts to reach a conciliation between the two governments to reunify the country, the 'Land of the Morning Calm' was again shattered by war.

In the pre-dawn hours of 25 June 1950, North Korean forces crossed the 38th parallel and invaded their neighbors to the south. The last American combat forces had been pulled out of South Korea in June of the previous year. The well-trained, Soviet-equipped North Korean army had no trouble forcing the South Korean troops to retreat as they rapidly advanced down the peninsula. On 27 June, President Truman ordered naval and air support for the South Koreans. He further ordered the 7th Fleet to protect Formosa from an attack by mainland China. Considering the decimated condition of the Navy's forces, especially Naval Aviation, imposed by the post-war policies dictated by the president's administration, the Navy had been assigned an almost impossible task.

Of the 15 carriers (three CVBs, four CVs, four CVLs and four CVEs) in commission on the day of the invasion, only *Valley Forge*, with Air Group Five embarked, was deployed to the Far East. The majority of the Navy's carrier forces were concentrated on the east coast, defending against the perceived threat of a Soviet invasion of Western Europe and the Scandinavian countries.

The three new 'Midway' class battle carriers were homeported at Norfolk, from where they deployed to the North Atlantic and Mediterranean. On 25 June, all three were in the Norfolk area, *Midway* with CVG-4 assigned, *Roosevelt* with CVG-6 and *Coral Sea* with CVG-17. *Leyte* and CVG-3 were deployed to the Mediterranean. *Cabot* (CVL 28), recommissioned 27 October 1948, and *Wright* (CVL 49), alternated ASW and training carrier duties while operating from Quonset Point and Pensacola. *Saipan* (CVL 48) was engaged in developing ASW

tactics out of Norfolk. Newly-recommissioned *Bataan* (CVL 29) was at Philadelphia where she would be immediately ordered to the west coast and on to Korea before the end of the year. She departed for San Diego on 5 July. The new escort carriers *Mindoro* (CVE 120) and *Palau* (CVE 122) completed the Atlantic Fleet's carrier force, where they too were engaged in ASW development.

On the west coast, *Kearsarge* had recently entered Puget Sound Naval Shipyard to commence an extensive modernization. *Boxer* and CVG-19 had just returned to Alameda from the Western Pacific. *Philippine Sea* and CVG-11 were at San Diego preparing for deployment. *Sicily* (CVE 118) worked with ASW squadrons out of San Diego and *Badoeng Strait* (CVE 116) was on her way to Pearl Harbor with a Marine fighter squadron aboard. In the Far East, the total number of Navy aircraft on 30 June amounted to only 108 of all types, including *Valley Forge*'s air group, two VP squadrons and two Fleet Air Service Squadrons (FASRON). The Navy was thus ill-prepared to fight another air war in the Pacific and Asia or, for that matter, anywhere else in the world.

As the North Koreans crossed the 38th parallel, Vice Admiral Arthur D. Struble's 7th Fleet striking force's only carrier was at Hong Kong. *Valley Forge*, under command of Captain L.K. Rice with Rear Admiral John M. 'Peg Leg' Hoskins, Commander Carrier Division 3 and acting Commander 7th Fleet embarked, departed for Subic Bay to replenish. Under way again on 27 June, she steamed north toward Japan. Launching a 'show of force' mission on 29 June, her Air Group Five planes covered the Formosa Strait in response to the president's directive to protect Formosa. Diverted to Buckner Bay, Okinawa, the carrier was joined on 1 July by the British light carrier HMS *Triumph*, which added its two squadrons to Task Force 77. By the morning of 3 July, aviators from the Anglo-American team conducted strikes against the North Korean capital city, Pyongyang. *Valley Forge* and *Triumph* thus carried the load of the carrier war until additional carriers could arrive in August.

With another full-scale war on their hands, (euphemistically termed a 'police action' by the government and press) the nation's leaders were suddenly and belatedly more receptive to a stronger military force. Admiral Forrest P. Sherman, who had relieved Admiral Denfeld as CNO, had already set into motion a plan for expansion and modernization of Naval Aviation for the future to include the recommissioning of some carriers. In July 1950, the Joint Chiefs of Staff approved Sherman's plan to keep *Leyte* in commission and to increase naval manpower. Since the end of World War II, the Navy's ships had been woefully undermanned, at

Below: *Valley Forge* (CV 47) and Air Group Five were the only US Navy carrier force in the Western Pacific at the outbreak of the Korean War on 25 June 1950. Joined by HMS *Triumph*, the two carriers shouldered the war until help arrived in August.

times to the point of being unable to meet operating schedules. *Philippine Sea*, commissioned 11 May 1946, was forced to remain at Quonset Point in a reduced-commission status until September because of a lack of personnel. During September 1950, President Truman replaced Louis Johnson as Secretary of Defense with General of the Army George C. Marshall. In July of the following year, the Congress passed a resolution for a major ship-building and modernization program which was signed into law by the president. Naval Aviation was on the road to recovery.

Strikes on Korea

Meanwhile, there was a war to fight. *Sicily*, under command of the famed Captain Jimmy Thach, was the first carrier to join *Valley Forge* and *Triumph*. Abandoning her anti-submarine role, *Sicily* stashed her VS-21 TBM-3S aircraft at Guam, then continued on to Japan where she picked up a Marine fighter squadron. By 2 August, her VMF-214 Vought F4U-4Bs were flying close air support missions for US and South Korean forces entrenched in the Pusan perimeter. She was assisted four days later by *Badoeng Strait* and VMF-323's F4U-4B fighter-bombers. Joined by the *Bataan* in December, and by *Bairoko* (CVE 115) and *Rendova* (CVE 114) in 1951, the five smaller carriers conducted strikes from the Tsushima Strait and the

Yellow Sea on Korea's western coast throughout the remainder of the war as part of Task Force 95, the Blockading and Escort Force.

Of the bigger decks, *Philippine Sea* arrived in Buckner Bay 1 August to begin workups for the combat zone. During the initial part of the war, the fast carriers operated from Okinawa, out of range of potential Chinese communist or Soviet land-based air attacks. There was distinct uncertainty of communist intentions at the time, or how widespread the war might become. US installations in Japan were well within bombing range of Chinese and Soviet bases. Despite this, the carriers moved to Yokosuka before the end of the year. Joining with *Valley Forge*, *Philippine Sea*'s CVG-11 launched its first strikes on 5 August against rail and highway bridges. At the outset of the war, the fast carriers launched strikes from both the Yellow Sea and the Sea of Japan. Later, their operating areas were limited to Korea's eastern coast.

The standard air group composition had been established on 20 July 1948 as three fighter and two attack squadrons. In January 1950 this changed to four fighter and one attack squadron. Two of the fighter squadrons flew F4U-4B Corsair fighter-bombers, backing up the two all-jet primary VF squadrons. Although the VBF designation had been dropped in 1946, the mission remained. In Korea, the Corsair was limited virtually to attack

US Navy

111

The Douglas Skynight would become the only fighter to serve in both the Korean and Vietnam Wars. VC-4 crews brought F3D-2s to Korea in 1953 in *Lake Champlain* (CVA 39), but operated from a land base.

missions, as were the majority of the jet fighter squadrons later on. Eventually, many of the Corsair units were redesignated as attack squadrons. The VA-designated squadron of the air group flew Douglas AD Skyraiders. Each squadron was authorized a complement of 18 aircraft for a total of 90 planes per air group. Additionally, there were detachments of F4U-5N night fighters and F4U-5P photo-reconnaissance versions of the Corsair. A mixture of AD-3N, AD-3Q/4Q and AD-5W special-mission Skyraiders filled out the combat load of the carriers. A Sikorsky HO3S-1 helicopter detachment was aboard, but was normally assigned to the ship and not the air group. In all, the 'Essex' class carriers could have over 100 airplanes aboard when deploying.

Valley Forge's CVG-5 was the Navy's most experienced jet air group. VF-51 had been the Navy's first squadron to operate jets from a carrier as VF-5A: the squadron's leader, Commander Evan 'Pete' Aurand, and Lieutenant Commander R.M. 'Bob' Elder conducted carrier suitability trials with the North American FJ-1 Fury 10 March 1948 aboard *Boxer*. The 'Screaming Eagles' traded their FJs to become the first Grumman F9F Panther-equipped squadron, receiving their first F9F-3 on 8 May 1949 at NAS San Diego. It was fitting that this squadron was also the first to take the Panther into combat and score its initial aerial victories. During the 3 July raid on Pyongyang, VF-51's Lieutenant (JG) Leonard H. Plog and Ensign E.W. Brown each bagged a Yakovlev Yak-9. However, it was VF-111's skipper, Commander W.T. Amen, flying an F9F-2 from *Philippine Sea* on 9 November 1950, who became the first naval aviator to shoot down a jet in combat. Amen brought down a MiG-15 on 9 November during the initial strikes against

the Yalu bridges at Sinuiju. As a precursor of years later in Vietnam, the communist pilots' normal tactic was a slashing, hit-and-run attack on the strike groups. In the course of the war, they did little damage although their attempts were at times frequent.

Navy and Marine Corps aviators distinguished themselves in aerial combat during the Korean War. Flying against North Korean, Chinese communist and Soviet pilots, the Americans challenged and beat the best the enemy had to offer. Although there were never a great number of aerial combats, Navy pilots flying from carriers shot down nine enemy aircraft: two Yak-9s, one Ilyushin Il-10 flown by a Soviet pilot and six MiG-15s, including two Soviet aircraft flying out of Vladivostok. The MiGs were all brought down by F9F pilots, who suffered no losses to enemy pilots. Two carrier-based Navy F4U-4s were lost to MiG-15s. VMF/A-312 Marine F4U pilots flying from *Sicily* and *Bataan* bagged three Yak-9s and a MiG-15 to the loss of one Corsair downed by a MiG. The Navy produced one ace for the war, Lieutenant Guy P. Bordelon, flying a VC-3 F4U-5N night-fighter. Bordelon, assigned to VC-3's *Princeton* (CVA 37) detachment, was land-based with the Marines at the time. In the last days of the war, VC-4's Douglas F3D-2 night fighter detachment in *Lake Champlain* (CVA 39) was transferred ashore to operate with VMF(N)-513. They lost one Skyknight to enemy aircraft. Navy and Marine Corps aviators (excluding those on exchange duty) confirmed 31 kills for the war. An additional 23½ MiG-15s were credited to Navy and Marine pilots attached to Air Force North American F-86 Sabre squadrons. Major John Bolt became the Marines' only ace as he acquired six victories over MiG-15s while on exchange duty.

Left: VA-195 AD-4 Skyraider deck launches from the *Boxer* in 1951 with three 500-lb (227-kg) and eight 265-lb (120-kg) general-purpose bombs. VA-195 became famed as the 'Dambusters' after its 1 May 1951 aerial torpedo attack against the Hwachon Dam.

Right: The recall to active duty of a substantial number of Reserve units in response to the Korean War of 1950 resulted in the F9F-2 Panthers of VF-781 seeing combat action from USS Oriskany (CV 34) as part of Carrier Air Group 102 (CVG-102).

Commander Robert E. Bennet, USN(Ret)

US Navy

Above: VF-193 F4U-4 launches from Princeton (CV 37) with a load of armor-piercing HVAR rockets during 1951 strike mission.

Above right: VF-51's 'Screaming Eagles' were first to bring the F9F-2/3 Panthers into combat and first to score aerial victories. On 3 July 1950 Lieutenant (JG) Leonard H. Plog and Ensign E. W. Brown each bagged a Yak-9 over Pyongyang.

Below: In this typical flight deck scene during the course of the Korean War, six Grumman F9F-2 Panthers of Navy fighter squadron VF-31 are seen aboard USS Leyte (CV 32) in 1950 shortly before launching for another ground attack mission over North Korea.

Total USN/USMC air-to-air losses were four (three Navy and one Marine) aircraft. Twelve years would lapse before naval aviators would again be tested by adversary pilots in a full-scale war.

Before the end of 1950, three more fast carriers joined Task Force 77. *Leyte*, ordered home from the Mediterranean in August, brought CVG-3's firepower to the line on 9 October. *Boxer*, with CVG-2, completed a hurried work-up to report on 15 September, and *Princeton*, only recommissioned on 28 August, arrived with CVG-19 on 5 December. *Valley Forge*, returning to North Island on 1 December, completed a five-day turnaround and returned to the line to relieve the *Boxer*, which was overdue for a scheduled overhaul. Air Group Two transferred to the ship known as the 'Happy Valley', a nickname that must have carried some irony for the ship's company.

The enemy's initial successes on the ground were soon reversed following a behind-the-lines invasion of Inchon by UN forces in September. By mid-October, US forces had captured the North Korean capital. ROK troops pushed ahead, forcing the enemy toward the Yalu. In late October, Chinese communists entered the war, sending ground troops across the Yalu and threatening the overextended South Koreans. In the next weeks, the UN forces attempted to hold back the onslaught of Chinese troops. The carrier strikes shifted from armed reconnaissance and attacks against supply routes to a heavier emphasis on close air support to relieve the pressure on the beleaguered troops. In November, the Yalu bridges were ordered destroyed. Relentlessly, the enemy pressed the offensive, and by the beginning of the New Year, they were once again south of the 38th parallel. In February 1951, the drive finally stalled and was partially reversed by the Allies. The war soon stagnated, with the enemy forces driven back slightly north of the dividing line. Here, for all practical purposes, the

US Navy

Left: Mariner flying-boats were in the Far East at the outbreak of the war. VP-46 flew patrols off Korea and the Chinese mainland in PBM-5S2s. Two FAW-6 Mariners attempted rescue of US Marines trapped at the Chosin reservoir in 1950, but were thwarted by frozen waters.

front remained static for the next 2½ years as seemingly endless rounds of peace negotiations were conducted. For the carrier aviators, however, nothing much would change. They faced 29 more months of flak and drudgery as they struck such targets as enemy lines of communications, hydro-electric power plants and troop concentrations in an attempt to pressure the communists into opting for a ceasefire.

VP missions

On the VP side of the ledger, Patrol Squadrons 28 and 46 were the only units of their type deployed to the Far East in June of 1950. VP-28 flew land-based Consolidated PB4Y-2S Privateers while VP-46 operated Martin PBM-5/5S Mariner seaplanes. The two squadrons were reinforced in July by VP-6 and VP-47. VP-6, flying Lockheed P2V-3/3Ws, introduced the Neptune into the combat zone. More squadrons reported to the area during the latter half of the year to operate under the direction of Commanders Fleet Air One and Six. The RAF also contributed Short Sunderland squadrons to serve with FAW-6.

The VP missions consisted primarily of coastal, anti-submarine and anti-mine patrol throughout the Korean area, the coast of mainland China and the Formosa Strait. Task Force 77 had been directed to prevent any attacks on Formosa by the Chinese communists and any offensive action by the Nationalists against the mainland. Heavy emphasis was placed by the VP units on this volatile area. VP squadrons also flew other missions, including flare-drop, aerial reconnaissance and search and rescue. Although their tasks were usually more mundane than those of the carriers, the VP squadrons brought versatility through their ability to operate from land and sea bases. Except for the harsh Korean winter, this versatility might have had a life-saving effect on many Marines trapped at the Chosin Reservoir by the Chinese offensive of 1950. On 1 December, FAW-6 attempted a rescue effort of the entrapped Marines by sending PBMs into the area to shuttle them out. The attempt was thwarted when, upon the arrival of the first two aircraft, the reservoir was found to be frozen solid. Not able to land, the PBMs were forced to leave the Marines to fight their way out over land.

From February 1951 until the ceasefire was finally signed, effective on 27 July 1953, there were 18 more fast carrier combat deployments to Korea. Most carriers made several return trips with new air groups. *Bon Homme Richard* (CVA 31) (CVB and CV attack carriers had been redesignated CVA on 1 October 1952), *Essex* (CVA 9), *Antietam* (CVA 36), *Kearsarge* (CVA 33) and *Lake Champlain* (CVA 39) were all recommissioned, some with modernizations, and brought their services to the war. *Oriskany* (CVA 34) was finally completed and commissioned 25 September 1950 as a virtually new-class carrier. She joined her sisters on the line 28 October 1952 with Reserve Air Group 102, which was commissioned in February of the following year as CVG-12 of the regular Navy. The 1951-3 deployments brought with them Air Groups 19 and 19X, and CVG-101 (another Reserve group, which became CVG-14) and CVGs 7, 9 and 4. A third all-Reserve air group, CVG-15, also served in Korea.

Soon after the beginning of the war, it was apparent that combat operations with five squadrons aboard an 'Essex' class carrier were proving difficult to manage. In fact, some aircraft were actually left in Japan until losses made room for them. Although authorized with 18 aircraft, the

A section of Grumman F9F-2 Panthers from VF-71 escort an F9F-2P photo-reconnaissance Panther of VC-61 during a mission over Korea in 1952. All three aircraft were operating as part of Carrier Air Group Seven (CVG-7) aboard *Bon Homme Richard* (CV-31).

Above: The requirement for more attack planes and fewer fighters operating from carriers in Korea brought about the anomaly of several VF-designated squadrons flying AD Skyraiders. Lieutenant Commander Hank Suerstedt, CO of VF-54, taxies forward after strike.

Above right: Some idea of the damage inflicted by Navy aircraft in the Korean War can be gained from this view of the Hwachon Dam following an attack with aerial torpedoes in May 1951. AD Skyraiders of VA-195 and VC-35 aboard USS *Princeton* (CV 37) were responsible.

Below: The only use of guided missiles launched against an enemy from an aircraft-carrier occurred aboard the *Boxer* in August 1952, as six GMU-90 Hellcats with 1,000-lb (454-kg) bombs were guided to targets by VC-35 mother planes.

squadrons normally operated with 14 to 16. The Navy was faced with a unique problem: too many squadrons to operate efficiently aboard the carriers and not enough air groups authorized by the Congress to man the carriers available. Naval Aviation, always the innovator, came up with a solution. The number of squadrons in the authorized air groups was reduced from five to four and a new type of unit was formed to circumvent the congressional limitation, the Air Task Group. Never officially commissioned, eight of these groups were formed between 1951 and 1955. Two of them, ATG-1 and ATG-2, served combat tours in Korea. In 1959, the ATGs passed quietly from the scene, having served their purpose. Another interesting aspect of the air group squadron reductions was that several VF squadrons assumed dedicated attack roles and flew AD Skyraiders while still carrying their fighter squadron designations. VF-54, VF-92 and VF-194 were examples of this anomaly.

Several other 'firsts' and unique aerial operations presented themselves in Korea. The F9F-2B version of the Panther became the Navy's first jet

fighter to be utilized in the bomber role: on 2 April 1951, two of these fighter-bombers assigned to VF-191 were launched from *Princeton*, each with four 250-lb (113-kg) and two 100-lb (45-kg) bombs to attack a railroad bridge near Songjin. *Princeton* was also the base for the only use of aerial torpedoes since World War II: five VA-195 AD-4s and three VC-35 AD-4Ns carrying Mk 13 aerial torpedoes were launched from *Princeton* 1 May 1951 to strike the flood gates of the Hwachon Dam. The attack was a success, with one gate completely destroyed and another damaged. The waters of the reservoir were released, flooding the valleys of the Han and Pukhan Rivers below, denying the enemy the ability to use the rivers for strategic purposes.

Another unique operation was the use of F6F-5K Hellcat drones, laden with 1,000-lb (454-kg) bombs, against enemy targets. Between 28 August and 2 September 1952 six radio-controlled Hellcats were launched from *Boxer* against a bridge, railroad tunnel and power plant in North Korea. Two direct hits and one near miss were scored by the drones, which were crashed into their targets by controlling AD-4Ns of VC-35. The operation, conducted by Guided Missile Unit 90, was the first use of guided missiles against an enemy from a carrier.

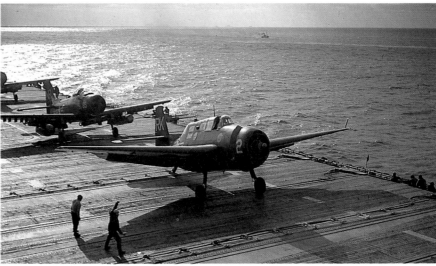

Two Naval Aviators earned the USA's highest award for their actions in Korea. Lieutenant (JG) Thomas J. Hudner of *Leyte*'s VF-32 was awarded the Medal of Honor for his gallant attempt to save the life of his wingman, Ensign Jesse L. Brown. Brown had been forced down behind enemy lines on 4 December 1950 near the Chosin Reservoir after being hit by AA fire. Hudner, circling the downed pilot, could see Brown trapped in his burning Corsair, struggling to free himself. Disregarding his own safety and completely aware of the presence of enemy troops in the immediate area, Hudner bellied his F4U-4 in nearby and rushed to free Brown from the fire. Unable to free the young pilot, whose leg was pinned in the crushed cockpit, Hudner packed snow around the injured Brown to keep the flames away from him. Returning to his own aircraft, Hudner called for assistance then resumed his frantic efforts to save Brown. Hudner's inspirational actions were to no avail. Brown died in the cockpit of his airplane before the rescue helo could arrive. With Brown's death, the Navy also lost its first black Naval Aviator.

The second Medal of Honor was awarded posthumously to Lieutenant (JG) John M. Koelsch, a helicopter rescue pilot assigned to HU-1 flying from the rescue ship LST-799 in Wonsan Harbor. Koelsch had already completed a combat tour with *Princeton*, but volunteered to remain in Korea

when the carrier was relieved. In the late afternoon of 3 July 1951, Koelsch and his crewman, AM3 George M. Neal, volunteered to attempt the rescue of a Marine pilot shot down behind enemy lines about 35 miles (56 km) south of Wonsan. In a darkening sky and with bad weather setting in, Koelsch lifted his HO3S-1 off the deck of the LST and headed south. Escorted by four Corsairs, Koelsch reached the rescue area. However, because of solid cloud cover beneath him, he was forced to leave his protective fighter cover and made the hazardous descent through the clouds in mountainous terrain heavily defended by enemy troops. Locating the downed pilot, the helo crew commenced the rescue attempt as they began taking intense small-arms fire. Despite having his aircraft struck once by enemy fire, Koelsch pressed his rescue and hovered over the survivor. As the pilot, Captain James V. Wilkins, positioned himself in the rescue sling, the frail helo was struck by a burst of anti-aircraft fire, causing it to crash. Finding that Wilkins' arms and legs were so severely burned that he was unable to walk, Koelsch and Neal fashioned a litter of sorts and headed for the coast. The airmen managed to avoid capture for nine days, but were finally taken prisoner. After his capture, Koelsch

Above: TBM-3R 'carrier-onboard-delivery' (COD) versions of the World War II torpedo bomber were used in Korea to transport men and equipment between land bases and carriers. VR-23 TBM-3R is about to launch from the *Essex* (CVA-9).

Above left: One of the US Navy's most successful types in Korea was the McDonnell F2H Banshee, which proved itself a useful fighter. The F2H-2P reconnaissance version provided much vital information for the attack squadrons.

Following the invasion of South Korea in 1950 a number of Reserve units were recalled to active duty. These were soon committed to action, being spearheaded by F4U-4 Corsairs of VF-791 and AD-2 Skyraiders of VA-702, seen here flying formation off the coast of North Korea in August 1951.

US Navy

Above: Carrier operations are dangerous at the best of times but during combat the danger increases dramatically. Here an AD Skyraider burns following a deck accident.

Below: Typical air group composition is seen in this 1953 photo of CVG-4 aboard 'The Champ'. VF-22 and -62 are in F2H-2 Banshees, VF-11 (on loan from CVG-11 in *Boxer*) is in F9F-5 Panthers, while VA-45 has AD-4 Skyraiders.

continued his valorous actions and actively inspired his fellow prisoners until he finally succumbed to dysentery and starvation in the hands of his captors.

Korea is described by history as a small war. Though it certainly never approached the proportions of World War II the size of a war is a matter of perspective. From the viewpoint of the soldier in the foxhole or the aviator in the cockpit watching incoming fire, one war is about as big as another. Only 15 carriers (including the five CVL/CVEs) were engaged in combat in Korea, as compared with the more than 100 that served in World War II. Yet comparative statistics are surprising. In 38 months,

as opposed to the 45 months of World War II, Navy and Marine aviators flew 276,000 combat sorties, dropped 177,000 tons of bombs and expended 272,000 rockets. While flying 7,000 fewer sorties, they had exceeded the World War II totals of bombs dropped by 74,000 tons and rockets fired by 60,000. So much for 'small' wars. The big difference in Korea, as it would be in Vietnam, was the length of time the carriers remained on station, as they launched several strikes daily against the enemy. World War II tactics centered largely around running in, hitting the target and moving on to the next one. In Korea it was 'out on the job' day after day for the carrier aviators.

24
The New Planes

US Navy

Between the end of World War II and Vietnam, Naval Aviation experienced a forward leap in technological advances the likes of which had not been seen in its previous 34 years. This technology took Navy fighters from 400-mph (644-km/h) prop-driven aircraft weighing less than 15,000 lb (6804 kg) to 55,000-lb (24948-kg) turbojet-powered behemoths capable of speeds over twice that of sound. The best the Navy had to offer in an attack plane in service on VJ-Day was an aircraft that could carry only 2,000 lb (907kg) of bombs at a speed of about 160 mph (257 km/h); within 11 years the Navy had operational carrier attack aircraft capable of carrying at high subsonic speeds, in one airplane, more destructive power than an entire World War II air group could deliver in a week of twice-daily strikes. The two areas of technology that were most responsible for these astonishing advances in the art of warfare were the development of jet aircraft and nuclear weapons.

Entry into the jet era began quietly and slowly for the Navy in November 1943, with the acceptance of two Bell YP-59A Airacomets from the Army Air Force. With the evaluation of America's first jet-propelled aircraft at Patuxent River, the Navy started the foundation of knowledge and experience necessary for it to produce jet aircraft suitable for its future needs.

The first steps into the jet age had been taken in January 1943 with a contract for a hybrid piston/jet-powered fighter. A year and a half later, on 25 June 1944, the first flight of the XFR-1 Fireball occurred at Ryan's plant in San Diego. Squadron deliveries of the FR-1 production models began with VF-66 in March 1945. Only a partial success, the FR-1s were used sparingly aboard a few CVEs and never in more than single-squadron strength until discarded in June 1947.

The slow, faltering steps into jet aviation continued with a surprising development in August 1943. The student of Naval Aviation history might

logically conclude that Grumman, with its relatively long history of development of fighter planes for the Navy, would have been the choice to design its first all-jet fighter. Instead, on 7 January 1943, a letter of intent to design and produce two jet prototype fighters was given to the McDonnell Aircraft Corporation, a company that had never in its history built a Navy airplane.

Originally designated XFD-1, McDonnell's fighter (later FH-1) took to the air at St Louis, Missouri 26 January 1945. A period of development and testing began at Patuxent River, culminating with Lieutenant Commander Jim Davidson launching and recovering aboard *Roosevelt* on 21 July 1946. These evolutions marked the first all-jet carrier operations in US history. Deliveries of the FH-1 Phantom began with VF-17A at Quonset Point on 23 July 1947. The 'Aces' were the first squadron to qualify aboard a carrier when, during 3-5 May 1948, the entire 16-plane squadron conducted carrier qualifications aboard *Saipan*.

The Phantom was quickly followed into service by the F2H-1 Banshee, a bigger, more powerful development of the FH-1 technology. Deliveries to VF-171 (formerly VF-17A) began in March 1949. Meanwhile, Vought had produced the XF6U-1 Pirate, first flown on 2 October 1946. Grumman produced the XF9F-2 Panther, first flown on 2 November 1947. North America's XFJ-1 Fury had flown on 11 September of the previous year. Of this

Above: The US Navy's entry into the jet era came in November 1943, with the evaluation of two Bell YP-59A Airacomets at Patuxent River. The Airacomet was the United States' first jet-powered aircraft.

Vought

Left: A Vought XF6U-1 Pirate flies formation with a McDonnell FH-1 Phantom and F2H-1 Banshee during VX-3 evaluations of all three aircraft. The Pirate never reached squadron service and only 30 were built.

Right: One of the more unusual types to see service in the immediate post-war era was the Ryan FR-1 Fireball, which employed mixed jet and propeller propulsion. Used in only modest quantities, it is represented here by an example from VF-41 during 1946.

Below: In the early post-war years, the US Navy wasted little time in exploring the possibilities offered by jet propulsion. One of the earliest types to be introduced to service was the FJ Fury, the example shown here featuring the markings of VF-5A in 1948.

Right: VF-5A 'Screaming Eagles' CO, Commander Pete Aurand, and his XO, Lieutenant Commander Bob Elder, conducted the US Navy's first carrier landings of an operational jet when they flew carrier suitability trials from the *Boxer* (CV 21) in March 1948.

courtesy Peter M. Bowers

US Navy – PHC J.C. Barnhill

Far right: Avengers were replaced by AD Skyraiders in fleet attack squadrons but assumed new duties in a variety of roles such as AEW and ASW. VS-32 TBM-3S and -3W Avengers are ready for launch from the *Salerno Bay* (CVE 110) on 2 March 1952.

plethora of jet fighters to enter the lists, only the Banshee and Panther experienced sustained operational service. The Phantom served only with VF-17A and the FJ-1 only with VF-5A on the west coast. Both types then went to the Reserves. Only 30 Pirates were built, none ever reaching a tactical squadron.

A typical air group composition for 'Midway' class CVBs in mid-1946 consisted of 65 Vought F4U-4s, four Grumman F6F-5Ps and 64 SB2C-5s, for a total of 133 aircraft. The smaller east coast 'Essex' class CVGs had 49 Grumman F8F-1s, four F6F-5Ps, 24 SB2C-5s, 15 Grumman/General Motors TBM-3Es and five TBM-3Qs assigned, for a total of 97. CVLG-58 had a total of 48 planes, with 11 F6F-5s, 11 F8F-1s, four SB2C-5s, four TBM-3Ns, 10 F4U-4s and four TBM-3Ws. On the west coast, the CVG composition was the same as on the east coast with the exception of CVG-5 and CVG-11, which operated all-Hellcat fighter squadrons. CVEG-41 had 18

Chuck McCandliss

Right: F4U-4 Corsairs continued their highly successful fighter-bomber roles with the fleet until after the Korean War, and here Air Group 82 F4U-4s are ready for launch from the *Randolph* (CV 15) in June 1946.

Post-war to Vietnam

A standard Gruman F8F-1 Bearcat, this aircraft is depicted in the 1953 markings in which it served with the US Navy Reserve at NAS Glenview, Illinois. Note the three whip aerials (one ventral) and HF wire aerial. At all times the Bearcat was an exhilarating aircraft to fly and more agile than anything it was likely to meet, but by the 1950s its all-round speed and firepower were looking decidedly deficient.

42

42

42

42

F8F-1
NAVY
94951

Keith Fretwell.

Vapor rings from the propeller shroud a Martin AM-1 Mauler on the deck of *Kearsarge* (CV 33). The date was 27 April 1949, at which time the Mauler was undergoing its four-day qualification cruise.

FR-1s and 12 TBM-3Es, while CVEG-42 had 16 F6F-5s, two F6F-5Ps and 12 TBM-3Es.

During 1949, the jet fighters slowly began replacing the conventionally-powered planes in squadron service. By the end of January 1950, VF-31 and VF-71 on the east coast were in Panthers, as VF-171 and VF-172 flew Banshees. On the west coast, four squadrons had transitioned to Panthers: VF-51, VF-52, VF-111 and VF-112. The typical air group mix by this time was four 18-plane fighter squadrons of either two jet or two F8F-2 units operating alongside two F4U-4B fighter-bomber squadrons. Douglas AD Skyraiders filled the 18-plane attack squadron complement. CVG-2 and CVG-4 had all-F4U-4/5 Corsairs in their fighter squadrons.

The mixture of jet- and piston-engined aircraft within the air groups raised a problem for the CAGs and strike group leaders. Since the development of the co-ordinated strike mission during World War II, escorting fighter cover had always had to cope with the differential in relative airspeeds between themselves and the bombers. With the advent of the jets and their even higher speeds, the problem became critical. Several methods of dealing with the problem were tried, such as launching the jets after the bombers were en route to the target. All experiments were only partially successful. During Korea, some air groups temporarily exchanged squadrons to give them more compatibility in aircraft composition. The speed differential dilemma was alleviated in later years as jet attack aircraft began fleet introduction. However, as the speed of the attack planes grew, so too did that of the fighters. The problem still exists in varying degrees within today's air wings.

Great and concurrent strides were made in the development of Navy attack aircraft and fighter technology. Development of history's most successful single-engine propeller-driven bomber began before the end of the war. As with the new fighters, several new attack designs were produced and discarded, including the Curtiss BTC, Kaiser-Fleetwings BTK, Douglas TB2D and Grumman TB2F. Two other aircraft, first flown in 1944 and 1945, showed great promise. The first appeared as Martin's XBTM-1, which later became the AM-1 Mauler. Following its initial flight of 26 August 1944, the Mauler began a lengthy development program which ultimately never achieved more than partial success. VA-17A (VA-174) at Quonset Point traded its SB2C-5s in March 1948 for AM-1s. Carrier suitability problems plagued the Maulers, and after limited service with VA-84, VA-85 and VC-4, the surviving aircraft were transferred to the Naval Air Reserve by 1950.

Left: VF-17A 'Aces' was the first squadron to operationally qualify jets aboard a carrier when they took McDonnell FH-1 Phantoms aboard USS *Saipan* (CVL 48) in May 1948. Here an FH-1 taxis to the catapult during CarQuals, on *Saipan*.

Right: Conceived during the closing stages of World War II, Martin's AM-1 Mauler saw only limited front-line service with the Navy, very quickly being relegated to Reserve elements such as that stationed at Grosse Ile, Michigan, in whose colors this example is depicted.

Right: Originally designed in 1941 as the two-seat XSB2D-1, the Douglas BTD-1 Destroyer was modified to a single-seat torpedo bomber in 1943. Only 28 were built and the program was closed in October 1945.

Far right: Douglas Skyraiders would enjoy a 23-year career with fleet squadrons from 1946 to 1969. As the AD-1, it first served with VA-19A in December 1946 at North Island. This is a VA-20A AD-1 off the California coast on 2 June 1947.

Below: The Air Group Two flight line at NAS Alameda shows the state of the evolution of carrier aircraft in 1954. VA-65 AD-4s are in the foreground with VF-64 F9F-5s and VF-24 F9F-6s in the background.

The tremendous success of the Douglas Skyraider, first flown 18 March 1945 as the XBT2D-1, more than compensated for the disappointment of the Mauler. A product of Ed Heinemann's Douglas design team, the Skyraider (originally called the Dauntless II) entered the fleet 6 December 1946 with VA-19A at North Island. Not flown until seven months after its Martin competitor, the Skyraider had beaten the Mauler to the fleet by almost a year and a half. The short development period was only a small indication of the future performance of the airplane that became the true 'workhorse of the fleet'. The AD quickly began replacing both the SB2C-5s and TBM-3Es with the fleet. VA-54 flew

the last SB2C in May 1949. ASW versions of the Avenger flew with anti-submarine squadrons until VS-27 retired the last one in October 1954.

The Skyraider continued to serve in first-line status with Navy attack squadrons until retired by VA-25 at NAS Lemoore 10 April 1968. This was not the end of the Skyraider's combat service with the Navy; the old warhorse was not finished yet. The last combat deployment of the 'Spad', as the Skyraider had become known, was with VAW-33 (later VAQ-33) in *Ticonderoga* (CVA 14). VAW-33 Detachment 14's three EA-1Fs flew ECM support missions off the coast of Vietnam for Air Wing Ten strike aircraft during the deployment which ended

Testing Times

Throughout the history of Naval Aviation, there has been a continuous line of experimental aircraft, research and development programs, and aircraft that never made it to production or the fleet. All of these aircraft have one thing in common, in that they have all contributed to the vast amount of aeronautical knowledge that has made possible the magnificent aircraft available to today's US Navy and US Marine Corps aircrews. The following pages provide only a glimpse at some of these programs between late World War II and the early 1960s.

Above: Follow-on to the BTD was the ungainly Douglas turboprop-powered XTB2D-1. The huge three-man bomber first flew in 1945, but was cancelled at war's end.

Above: Proposed replacement for the Avenger was Grumman's XTB2F-1, which never got past the mock-up stage of 1944. Heavily armed, the aircraft was cancelled as being too large to operate from the carriers of its day.

Above: One of the most bizarre projects was Vought's XF5U 'flying pancake'. The full-size aircraft never flew but the V-173 test aircraft made several flights.

Above: Redesigned from the XBTV-2, the XBT2C-1 met with no more success than its predecessor. Ten prototypes were ordered in 1945, but only nine were delivered by the end of the program in October 1946.

Above: An attempt at a turboprop follow-on to the mighty 'Able Dog', or AD Skyraider, brought about the XA2D Skyshark. First flown on 26 May 1950, it was cancelled in September 1953 after five had been built.

Above: The XF14C-2 with contrarotating propellers. The redesign still did not provide adequate performance and the XF14C-2 was abandoned in favor of the F4U-4.

Above: The last Curtiss attempt to build a US Navy fighter was the XF15C-1, first flown on 28 November 1945, with an R-2800 radial piston engine forward and a de Havilland Halford jet engine in the fuselage. All-jet fighters were the coming thing and the Curtiss hybrid did not make it.

Left: The last aircraft to be built for the US Navy by Boeing was the XF8B-1, first flown on 27 November 1944. The long-range fighter-bomber was cancelled after only two examples had been built.

Above: Variable-sweep wing technology derived from Grumman's XF10F-1 Jaguar, which first flew 19 May 1952, contributed to the company's success 16 years later with its F-14A Tomcat design. The Jaguar suffered from several development problems, one of which was the nefarious Allison J40 engine.

The world of vertical take-off (VTO) was explored in the early 1950s by two US Navy 'fighter' proposals which, in reality, were research designs. Convair's XFY-1 'Pogo' on 1 August 1954 made its first free flight after several tethered hovers. Although flown in the vertical take-off and landing mode and transitioned to horizontal flight, the 'Pogo' was powered by the T40 engine, which provided insufficient power, and the program was cancelled.

US Air Force

Douglas

Martin

Above: Lockheed paralleled Convair's Pogo with its XFV-1 VTO fighter program. Closely resembling the Pogo, the XFV-1 was never flown in the vertical take-off or landing mode. A special dolly was affixed to the airplane and it first flew conventionally on 16 June 1954.

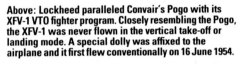

Left: Convair's penchant for novel US Navy fighters continued with the waterborne F2Y-1 Sea Dart. Lifting from San Diego Bay on 9 April 1953, the Sea Dart was a spectacular sight on its first flight. Three Sea Darts were flown, with one fatal crash.

Above: Designed as a high-speed research aircraft, the turbojet-powered Douglas D-558-1 was first flown on 15 April 1947, at Muroc Dry Lake (later Edwards AFB). Three of the highly-successful Skystreaks were flown by Douglas, US Navy, US Marine and NACA test pilots.

Above: The last new seaplane for the US Navy was Martin's P6M Seamaster. Designed as a high-speed minelayer, the XP6M-1 first flew on 14 July 1955. Both XP6M-1 prototypes were destroyed in fatal crashes but development continued with six YP6M-1s. Twenty-four P6M-2s were ordered but the program was cancelled in August 1959, after only four had been completed.

courtesy Harry Gann

Above: The D-558-2 Skyrocket followed its scarlet-red predecessor in flight on 4 February 1948. Three of the sleek research aircraft were built, all powered by combined J-34 turbojet and XLR-8-RM rockets, the first two aircraft being retrofitted with the rocket engine after jet-only flights.

Left: Vought's XC-142A was a tri-service research effort into the feasibility of a V/STOL transport. The four-engine tilt-wing design first flew 29 September 1964, and on 11 January 1965 it made its first transitional vertical-to-horizontal flight. Carrier suitability flights were made aboard *Bennington* (CVS 20) before the project was abandoned in 1968.

US Navy

17 August 1968. The last carrier deployment of the Skyraider was with VAQ-33 Detachment 67 assigned to *John F. Kennedy* (CVA 67) and CVW-1. The final Spad launch was made 20 December 1969 from *Kennedy*'s flight deck.

With the advent of atomic weapons, the Navy was suddenly faced with a serious dilemma: it had no long-range or strategic mission capability in an atomic war. As recounted above, the Army and the struggling-for-independence Air Force had joined in an attempt to convince Congress of the need for unification of the armed forces centered around strategic bombing provided by the Air Force. A strong army would be retained to act as an occupying agency. A navy would be required to serve only in support functions.

The Navy, fighting for its very existence, countered with the 'super-carrier' *United States*, which would be required to support an all-new long-range airplane with a strategic mission capability, the North American AJ-1 Savage. An order for three XAJ-1 prototypes was let 24 June 1946, the first flight occurring on 3 July 1948.

Meanwhile, the long-range nuclear strike capability concept had to be made viable aboard existing carriers. The large-deck 'Midway' class was the logical choice for the launch point and the Navy's newest patrol plane was chosen as the delivery vehicle. Twelve specially-modified P2V-3C Neptunes were made available for the mission to VC-5, formed on 9 September 1948 under Captain John T. 'Chick' Hayward at NAS Moffett Field. Choice of the P2V was necessary because of the size of the few nuclear weapons available to the Navy, some weighing as much as 10,000 lb (4536 kg). The P2Vs were to launch from the carriers, make their runs to the target, then fly on to land bases or ditch alongside ships at sea.

As modifications were made to enable the three 'Midways' to handle nuclear weapons, Hayward's crews began training in short-field jet-assisted take-offs (JATO) in P2V-2s and then P2V-3Cs when the latter began arriving in November. A plan was also evaluated to bring the P2V back aboard the carrier, a feat Hayward believed to be feasible. One Neptune (BuNo 122969) was equipped with a tail-hook. Field arrestment tests were conducted by Lockheed at Burbank and Hayward at Patuxent River. The concept was proven by Hayward making 128 landings into the short-field gear at Patuxent. He also made approaches and a touch-and-go landing aboard *Franklin D. Roosevelt*. No arrested landings were actually made aboard ship.

In April 1948, before VC-5's commissioning, P2V-2s were flown to Norfolk where, on 27 April they were loaded aboard *Coral Sea* by crane. The next morning, two of the largest aircraft ever to launch

from a carrier left *Coral Sea*'s deck, flown by Commanders Tom Davies and J.P. Wheatley. The 100-ft (30.48-m) wingspan and 60,000-lb (27216-kg) Neptunes lifted easily from *Coral Sea*, assisted by JATO.

A series of long-range record-setting flights were made during the next two years from all three CVBs by VC-5 and VC-6. The latter outfit was commissioned on 6 January 1950 to assist in fulfilling the nuclear mission requirement. The record flights conclusively proved the concept to Congress and the public through the publicity generated. In so doing, the Navy used a page right out of the Air Force's game book!

The Savage arrives

Finally, after several developmental problems, the first AJ-1s began arriving at VC-5 in September 1949. Powered by two wing-mounted Pratt & Whitney R-2800s and an Allison J33 auxiliary jet in the fuselage, the Savages relieved the Neptunes of their shipboard duties. Fulfilling their mission to keep the Navy in the nuclear-strike role, the AJs were never popular with carrier skippers because of their huge size. They remained in service in their original role until the mid-1950s, operating mostly from overseas land bases. In 1958, the Navy began conversion of the surviving AJs to fulfill the role of carrier-based aerial refuelling tankers. Two photo-reconnaissance squadrons operated the AJ-2P aerial reconnaissance version until the last Savages retired 31 January 1960 from VAP-62 and VCP-61.

As the P2V was an interim measure until the AJ was available, the Savage performed the same function until the next-generation heavy attack bomber could be made ready. The Douglas A3D-1 Skywarrior brought the attack community into the realm of pure jets and heavy attack. Even with its

Above: Replaced by newer jet attack aircraft, the AJs began conversion in 1958 to the role of aerial tanker, which made them more popular around the carriers. Here a VAH-7 AJ-2 refuels a VFP-62 F9F-8P photo Cougar in the late 1950s.

Left: P2V-3C Neptunes of VC-5 and VC-6 filled the role of interim carrier-based strategic bombers until AJ-1 Savages were ready for squadron service. Here a VC-5 Neptune launches for nonstop record distance flight from the Virginia coast to Panama Canal and Moffett Field, 5,156 miles (8298 km) on 2 April 1949.

Right: Long-range attack capability was initially vested in the North American AJ-2 Savage, which equipped several Heavy Attack Squadrons in the mid-1950s. A typical example is depicted here in the markings of VAH-6, which served aboard USS *Lexington* (CVA 16) in 1956.

Right: The US Navy pursued a course of development of both large 'heavy attack' aircraft such as the Skywarrior, and small 'light attack' aircraft such as the Douglas A4D-1 shown here with a simulated Mk 7 nuclear weapon. The advent of reduced-size nuclear weapons made smaller attack aircraft possible.

70,000-lb (31572-kg) maximum weight and 72½-ft (22.1-m) wing span, the A3D could operate from both the modernized 'Essex' and 'Midway' class carriers. The appearance of newer and smaller nuclear weapons in the early 1950s made the production of the Skywarrior controversial among Naval Aviation leaders. Proponents of the 'heavy attack' concept argued for an aircraft large enough to carry bigger Mk 4 type weapons and to operate at 1,500-mile (2415-km) range. Fulfilment of these requirements would provide the Navy with the capability of striking almost any Soviet target in the world from its carriers. Others felt that this plan would not be workable and pressed for a smaller aircraft with smaller weapons. The Navy wisely progressed with the development of both concepts. The first Douglas XA3D-1 flew 22 October 1952, with fleet introduction to VAH-1 on 31 March 1956 at Jacksonville.

As the Skyraider was to prop-driven carrier aviation, so was the Skywarrior (or 'Whale' as it became more popularly known) to jet carrier aviation. Thirty-two years after its first flight, the Whale is still in service aboard carriers. Following a pattern similar to, but far more successful than its AJ predecessor, the A3D served in its designed heavy attack role, then shifted to the aerial tanker mission. Later, it functioned as an electronics countermeasures aircraft. For a period of time during the Vietnam War it did both, designated EKA-3B.

Paralleling its oversized sister in development, the diminutive Douglas A4D Skyhawk series filled the 'small nukes' delivery role for which proponents had called. Like the A3D and AD before it, it was a product of the genius of Douglas design engineer Ed Heinemann. Designed as a lightweight, low-cost tactical nuclear weapons delivery platform, the first XA4D-1 flew 22 June 1954. Thirty years later, its

A-4M progeny is still in first-line service with the Marine Corps. The A4D-1 weighed only about 20,000 lb (9072 kg) at maximum gross and could carry Mk 7 or Mk 8 nuclear weapons or nearly 6,000 lb (2722 kg) of bombs. Deliveries of the Skyhawk began to VA-72 on 27 September 1956. The 'Scooter', as fleet pilots liked to call them, last served in a Navy carrier squadron as the A-4F with VA-212, VA-164 and VA-55 in *Hancock* (CV 19) during that carrier's 1975 cruise, which ended on 20 October.

The last attack aircraft designed for the long-range strategic strike mission was the North American A3J-1 Vigilante. The airplane would never deploy in that role. Esthetically, the 'Vigi' was possibly the most beautiful aircraft ever to land aboard a carrier. In 1954, North American offered to the Navy an unsolicited proposal called NAGPAW (North American General-Purpose Attack Weapon), a concept developed by its engineers. The proposal called for an all-weather bomber capable of nuclear delivery using the new LABS (low-altitude bombing system) utilizing the 'loft' bombing technique and inertial navigation

Below: Even with 70,000-lb (31752-kg) maximum weight and 72½-ft (22.1-m) wingspan, A3D Skywarriors could operate from both modernized 'Essex' class and 'Midway' class carriers. Here a VAH-1 A3D-1 comes aboard the *Saratoga* (CVA 62) on 15 November 1956.

systems. Four years later, the first YA3J-1 became airborne on 31 August 1958. Fleet introduction began with Heavy Attack Squadron Seven in August 1961, following delivery to VAH-3, the Fleet Replacement Squadron at NAS Sanford, Florida.

The A3J-1 (A-5A) was designed to carry either a Mk 27 nuclear weapon externally or a Mk 28 stored in an internal linear bomb bay located between the General Electric J79 engines in the rear fuselage. A totally innovative design, the Vigilante was to make a supersonic run into its target at treetop level, pull up into an 'idiot loop' as it ejected it weapon rearward, then depart the area on a reverse course. Problems inherent with this concept were never completely resolved, and the linear bay later became a storage area for extra fuel tanks. The Vigilante represented the Navy's only level-flight supersonic attack aircraft until the advent of the F/A-18A Hornet 20 years later. Deployment as a bomber occurred with only two squadrons, VAH-7 and VAH-1. 'Heavy Seven' made the first of three deployments with the 'Vigi' to the Mediterranean in *Enterprise* (CVAN 65) from 3 August to 11 October 1962.

In 1962, the Vigilante suddenly became an airplane without a mission when Naval Aviation's strategic role was dropped in favour of the nuclear submarine-launched Polaris missile. However, the large two-place bomber lent itself nicely to conversion as an all-weather reconnaissance platform capable of carrying a multitude of aerial cameras and sophisticated sensor packages. Converted to RA-5Cs, the Vigilantes began assuming their new intelligence role in 1964; former heavy attack squadrons were redesignated as RVAH (Reconnaissance Heavy Attack).

The last attack aircraft to be developed between World War II and Vietnam was the Grumman A2F-

1, which became the A-6A Intruder after October 1962, under the new Department of Defense aircraft redesignation system. The Intruder resulted from a 1956 request to industry for a new medium attack bomber. The lessons learned from the Korean War indicated the need for a low-level, all-weather bomber capable of penetrating the enemy's radar defenses. The Intruder's first flight was on 9 April 1960, with initial squadron deliveries going to VA-42, the A-6 RAG at Oceana, on 1 February 1963. The Intruders began primarily to replace the Navy's A-1 Skyraider squadrons. The A-6 soon became the most capable attack plane ever to operate from an aircraft-carrier, and it arrived none too soon. The volatile situation in South East Asia was rapidly deteriorating and the Intruder's services would be sorely needed.

Grumman's feline fighters

As the attack aircraft made giant strides in their progression from the Skyraider to the Intruder, so did the fighters, who had started it all with the Fireball and Phantom.

Grumman's initial success with the F9F-2 Panther and its fine record in Korea led to the development of the F9F-5 and, in 1951, of the swept-wing F9F-6 version, renamed Cougar. The Cougars began appearing in the fleet in November 1952, with VF-32. A further modification of the successful Cougar design in 1956 produced the two-seat F9F-8T (TF-9J) trainer version, which remained in service until 1974. Another model of the Cougar, the F9F-8B with a LABS nuclear-delivery capability, was also produced, as were photo versions of both the Panther and Cougar. The F9F-8 Cougar was the first fighter capable of operational use of the Sidewinder air-to-air heat-seeking missile.

Although the Cougar could be induced to exceed Mach 1 in a vertical dive, the Navy's first truly-

Above: On 12 September 1955, the US Navy directed that all its fighters in production would be fitted with an inflight-refuelling capability. Here a Convair R3Y-2 Tradewind performs the first four-point refuelling with VF-123 F9F-8s off San Diego, California, on 31 August 1956. R3Ys were developed from the early 1950s XP5Y-1 patrol seaplane which never reached production.

Above left: Development of Grumman's A2F-1 (A-6A) Intruder all-weather medium attack bomber began in 1957. Fleet delivery was first with VA-42, the fleet replacement squadron, at NAS Oceana on 1 February 1963.

Right: Immaculate station-keeping is displayed by this four-ship formation of F9F-8B Cougars of VF-81 during August 1958. Less than a year later, this unit became a fully-fledged attack squadron (VA) and converted to the Douglas A4D-2 Skyhawk.

Below: Cancellation of the US Navy's strategic nuclear strike role for carriers left the Vigilante without a mission in 1962. The large two-place bombers were converted into highly-successful reconnaissance aircraft and became RA-5Cs.

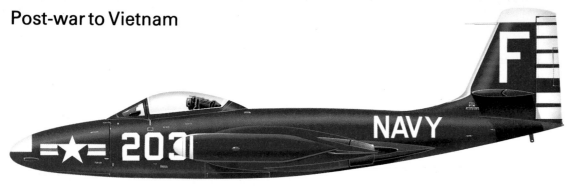

US Navy

The McDonnell F2H-2 Banshee performed well in the fighter-bomber role over Korea, but it is not thought that it encountered MiGs in combat. The F2H-2P photo-reconnaissance version provided much useful information for the fleet.

US Navy

Above: Douglas' first post-war fighter design was the F3D-1 Skyknight. The two-man, twin-engine night fighter served in only two carrier squadrons, of which VF-14 'Tophatters' was one, but never deployed.

Above left: The Gruman F11F-1 (F-11A) 'Tiger' was the Navy's first supersonic fighter and began fleet service with VA-156 in March 1957. Suffering from 'short legs', the Tiger was quickly relegated to the Training Command, where it was flown until 1967. These aircraft belong to VF-21.

supersonic fighter was the Grumman F11F-1 Tiger. Originally designated F9F-9, the new fighter was first flown 30 July 1954. Redesigned, incorporating the area-rule 'coke bottle' fuselage, the production models were delivered as F11F-1s. Suffering from a lack of range and competition from the better-performing Vought F8U Crusader, the Tiger served in only seven fleet squadrons, the first (VA-156) in March 1957. Four years later it was out of the fleet and relegated to the Training Command as an advanced trainer. The Tiger served well in its training role until finally retired by VT-26 in mid-1967. The 'Blue Angels' flew Tigers until that same year.

McDonnell's F2H Banshee met with success similar to that of the F9F. It too performed capably as a fighter-bomber in Korea. There are no known engagements between Banshees and MiGs during the war, and it was used mainly in the bombing and photo-reconnaissance roles. The F2H-2 also appeared in the F2H-2N night fighter and F2H-2B nuclear attack versions. An all-weather capability was designed into the Banshee in the larger F2H-3 and F2H-4 versions of 1952.

Douglas never achieved the degree of success with its Navy fighters that it did with its attack planes. Its first post-war effort was the F3D-1, a two-seat night fighter first flown 23 March 1948. VC-3 received the first fleet aircraft in 1949. Designed as a carrier fighter, the F3D-1 never deployed in squadron strength aboard ship. Only two air group squadrons used the airplane, VF-11 and VF-14. The Skyknight's employment in the Navy came primarily with VC-3 and VC-4 at shore stations on both coasts. The F3D-2 (later F-10B) was used extensively by the Marines as a night fighter in Korea, scoring six and possibly seven kills. Missile and ECM versions were produced and the TF-10B was used by both the Navy and Marines for Radar Intercept Officer training. Disparaged by outsiders, the Skyknight, or 'Drut' as it became known, was beloved by its crews. It became the only fighter to serve in combat in both Korea and Vietnam, finally retiring from the Marines in 1970.

Douglas' next fighter was the advanced-design F4D-1 Skyray, conceptualized as a short-range interceptor. The Skyray introduced the delta-wing to carrier aviation and was first flown 23 January 1951. The problem-plagued Allison XJ40 engine caused delays in the Skyray program. The aircraft, then powered by a Pratt & Whitney J57, did not enter squadron service until 16 April 1956 with VC-3. Magnificent in appearance, an XF4D-1 set a world speed record of 753 mph (1212 km/h) over a 3-km (1.86-mile) course on 3 October 1953. This record-setting flight, the first for a carrier aircraft, was flown by Lieutenant Commander James B. Verdin. Only achieving limited operational success, (primarily a result of its 'short legs'), the F4D-1 served until February 1964, when VMF-115 trans-

courtesy Harry Gann

Left: The F4D-1 Skyray brought the delta wing to carrier aviation. VC-3 received the first 'Fords' on 16 April 1956. Later, as VF(AW)-3, the squadron became the top squadron assigned to the USAF Air Defense Command, and here a squadron Skyray launches 2.75-in (70-mm) rockets over the Pacific.

Much of the responsibility for introducing effective missile armament aboard ship fell to the FJ-3M Fury, this being compatible with early versions of the Sidewinder AAM. The example shown here is from VF-142, which was assigned to CVG-14 aboard USS *Hornet* in 1957.

Above: Showing obvious parentage to the F-86 Sabre, the FJ-4 Fury introduced greater fuel capacity over its predecessors. This VA-63 FJ-4B had Bullpup capability and LABS nuclear delivery.

Below: The basic Fury design was modified to the swept-swing FJ-2 which served with the US Marines beginning in January 1954. A further modification produced the FJ-3, flown by both US Navy and US Marine units. Here a GMGRU-1 FJ-3D Regulus-control Fury traps aboard *Lexington* (CVA 16) in 1957.

ferred its last 'Ford' from tactical service. The Skyray's most notable achievement came with VC-3, later VF(AW)-3, at North Island. Assigned the continental air-defense mission, VF(AW)-3 was the only Navy unit attached to the Air Force's Air Defense Command (ADC). The squadron earned ADC's top honors two years running as the best outfit in the command. A larger version of the basic Skyray airframe appeared in 1956, originally designated F4D-2. The aircraft became the F5D-1 Skylancer, but was cancelled after only four pre-production models had been built.

A final attempt by Douglas to produce another Navy fighter came with the F6D-1 Missileer proposal of 1960, which never got off the drawing boards. The three-man interceptor was designed specifically around the Eagle long-range air-to-air missile. Both the Missileer and Eagle programs were cancelled in 1961 as not cost effective.

Jet successes and failures

North American followed its straight-wing FJ-1 Fury with the swept-wing FJ-2, FJ-3 and FJ-4 series. The FJ-2 was a development from the USAF F-86E, and began appearing, during January 1954, in Marine fighter squadrons. The type was not used by Navy squadrons. Improved FJ-3s went into service with VF-173 in September of the same year at Jacksonville. Following the missile-capable FJ-3M, the refined FJ-4 with an increased fuel capacity also went to the Marines. The final version of the Fury, the FJ-4B (AF-1E), incorporated the LABS nuclear delivery capability and Bullpup air-to-ground missile. VA-126 received the first of the 'Fury Bravos' in 1957. The Furies left operational service 30 September 1962, being last assigned to VA-216.

Continuing Corsair

Production of the Vought F4U Corsair had continued during the abortive development of the F6U Pirate. After more than 10 years of operation, the Corsair production line finally closed in December 1952, with the AU-1 ground attack version of the famed World War II fighter-bomber. The company's next effort was the radical, swept-wing F7U Cutlass, with no tail but twin vertical stabilizers. The initial XF7U-1 flight was made 1 March 1950 at Vought's new Dallas, Texas facility. Suffering developmental program tragedies, five early F7U-1s crashed, killing three test pilots. The planned F7U-2 was cancelled, and an improved F7U-3 appeared in the fleet with Project Cutlass at

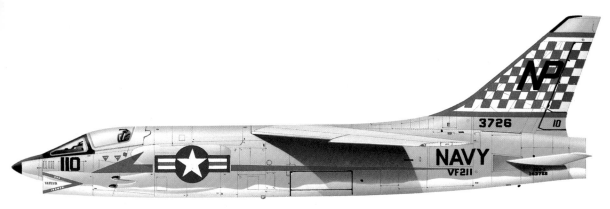

Left: A VF-211 Vought F8U-1 (later F-8A) Crusader with the prominent checkerboard design of the squadron applied to the fin, showing the Crusader's heyday of the early 1960s. Production of this model was to total 318.

Below: Vought's F7U Cutlass was radical, but not successful. First flown on 1 March 1950, the F7U did not reach the fleet until 1954 with VC-3. After limited service, it was dropped by November 1957. Here a VX-4 F7U-3M taxies out of the gear aboard *Lexington* on 30 April 1956.

Miramar in February, 1954. Heroic efforts by Patuxent River and VC-3 pilots to make the Cutlass a workable fleet aircraft were never completely successful. After limited fleet service, the Cutlass was finally dropped in November 1957, last serving with VA-66.

Undaunted by its previous two failures to produce a first-line naval jet fighter, Vought next gave the Navy what many consider its finest pure fighter of the jet age, the F8U Crusader. Equipped with both guns and missiles, the Crusader was the Navy's last 'gunfighter' until the appearance of the Grumman F-14A Tomcat in 1973.

The XF8U-1 lifted from Rogers dry lake at Edwards AFB on 25 March 1955 for the Crusader's first flight. The new fighter was pushed through Mach 1 on its maiden flight, the first aircraft ever to do so. The Crusader also became the Navy's first aircraft capable of more than 1,000 mph (1609 km/h). VF-32 received the fleet's first F8U-1 (F-8A) in March 1957. The Crusader remained a front-line fighter through several designations until the last F-8Js were retired in early 1976 from VF-191 and

VF-194 at Miramar. The RF-8G photo version served with VFP-63 until 26 May 1982 and continues in service with Reserve squadron VFP-206.

Another version of the Crusader which appeared as the XF8U-3 was first flown 2 June 1958. By rights, this airplane should have been designated the F9U-1, as it bore little resemblance to its namesake. Powered by a single J79-P-6 engine, the new Crusader III was a superbly performing missile-fighter. However, it found itself in competition with the McDonnell F4H-1 Phantom. A Navy decision to develop the two-engine, two-man fighter concept killed the F8U-3 in December 1958 after only three examples had been built.

McDonnell's success with the Banshee was followed by near-disaster in its F3H Demon interceptor. The XF3H-1 was first flown 7 August 1951, but it was five years before a Demon entered a fleet squadron. First utilizing the underpowered West-

Above left: The last fighter built by Vought was the XF8U-3 Crusader III of 1958. Bearing virtually no similarity to the Crusader, it probably should have been designated the F9U-1. A superbly performing missile-fighter, it lost out in competition with the F4H-1 Phantom II.

Below: McDonnell's success with its first US Navy fighters was followed by the less-than-successful XF3H-1N Demon, first flown on 7 August 1951. Here is Lieutenant F. A. W. Franke, Jr. off the angle in a VF-61 F3H-2M Sparrow missile version of the Demon on 10 April 1957.

Right: Existing for little more than a year during 1961-62, VF-131 was intended to operate the F3H-2 Demon from USS *Constellation* (CVA 64) as part of CVG-13. In the event, the 'Conny' was transferred to the Pacific Fleet, CVG-13 and its constituent squadrons being decommissioned.

Above; First flight of a long line to follow. XF4H-1 BuNo. 142259 shows its small nose and rear canopy as well as the curved intake of the early Phantom II design over St Louis, Missouri, on 28 May 1958.

Below: Fleet deliveries of F4H-1s began on 8 July 1961 to VF-74's 'Bedevilers' at Oceana. More than 5,000 Phantoms would eventually be produced by McDonnell over the next 20 years for the Navy, Air Force and other West-aligned nations.

inghouse XJ40-WE-6 engine, the Demon program was fraught with developmental problems and crashes which killed four test pilots and destroyed six aircraft in 11 accidents. In July 1955 the all-weather F3H-1Ms were permanently grounded, most of them ultimately being barged from St Louis to NATTC Memphis for use as mechanics training aids. The J40 engine and its T40 turboprop equivalent never proved successful in any Navy aircraft.

A new engine, the Allison J71-A-2 producing 14,400 lb (6532 kg) of thrust with afterburner, was assigned to the F3H-2N to alleviate the Demon's power problems. Fleet introduction began with VF-14 on 7 March 1956. The F3H-2N was equipped with 20-mm guns and could carry Sidewinder air-to-air missiles. The later F3H-2M missile version was designed to use the longer-range Sparrow. Its 'widow maker' status established, the Demon was generally regarded as less than popular by fleet pilots and was retired in August 1964 by VF-161 at NAS Miramar.

As is the case with many things in life, something good frequently comes from adversity. So it was with the Demon. The Demon provided the next step in the art of aeronautical progress that led to the highly-successful F4H-1 Phantom II. Originally proposed and ordered as the single-seat AH-1 attack aircraft in 1954, the Phantom's role and designation were changed the following year before

prototype production had started. First flight of McDonnell's F4H-1 took place at St Louis on 27 May 1958. A second seat and rear cockpit had been added to allow for a Radar Intercept Officer (RIO) to control the interceptor's weapon system. Thus, with the Phantom, the Navy had reverted to a two-man fighter concept virtually abandoned for more than 20 years but had introduced an entirely new concept, a fighter aircraft without guns. The Navy Phantoms were to carry missiles only. Three basic models of the Phantom were built for the Navy, the F4H-1F (F-4A), an interim model with J79-GE-2A engines, the F4H-1 (F-4B) with J79-GE-8B/C engines and the F-4J with AWG-10 pulse-Doppler fire control and other refinements as well as the J79-GE-10 powerplant. Additionally, 12 F-4Gs were produced, which were basically F-4Bs with two-way data link. An RF-4C photo version was built for the Marines.

The Mach 2.2 Phantom was destined for success from the beginning. During its developmental stages, the airplane claimed one time-to-climb, altitude and speed record after another. After delivery of the first squadron Phantoms to VF-121, the replacement squadron, in December 1960, VF-74 was selected to be the first fleet outfit to get the airplane. The 'Bedevilers' received their first F-4B on 8 July 1961 and the Phantom was on its way to becoming the most versatile fighter in the Navy's inventory.

The Phantom arrived on the scene none too soon. As the storm clouds gathered over South East Asia, the 'Great Smoking Thunderhog' began relieving Demon and some Crusader squadrons. On 5 August 1964, as aircrews from *Constellation* (CVA 64) and *Ticonderoga* (CVA 14) were launching for the first retaliatory strikes against North Vietnam, the Navy's fighter squadrons were about evenly divided at 15 F-4 and 16 F-8 squadrons. By the end of the US participation in Vietnam in January 1973, the numbers were 24:4 in favor of the Phantom. All four F-8 squadrons were on the west coast; the Atlantic Fleet was all-Phantom.

25
Evolution of the Carriers and New Weapon Systems

Early in World War II a new class of carrier was designed utilizing some of the hard-learned damage control lessons from *Lexington* at Coral Sea and *Yorktown* at Midway. In August 1942 *Midway* (CVB 41) was ordered as a heavily armored battle carrier; two sisterships, *Franklin D. Roosevelt* (CVB 42) and *Coral Sea* (CVB 43) were ordered the following year. *Midway* was commissioned 10 September 1945, *FDR* 27 October 1945 and *Coral Sea* 1 October 1947.

Upon commissioning, the three CVBs were the largest warships in the world at 55,000 tons full load displacement. *Midway* and *FDR* had 18 5-in (127-mm) anti-aircraft guns arranged along each side of the hull, *Coral Sea* had 14. Additionally, they carried 84 40-mm and 28 20-mm gun mounts. Designed to operate 137 aircraft, the 'Midway' class carriers had an overall length of 986 ft (300.5 m) and were the first US carriers with armored flight decks.

Also in 1943, two CVLs were ordered as a new class. *Saipan* (CVL 48) and *Wright* (CVL 49) differed from their 'Independence' class predecessors in that they were built from the keel up as carriers. Fully loaded, they displaced 20,000 tons and were 683½ ft (208.3 m) long. *Saipan* joined the fleet on 14 July 1946, *Wright* followed on 9 February of the following year. Nine 'Commencement' class CVEs were also placed in commission after the war ended.

With all the furor over the 1948 cancellation of the new 'super-carrier' *United States*, a significant point is often overlooked. By late 1949 Admiral Forrest P. Sherman had as Chief of Naval Operations inaugurated a plan to modernize the Navy's carrier fleet. The detonation of an atomic weapon by the USSR on 23 September had helped bring to Congress and the Truman administration an increased awareness of the nation's drastically weakened defense posture. This event, followed

closely by the Korean War, clearly identified the requirement for the nation to have several major weapon systems in the defense arsenal and for the abandonment of a policy of reliance upon a single-weapon strategy controlled by one agency. One of the most important programs to be revitalized was the modernization of the 'Essex' class carriers.

During the three years of the Korean War (1950-3), the active carrier strength of the Navy rose from 15 of all types in June of 1950 to 39 by the end of hostilities. Furthermore, seven of the 'Essex' class ships then in the fleet had received extensive modernizations under the Project 27A program. Two others were in the yards undergoing the same overhaul. Fifteen of the 'Essex' class carriers would undergo, by 1957, one of the modernization programs termed 27A, or 27C.

The basic SCB 27 program had been planned as early as 1946 for *Oriskany*, whose construction had been suspended the year before. Funding was withheld until 1947 and building resumed on 1 October under Project 27A. The major improvements of Project 27A provided new Mk 5 arresting gear and more powerful H-8 hydraulic catapults. The flight deck was strengthened to handle the new heavy attack aircraft with planned weights of up to 52,500 lb (23814 kg). Elevator capacity was increased to handle 30,000 lb (13608 kg), and fuel storage was expanded to accommodate the new jets. Additionally, improved radar provided increased

Above: Joining her sisterships on 1 October 1947, *Coral Sea* (CVB 43) had 84 40-mm and 28 20-mm anti-aircraft gun mounts as well as 14 5-in (127-mm) mounts. Her sisters had 18 5-in (127-mm) guns. They were designed to operate 137 aircraft.

Left: Comparative sizes of 'Saipan' class CVL and 'Essex' class CV is seen with *Wright* (CVL 49) and *Leyte* (CV 32) alongside the pier at NAS Quonset Point, Rhode Island, in 1950.

Right: Steam catapults were one of three British innovations that virtually saved jet carrier aviation, and here Commander H. J. Jackson makes the US Navy's first steam catapult launch from *Hancock* (CVA 19) on 1 June 1954, in a VS-38 S2F-1 Tracker.

US Navy

self-defense capabilities. The most noticeable change was the streamlined island and removal of the twin 5-in (127-mm) gun mounts from the flight deck. The loss of these mounts was compensated by four single 5-in (127-mm) mounts in sponsons added to the starboard side to maintain adequate anti-aircraft protection. Small jet blast deflectors (JBD) were installed behind each catapult to prevent injury of flight deck personnel. The combined modernization features resulted in a growth of the full load displacement to 40,800 tons. This forced BuShips designers to widen the hull by 9 ft (2.74 m) to a total of 102 ft (31.09 m). Nine 'Essex' class ships received the Project 27A modernization, all completed by November 1953.

Progress in launching and landing

Meanwhile, the innovative British had been working on the development of three major programs that would virtually save jet aviation aboard carriers: the angled deck, mirror landing system and steam catapults. *Hancock* was chosen to be the first US carrier to be fitted with steam catapults.

Intrepid and *Ticonderoga* followed, the only three ships to have the C-11 steam catapults as straight-deck carriers under the 27C program. With the jets had come an alarming increase in carrier aviation accidents. There were many naval leaders of the day who were skeptical of the carrier's continued potential for success. Had it not been for the three British inventions, they could easily have been proved correct.

Following tests during May 1951 aboard *Midway*, with a painted simulated angled-deck, *Antietam* was chosen in June 1952 to have an extension installed to her port side to evaluate the feasibility of the angled-deck concept. Originally called the 'canted deck', the name was changed by CNO direction in 1955. Successful completion of the test program on 1 July 1953 led to the Project 125 program.

Eight of the nine Project 27A carriers received angled decks and enclosed 'hurricane' bows under the 125 program; *Lake Champlain* remained a Project 27A ship until her decommissioning in 1966. Additional refinements were removal of the

Below: Jet aircraft brought an alarming accident rate to carrier aviation. Early jet engines were slow to respond ('spool-up') to power increase commands by pilots, resulting in horrifying ramp strikes such as this VF-124 F7U-3 aboard *Hancock* on 14 July 1955.

US Navy

Evolution of the 'Essex' class

The WWII 'Essex' class carrier design underwent several improvement and modernization programs following the war. The major programs were SCB-27A, 27C and P125. Fifteen of the 'Essexes' received at least one of these programs, some received two of them. Listed right are the carriers which were modernized and the programs they underwent in the order received.

USS *Essex*	SCB-27A February 1951
	P125 March 1956
USS *Yorktown:*	SCB-27A January 1953
	P125 October 1955
* USS *Intrepid:*	SCB-27C June 1954
	P125 May 1957
USS *Hornet:*	SCB-27A October 1953
	P125 August 1956
* USS *Ticonderoga:*	SCB-27C December 1954
	P125 February 1957

USS *Randolph:*	SCB-27A July 1953
	P125 February 1956
** USS *Lexington:*	SCB-27C/P125 September 1955
USS *Wasp*	SCB-27A September 1951
	P125 December 1955
* USS *Hancock:*	SCB-27C March 1954
	P125 November 1956
USS *Bennington:*	SCB-27A November 1952
	P125 April 1955
** USS *Bonne Homme Richard:*	SCB-27C/P125 November 1955
USS *Kearsarge:*	SCB-27A March 1952
	P125 January 1957
*** USS *Oriskany:*	P125A March 1959
** USS *Shangri-La:*	SCB-27C/P125 February 1955
USS *Lake Champlain:*	SCB-27A September 1952

* Three ships first became SCB-27C straight decks, later receiving the P125 program

** Three ships received all SCB-27C and P125 modernizations at one time

*** USS *Oriskany* underwent a special P125A conversion that essentially gave her SCB-27C features with added

Left: USS *Essex* (CV 9) name-ship of her class during builder's trials on 1 February 1943 in Hampton Roads. Basic straight deck, open bow and flight deck 5-in gun mount design is apparent. Deck edge elevator is folded upward in stored position.

Right: USS *Lake Champlain* (CVA 39) underway off Guantanamo, Cuba on 18 December 1952 following 27A conversion. Visible improvements are streamlined island, removal of 5-in flight deck gun mounts and addition of 3-in .50 sponsons on starboard side. 'The Champ' received no further improvements and became the last straight deck attack carrier in the Navy.

Left: USS *Intrepid* (CVA 11) underway on 10 August 1956 with 27C steam catapults and aft starboard deck edge elevator modifications. She was one of three straight deck 27 Charlies, receiving the P125 improvements in a later second fitting.

US Navy

Above: Although never modernized, USS *Antietam* (CVA 36) was selected to receive an experimental angled deck which led to the P125 program. Seen here on 14 January 1953 she conducts trials of the angled deck.

US Navy

Right: Eight carriers received 27A and 125 modernizations in two fittings. USS *Yorktown* (CVA 10) clearly shows the angled deck and enclosed 'hurricane' bow of the 125 program. However, she and her seven sisters did not get the C-11 steam catapults of the 27C program, thus causing their ultimate reclassification as CVS ASW carriers unable to operate the later, heavier jet aircraft.

US Navy

Right: Three ships received the 27C and 125 improvements in one fitting, USS *Shangri-La* (CVA 38), *Bon Homme Richard* (CVA 31) and *Lexington* (CVA 16), seen here launching an A3D-2 Skywarrior 30 November 1958. Serving today as a training carrier in the Gulf of Mexico, *Lexington* (CVA 16) is the last Essex-class carrier still in commission.

aft centerline elevator and installation of a new elevator aft of the island on the starboard deck edge. The 125 program did not provide for steam catapults, leaving these ships with the less powerful H-8. This factor contributed to these eight carriers ultimately being reclassified as CVSs, anti-submarine warfare support carriers. They would not be required to handle the forthcoming heavier jet aircraft.

The final modernization of the 'Essexes', the '27 Charlies' as they became known, provided all of the refinements of the 27A and 125 programs with up-to-date improvements plus C-11 steam catapults. *Lexington*, *Bon Homme Richard* and *Shangri-La* all received the 27C improvements in one fitting. By May 1957 *Intrepid*, *Ticonderoga* and *Hancock* had also received the complete 27C program. The *Oriskany* remained a 'one-of-a-kind' ship when she underwent a special 125A program in 1958-9 that essentially gave her the 27C conversion with further upgraded features. Her CIC was relocated beneath the armored hangar deck and the hull double-blistered for added torpedo protection.

Third of the British contributions to carrier safety was the mirror landing system. The first mirror was installed aboard *Bennington* for evaluation and, on 22 August 1955, Commander Bob Dosé, leader of VX-3, flying a North American FJ-3, made the first landing using the system. Later that year, CNO directed the installation of the system on all angled-deck carriers.

As improvements were required for the 'Essex' class, so were they for the 'Midways'. In September

1953 Project 110 was implemented to upgrade the big CVAs. *Roosevelt* began rework at Puget Sound in May 1954 to increase her capabilities. She received improvements similar to those of the '27 Charlies' with the addition of a third catapult in the angled deck. *Midway* followed in July 1955. *Coral Sea* received a 'one-of-a-kind' overhaul (SCB-110A) which virtually rebuilt the ship and vastly increased her warfare capabilities. *Midway* was again extensively modernized during 1966-70. *Roosevelt* received no such future renovation which doomed her to the scrappers in 1977. After all moderniza-

Above: Third of the British-designed carrier aids was the mirror landing system which provided glide-slope information to pilots. Commander Bob Dosé, CO of VX-3, makes the first mirror landing on 22 August 1955 aboard *Bennington* (CVA 20).

The *Midway* departs Alameda, California, on 14 August 1958 bound for the Western Pacific. The mixture of AD Skyraiders, A3D Skywarriors, F3H Demons, FJ-4B Furies and F8U Crusaders was typical of the deck load out in the late 1950s.

Above: The US Navy entered the super carrier era on 1 October 1955, with the commissioning of the *Forrestal* (CVA 59). With four deck-edge elevators and four catapults, the four Forrestals were 1,039 ft (316.7 m) overall and 76,000 tons fully loaded.

Above right: The US Navy's first nuclear-powered carrier was *Enterprise* (CVAN 65), commissioned on 25 November 1961. She remains dimensionally the world's largest warship at 1,123 ft (342.3 m) and 85,600 tons fully loaded, despite the appearance of the greater-displacement 'Nimitz' class in 1975.

Below: Sikorsky HO3S-1s brought helicopters to carrier aviation in the late 1940s. Since that time, helicopter detachments or squadrons have been deployed in every carrier. Here an HU-1 HO3S-1 lifts from the *Princeton* (CV 37) during the 1950-1 Korean deployment with CGV-19.

tions, the three original 'Midway' class carriers became singular ships in appearance and capability.

The Navy finally entered the super-carrier era on 1 October 1955, with the commissioning of the *Forrestal* (CVA 59). *Forrestal* represented an advance in carrier technology of a magnitude surpassing even that of the 'Midway' over the 'Essex' class. With an overall length of 1,039 ft (316.7 m), the fully loaded *Forrestal* weighed in at 76,000 tons. She had four catapults and four deck-edge elevators which could handle any aircraft in the inventory or postulated. *Forrestal* was followed by three sister-ships: *Saratoga* (CVA 60) in 1956, *Ranger* (CVA 61) in 1957 and *Independence* (CVA 62) in 1959.

Conventional to nuclear carriers

A slightly larger and improved 'Forrestal' class appeared in 1961 with the commissioning of *Kitty Hawk* (CVA 63) on 29 April. Name-ship of her class, *Kitty Hawk* also had two sisters, *Constellation* (CVA

64) of 1961 and *America* (CVA 66) of 1965. *John F. Kennedy* (CVA 67) followed in 1968. *Kennedy* was the last conventionally powered attack carrier built for the Navy. Changes in the *Kennedy*'s construction make her a one-ship class. A unique propulsion plant and foam torpedo protection system (adopted in the later 'Nimitz' class) clearly separate her from earlier big-deck carriers. Debate over the use of nuclear power in *JFK* was terminated by the decision in 1963 of Secretary of Defense Robert Strange McNamara to have her conventionally powered. McNamara's edict caused the resignation of Secretary of the Navy Fred Korth; it was 1948 all over again.

But Naval Aviation was already in the nuclear power business to stay. Construction had begun 4 February 1958 on *Enterprise* (CVAN 65) at Newport News. Commissioned on 25 November 1961, she remains dimensionally the world's largest warship despite the appearance of the greater-displacement 'Nimitz' class in 1975. Originally built as an improved *Kitty Hawk* design, *Enterprise* has a length of 1,123 ft (342.3 m) and a full-load displacement of 85,600 tons.

The USSR's increased emphasis on her submarine fleet brought about the establishment of hunter-killer (HUK) groups, built around the 'Essex' class CVS, equipped with CVSG anti-submarine air groups. The postwar efforts of the CVLs and CVEs with Grumman/Eastern TBM-3Es and -3Ws led the way for their larger sisters with their more sophisticated aircraft.

Helicopters had come to carrier aviation with the

assignment of Sikorsky HO3S-1s to plane guard duties in the late 1940s. Since that time, helicopter detachments or squadrons have deployed in every carrier. The first operational ASW helo was the sonar-dipping Sikorsky HO4S which performed ASW services off Korea in *Sicily* during the Korean War. They were replaced with the HSS-1 Seabat with HS-3 in 1955. The first ASW-dedicated fixed wing aircraft was Grumman's AF-2S/2W Guardian, which had reported to VS-24 in 1950. These types were followed by the S2F Tracker in 1954 and Sikorsky SH-3A Sea King in 1961 which, with the Douglas AD-5W and Grumman E-1B Tracer with its APS-82 radar, became the backbone of the CVS program.

The first 'Essex' class carriers to assume the CVS role were the unmodernized *Leyte* and *Antietam* on 8 August 1953. They were followed closely by *Princeton, Boxer, Tarawa, Valley Forge, Philippine Sea* and *Lake Champlain*. Except for *Lake Champlain*, none of these carriers had ever been modernized. The decommissioned *Franklin, Bunker Hill* and *Enterprise* were all redesignated CVS on 8 August 1953, but never put to sea with this designation.

Eventually, these ships were replaced by the '27 Alphas' which served throughout the next two decades. Two '27 Charlies' also became CVSs,

Intrepid in 1963 and *Ticonderoga* in 1970. Although *Shangri-La* was redesignated CVS, this was an administrative maneuver to meet the congressionally-mandated number of active CVAs. *Intrepid* made three Vietnam War cruises as a limited-capability attack carrier. The CVSs deployed regularly to the Mediterranean and Western Pacific until the early 1970s, when the program was abandoned in favor of the CV concept which integrated the HS and VS squadrons into the attack air wings.

The aircraft-carrier has made Naval Aviation one of the most potent forces the world has ever seen. The 'Essex' class, and 'big decks' which followed, contributed to the advances in the state of carrier technology that would lead to the 'Nimitz' class of the 1970s, the most powerful warships afloat.

Above: The Sikorsky HSS-1 Seabat replaced the HO4S in HS squadrons aboard CVSs beginning with HS-3 in 1955. HS-5 'Hisses' are spotted on *Lake Champlain* (CVS 39).

Above left: The first operational sonar-dipping helicopter was the Sikorsky HO4S, which performed ASW services off Korea in the *Sicily* (CVE 118). This is an HS-4 HO4S-3 lowering its sonar dome during ASW exercises off Japan.

Below: The Grumman AF-2S and -2W Guardian was the first designed-for-the-purpose ASW carrier aircraft. It began fleet service with VS-24 in 1950, and here VS-20 Guardians make ready for launch from the *Badoeng Strait*.

Antietam (CV 36) with Air Group 89 joined the 7th Fleet at the end of the war, but too late for combat. Accompanied by *Intrepid* (CV 11) and *Cabot* (CVL 28), they formed TF-72 to assist the occupation forces on mainland China.

26
The Seventh Fleet: TF-77 Towards the Abyss

After the close of World War II, two US Navy units emerged as the most potent instruments of naval air power in the world, the 6th Fleet in the Mediterranean and the 7th Fleet in the Western Pacific. Of the two, the 7th Fleet and its Task Force 77 would carry the major burden of the nation's wars for the next three decades, while the 6th Fleet was on station guarding the opposite side of the world from Soviet aggression in that area.

The 7th Fleet carriers trace their history back into mid-World War II, when they served under Rear Admiral Thomas L. Sprague as part of 'MacArthur's Navy' during the invasion of the Philippines. During the 2nd Battle of the Philippine Sea, 16 escort carriers of TG-77.4 earned their niche in Naval Aviation history off Samar, when they held off a vastly superior Japanese battleship force on 25 October 1944.

As the Japanese capitulated, *Antietam*, *Intrepid* and *Cabot* formed TF-72 to support the occupation of China and Korea, the first assignment of fast carriers to the 7th Fleet. These three ships headed a long list of illustrious names to follow in their wakes to support their nation's policies in the Far East. TF-72 aircraft flew sorties from the Yellow Sea over the Chinese mainland until mid-October, overseeing compliance by Japanese troops of the peace terms. On 11 October, *Boxer* relieved *Intrepid*, with *Cabot* returning home the same month. *Antietam* and *Boxer* supported TF-72 operations until August and September 1946 respectively.

The 7th Fleet underwent a series of name

changes between 1947 and 1950, first as Pacific Task Fleet on 1 January 1947, when fleet numerical designations were temporarily abolished. In the summer of 1948 it became the 7th Task Fleet, the word 'Task' being dropped 11 February 1950, returning the name to its original World War II 7th Fleet form.

Boxer returned to the 7th Fleet in January 1950, following the Chief of Naval Operation's directive of the month before that one carrier be permanently deployed to the Western Pacific. This assignment was a result of the collapse of the Nationalist Chinese government on mainland China and its exodus to Formosa. *Boxer*'s assignment began a continuous carrier presence in the Western Pacific that has been maintained to this day.

Shortly after the beginning of the Korean War, the Fast Carrier Task Force was re-formed and soon became Task Force 77. Nearly 26 years later, in January 1976, TF-77 was finally established as a permanent entity. Commander Carrier Division Five was assigned this permanent responsibility.

From TF-77's first inception under the stress of war in 1950, until its next call to battle 14 years later, many historical events occurred which influenced the Navy's air arm and shaped the course of TF-77.

The Navy's first hesitant steps toward entering the realm of helicopters came in October 1943, with the delivery of a Sikorsky HNS-1 to the Coast Guard at NAS Floyd Bennett Field. The Coast Guard fulfilled the Navy's needs for helo services and pilots until 1 July 1946, when Experimental Squadron Three (VX-3) was commissioned 'to expedite the evaluation of helicopter operating techniques for fleet uses and land-based operations'. The first operational helicopter squadron, Helicopter Utility Squadron One (HU-1), was commissioned 1 April 1948 at NAS Lakehurst. Less than four years later, Helicopter Antisubmarine Squadron One (HS-1) was established at NAS Key West as the first unit of its type.

Helicopters soon became common sights in the fleet with the appearance of HU-1 and sister-squadron HU-2 Sikorsky HO3S-1 detachments aboard surface units and carriers on both coasts. The advent of the versatile 'whirly-bird' led to the demise of one of the oldest sea-going traditions in Naval Aviation, namely the catapult scout planes aboard cruisers and battleships. On 5 April 1949 the last observation squadron, VO-2, was decommissioned. The Curtiss SC-1 Seahawk faded from the scene as the last scout plane of the Navy.

By 1943, Patuxent River, Maryland had been firmly established as the center of activity for testing of the Navy's aircraft. On 16 July 1945 the Naval Air Test Center (NATC) was commissioned

Evolution and post-war technology brought about the demise of many long-standing traditions of Naval Aviation. VO-2 was decommissioned on 5 April 1949 as the US Navy's last scout plane squadron. This is an SC-1 of VCS-15 from *Topeka* (CL 67) during the spring of 1947. Seahawks were the US Navy's last scouts.

at Patuxent River. Less than two years later, on 4 March 1948, the Test Pilot Training Division was established at NATC to provide pilots qualified in aeronautical engineering and flight testing. Ten years later, the name was officially changed to the US Naval Test Pilot School. From its humble wartime beginnings in spartan surroundings, Patuxent River would produce men who would continually probe the limits of Naval aircraft by taking them to unbelievable heights and speeds. One day, such a man would walk on the moon.

VF-171, the first jet-qualified squadron, produced the Navy's first emergency ejection on 9 August 1949, when Lieutenant J.L. 'Pappy' Fruin experienced control difficulties with his McDonnell F2H-1 Banshee over Walterboro, South Carolina. Fruin owed a debt of gratitude to a host of Navy test parachutists of the Parachute Experimental Unit who tested the life-saving equipment used by Naval Aviators. He owed a special debt to Lieutenant (JG) A.J. Furtek who, on 30 October 1946, made the first live ejection in the US during a test from a Douglas JD-1 5,000 ft (1525 m) over Lakehurst.

South China Sea

In a prelude of things to come all too soon, two carriers and destroyer escorts were ordered into the South China Sea on 15 February 1954, for possible contingency actions in support of French forces in their struggle against the Viet Minh in North Vietnam. As Attack Carrier Striking Group TG-70.2, the *Essex* and *Wasp* (joined later by *Boxer*) began 'training operations' off the Philippines in the spring of the year. On 18 April the light carrier *Saipan* arrived at Tourane (later DaNang) to deliver 25 Vought AU-1 Corsairs to the French navy. In the midst of an around-the-world cruise with VMA-324 embarked, *Saipan* had been diverted to Japan to onload the ground-attack versions of the F4U and speed them to the French. Marine pilots flew the AU-1s into Tourane's airfield, turning them over to waiting French pilots.

In March, as *Boxer* and *Essex* stood by on 12-hour alert in the South China Sea, the French requested air support from the US for their troops trapped at Dien Bien Phu. Several proposals for assistance

were considered by Washington, including a nuclear strike (VC-6 with three North American AJ-2s was at Atsugi, Japan in position to fly aboard the carriers to load nuclear weapons), but no armed support was approved. Although intervention by the US was recommended to President Eisenhower by Admiral Arthur W. Radford, Chairman of the Joint Chiefs of Staff, assistance was limited to covert reconnaissance flights from the carriers over the border area, Dien Bien Phu and Tonkin Delta. The flights were to observe Viet Minh positions as well as Chinese airfields and staging areas. However, the fate of France's colony was sealed when Dien Bien Phu fell on 7 May.

After the French collapse at Dien Bien Phu, the Chinese communists increased their attention in the area of Formosa and the offshore islands. Intelligence indicated a possible Chinese invasion attempt and the *Tarawa*, along with *Boxer*, were ordered into the area. On 22 July, Chinese fighters shot down a British Air Cathay Douglas DC-4 airliner 20 miles (32 km) south of Hainan. The *Hornet* (with CVG-9) and *Philippine Sea* (with CVG-5) were in the South China Sea as part of the four-carrier requirement in the Western Pacific in force at the time. Responding to the British airliner's mayday call, the two carriers launched search and rescue efforts. On 26 July, Air Group Five Douglas Skyraiders, led by Commander George C. Duncan,

Above: The US Navy's first emergency ejection was made 9 August 1949 by VF-171 pilot Lieutenant J. L. 'Pappy' Fruin from a F2H-1. Fruin owed his life to the work done by test parachutists at the Parachute Experimental Unit, and here CHMAC C. E. Storm ejects from a PEU JD-1 on 23 January 1952 during a test near NAS El Centro, California.

USS *Saipan* (CVL 48) arrives at Tourane, Vietnam, with 25 AU-1 Corsairs for the French navy. Flown into Tourane (later DaNang) by VMA 324 pilots, the Corsairs were an attempt to aid the French in their fight against the Viet Minh communists in the North.

Above: Electronic reconnaissance of communist defenses is risky business. VQ-1 lost one P4M-1Q with entire crew and had another plane badly damaged by MiGs in the Far East. A ploy used by the squadron was to paint similarly appearing Mercators in markings of deployed P2V squadrons, and the VQ-1 P4M-1Q in this photo is in markings of VP-9 at Shema, Alaska, in 1959.

Above right: Between 1950 and 1959, numerous attacks were made by Soviet and Chinese aircraft and surface forces on US Navy aircraft as well as civilian airliners. Several downings occurred with heavy loss of life. VP-22 lost a P2V-5 on 18 January 1953, with most of its crew when hit by AA fire.

were attacked by two Chinese Lavochkin La-7 fighters. Both of the attackers were destroyed by the Navy pilots.

The 'Hainan Incident' was only one of a long list of communist attacks on military and civilian aircraft that ventured or strayed near their borders during the 'cold war'. Other such actions against US Navy aircraft include:

8 April 1950: a VP-26 Consolidated PB4Y-2 was lost with its crew of 10 men after being attacked over the Baltic Sea by Soviet aircraft

6 November 1951: a VP-6 Lockheed P2V-3 was downed in the sea off Siberia after an attack by Soviet aircraft

31 July 1952: a VP-731 Martin PBM-5S2 was attacked by two MiG-15s near Formosa, killing two of its crewmembers and seriously wounding two others; this followed an unsuccessful attack on 16 July by a MiG-15, which made several firing passes at another FAW-6 patrol plane over Korea Bay

18 January 1953: a VP-22 P2V-5 patrolling the Formosa Strait was shot down by AA fire and ditched near Swatow; a Coast Guard PBM-5 attempted rescue of the downed crew in the face of gunfire from the shore and heavy 8-12 ft (2.4-3.7 m) seas; the Mariner crashed on take-off and only 10 survivors of the combined 21-man crews were finally rescued by a destroyer; another search aircraft was fired upon during the rescue operation by Chinese planes, but escaped un-

harmed

20 September 1952: a VP-28 P4Y-2S was attacked by two Chinese MiG-15s while on patrol; the aircraft escaped without damage and returned to Naha, Okinawa; a similar incident occurred 23 November when another MiG made eight firing passes at a P4Y over the China Sea off Shanghai; no damage or casualties were sustained by the Privateer

19-28 June 1953: a VP-46 PBM-5S2 and two VP-1 P2V-5s while on patrol over the Formosa Strait fired upon by surface vessels; none of the aircraft received any damage during the encounters and did not return fire

8 July 1953: a VP-1 P2V-5, on a routine photo mission, received light flak off the Chinese mainland near Nantien; on 21 July another VP-1 photo plane was fired on from Amoy; neither plane was damaged

4 September 1954: a VP-19 P2V-5 was shsot down off Siberia by two MiG-15s; one crewmember was lost with the plane and the other nine men were rescued

22 June 1955: a P2V-5 crash-landed on St Lawrence Island in the Aleutians after being set afire by two Soviet MiG-15s; all crewmembers escaped unharmed

22 August 1956: a VQ-1 Martin P4M-1Q disappeared on a night patrol out of Iwakuni, Japan, after reporting an attack by aircraft 32 miles (50 km) off the Chinese coast; no survivors were found

26 June 1959: a VQ-1 P4M-1Q made an emergency landing atMiho, Japan, with one wounded crewmember after being attacked by two MiGs off

Right: VP-26 lost a PB4Y-2S and its crew of 10 men on 8 April 1950, after being attacked by Soviet aircraft over the Baltic Sea. Seen here in the form of an aircraft of VP-26 at NAS Norfolk, Virginia in 1951, the Privateer was a World War II outgrowth of the USAAF B-24 Liberator.

Post-war to Vietnam

One of the most successful anti-submarine warfare aircraft of all time, the Lockheed Neptune enjoyed a lengthy and distinguished career with the US Navy, seeing service in both Korea and Vietnam. The aircraft depicted here is a late production example of the SP-2H variant, this being the final US-built sub-type as well as the most sophisticated derivative. It appears in the colours and markings of Patrol Squadron VP-1, which operated this model of the Neptune from Whidbey Island NAS, Washington from 1960 to 1969 when it converted to the Lockheed P-3B Orion.

NAVY
VP-I
140967
YB
140967
8

Keith Fretwell

Left: A total of 142 Lockheed WV-2 Warning Stars was procured by the US Navy, acting as airborne early warning (radar picket) platforms. The radar involved for such operations necessitated the large dorsal and ventral bulges.

Korea; the Mercator pilot brought his aircraft in with the starboard engines and some flight controls shot out.

The message from the Soviets and Red Chinese was loud and clear.

Two days after Christmas 1954, *Midway* departed Norfolk with CVG-1 embarked to begin a round-the-world cruise and service with the 7th Fleet. Arriving off Formosa 6 February 1955, *Midway* joined TF-77 to become the first ship of her class to operate in the Western Pacific. She accompanied *Kearsarge, Yorktown, Essex* and *Wasp* in providing protection over Formosa and the Pescadores in response to Chinese communist bombardment of the Tachens and seizure of Ichiang Island. On 28 January, a joint congressional resolution had authorized the President to use US armed forces in the defense of the area. TF-77 aircraft covered the evacuation of nearly 27,000 Chinese Nationalists from the offshore islands to Formosa during 6-12 February.

During the month of September, two unique squadrons were established under the Naval Aviation organization: Guided Missile Group One on 16 September and GMGRU-2 on 26 September. These units combined the talents of surface fleet guided missilemen, with those of aviation personnel and equipment, to launch and control Regulus assault missiles (RAM). The Regulus was the nation's first nuclear guided missile to be deployed operationally. GMGRU-1 detachments deployed regularly in Western Pacific carriers from Barbers Point, Hawaii, while GMGRU-2 provided Atlantic Fleet carriers with detachments from NOTS Chincoteague, Virginia until the Regulus was phased out in 1960 in favor of the Polaris program.

The nation's continental air defense capabilities were expanded when, on 10 January 1956, Airborne Early Warning Wing, Pacific was established at Barbers Point. VW squadrons under this command flew Lockheed WV-2 (EC-121K) barrier patrols

from Midway Islands and Adak, Alaska, providing early warning protection of the Hawaiian Islands and continental US against surprise attack. The AEW 'Connies' flew round-the-clock patrols until they were replaced by advanced technology detection systems in the mid-1960s. Additionally, the threat of a massive Soviet bomber attack was replaced by ICBMs, which hastened the obsolescence of the graceful 'Willie Victors'. On 30 June 1965, the Pacific extension of the 'Dewline' was disbanded and, in the Atlantic, VW-11 flew the last barrier patrol on that coast on 26 August.

An event of great significance occurred without fanfare on 14 July 1956, when the 'Clansmen' of VA-46 deployed with Sidewinder air-to-air missile-equipped Grumman F9F-8 Cougars in the *Randolph* to the 6th Fleet. In the following month, VF-211 deployed in *Bon Homme Richard* to the Western Pacific with Sidewinder-capable North American FJ-3Ms. The heat-seeking Sidewinder was a quantum leap in the art of aerial warfare and became the Navy's most successful weapon in the aerial war over Vietnam.

The virtual dismantling of the Fleet Logistics Air Wings and Naval Aviation's transport capabilities was expedited 7 December 1956, when the Secretary of Defense ordered air transport operations to be placed under USAF MATS control from 1 July 1957. All US Navy transports operating under MATS would be transferred to the Air Force,

Above: Two unique squadrons were formed to deploy the Regulus assault missile in US carriers: Guided Missile Group One on the west coast and GMGRU-2 on the east coast. GMGRU-1 TV-2D and FJ-3D control aircraft here bring a Regulus training missile in for landing at ALF Bonham, Kauai, T.H. following a 1958 training mission.

Below: Virtual dismantling of Fleet Logistics Air Wings occurred 7 December 1956 with an order from the Secretary of Defense placing the US Navy's transport operations under USAF control. The Navy was left with only a few VR squadrons and 30 four-engine transports.

UNITED STATES NAVY

together with all but 30 of the Navy's four-engine transport aircraft.

The end of two more eras came with the decommissioning of *Badoeng Strait* on 17 May and *Saipan* on 30 September 1957. These carriers represented the last of the escort and light carriers to serve with the Navy in those roles. One CVL, *Cabot*, is still active as *Dedalo* with the Spanish navy. Several CVEs remained in service as aircraft transports under the designation of CVU, which was changed to AKV on 7 May 1959. Additionally, *Thetis Bay* (CVE 90) was converted in 1955 to become CVHA-1, the first helicopter assault ship, and was redesignated LPH-4 on 28 May 1959.

The training of fleet aircrew and maintenance personnel was reorganized on 10 March 1958, with the approval by CNO of the establishment of two Replacement Air Groups (RAG). This event followed the precedent established toward the end of World War II of replacement training air groups. RCVG-4 was formed at Oceana for east coast squadrons and RCVG-12 at Miramar for the west coast. This event, combined with the Naval Air Training and Operating Procedures Standardization (NATOPS) program instituted in 1961, provided standardized training for all fleet squadrons and promoted a dramatic improvement in the Naval Aviation safety record.

The seeds of discontent

Events in the Middle East for the 6th Fleet through the 1950s paralleled those in the Western Pacific. As hot spots continually flared and 'wars of liberation' broke out throughout the area surrounding the Mediterranean, the 6th Fleet carriers were unfailingly on the scene. Two of their most prominent attempts to bring stabilization to events in the area and to protect US interests were the Suez War of 1956 and the Lebanon crisis of 1958.

The Bureau of Aeronautics, or 'BuAer' as it was more commonly known, ceased to exist on 1 December 1959. Formally established 1 September 1921, BuAer's chiefs had guided Naval Aviation to preeminence in the world. Once again, the age of technology had overtaken a tried and true entity, and BuAer was combined with the Bureau of Ordnance (BuOrd) into a new unit, the Bureau of Weapons (BuWeps), under Rear Admiral P.D. Stroop. In turn, BuWeps became Naval Air Systems Command (NavAirSysCom) on 1 May 1966.

The Navy's small step into the space age in 1946 became an increasingly larger investment over the years as the lure of space attracted attention to its military potential. After an unpromising beginning, the Navy launched a 3¼-lb (1.47-kg) satellite into orbit on 17 March 1958 atop a Vanguard missile. On 5 May 1961, the nation's hopes and aspirations were realized when Naval Aviator Commander Alan B. Shepard became the first American into space. After a 116-mile (187-km) flight downrange from Cape Canaveral, Florida, Shepard's Freedom 7 space capsule was recovered at sea by an HMR(L)-262 Sikorsky HUS-1 and flown to the recovery ship *Lake Champlain* (CVS 39), where a jubilant crew greeted the country's first astronaut. Almost one year later, on 20 February 1962, another Naval Aviator, Lieutenant Colonel John H. Glenn, USMC, became the first American to orbit the Earth in a spacecraft. On 24 July 1969, mankind set foot upon the moon for the first time. Once again a Naval Aviator led the way, as former Navy pilot Neil A. Armstrong took a 'giant step for mankind'.

As Naval Aviation grew older, more and more of its institutions fell by the wayside. Another tradition disappeared with the decommissioning, on 31 October 1961, of Fleet Airship Wing One and LTA patrol squadrons ZP-1 and ZP-3 at Lakehurst. These organizations represented the last operational units of the LTA service. The final flight of a Navy lighter-than-air ship came 31 August 1962, when one of two airships retained for research and development purposes moored at Lakehurst for the last time. A 45-year tradition of ungainly grace was gone.

Slightly more than two years later, on 20 December 1963, another institution fell with the renaming of carrier air groups to carrier air wings (CVW).

US Navy

Right: Standing guard against Soviet ventures in the eastern hemisphere, the 6th Fleet carriers were on hand to bring stability to the Suez War of 1956 and Lebanon Crisis of 1958. *Saratoga* (CVA 60) with CVW-3 steams off Lebanon in 1958 during her first cruise.

Left: The Cuban Missile Crisis of October 1962, brought the USA and Soviet Union to the brink of war. VFP-62 earned a Navy Unit Commendation for recon flights over Cuba during the confrontation, and here a VFP-62 RF-8A pilot gets the catapult signal aboard *Independence* (CVA 62).

However, the air group commanders are still (and probably forever more will be) known as CAGs.

Suddenly, in the fall of 1962, the Cold War became more real for the citizens of the United States as President John F. Kennedy announced the presence of Soviet offensive nuclear missiles in Cuba. Ordering a naval and air quarantine of the communist country, President Kennedy established a naval blockade to prevent the introduction of more weapons. Photo-reconnaissance squadrons VFP-62 and VMCJ-2 flew intensive intelligence-gathering sorties over Cuba, as *Enterprise* and *Independence* positioned themselves to ward off any attack on the US naval base at Guantanamo Bay. *Essex* provided ASW support to the blockade force. A total of eight carriers, CVA and CVS, took part in the 'Cuban Missile Crisis' before Soviet Premier Nikita Krushchev relented and agreed to remove the weapons. On 20 November the crisis, which brought the nation perilously close to war with the Soviet Union, was officially declared ended.

Meanwhile, in the Western Pacific, the 7th Fleet and Task Force 77 continued in their role as America's sentinel in the Far East. During the latter part of the 1950s they responded to events in the Indonesian, Thai, South China Sea and ever-troublesome Formosa areas. A threatened invasion of Quemoy by China on 27 August 1958 was coun-

tered by moving *Essex* through the Suez Canal and *Midway* from the Eastern Pacific into the area with a US Marine amphibious force. With American resolve to protect the area demonstrated, the communists backed off and tensions once again were eased temporarily.

US naval support of the Southeast Asia Treaty Organization (SEATO) led to several joint ASW and amphibious exercises in that area. Squadrons from CVS carriers operated with hunter-killer (HUK) groups in the South China Sea into the early 1960s alongside forces from other SEATO nations. Additionally, the US had assumed the task of training and providing advisors to the Army of the Republic of Vietnam in their struggle against communist-inspired insurgency in that country which was supported by the communist regime in the North.

Fighting broke out in neighboring Laos between the government and communist Pathet Lao forces, also supported by North Vietnam. A request for aid from the Laotian government, coupled with the US commitment to South Vietnam, increased the presence of American naval forces in the South China Sea.

On 2 August 1964, North Vietnamese torpedo boats attacked USS *Maddox* (DD 731) patrolling in the Gulf of Tonkin . . .

Right: Taken during Operation 'Sea Orbit' in August 1964, this view of the aft flight deck of USS *Enterprise* (CVAN 65) shows just how crowded aircraft carriers can be. A-4C Skyhawks of VA-64, VA-66 and VA-76 can be seen alongside A-1H Skyraiders of VA-65 and E-1B Tracers of VAW-12 Detachment 65.

Below: A tradition of 45 years ended with the flight of the US Navy's last blimp on 31 August 1962. The last lighter-than-air squadrons were decommissioned during the previous year. ZPG-3W, in flight here, was the largest non-rigid airship ever built and the last LTA type delivered to the US Navy.

U.S. NAVY

VF-111 'Sundowner' F-4B buddy bombs with its VF-51 sister squadron Phantom II.
This type of bombing, usually using navigation fixes, was relatively inaccurate and
used only as a last resort in lightly defended areas. The four Mk 82 bombload was
typical for *Coral Sea*'s F-4s due to that ship's limited catapulting capacity.

Vietnam- All for Naught

US Naval Aviation, and particularly the tactical squadrons of the carrier fleet, bore the brunt of the Navy's combat action in the Vietnam War. All but one of the 12 larger carriers in commission, five of the smaller 'Essex' class and one converted CVS launched strikes against targets in Vietnam. Other anti-submarine warfare carriers served in support and ocean surveillance roles, whilst LPHs supported the amphibious forces and former CVEs ferried aircraft. In short, the Navy fought a carrier war in Vietnam.

Naval aviators carried the action to the enemy, and while flying missions in the North faced the most formidable air defense system ever devised. From their carrier decks they launched to press home attacks, dodging surface-to-air missiles and flying through dense clouds of anti-aircraft fire. Against the MiG pilots, the carrier aviators acquitted themselves well as they battled an elusive enemy who had all the advantages of fuel and usually of surprise.

For nearly 10 years aircrews manned their aircraft on windswept flight decks and took to the skies over South-East Asia. In spite of political vacillation and sparse public support from home, they distinguished themselves. Once again, they had met the challenge and defeated it, as they had done so many times before.

27
Tonkin Gulf

Long before the US Congress overwhelmingly approved the Gulf of Tonkin Resolution which granted the President the power to take the necessary measures to repel further Communist aggression in South East Asia, the United States was politically and, indirectly, militarily involved in Vietnam.

Toward the end of hostilities in World War II, the weakened Japanese were challenged for control of Indochina by various rebel groups. Strongest of these groups was the Communist revolutionaries known as the Viet Minh led by Ho Chi Minh. Taking advantage of the political instability, Ho and his followers established a strong influence in Tonkin, the northern area of Vietnam.

With the end of the war and the surrender of Japan, France began the struggle of rebuilding itself as a European power and re-establishing its colonial authority on the Indochina peninsula. In early 1946, a small French task force, including the aircraft-carrier *Béarn*, used as a troop and supply ship, had returned French colonial control to Saigon. The task force then proceeded north to Haiphong. As the French ships approached the port city on 6 March, they came under heavy hostile fire but were able to land enough troops to overcome the opposition and regain control of the northern area.

During the following year, the Viet Minh employed disruptive tactics against the French, forcing them to send the aircrft-carrier *Dixmude* to bolster their forces. Use of the *Dixmude*, an escort carrier converted in the United States from a merchant hull, and her US-built Douglas SBD bombers, marked the first combat use of aircraft-carriers in French history and provided the power of a mobile striking force. With the lack of suitable land airfields, the *Dixmude* demonstrated the importance of carrier aviation and its ability to move freely and concentrate its air power where needed. The *Dixmude* operated along the northern coast of Vietnam until May 1947, when she returned to France for overhaul.

In September 1951, the *Dixmude* returned to Vietnam after having picked up more modern Grumman F6F Hellcats and Curtiss SB2C Helldivers in the United States. Alternating forces with the carriers *Arromanches* and *LaFayette (former USS Langley* (CVL 27)) French carrier planes continued to support ground forces against the Viet Minh until 1954 when the French defeat at Dien Bien Phu marked the end of French influence in Asia.

French forces made their final valiant stand in Indochina at Dien Bien Phu, a remote outpost located 170 miles (275 km) west of Hanoi. With the rainy spring of 1954 and the extreme distance from firmly held French territory, the beleaguered troops found themselves surrounded with only limited resupply and air support. Although French pilots flew through the heavy defenses in a vain effort to support the ground troops, their aging aircraft proved inadequate for the task.

The French pleas for support from US carriers in the Tonkin Gulf was denied. American carriers were operating in the South China Sea loaded with the latest jet aircraft and tactical weapons. However, because of political considerations the carriers were not allowed to launch the strikes which could have saved the French outpost. In Washington, a proposal to use nuclear weapons from the carriers was also rejected.

On 7 May 1954, Dien Bien Phu fell to the Viet Minh. At home, public clamor forced the French to sue for peace with the triumphant Communists. As a result of these peace negotiations, the Geneva Agreement of 1954 partitioned Vietnam into North and South Vietnams with a Demilitarized Zone (DMZ) at the 17th parallel. Now with control over the northern sector the Communists largely ignored the Geneva agreements and continued their terrorist attacks in the South.

Throughout the 1950s, US foreign policy called for a naval presence in the western Pacific and a carrier task force routinely patrolled South East Asian waters. With the defeat of the French, the United States showed an ever-increasing interest in the area. American carrier task groups demonstrated that interest through routine flight operations in and around the South China Sea.

As part of the intelligence-gathering efforts during the 1950s and into the early 1960s, unarmed reconnaissance flights were launched from carriers operating in the South China Sea. Flying the RF-8 Crusader, a camera-carrying version of the Vought-built F-8 fighter, pilots brought back valuable photographic coverage of Communist activities, providing US foreign policy makers with accurate and timely information on infiltration of personnel and military supplies from north of the 17th parallel.

By the spring of 1962, the first US military advisors and American air support were operating in South Vietnam. US Army advisors were directly involved with training the young South Vietnamese troops. In April 1962, the US Marines provided the initial use of helicopters under Operation 'Shufly'. Based at DaNang airfield, which was to become a major staging point for Marine and Air Force aircraft, Operation 'Shufly' helicopters gave the relatively ill-equipped South Vietnamese army a much needed boost in mobility and logistic sup-

US Navy

Left: An F8U-1P (RF-8A) rotates from the deck of *Midway* (CVA 41) on an intelligence-gathering mission. Reconnaissance squadrons provided intelligence information for Washington policy makers throughout the 1950s and early 1960s. Their mission was critical to accurate battle damage assessment of large Alpha strikes within North Vietnam in later years.

Above: Alert posture was a daily fact of life for the squadron and carrier crews. Various levels of alert posture were set depending on the expected threat and distance from land. This 1964 photograph of USS *Ticonderoga* (CVA 14) taken in the Tonkin Gulf shows F-8 Crusaders manned on the bow catapults in Alert 5 status (capable of launching in less than five minutes).

port in its struggle to counter the growing guerrilla threat supported from the North.

The US Navy became indirectly involved in the Indochina situation in the early 1950s through the use of US Navy aircraft by the French. Supplied through the Mutal Defense Assistance Program (MDAP), these aircraft were operated by the French until their defeat in 1954. Following the partitioning of Vietnam, the US Navy aircraft were turned over to the fledgling South Vietnamese air force (VNAF).

A more direct involvement by the US Navy came in August 1960, when a contingent of Navy personnel led by Lieutenant K.E. 'Ken' Moranville arrived at Bien Hoa to instruct the Vietnamese in flying and maintaining Douglas AD Skyraiders. The use of Skyraiders by the Vietnamese had been recommended by Captain H. 'Hank' Suerstedt, Asian

Training Officer on the staff of Admiral Harry D. Felt, Commander-in-Chief Pacific. Moranville, the only officer and pilot, was assisted by four chief petty officers and two first class petty officers. The first Skyraiders began arriving in September to bolster the Grumman F8F Bearcats then in use by the VNAF. The skies of Vietnam would be filled with many more of the powerful Douglas bombers in the years to come, flown both by the Vietnamese and US Naval Aviators.

By mid-1964, American naval units were a common sight in the Tonkin Gulf off the coast of Vietnam. Commander Task Force 77 (CTF-77), the US Navy's presence in the Western Pacific and South East Asia since World War II, had the responsibility for gathering intelligence on Communist activities and estimating their capabilities. Daily carrier-based reconnaissance flights provided photographic intelligence information while surface units, named DeSoto Patrol, roamed the waters off the coastline gathering intelligence on enemy electronic signals.

On the afternoon of 2 August 1964, while on DeSoto Patrol, *Maddox* (DD 731), a 2,200-ton destroyer, detected three unidentified high-speed surface craft approaching her position in international waters off the coast of North Vietnam's Hon Me Island. Identifying the targets as North Vietnamese torpedo boats, *Maddox* fired a warning shot at the onrushing targets and began to take evasive action. Undaunted, the torpedo boats pressed their attack, two of the boats launching torpedoes which missed the destroyer.

Maddox took the three craft under fire, inflicting probable damage on one of the boats. At the same time, four Vought F-8E Crusaders, which had launched on a normal training flight from *Ticonderoga* (CVA 14), were dispatched to the scene. The Crusaders attacked the PT boats with their 20-mm cannon and 5-in (127-mm) Zuni rockets as the boats tried to flee toward the north. One boat was reported sunk.

Even though the attack took place on the high seas, the United States took no immediate retalia-

Right: Smaller-deck CVS carriers, normally used for anti-submarine warfare, served during Vietnam in both a support role and configured with detachments of fighter and light attack aircraft for special operations. Shown here is *Hornet*'s VAW-11 detachment E-1B 'Willy Fudd' airborne early warning aircraft.

tory action. The *Turner Joy* (DD 951) and *Constellation* (CVA 64), in port in Hong Kong, were ordered to the area. DeSoto Patrols resumed and were provided air cover by *Constellation* and *Ticonderoga*. All units were authorized to return fire if attacked while in international waters. To preclude any possible misunderstanding of US intent, the destroyer captains were directed to go no closer than 11 miles (17.7 km) from the North Vietnamese coast. On their own initiative the destroyers remained outside 16 miles (25.75 km) during daylight hours, retiring as directed to around 100 miles (160 km) at night.

Two nights later, in the early evening while some 60 miles (96.5 km) from the coast, the two destroyers picked up five surface radar contacts as the US ships were retiring to the east. The *Maddox* and *Turner Joy* increased their speed and turned sharply to the south in attempts to outdistance the incoming craft. When they could no longer avoid the inevitable, and the enemy was within 6,000 yards (5485 m) of *Maddox*, the two destroyers opened fire. In the ensuing four-hour battle, with torpedo sightings reported coming within 300 ft (90 m) of *Turner Joy*, two of the enemy patrol boats were sunk. Neither US destroyer received any damage.

With now two unprovoked attacks on American ships in international waters, President Johnson announced his response. At the same time, aircraft from *Constellation* and *Ticonderoga* were launching to attack four major PT boat bases along the North Vietnamese coastline and their supporting fuel installation at Vinh. The bases ranged along the coast from Quang Khe, 50 miles (80 km) north of the DMZ, to Hon Gai, just north of the port city of Haiphong.

In 64 sorties, Douglas Skyraiders, Douglas Skyhawks and Crusaders from the two American carriers bombed and rocketed the bases, sinking or seriously damaging 25 PT boats and destroying a major portion of their petroleum stores and storage facilities. Pilots reported that fuel oil tanks were burning profusely at Vinh as they left the area, and intelligence confirmed an estimated 90 per cent of Vinh's fuel installation had been destroyed.

During these strikes two US aircraft were shot down, including the A-4C Skyhawk flown by 26-year-old Lieutenant (JG) Everett Alvarez. In the raid against the PT boat facilities at Hon Gai his aircraft was hit by enemy fire. Alvarez ejected and was captured by the North Vietnamese, becoming the first confirmed POW of the war. He would not leave Hanoi until eight and a half years later as a lieutenant commander.

Later that same day, President Johnson sent a message to Congress asking for passage of a joint resolution in support of US policy in South East Asia. The resolution, known commonly as the Tonkin Gulf Resolution, was passed by nearly unanimous vote by both houses of Congress. This document gave the President the necessary power to halt the Communist advances in South East Asia. But, if the overwhelming resolve of Congress was there, as well as the necessary military means to achieve the US objectives, determination was diluted by the controlling powers in Washington and the Pentagon itself. As the war progressed with its periods of 'escalation', the tactical control was more and more held by the politicians in Washington. For the professional aviator trained to execute appropriate options in light of the tactical situation, the seemingly thoughtless civilian operational control of the war and overly restrictive 'rules of engagement' would become a nightmare which often led to a death trap. Militarily significant or politically sensitive targets were off limits for much of the war. Targets were often selectively doled out from Washington for a particular day and if not hit that day authorization was cancelled. No follow-up

Above: The catapult tension signal is given for a VA-25 A-1H Skyraider loaded for an attack mission. VA-25 transitioned to the A-7E Corsair II light attack aircraft after flying the Skyraider's last attack squadron combat missions. Commode attached to bomb tack was dropped on Viet Cong positions in disdain of the enemy.

Left: Flight deck crew launch an RF-8A Crusader from *Constellation* (CVA 64) as squadron maintenance personnel from VA-146 ready their A-4Cs for launch. Numerous models of the F-8 Crusader and A-4 Skyhawk were the mainstay of Naval Aviation through the 1950s and 1960s. Both the F-8 and A-4 were in action to the war's end. They were replaced by new-generation aircraft as the smaller 'Essex' class carriers were retired.

Right: VA-144 A-4C Skyhawk is airborne off the waist catapult of *Constellation* (CVA-64). *Connie* aircraft participated in the first retaliatory raids against North Vietnam on 5 August 1964 following the Tonkin Gulf incidents with *Turner Joy* and *Maddox*. LTJG Everett Alvarez was flying a VA-144 A-4C during these raids when he became the first US POW of the war.

US Navy

strikes were allowed. Pre-strike intelligence photography was not allowed, and the rules of engagement often prevented pilots from initiating any action unless they were fired upon first. The key element of surprise did not exist. In many cases the men with the required expertise, the Naval Aviators leading the strike or planning the mission, would not be allowed to exercise the best tactical options, those learned at great costs in previous combat. Added to these restrictions was the naive philosophy that given a respite, the Communists would not take advantage of a bombing lull to rebuild and resupply. At every halt in the bombing, of which there were many, massive resupply and reconstruction efforts were pushed forward by the Communists. To the professional military aviator the war was seldom satisfactory. With the resumption of air strikes following every fruitless bombing halt, he was faced with making up the lost ground that was given away, and nearly always at much

greater odds as well as cost in lives.

28
The MiG Threat

In September 1964, to provide for any eventuality, the attack carrier *Ranger* (CVA 61) was dispatched to the Tonkin Gulf to bolster the force of Task Force 77, arriving on 18 September. But for a period there was no call for the naval forces. Several Air Force units were moved into South Vietnam along with support equipment and personnel. The long, slow buildup was beginning.

In the waning months of 1964, the Communists pressed their terrorist attacks and took every advantage of the unstable political situation within South Vietnam. On 7 February 1965, the Com-

Below: With 'everything down', an A-1H approaches the aircraft carrier deck. An incredibly sturdy aircraft, the 'Spad' could absorb much battle damage as well as delivering a vast array of ordnance from the 14 underwing hardpoints.

US Navy

Vietnam

'CAG-bird' multi-coloured stripes are a prominent feature of the markings adorning this VA-52 Douglas A-1H Skyraider, which operated from *Ticonderoga* (CVA 14) as part of CVW-19 during this vessel's 1966-7 combat cruise to the Western Pacific. Despite its age, the trusty 'Spad' compiled an impressive record in the Vietnam War, seeing extensive service with the US Navy, US Air Force and South Vietnamese Air Force; indeed, it even succeeded in downing a couple of MiG-17s no mean achievement for what was essentially a World War 2 design. This particular specimen carries the name of CVW-19's boss, Commander Bill Phillips, below the cockpit canopy.

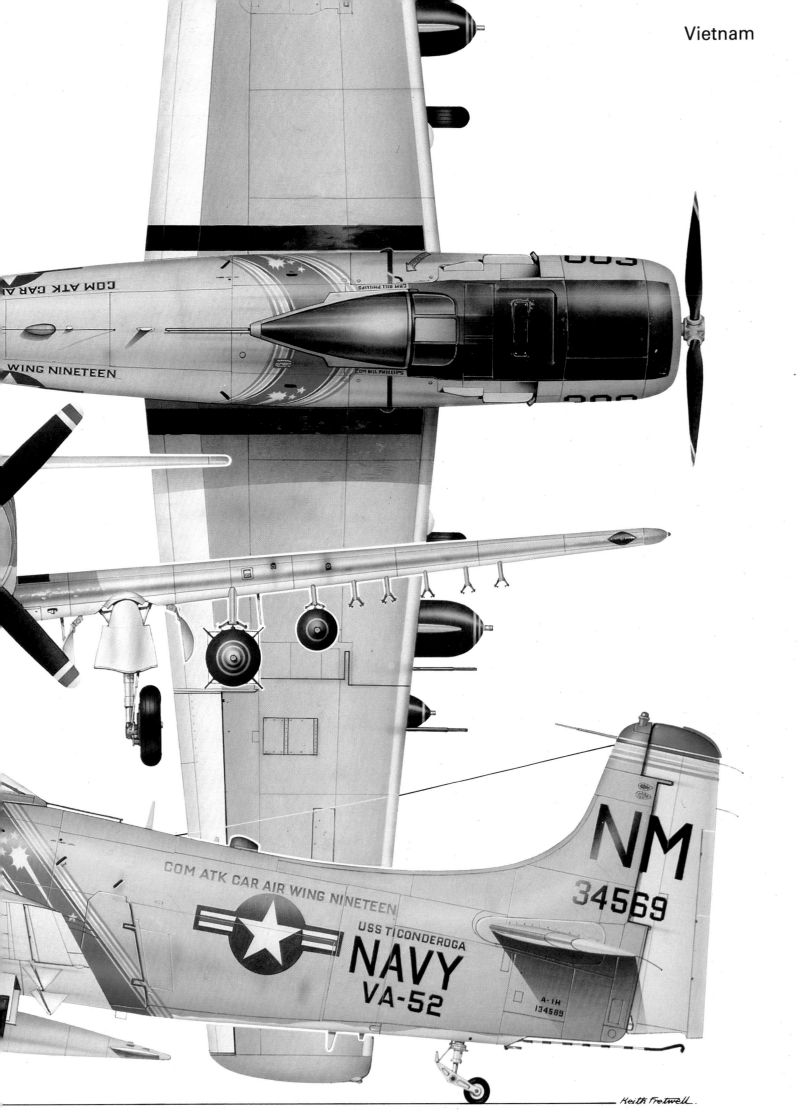

Vietnam

COM ATK CAR AIR WING NINETEEN
USS TICONDEROGA
NAVY
VA-52
NM
34569
A-1H
134569

Keith Fretwell.

munists attacked the US military advisors' compound at Pleiku, killing nine and wounding 76 US advisors. Six helicopters were destroyed in the attack and another 15 damaged. From this attack emerged the US policy of 'sustained reprisal' and for much of the war US attacks, particularly in the North, were retaliation to the level and type of Communist actions in the South. It would be only near the end of American involvement that air power would turn from this reactive policy to one of true power projection and would exercise the full political strength necessary to drive the Communist regime to negotiate a ceasefire.

In answer to the attack on Pleiku, President Johnson authorized a combined US Navy-South Vietnamese air force strike on the military barracks and staging area just north of the DMZ. The strike was codenamed 'Flaming Dart One'. Aircraft from *Coral Sea* (CVA 43) joined aircraft from *Hancock* (CVA 19) and *Ranger* forming the largest single US Navy air effort since the Korean War. *Ranger*'s planes were unable to reach their assigned target at Vit Thu Lu, a barracks 15 miles (24 km) inland from the Gulf, but the strike aircraft from *Coral Sea* and *Hancock* destroyed much of the facility at Dong Hoi.

Plans had been in existence for some time to co-ordinate naval strike forces off the coast of Vietnam. Two primary geographic points were used for the general stationing of the carrier battle groups. North of the DMZ in the Tonkin Gulf there

was Yankee Station. From this point the carrier planes could reach targets in North Vietnam, Laos and the northern regions of South Vietnam. Dixie Station was located off South Vietnam. Here carrier battle groups could support operations in the southern areas of South Vietnam, Laos and Cambodia. In later months, as the war heated up and daily strikes were flown against the heavy defenses in the North, newly arriving carriers would first be assigned to Dixie Station, warming up slowly in the relatively permissive atmosphere of South Vietnam and Laos. Pilots could refine their bombing skills and practise their tactics before graduating to the intensive anti-aircraft artillery, surface-to-air missiles (SAMs) and MiGs of the North.

For ease in command and control and for assigning targets and co-ordinating South Vietnamese, US Air Force and US Navy strikes, South Vietnam was divided into four corps areas. The northernmost, I Corps (pronounced 'eye' corps) covered the area near the DMZ south, past the ancient capital city of Hue and the US airfield at DaNang to a point south of the Marine Corps airfield at Chu Lai. II and III Corps covered the central highlands. Saigon and the rice-rich Mekong Delta to the south were in IV Corps. North Vietnam was divided into six route packages. For most of the war, the US Navy was

Above: Early in the war, Skywarriors performed bombing missions, even into targets in the heavily defended Hanoi-Haiphong area. This VAH-1 A-3B from *Oriskany* (CVA 39) drops Mk 83 1,000-lb (454-kg) bombs over the jungles of South Vietnam.

Above left: The remains of an RF-8 photo Crusader from VFP-63. This aircraft was reported by Vietnam news agencies to have been the 500th US aircraft brought down over the North. Reconnaissance aircraft were particularly vulnerable to enemy defenses as they were unarmed and were required to fly straight and level at set altitudes in order to get the necessary photographic and electronic images.

Right: An Attack Carrier Air Wing 15 Douglas EA-1F Skyraider prepares for launch from USS *Coral Sea* (CVA 43). VAW-13 flew electronic countermeasures (ECM) missions in support of air wing strikes.

Left: VA-153 A-4C Skyhawk is shot from *Coral Sea* (CVA 43) en route to targets in North Vietnam. The 12,000-lb (5443-kg) Skyhawk could carry its own weight in ordnance, though a typical load was a single centerline, or two wing mounted gas tanks, and between six and 10 500-lb (227-kg) bombs. This aircraft is loaded with a 400-US gal (1514-litre) centerline tank and two Mk 83 1,000 lb (454-kg) bombs.

Vietnam

Conventional free-fall iron bombs and Bullpup air-to-surface missiles are carried on the underwing hardpoints of this McDonnell Douglas A-4F Skyhawk of VA-212, which features the markings carried when it deployed to South-East Asia for a combat tour aboard *Hancock* (CVA 19) in 1969-70. Extensively used by both the Navy and Marine Corps, variants of the Skyhawk saw action through the entire Vietnam War, although the Navy machines were progressively replaced by the rather more capable Ling-Temco-Vought A-7 Corsair II from 1967 onwards. Nevertheless, some examples of the type did remain in front-line Navy service right up until the cease-fire in 1973.

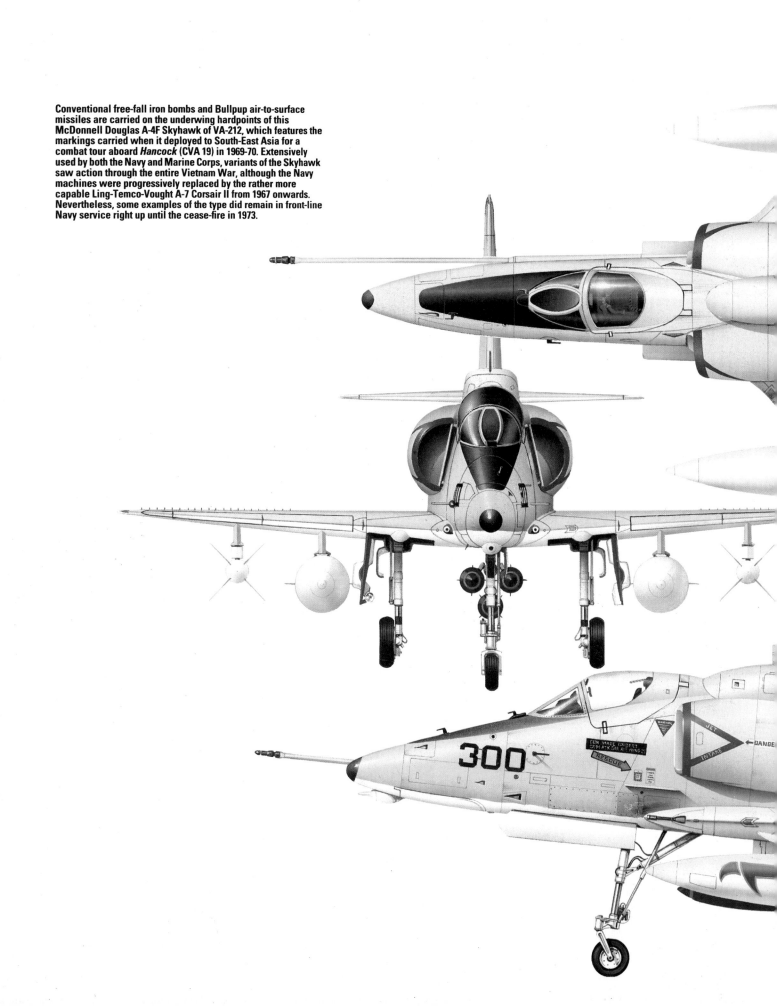

assigned responsibilities over Route Pacs 2, 3, 4 and 6B, generally the coastal areas which included the major urban areas of Dong Hoi, Vinh, Thanh Hoa, Ninh Dinh, Nam Dinh, Haiphong and Hon Gai. Route Pac 6, which covered the north eastern portion of North Vietnam, was split into Alfa and Bravo sectors by a line drawn over the north east rail line from Hanoi to China. The US Navy was assigned 6B. It must be remembered that throughout the majority of the war targets were handpicked in Washington and that much of the war-critical industry and large supply areas were located inside the Hanoi and Haiphong restricted areas, off limits to aerial strikes.

'Rolling Thunder' commences

The bombing campaign in the North can be followed chronologically through the codename 'Rolling Thunder', a name picked to indicate the psychological effect of the tactical bombing campaign as it stepped closer and closer to the geographical and political heart of the country, Hanoi. Unfortunately, the numerous restrictions weakened the full military significance of the campaign. Throughout the war, the full psychological impact was never achieved. The initial strikes of 'Rolling Thunder' began in March 1965 for air units of Task Force 77. A-4C Skyhawk aircraft from VA-153 and A-1 Skyraiders from the *Hancock* and *Coral Sea* flew co-ordinated strikes along with aircraft from the South Vietnamese air force against weapons and radar installations on Tiger Island, a small island off the coast of the DMZ. An ammunition depot near Phu Qui in the southern panhandle of North Vietnam was hit at the same time.

Weather over the South China Sea and the South East Asian peninsula was a key factor in the Vietnam War and greatly affected air operations. The winter north east monsoon season between early December and mid-May brings with it violent storms with cloud cover which often extends from 2,000 or 3,000 ft (610 or 915 m) above the ground to 40,000 ft (12190 m). During bomb runs sufficient visual warning of SAMs or MiGs, under these conditions, left no time for defensive maneuvering. This painful lesson was relearned numerous times as the war progressed. Either the Washington planners would disregard weather minimums or the overly aggressive pilots would often press their attacks beyond the established limits. The long periods of poor visibility and the small numbers of all-weather attack aircraft limited air strikes for days and occasionally weeks. Considerable supply movement and rebuilding could be accomplished during these periods without the presssure of daily bombing. Then as June nears the winds shift, bringing clearing weather and the south west monsoon to Vietnam. (Monsoon means a wind that blows from one direction part of the year and alternating to the opposite direction for the remainder.) During these summer months visibility over land is still plagued by a chronic low-lying haze, but the torrential monsoon downpours and the overcast cloud cover is replaced by generally clear sky and good flying weather.

There is little doubt that tactical Naval Aviation had a pronounced effect on North Vietnam's war-making capability. But as with any extended conflict, countermeasures are quickly applied when the opposition's plan or tactics become familiar. In Vietnam this became reality for both sides.

With the heavy defensive forces in North Vietnam and the triple threat of anti-aircraft artillery, SAMs and MiGs, US forces relied heavily on saturating the target area with large concentrations of aircraft. From this concept grew the Alpha or co-ordinated strike used extensively throughout the war by tactical air units of both the Navy and the Air Force. The Alpha strike was composed of as many as 40 aircraft, each assigned a specific mission such as flak suppression, target combat air patrol, or actual strike once in the target areas. Through the use of relatively tight formations during ingress and egress from the target area, defenses would be saturated with each aircrew relying on the mutual support of the other aircraft's deceptive and defensive electronic gear, chaff and

Above: An E-2A Hawkeye is about to trap aboard *Kitty Hawk*. The E-2 provided radar coverage of carrier battle groups off the coast of Vietnam and early warning of intruding aircraft. It effectively increased the carrier's radar range well beyond the horizon.

Above left: Introduced to service soon after the end of World War II, the Douglas Skyraider enjoyed a lengthy and illustrious career and was still widely used at the start of the Vietnam War. This A-1H of VA-176 is shown over Vietnam whilst serving aboard USS *Intrepid* (CVS 11) in 1966.

Left: The anti-aircraft artillery and surface-to-air missile defenses within North Vietnam were the most formidable ever faced by US aircrew. Here Lieutenant (JG) Michael Weakley stands in a hole in the wing fuel cell of his battle-damaged A-4 Skyhawk aboard *Midway* (CVA 41). Aircraft and electronic warfare modifications based on experiences during the war, resulted in increased survivability and safe return of US aircraft. Skyhawks hit in the wing fuel cell such as this would lose all their wing fuel followed by engine flame-out – even with fuel in the drop tanks. A modification to the A-4 known as the 'Vietnam switch' allowed transfer of drop tank fuel to bypass the damaged wing cell and go directly to the engine-feeding fuselage cell.

anti-radiation missiles. It was a distinct advantage to have other aircrew to help spot the oncoming MiGs and SAMs, a necessity if they were to defeat them.

The first photographic intelligence of Soviet-supplied surface to air missile installations was brought back 5 April 1965 to *Coral Sea* by a VFP-63 Detachment Delta Vought RF-8A. An immediate plan to strike the missile sites was developed. However, permission to hit the SAM sites was not given by Washington until mid-August, after several US planes had been downed by the lethal missiles.

As the war progressed, major developments in tactics and innovations in weapon systems resulted, followed soon afterwards by counter-tactics and new opposing weapons. Introduction of sophisticated SAM missiles created the need for electronic countermeasures to warn US pilots when a SAM was being fired at them, and from which direction. The large size of the SA-2 'Guideline' missiles led pilots to comment that defeating the intercepting missiles was like dodging 'flying telephone poles'. When pilots discovered they could defeat the supersonic missiles by rolling and pulling hard down into the missile, causing it to overshoot its mark, the ground-based missile crews developed new tactics. Firing one missile high at an incoming plane and one missile low after a short delay, the missile battalions knew that pilots would descend while trying to counter the first missile and predictably fly into the lethal zone of the second, possibly unseen missile.

Introduction of the AGM-45 Shrike anti-radiation missile was effective in either eliminating threat radar signals or significantly reducing their 'on air' time. The Shrike was designed to home in on enemy radars located on top of SAM battalion electronic vans. Operators soon became reluctant to shine their radar in an indiscriminate fashion while searching for intruding aircraft, for fear of becoming victims of the lethal Shrikes. In order to limit the radar transmitter on time and avoid the Shrike threat, an optical sight was designed and added to the SAM's radar tracking antenna. This sight allowed the ground operator to track aircraft visually and so position the antenna. The SAM would then be launched at close range and radar guidance

signals turned on only at the last possible second, thus avoiding exposure to anti-radiation missiles and giving the unsuspecting pilot little time to react against the incoming SAM.

Dueling with SAMs was not 'choice duty' and those aviators who performed this mission braved fierce odds. One such man was Lieutenant Commander Michael J. Estocin, of VA-192's 'Golden Dragons'. On 20 April 1967, Estocin was flying an anti-SAM ('Iron Hand') mission from *Ticonderoga* against thermal powerplants at Haiphong. Providing continuous SAM warnings to other members of the strike group, he personally neutralized three SAM sites. Estocin's A-4E received extensive damage but he elected to remain over the target area and made another Shrike attack, all the while receiving heavy flak fire. Depleting his ordnance, the Skyhawk pilot managed to return the crippled plane safely to the *Ticonderoga*.

Six days later, on another strike against Haiphong, Estocin once again pitted himself against the deadly missiles. Hit by an exploding SAM, he managed to retain control of his now burning aircraft to launch his Shrikes. Engulfed in the fireball of detonating SAM, Estocin's Skyhawk was seen to commence four or five aileron rolls in a 45° nose-down attitude. Recovering, Estocin called he had a fire-warning light and headed for the safety of the sea with fire streaming behind his aircraft. However, before he could reach this haven, the stricken A-4 once again began a series of rapid rolls, disappearing inverted into the undercast at 3,500 ft (1065 m). Listed as MIA, Estocin was declared dead after the war and posthumously awarded the Medal of Honor.

Possibly the most effective weapon system introduced by the Navy into the Vietnam War was the Grumman A-6 Intruder. For the first time, Naval Aviation had a truly all-weather, day and night, state-of-the-art attack plane. This ultra-sophisticated aircraft was an outgrowth of requirements made evident by the Korean War and the rapid technological advances in warfare experience in the years immediately following.

First flown in 1960, the Intruder was introduced into combat five years later with VA-75. Deployed in the *Independence* (CVA 62) with CVW-7, the bomber performed its mission well, reporting on-

Below: The Catapult Officer touches the flight deck as signal to launch a VA-75 A-6A Intruder. The Intruder's advanced computerized weapons system and the addition of a bombardier/navigator was responsible for its pinpoint bombing accuracy. VA-75's 'Sunday Punchers' were the first squadron to fly the A-6A in combat.

US Navy – PH CAR. C. Lister

One of the first Intruder squadrons to undertake combat duty in South-East Asia was VA-35 'Panthers', which completed successive tours of duty aboard USS *Enterprise* (CVAN 65) in 1966-7 and 1968. The aircraft shown here with an impressive array of 18 Mk 82 500-lb free-fall bombs is a standard production A-6A Intruder and features the markings employed during the second combat cruise, VA-35 returned to Oceana, Virginia and completed a Mediterranean deployment before again seeing action from USS *America* (CVA 66) in 1972-3.

USS ENTERPRISE
NAVY
VA-35
152940
10

Left: VF-21 pilots accounted for the first MiG kills of the war with AIM-7 Sparrow missiles, but the unit was typical of F-4B Phantom squadrons in that its aircraft were employed in several roles. Here an F-4B drops its load of 500-lb (227-kg) Snakeye bombs on surface targets.

station 27 June 1965. However, the first days of combat were disastrous. During the initial 28 days of combat employment, the 'Sunday Punchers' lost three A-6As because of premature explosion of Mk 82 500-lb (227-kg) bombs.

The problem was found to be with non-ejector bomb racks and electrical fuses. Use of non-ejector style racks, combined with instantaneous-arming electrical fuses, presented situations where, under certain conditions, the bombs could strike the drop aircraft after release. A modification of drop tactics requiring positive-g forces on the aircraft before release, and a switch to mechanical fuses eased the immediate situation. Later, multiple-ejector racks were employed to further aid in alleviating the problem. However, to this day, the basic problem of prematurely exploding ordnance still exists.

One other A-6 was lost during VA-75's deployment: this aircraft was lost in September to 37-mm anti-aircraft fire while making a night attack against PT boats south of Bach Long island. Of the eight VA-75 aircrew downed, four were returned safely to the *Independence*, two were captured and the last two were listed as KIA.

The Intruder's second combat cruise came with VA-85's 'Black Falcons' during 1965-6 in *Kitty Hawk* (CVA 63) and CVW-11. A loss of six aircraft during this cruise, combined with VA-75's experiences, brought a re-evaluation of the A-6's employment. All the sophistication in the world would not protect the aircraft against a chance hit in the right place from a rifle. Sending multi-million dollar airplanes against high-risk, low-value targets did not make sense, and Navy planners soon realized this. A shift to better utilization of the Intruder's capabilities against more worthwhile targets brought about a marked improvement in the combat performance of the A-6 program. This change, combined with the previously mentioned tactics and equipment changes, also resulted in a substantial reduction in losses of A-6 crews for the remainder of the war.

The McDonnell Douglas F-4 Phantom II was the newest-generation fighter for the Navy during Vietnam and would eventually replace the Vought F-8 Crusader. The F-4 proved to be a very capable bombing platform and was used in multiple roles during the war. It also became the standard fighter-bomber for the Air Force.

The AWG-10 radar and the radar-guided Sparrow missile gave the Phantom the capability of engaging enemy aircraft well beyond visual range. In all but a few isolated cases the rule of engagement, however, required aircrew first to identify their intended target visually before firing a missile. Thus, the advantage of firing a longer-range Sparrow (one which the North Vietnamese did not have) was blunted by these restrictions. This directive, in part, was why Navy fighter pilots tended to favor the heat-seeking Sidewinder.

The Phantom was fast. Even loaded with bombs it could outrun the other air wing attack aircraft. Equipped with the standard J79 turbojet engines, each producing 16,000 lb (7258 kg) of thrust, the Phantom reached a speed of Mach 2.6 during initial testing.

The F-8 Crusader became known as the 'MiG Master' during Vietnam, but it was actually the Phantom which racked up the most Navy MiG kills: Crusaders accounted for 18 confirmed MiGs downed, and Phantoms for 36.

In early April 1965 US Air Force strikes coming in the 'back door' to Hanoi from bases in Thailand had encountered the first MiG threat, but it was not until 17 June that the Navy provided the first MiG kills of the war. Two F-4B Phantoms of VF-21 from USS *Midway* (CVA 41) engaged four MiG-17s south of Hanoi. In the ensuing air battle, two of the MiGs were downed by the two Phantoms' radar-guided AIM-7 Sparrow missiles. Commander L.C. Page and his Radar Intercept Officer, Lieutenant J.C. Smith along with Lieutenant J.D. Batson and Lieutenant Commander R.B. Doremus, scored the first US victories over MiGs in Vietnam and were awarded the Silver Star Medal.

Left: MiG-killers Commander Louis C. Page and his Radar Intercept Officer Lieutenant J. C. Smith pose on the cockpit rail of their VF-21 F-4B Phantom II. The kill came on 17 June 1965, when they downed a MiG-17 with a Sparrow air-to-air missile. Theirs was the first downing of a North Vietnamese aircraft by a US Navy aircrew.

Right: A VA-85 A-6A Intruder taxies towards *Kitty Hawk*'s number one catapult shuttle in preparation for launch. Dark camouflage paint was applied to CVW-11 aircraft in order to evaluate its effectiveness in blending with the dark jungle terrain. It was thought that such camouflage would make US Navy aircraft less likely to be spotted and attacked from above by enemy MiGs.

In early December 1965, the nuclear-powered USS *Enterprise* (CVAN 65), carrying the largest air wing (CVW-9) ever deployed to the Western Pacific, brought the latest in warfare technology to the Tonkin Gulf. Arriving at Yankee Station following initial workups on Dixie Station, *Enterprise* joined *Kitty Hawk* and *Ticonderoga* in winding up the end of the year with one of the biggest strikes yet against the North Vietnamese. Until this point, the only targets on the 'authorized' list were bases and support installations. On 22 December a major industrial target was struck for the first time, the target being the thermal powerplant at Uong Bi, using the combined forces of the three carriers. That afternoon, when the strike aircraft departed the target 15 miles (24 km) north east of Haiphong, pilots debriefed that the sky was full of billowing smoke and that major portions of the plant had been destroyed. Two of *Enterprise*'s Douglas A-4s did not return from the strike.

Two days later, on 24 December, a bombing pause of indeterminate length went into effect. Through diplomatic channels, the US government asked North Vietnam to 'reciprocate' by making a serious contribution to peace. The supply of material and arms to the South intensified and the bombing halt ended on 31 January 1966. Only then did the Communists reply to the peace initiative with a terse diplomatic note from Hanoi totally denouncing the offered US peace terms.

During the 37-day bombing lull, continuing reconnaissance flights brought back ample evidence of the intensified military buildup in the North. Additional anti-aircraft artillery emplacements were built in and around Hanoi. Underground facilities for storage of petroleum products were constructed, increasing the difficulty for American aircrews to locate and destroy the POL. Bridges, which had been interdicted at such high cost in American aviator's lives and equipment, were rebuilt with impunity. The major accomplishments gained in the last months of 1965 were thrown away. And when the bombing resumed, none of the previous restrictions were lifted: foreign shipping (often with SAMs strapped to the decks) were to be avoided, MiG bases could not be hit, and

Below: *Kitty Hawk* (CVA 63) A-4 Skyhawks were painted in an experimental camouflage in hopes the aircraft would blend with the jungle terrain of South East Asia. Most of Attack Carrier Air Wing 11's aircraft were similarly painted for six months, but US Navy officials concluded the paint scheme was not effective and the aircraft were returned to US Navy gray following *Kitty Hawk*'s deployment. Oil from the engine oil breather on the Skyhawk's starboard fuselage has streaked the camouflage paint.

the large industrial targets surrounding Hanoi and Haiphong were off limits. In fact, as the strikes resumed, the limits were more restrictive than in 1965. Only armed reconnaissance strikes, which limited force only to the extent of protecting the photo planes, were authorized and then only south of 21° North. Essentially, this restriction eliminated all military pressure on the movement of war supplies to the South, as well as making US aircraft more vulnerable to the North's defenses.

Throughout the early months of 1966, US forces were hampered by the monsoon season. As the clouds began to clear in April, a new political philosophy was applied to the air war in the North. Where previously the emphasis had been on reactive strikes, now the emphasis was on interdiction, the cutting off of lines of supplies and communication.

On 1 April, little over a year after the beginning of the 'Rolling Thunder' campaign, 'Rolling Thunder 50' was authorized. For the first time, strikes against four key bridges and armed reconnaissance along the major lines of communication were allowed.

At this time also, the Navy began an experiment in aircraft camouflage. Half of the aircraft on board *Kitty Hawk* in Attack Carrier Air Wing 11 were repainted in dark green camouflage. It was hoped that the color would render the aircraft less visible over the jungle background of South East Asia. At the end of *Kitty Hawk*'s deployment the results were inconclusive. The green camouflage schemes were

Left: Rare F-4G Phantom II from VF-114 is taxied forward to the bow for parking following arrested landing on *Kitty Hawk*. The F-4G was similar to F-4B but had a modified, smaller fuel cell directly aft of the Radar Intercept Officer's cockpit which contained data link equipment. Note experimental camouflage paint scheme.

also evaluated by CVW-15 in *Constellation* and CVW-14 in *Enterprise*. Even though a similar US Air Force study resulted in a green camouflage paint scheme for all its tactical aircraft, the Navy retained gray aircraft with white underbellies for all of its tactical aircraft.

Victories over MiGs

In March 1966, the more capable, higher speed MiG-21 was sighted for the first time over North Vietnam. Although the Navy Phantom and Crusader fighter pilots itched for the chance to go against this new threat, it would be a US Air Force Phantom pilot who would down the first sleek MiG-21 nearly a month later.

Commander H.L. Marr, commanding officer of VF-211 at the time, related the first F-8 MiG kill in *Grumman Horizons*: 'We're roaring into the backwoods at about 1,500 feet in very poor weather. North of Haiphong, the A-4s make their bombing runs and the strike group comes off the target as briefed and the fighters fall in behind. Passing about 040 degrees (heading) LTJG Phil Vampatella, God bless his soul, calls "Tally Ho. Bogies at seven o'clock."

'I look down and see four MiG-17s about a mile and a half at 2,000 feet. We pull hard into them and the fight's on. I fire a short burst of cannon at one MiG, more for courage than anything else – just to hear my four cannon bang.

'We're doing about 450 kts and pulling seven to eight Gs and reverse hard right in a sharp scissors. I get a good 90° deflection gunshot but my cannon misses again and Phil goes after one and I after the other.

'Now I'm at 2,500 ft at his eight o'clock and the MiG is down around 1,500 ft with nowhere to go. I fire the first of my two Sidewinders, but the missile can't hack it and falls to the ground.

'The MiG has been in (after) burner for four or five minutes now and is mighty low on fuel, so he rolls and heads straight for his base. I roll in behind, stuff in burner and close at 500 kts. At a half mile, I fire my last 'Winder and it chops off his tail and starboard wing. He goes tumbling end over end. The poor pilot doesn't even have a chance to eject.

'With nothing more to fire, I light burner again and make a hasty retreat out the back door. By the time I got back to the *Hancock* our whole strike group was aboard without a scratch. After "telling" the (Air) Boss I'm going to make a victory flyby, I come down the port side below the elevator, big victory roll, break and come aboard to the wildest reception the world's ever seen to celebrate the first MiG kill by an F-8 Crusader.'

Just nine days later, Lieutenant (JG) Vampa-

Below left: Commander H.L. Marr (right) is congratulated by his wingman, Lieutenant (JG) Phillip Vampatella, after his victory over a MiG-17 in June 1966. Vampatella equalled the score just nine days later.

Below: An RVAH-11 RA-5C Vigilante in experimental paint scheme grabs an early arresting wire on *Kitty Hawk*. The Vigilante was one of the largest and fastest aircraft ever to have been routinely flown on and off carrier decks.

Above; Safely back on the deck of USS *Oriskany* (CVA 34), Commander Dick Bellinger recounts the maneuvers of his victory over a MiG-21 on 9 October 1966.

Below: Douglas A-3 Skywarriors performed a variety of missions in Vietnam, including bombing, tanking, electronic sensing, radio relay and surface-to-air missile warning. This black RA-3B of VAP-61 was used for night photo-reconnaissance.

tella, Marr's wingman, would score another MiG-17 kill. In a treetop level, high-speed engagement, the young fighter pilot maneuvered his crippled fighter into a firing position, blasting the MiG out of the sky. His heroic dogfight while low on fuel made numerous headlines in the United States and became strong motivation for the fledgling fighter pilots yet to make their first combat cruise.

On 23 June 1966, permission from Washington was finally granted to strike petroleum, oil and lubricants (POL) targets. But, before the strikes could be executed, word of the mounting attacks was somehow leaked to the press, and the North Vietnamese, in fact all the world, knew the US plans. While Washington planners directed utmost care be taken to minimize civilian casualties, leaks to the press often resulted in missions many times more dangerous to US pilots. Following the initial permission to strike the POL targets came indecision, cancellation of the strikes on 25 June, then shortly after their approval once again.

On 29 June 1966, Navy attack aircraft and fighters struck the POL storage facilities near Haiphong. Aircraft from Attack Carrier Air Wing 14, off *Ranger* (CVA 61), hit the complex. VA-146 and VA-55's Douglas A-4Cs unleashed 19 tons of iron bombs and fired 5-in (127-mm) Zuni rockets, leaving the facility a burning shambles with columns of black smoke billowing skyward.

Throughout the summer months the direction from Washington in the bombing campaign was toward POL storage. Unfortunately, the North had ample warning over the previous year and had been able to disperse its supplies as well as build underground storage areas. With the restrictions placed on foreign shipping, resupply countered the effects of the bombing. A combined strategy of interdiction and POL strikes as recommended by the military leaders would have been more effective in slowing

or stopping resupply of the Communists in the South. This, however, was not approved by Washington.

In the fall of 1966, Commander Dick Bellinger, Skipper of VF-162, was credited with the first Navy-versus-MiG-21 victory. Bellinger's victory was even more rewarding as he was able to 'turn around' a previous mission. On 17 July, a MiG-17 severely damaged his F-8E in dogfight. Unable to aerial-refuel his jet, Bellinger was forced to eject before he could nurse the plane to a landing at DaNang.

Now, on 9 October, Bellinger intercepted MiGs while providing air cover for a strike group from *Intrepid* (CVS 11). *Superheat* 210, in company with three other F-8s from *Oriskany* (CVA 34), met the MiGs as they jumped *Intrepid*'s A-4s. Spotting a MiG-21 breaking off its attack on the strike group, 210 chased the MiG toward the ground, firing two heat-seeking missiles. Pulling back on the stick, Bellinger maneuvered to avoid hitting the ground. Looking back over his shoulder he sighted the burning wreckage of the Soviet-built interceptor in the rice paddies below.

Even without any real threat to its task groups off the Vietnamese coast, the Navy suffered casualties there as well as over land. On 26 October, as two sailors were stowing parachute flares in a storage locker on board *Oriskany*, a massive fire erupted in the space. Ordnance was touched off by the inferno and the fire spread to the hangar deck below and into several living quarters. Flames engulfed the fantail and spread below decks, igniting bombs and ammunition. Through heroic efforts the fire was brought under control, but damage to aircraft and the ship was severe. At final count 132 were dead, two missing and presumed dead, and 62 injured.

Early 1967 brought with it little MiG activity. The MiGs had become adept at engaging the incoming American strike aircraft, only attempting

US Navy

to fight when it was to their advantage. Despite pleas to allow strikes on the MiG bases, as well as on other significant targets, the MiG fields were sanctuaries until April 1967. Finally succumbing to the persistent requests of the Pacific commanders, the Washington planners gave the go ahead to strike Kep, the North's biggest MiG field.

Planes from the *Kitty Hawk* and *Bon Homme Richard* (CVA 31) co-ordinated a strike against the airfield located 37 miles (60 km) north east of Hanoi. The attacks were delivered by Grumman A-6A Intruders and A-4 Skyhawks in the daylight of 24 April, followed by an A-6 attack that same night. The attacks left craters in the 7,000-ft (2135-m) single main runway and damaged several MiGs and support facilities on the ground. Two F-4B Phantoms from VF-114 escorting the strike group caught two MiG-17s attempting to take-off to intercept the incoming planes. The MiGs were quickly downed before any damage could be done.

The skies soon became the scenes of major air battles. During the January to June period the Air Force downed 46 MiGs. In the April to July time-frame the Navy accounted for another 12 kills. Even though these numbers amounted to a major portion of the North's air force, the lost planes were soon replaced by the Chinese and Soviets.

During a strike on Kep airfield on 1 May, Lieutenant Commander Ted 'T.R.' Swartz scored one of the most unusual MiG kills recorded during the war. While rolling in on his assigned target on the airfield in his A-4C, Swartz was advised by his wingman that he had a MiG-17 closing behind him. Aborting his attack, he pulled his Skyhawk hard into the attacking MiG and rolled the aircraft, causing the MiG to overshoot its intended target. Now inside the MiG's turn, Swartz armed his 5-in (127-mm) Zuni unguided rocket pods, pointed the A-4's nose at the MiG and fired. The hail of rockets streaked toward the MiG, exploding it on impact. The jubilant Skyhawk pilot returned to 'Bonnie Dick' with the only MiG kill by unguided rockets that would be scored during the Vietnam war.

29
Support Missions and Continuing Action

Land-based Naval Aviation units also saw action in Vietnam and if not as much in the limelight as their carrier counterparts, they served no less important functions. From the early stages of US participation in the war, VP units based out of such American-built fields in South Vietnam as Cam Rahn Bay and Da Nang, flew maritime surveillance missions. These flights were an effort to help stem infiltration of personnel and equipment transported via small craft down the Vietnamese coastline and rivers. Lockheed P-2 Neptunes, Martin P-5 Marlins and later, after 1967, Lockheed P-3 Orions, all were deployed in this capacity, their long endurance being ideal for these missions. The Vietnam War was also the scene of the Navy's last seaplane operations. The last of the graceful 'big boats' left the country in 1967, having operated from Cam Rahn Bay and Sangley Point in the Philippines. The final

Above: RIO Ensign James Lainge ejects from a VF-114 F-4B Phantom following a raid on Kep airfield, North Vietnam, in April 1967. AIM-7 and AIM-9 missiles are carried by the stricken aircraft, which was operating from USS *Kitty Hawk* (CVA 63). Pilot, Lieutenant Commander 'Ev' Southwick, followed soon after when he was unable to transfer fuel. The crew had downed a MiG-17 on this flight.

Below: Martin's highly distinctive SP-5B Marlin was the last flying-boat to see active service with the Navy's patrol force, finally being retired by VP-40 at the end of October 1967. In this evocative view, an SP-5B gets airborne for a night patrol off the coast of Vietnam.

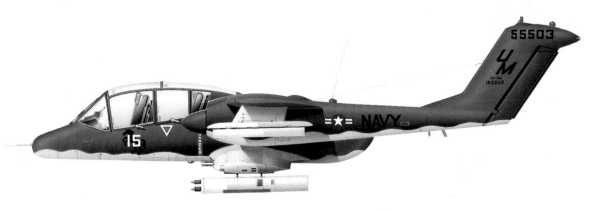

Right: Employed mainly in the light attack role, the Rockwell OV-10A Broncos of VAL-4 'Black Ponies' were stationed at Binh Thuy, South Vietnam, between 1969 and 1972. Apart from a handful of similar aircraft employed by VS-41 for training, these were the only OV-10s used by the Navy.

Below: The seaplane tender USS *Currituck* provides support to an SP-5B Marlin of VP-40 during the last combat deployment of this seaplane. Much of the work performed by patrol squadrons was tedious, but they played an important part in cutting down the flow of supplies to the Viet Cong.

Above right: In addition to carrier-based aircraft, VQ-1 provided land-based electronic eavesdropping. EP-3B aircraft patrolling offshore in the Tonkin Gulf would detect surface-to-air missile launches.

Below: A variety of aerial cameras could be concurrently used by this VAP-61 RA-3B reconnaissance version of the Skywarrior. The Skywarrior proved to be a stable photographic platform but was slower and more vulnerable to ground defenses than the RF-8 Crusader and RA-5C Vigilante.

operational flight of a Navy seaplane came 6 November 1967, when a VP-40 SP-5B lifted from San Diego Bay.

Operating under the title of 'Market Time', the VP squadrons patrolled from southern Cambodia to the DMZ and out into the Gulf of Tonkin. Another function of their mission was ocean surveillance patrols monitoring Communist-bloc nations' shipping as well as keeping a general overview of the sea-lanes near Vietnam.

As the war in the North escalated, several types of special supporting missions were flown by the land-based Navy units. Once again ocean surveil-lance was critical to accurate intelligence on the movement of Communist-bloc shipping and the import of war supplies. The vast majority of North Vietnam's war matériel was processed through the port of Haiphong. VQ-1's Lockheed EC-121s and EP-3s were used to gather enemy electronic signals and radio transmissions, supplementing their carrier counterpart, the Douglas EA-3. Giving direct support to the tactical aircrew were two important missions flown by the ECM outfits: 'Luzon' and 'Motel'. Orbiting high in the Tonkin Gulf, 'Luzon' relayed critical radio transmissions, extending the radio range and passing time-critical information. 'Motel' used sensitive electronic eavesdropping equipment to detect the launch of SAMs, pinpointed their location and broadcast the launch to unsuspecting aircraft over the beach.

In 1971, the Navy received North American OV-10A Broncos and commissioned a new type squadron, VAL-4 (Light Attack Squadron 4). Serving alongside another new Navy squadron, HAL-3

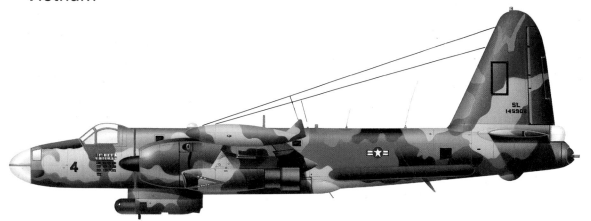

Right: Equipped with cannon, grenade launchers, forward-looking infra-red and low-light TV gear, this AP-2H Neptune gunship was employed by VAH-21 at Cam Ranh Bay on night missions against the trucks plying the Ho Chi Minh Trail.

Below left: VAL-4 OV-10A Broncos over the IV Corps area in South Vietnam. VAL-4 flew attack and reconnaissance missions and provided Forward Air Control for aircraft flying off US carriers on Dixie Station.

(Helicopter Light Attack Squadron 3) flying Bell UH-1B 'Hueys', the two in-country Navy units were responsible for providing protection for the river convoys travelling the Mekong River from the South China Sea to the inland port of Saigon.

Two other unique land-based squadrons were commissioned for participation in the Vietnam War. They were VO-67 and VAH-21, both of which flew P-2 Neptunes specially modified for counter-insurgency operations.

The first of these special operations squadrons, VO-67 (the first use of the Observation Squadron designator since 1948) began operations from Nakhon Phanom in Thailand in November 1967. Flying OP-2Es, the squadron's mission involved dropping Spikebuoy and Adsid acoustical sensors

along the Ho Chi Minh Trail in a vain attempt to build an 'electronic field' around North Vietnam. After quickly sustaining three losses, and with a lack of identifiable results, the short-lived squadron was decommissioned in July 1968.

The second special operations squadron was VAH-21, which appeared in September 1968 as an outgrowth of Naval Air Test Center 'Project TRIM'. An acronym for Trails and Roads Interdiction Multisensor, TRIM was an electro-optical sensing system designed to ferret out night insurgency

Above: VO-67 OP-2E Neptunes provided support for tactical forces through electronic sensing devices dropped along the Ho Chi Minh Trail.

As well as offshore surveillance by patrol aircraft, the Navy was also responsible for monitoring inland waterways during the Vietnam War. Code-named 'Game Warden', this mission was fulfilled by Bell UH-1B Iroquois helicopters assigned to HAL-3 at Binh Thuy.

A Bell UH-1B 'Huey' in company with a Navy Swift Boat on the Cua Lon River. Navy Hueys worked in co-ordination with Swift Boats in patrolling enemy river and coastal access for South Vietnam.

Left: In addition to being a fine attack aircraft, the Douglas Skyraider proved highly adaptable to other missions. One of many variants was the EA-1F ECM version. VAW-33 EA-1F here is about to launch from USS *Intrepid* (CVS 11) for the last combat mission of a Skyraider in the Vietnam war, on 18 September 1967.

operations by the North Vietnamese and Viet Cong. Four SP-2Hs were extensively modified with electronic sensors and specialized weapons for night interdiction missions and redesignated AP-2H. Primarily designed as a combat operational test unit for the electronic equipment, the squadron staged from NAS Sangley Point and operated the AP-2Hs from Cam Rahn Bay until May 1969. By July 1969, VAH-21 had been disbanded. Much of the squadron equipment was transferred to the Army which flew AP-2Es, another Neptune version modified for night attack. Much of the technology perfected by VAH-21's AP-2Hs was later used in the A-6C TRIM version of the Intruder and paved the way for today's A-6E TRAM aircraft.

Retirement of the CVS

It was during the Vietnam War that the Navy began the phaseout of the CVS program. The carriers, although modernized in the 1950s, were still basically World War II 'Essex' class ships. By

the late 1960s they were growing old and had become expensive to maintain. With neither the Soviet Union nor the Chinese Communists presenting any submarine threat in the Gulf of Tonkin, the Grumman S-2 squadrons were utilized mostly in support roles such as 'Market Time' and ocean surveillance. The helos, as mentioned, assumed the combat SAR mission. Some ASW work was performed by the CVSs throughout the war, but on a very limited basis.

The war continued to drag on, devouring the Navy's limited funds. The CVS program suffered from this as sufficient monies were never allocated to develop new ships and aircraft to replace the obsolescent ASW forces. During the mid-1960s the CVSs began to rapidly disappear from both the Atlantic and Pacific Fleets. *Ticonderoga* (CVS 14), converted from a CVA in 1969, was the last Pacific Fleet CVS and was decommissioned on 1 September 1973. *Intrepid*, after her three war cruises as a limited-CVA, returned to her CVS role with the

Right: Patrol Squadron VP-1 was one of many such units which deployed to South-East Asia in support of the Vietnam War effort. Here, a VP-1 Lockheed SP-2H Neptune overflies some Vietnamese junks during the course of a 'Market Time' offshore surveillance mission.

Left: S-2E Trackers turn up on aft end of the flight deck of *Hornet* (CVS 12) in preparation for ASW mission. Trackers were the US Navy's primary carrier-based ASW aircraft for more than 20 years, until retired from VS-37 in 1976.

Vietnam

Atlantic Fleet and was decommissioned on 30 March 1974. With the demise of *Intrepid*, the CVS program had come to its end. New, more capable models of the P-3 Orion, coupled with development of sophisticated offshore underwater detection systems, replaced the CVS's detection and tracking role. The carrierborne ASW squadrons were integrated into the big-deck carrier air wings in the mid-1970s to assume the function of ASW protection for the carrier battle groups.

As the war developed, much of the campaign to interdict the flow of supplies and materials concentrated on North Vietnam's bridges. The two main lines from China to Hanoi, the north east and north west rail lines, were built on numerous bridges which spanned the large gorges in the mountainous terrain. As the terrain flattens toward the industrial center of Hanoi, the bridges cross the many tributaries of the Red River. South of Hanoi and Haiphong, several bridges forded the paddies of the rice-rich delta area. Most of the bridges were narrow, built for only one rail track; but for the North Vietnamese the bridges were multi-purpose. Planks laid along the rails allowed vehicles and pedestrians to use the bridge between trains. Bridges became choke points for moving supplies and thus became a major focus for the interdiction campaign. But the bridges were not easy targets. Generally built with a steel framework, they were then covered by wooden planking. Unless the bombs hit precisely in a critical structural member, they did little damage. Bombs which struck the bridge surface simply went through the wood planking, detonating harmlessly below. The North also knew the value of the bridges and was always prepared. The approaches to the critical bridges were lined with anti-aircraft gun emplacements. Repair equipment and materials were stockpiled so any damage done to the bridge during daylight could be quickly repaired at night. Pontoon bridges were kept along the river banks, ready to be put into place across the waterways at night, either to supplement the normal bridge traffic or to provide a detour while repairs were in progress. Many of the bridges were hit and damaged innumerable times only to be put back into operation a short time later.

One such bridge symbolized both the frustration of the military and how resolute were the defending Communists. This was the Thanh Hao Bridge, a target that became infamous with Navy and Air Force aircrews. The structure had been built by the French of steel girders on massive concrete piers. It spanned the Song Ma River on the coastal Route

One, 75 miles (120 km) south of Hanoi and was used for both rail and highway traffic. It was called the 'Dragon's Jaw' by the Vietnamese.

The Thanh Hoa Bridge was an important link in the daily movement of military supplies southward. Even though photographic reconnaissance showed a pontoon bridge nearby could be used to reroute truck traffic, elimination of the rail passage and its impact on morale became an overriding obsession.

The bridge was heavily defended. Anti-aircraft artillery positions lined the approaches to the bridge with 23- and 37-mm guns, making it both one of the toughest targets to hit and one of the best defended in all of North Vietnam.

Authorization to attack the Thanh Hoa Bridge first came on 1 April 1965 with 'Rolling Thunder 9'. For the next year the bridge was targeted an average of twice a month with little success. The minor damage was quickly repaired and the span was never out of service for any great length of time. The massive concrete abutments took numerous direct hits, but the ordnance lacked the force required to knock out such a massive target. Until the 1968 bombing halt temporarily stopped all attacks, over 600 sorties were directed on the bridge. The resulting damage was minimal, but the price paid high: 39 aircraft and 57 aircrew were lost to the Thanh Hoa Bridge.

When bombing resumed in 1972, new technology had paved the way for the bridge's destruction. Air Force McDonnell Douglas F-4s, using the pinpoint accuracy of laser-guided 'smart' bombs, finally dropped the 540-ft (165-m) span, cutting off rail traffic for the remainder of the war. The flow of

Above: Two F-4s from VF-21 skirt some 'dirty' weather over South Vietnam on their way back from an 'in-country' strike. The triple-ejector racks (TERs) which allowed the carriage of bombs can be seen on the wing pylons with a centreline multiple-ejector rack (MER).

Below: VQ-1 Douglas EA-3B Skywarrior comes aboard USS *Hancock* (CVA 19). The squadron's EA-3s, with the call-sign 'Peter Rabbit' (derived from the 'PR' tail codes), were deployed in small numbers aboard carriers in the South China Sea. Their primary mission was electronic eavesdropping.

Far left: Thanh Hoa railroad and highway bridge after one span was dropped by laser-guided bombs. The Thanh Hoa bridge defied attempts to destroy it from March 1965 until it was finally dropped on 13 May 1972. Note the barges (tied to the bridge) used to move supplies across the waterway.

supplies was not slowed, however, as the Communists employed alternative methods of moving the materials across the waterway.

On 29 July 1967, CTF-77 suffered its second catastrophic carrier fire. *Forrestal* (CVA 59) had left Norfolk, Virginia the month before with CVW-17 embarked and joined the Pacific units on Yankee Station. After just four short days of combat operations, tragedy struck.

Aircraft had been spotted on the flight deck, armed and fuelled, and were in final preparations for start-up before the second launch of the day. The jet starting units were fired up and as one unit was backed into position to start an F-4, its hot exhaust blew directly on the Phantom's loaded Zuni rocket pack. A Zuni, ignited by the starter's exhaust heat, streaked across the crowded flight deck and slammed into a loaded Douglas A-4, which burst into flames. The fire engulfed the fantail and spread quickly below decks, touching off bombs and ammunition. Aircraft and ordnance exploded, blowing men overboard. Others were caught in the searing flames and choking smoke in the decks below.

Nearby units quickly came to assist in helping both to fight the fire and to care for the injured. Above deck, the fire was controlled and put out within an hour, but the fire in the bowels of the giant carrier raged on for another 12 hours.

It was only through efforts of extreme heroism by ship and air wing personnel that the fire and damage were contained. Ordnance was literally pulled off the loaded and sometimes burning planes and jettisoned overboard. Searingly heated 250- and 500-lb (113- and 227-kg) bombs were carried or rolled to the deck edge to be thrown over the side.

Aircraft and the ship suffered severe damage: 134 men were lost and 62 injured, and 21 aircraft were totally destroyed with another 43 damaged. The estimated cost of repair was over $70 million.

Forrestal left the line, pulling into Subic Bay, Philippines for temporary repairs and returned to Norfolk on 14 September 1967.

The vital role of SAR

The Navy pilots who took the risks and flew the hazardous missions over hostile territory could take comfort that all stops would be removed if there was even the faintest chance that a downed aviator could be rescued. The real heroes of these efforts were the pilots and aircrew of the search and rescue helicopters, better termed Combat SAR.

At the war's beginning there were no dedicated SAR forces. Helicopters, whose primary mission was anti-submarine warfare, were quickly converted to the Combat SAR mission. Armor plating was added along with machine-guns, and various camouflage schemes usually replaced the standard gray and white paint.

The Sikorsky SH-3A Sea King became the primary Navy rescue vehicle although Kaman HU-2Bs made numerous pickups and some were modified with a chin turret, becoming HH-2Cs. The first Combat SAR Sea Kings arrived in Vietnam in 1966 with HS-6 aboard the anti-submarine warfare carrier *Kearsarge* (CVS-33). Five SH-3A Sea Kings had been modified for the SAR mission by the removal of their sonar and addition of armor plating around the engines, transmission and seats. A 7.62-mm (0.3-in) machine-gun was added for the door gunner. A large fuel capacity and 140 mph (225 km/h) top speed, along with an all-weather hover

Below: The still-smouldering and charred remains of three F-4Bs lay testament to the tragedy aboard USS *Forrestal* after the inadvertent firing of a Zuni rocket and the ensuing fire and explosions.

capability, made the Sea King ideal for the mission. Its night rescue capability was improved as well. The night low-visibility hover proved much easier by using the hover coupler developed for ASW sonar dipping.

Haiphong harbor became the site of several daring rescues. On 26 April 1967, Lieutenant Steve Millikin, of HS-2, earned the Silver Star and his copilot a Distinguished Flying Cross for the dramatic rescue off Haiphong of a downed A-4 pilot.

Millikin and his crew were operating from the north SAR station ship *Mahan* (DLG 11) in the northern Gulf. The A-4E of Lieutenant (JG) J.W. Cain, assigned to VA-192 in *Ticonderoga*, had been hit while on the morning Alpha strike against POL targets at Haiphong. Cain headed his stricken A-4 back toward the sea. But before he could make it to the safety of the Gulf, he was forced to eject as the Skyhawk's cockpit filled with smoke and the aircraft began an uncontrollable roll.

The SH-3A was orbiting the pre-assigned area when word came of the A-4 in trouble. Millikin immediately turned the helo in toward the harbor and was soon joined by four ResCap Douglas A-1s from VA-15 and VA-52 from 'Tico' and 'Bonnie Dick'. They crossed the mouth of the harbor at about 200 ft (60 m) at full bore; in Millikin's words, 'I saw 145 kts . . . redline (is) 144 . . . and I'm sure we went faster.' The helo crew sighted Cain in the water between a peninsula and a small island and brought the Sea King into a hover. Just 250 yds (230 m) from the shoreline, the helo immediately came under heavy enemy fire, from both the neck of land and from the island. The ResCap 'Spads' immediately brought their awesome firepower to bear, delivering rockets, bombs and strafing during their runs.

Enemy mortar shelling continued, some landing within yards of the helo. Big geysers of water erupted nearby as the shore gunners zeroed in on their stationary target. Millikin struggled to hold the helo steady over the downed aviator, but at each 'whomp' from the incoming shells and the splash of cascading water, he instinctively pulled up on the collective, rising up from the hover.

The helo pulled the rescue sling several times and the desperate A-4 pilot grabbed anxiously for the cable. The mortar splashes came closer as the

gunners now found the correct range. Meanwhile, the copilot directed the 'Spads' in their runs on the island, indicating the sources of ground fire. Then, with the downed pilot scrambling into the side door off the hoist, Millikin beat a hasty retreat to the safety of the Gulf.

As the helo exited, a late-arriving A-4 unloaded its four 750-lb (340-kg) bombs on the source of the intensive fire. The whole side of the island slid into the sea.

With the exhausted but happy Cain safely aboard and his crew unscathed, Millikin wheeled his shrapnel-punctured Sea King around and headed for the *Mahan*. Once back over the destroyer, the shaken Millikin looked at the tiny helo spot on the aft end and asked his copilot if he would like to make the landing. In quick reply, the equally shaken copilot responded, 'Not me, you're the Pilot in Command!'

Another helo pilot, Lieutenant (JG) Clyde E. Lassen of HC-7, put new meaning into the phrase 'above and beyond the call of duty'. On the night of 19 June 1968, Lassen and his crew were launched from *Preble* (DLG 15) in a UH-2A to rescue an F-4 crew down 20 miles (32 km) inside North Vietnam. Attempting the rescue by illumination flares, and under heavy enemy fire, the helo struck a tree in the darkness after the flares burned out. Maintaining control of the badly vibrating Seasprite, Lassen

Above: An HC-7 HH-2C Seasprite. HC-7 flew combat search-and-rescue missions throughout the war, picking up downed US aircrew while flying Seasprite and Sea King helicopters.

Left: An HS-2 SH-3A Sea King is tied down to the destroyer *Mahan* (DLG 11) located in the northern Tonkin Gulf. The aircraft was used for combat search-and-rescue missions into North Vietnam and the waters near Haiphong. This aircraft was lost at sea with no trace of survivors two weeks after this photograph was taken.

US Navy

Above: USS *Intrepid* sails in her 'special' attack carrier capacity with McDonnell Douglas A-4 Skyhawks from CVW-10 on deck along with E-1Bs and RF-8As. The A-4s were to see particularly heavy action, resulting in several losses.

made another attempt under new flares, which also burned out before the rescue could be completed. All the while still under intense fire, Lassen, realizing the danger involved, turned on his landing lights and effected the rescue. Unscathed, the crew beat a hasty retreat with the Phantom crew to land aboard *Jouett* (DLG 29) with only five minutes fuel remaining.

These are only two of the incredibly courageous rescues and attempts made by US Navy helo pilots during the Vietnam War. During the 10-year conflict US Navy SAR forces rescued over 200 downed aircrewmen from the Gulf of Tonkin and 27 from inland North Vietnam. The price was dear, however. Over land, the Navy lost two SAR aircraft for every three aircrewmen rescued. Many more rescues were attempted than were successful.

If it was the MiGs that the US fighters were after, the reverse was not true for the MiGs. If the MiG pilot could momentarily divert the bomber pilot's attention, force him to jettison his ordnance load short of the target, or even break up his formation, at least part of the MiG pilot's mission was a success. It was the attack aircraft the MiGs were after. In fact, the North Vietnamese pilots avoided the fighters.

The MiGs attacked when and where it was to

their advantage, employing similar tactics to their comrades on the ground: hit and run. The tactical advantage belonged to the North Vietnamese, who enjoyed the benefits of accurate ground-controlled radar intercept (GCI) for short-range missions with lots of fuel for combat, and they usually had adequate forewarning of incoming strikes. That advance warning came either from a Soviet intelligence gathering ship (AGI) which shadowed the carriers, or from numerous North Vietnamese fishing junks throughout the Gulf.

The strike groups were severely limited in mission planning. The targets, in particular those of any significance, were hand-picked in Washington. It was not unusual that even the specific tactic used to strike the target was directed from half the world away. Against the massive air defenses of the North, Navy pilots came to realize that 'speed was life'. But often all the speed they could muster was not enough. The fully loaded A-4, typically carrying six to ten Mk 82 500-lb (227-kg) bombs, could reach barely 400 mph (644 km/h). Against a Mach 2.5 'Guideline' SAM, or a 690-mph (1110-km/h) MiG-21 in a slashing attack, the Skyhawk often came up short.

In mid-1967 *Intrepid*, which normally carried a CVSG complement of Grumman S-2s and Sikorsky SH-3s for its anti-submarine mission, was outfitted with A-4s, Air Wing 10 being temporarily assigned to this 'special' attack carrier.

Intrepid reported on Yankee Station with its three embarked A-4 squadrons: VA-34, VA-15 and VSF-3. The A-4s flew against the same type targets that the other air wings did from the DMZ north to Hanoi and Haiphong. Trans-shipment points, power stations, small shipping bridges, electrical relay stations, truck parks, trains and oil and ammo storage areas all became CVW-10 targets.

For VA-34, the '*Blue Blasters*', the six-month cruise would cost them four aircraft lost to enemy fire. All four pilots ejected safely from their battle damaged planes, but two pilots would be forced to wait out the remainder of the war as POWs.

One of these more fortunate to get his crippled plane to the coastline was Lieutenant Commander Sam Hawkins. On a flak-suppression mission against the Haiphong railroad yards, on 18 September 1967, Hawkins' A-4C took a lethal hit from a SAM. Inbound to the target at 5,000 ft (1525 m) and doing 370 mph (595 km/h) Hawkins received a SAM warning off his right. Maneuvering his A-4

Lieutenant Clark Van Nostrom

Right: Bombs explode in the city of Haiphong. It was only near the war's end that major targets in the cities of Hanoi and Haiphong could be struck.

hard down and to the right against the upcoming missile, he reversed back left at 3,000 ft (915 m). Off to his left he spotted two more SAMs. Hawkins was unable to react in time to this new threat, and one of the missiles detonated with a shattering explosion within 100 ft (30 m) of his plane. With heavy damage over the entire fuselage, no radio or oxygen, and the ailerons frozen, Hawkins fought for control of the plane as it headed toward the ground in a 40° dive. Struggling to get the nose of the stricken plane back toward the horizon, he forced the A-4 back toward the water using all the rudder he could jam in.

Joined by his wingman, who signaled for him to eject, Hawkins asked back if he was on fire, and again his wingman gave the eject signal. Hawkins, by now 10 miles (16 km) out into the Gulf, initiated ejection and was rescued uninjured by a SAR helicopter.

The strike continued and MiG activity was constant, if light. Two MiG-21s fell to Navy fighter pilots in August and another two in October. On 24 October 1967, the largest MiG base, and the only major airstrip not previously hit, was finally given the OK. Phuc Yen airfield 11 miles (18 km) north of Hanoi, was attacked in a massive co-ordinated strike with Navy and Air Force aircraft. Pilots flew through some of the heaviest SAM barrages of the war to deliver their bomb loads. On debrief, crews estimated at least 30 SAMs were launched as they pounded the 10,500-ft (3200-m) runway with 500- and 750-lb (227- and 340-kg) bombs. The next day, US Navy bombers and fighters from *Coral Sea* again struck Phuc Yen, battering a large aircraft revetment area and taxiway north of the strip. This time the aircraft found only moderate resistance. MiGs were sighted airborne but none attempted to close on the strike group. In the two raids, two VF-151 F-4Bs were hit and downed by surface-to-air missiles.

In December *Ranger* returned to Yankee Station. In the time she had been away from Vietnam, her

two light attack squadrons, VA-146 and VA-147, had transitioned to the new Vought A-7A Corsair II.

Debut of the A-7

In 1963 the Navy had sought a replacement aircraft for the aging A-4, one which would have a greater payload and range. *Ranger* now was the first carrier to deploy this new aircraft. The Corsair II, its outward appearance resembling the Vought-built F-8, was designed with six underwing hardpoints to carry ordnance, two more than the A-4. Its combat range of 700 miles (1125 km) gave an enhanced range and endurance which proved ideal in the Vietnam theater. It could carry all the latest weapons in the Navy inventory: general-purpose and nuclear bombs, 2.75-in (70-mm) and 5-in (127-mm) Zuni rockets, AGM-45 Shrike anti-radiation

Above: Lieutenant (JG) D. R. Earl, wounded by ground fire over North Vietnam, takes a barricade engagement aboard the *Oriskany*. Such engagements normally resulted in only minor aircraft damage and the planes were usually flying again within days.

Below: 'Ironhand' A-7 launching from *Ranger*: the aircraft is configured with Shrike anti-radiation missiles and cluster bombs. Cluster bombs were used effectively against anti-aircraft artillery.

Above: A pair of bomb-laden Grumman A-6A Intruders from VA-196 aboard USS *Constellation* (CVA 64) head for North Vietnam during the latter half of 1968. Introduced to combat in 1965, the Intruder overcame an unhappy debut to compile an impressive war record.

Below: A diamond formation of VF-211 F-8 Crusader aircraft, which flew fighter missions from the smaller 'Essex' class carriers *Hancock*, *Bon Homme Richard*, *Oriskany*, *Intrepid* and *Ticonderoga*.

missiles, Walleye glide bombs, cluster bombs and Bullpup air-to-surface missiles. It also had an internally-mounted 20-mm Gatling gun and two fuselage Sidewinder stations. Its normal armament load was 4,000 lb (1814 kg), but it could carry up to 15,000 lb (6804 kg) for short missions. Incorporation of advanced avionics made it a very accurate clear-air-mass bombing platform. With a 12,000-lb (5443-kg) thrust Pratt & Whitney TF30 turbofan engine, later upgraded in the A-7E to a 15,000-lb (6804-kg) thrust TF41, the Corsair II could maintain a somewhat faster attack speed than the older A-4.

The new attack aircraft went into combat for the first time with VA-147 from *Ranger* on 4 December 1967. VA-97 and VA-27 were next to get the new A-7A. During the six-month *Ranger* combat-deployment of VA-147, only one Corsair was lost to enemy fire.

Reconnaissance flights over the Christmas and New Year's truce brought back information that the Communists were pouring into South Vietnam unabated through the Ho Chi Minh Trail in Laos. Movements were especially heavy during the first two weeks of January 1968.

On 29 January, a 36-hour ceasefire for the *Tet* religious holiday began with many of the South Vietnamese going home on leave. Enemy activity soon forced cancellation of leave and the ceasefire. Two days later, just before the beginning of *Tet*, the Communists launched massive ground attacks throughout South Vietnam. Viet Cong local insurgents and North Vietnamese regulars attacked every important city, provincial capital and military installation in South Vietnam. The cities of Pleiku, Nha Trang, DaNang, and Qui Nhon were attacked. The ancient city of Hue in I Corps was overrun. In Saigon, Viet Cong blasted holes in the palace and US Embassy walls and entered the courtyards. The insurgents were soon repulsed, but harsh fighting continued throughout the provinces.

In north western I Corps, near the Laotian border and just below the DMZ, North Vietnamese troops stormed the Ashau Valley and the American outpost at Khe Sanh. Khe Sanh was manned initially in 1962 by the Army and augmented in 1967 with Marines. After 71 days of intensive fighting, extensive airborne resupply, and large amounts of tactical and strategic support, the invading Communists were repulsed. For Khe Sanh, unlike Dien Bien Phu, there had been massive air support.

The *Tet* Offensive by the Communists in 1968 was a tactical disaster for them. The enemy sustained wholesale losses of manpower and were unable to gain any permanent tactical advantage. Within weeks they lost any territory they had been able to occupy. However, the propaganda effect of the offensive gained them advantages beyond their

Chance-Vought's classic Crusader was the last pure single-seat fighter to be developed for the US Navy, and served with front-line elements of this air arm for almost 20 years, with well over 1,000 being built. The example shown here, carrying Sidewinder air-to-air missiles, is an F-8E of Fighter Squadron VF-53 'Iron Angels' and is shown in the markings applied during the course of a combat cruise aboard USS *Hancock* (CVA 19) as part of Carrier Air Wing Five (CVW-5) between January and July 1967.

Keith Fretwell

imagination. Their supposed ability to strike wherever and whenever they chose was reported by the press and TV media in the US, according them a strength they did not possess. In the South, they were a beaten force. Anti-war protests mounted in the US, pushing an already vacillating government into indecisiveness that would cause the loss of many more Naval Aviators over the next five years.

30
Bombing Halts and Politics

Once again questioning the use of tactical air power as a means to force the Communists to the conference table, on 31 March 1968, President Johnson called for a halt in all bombing north of the 20th parallel; essentially all of North Vietnam except for the extreme southern panhandle was off-limits. It was a futile hope once again that the gesture of good faith would motivate the Communist regime to seek resolution of the conflict at the peace table.

Under great political pressure on the home front and with conflicting advice from his civilian and military advisors, President Johnson went on the air 31 March to deliver one of the most important speeches of his career. He stated he had called a halt to the bombing of North Vietnam except in the area near the DMZ which posed an immediate threat to allied forces in South Vietnam. He went on to say that even this limited bombing would cease if the US initiatives were matched by restraint in Hanoi. The US's intent, he said, was not to annihilate the enemy but to elicit a recognition by Hanoi that South Vietnam could not be taken over by force. Then, at the end of his speech, President Johnson made his most grave and unexpected pronouncement. With America's sons fighting in far off countries, he said he could not spare a moment's time for political aspirations and therefore would

not seek nor accept his party's nomination for another term as president.

History would show that the president's remarks did not signal the end to the war. But with this major decision, one which committed American policy irrevocably toward a negotiated peace, significant concessions were made. A military solution to the conflict was no longer an option. On 1 April 1968, combat air operations north of 20° North were discontinued. The president's advisors, motivated at least partly by political conditions within the United States, had led him into making concessions to the enemy in the hope of getting negotiations started. In the end, the long bombing halt proved to be more costly in American lives and equipment as well as prolonging resolution of the conflict four more years.

In April 1968, VA-25 retired the last examples of the aging Douglas A-1 Skyraiders, or 'Spads' as they had become known, from an attack squadron. (VAW-33 would continue to operate electronic versions of the A-1 until December 1967.) The Skyraiders first entered production at the end of World War II, but came too late to fly combat in that war. After nearly 23 years of service the A-1 had extensive use in the Korean War and in South East Asia. It remained in service with the US and Vietnamese

Above: Commander L. R. 'Moose' Meyers traps his F-8H Crusader aboard the *Bon Homme Richard* (CVA 31) following his 26 June 1968 MiG-21 kill. He downed the MiG with a heat-seaking Sidewinder air-to-air missile while flying MiG CAP with Attack Carrier Air Wing Five.

Right: Cdr Harry E. Ettinger, CO VA-25, unleashes 12 Mk 81 bombs on a VC target in South Vietnam. A-1 Skyraiders, because of their vulnerability to radar-controlled AAA, were restricted to the war in the South during their last deployments to Vietnam.

Left: Light attack aircraft were assigned the role of 'Ironhand', or defence against anti-aircraft and surface-to-air missiles. The anti-radiation missiles were very effective in homing in on enemy radar signals with lethal results. Near the war's end simply broadcasting 'Shotgun' (the term used to signal anti-radiation missile launch) over the radio – was enough to cause defending radars to shut down.

Vietnam

air forces throughout the war and proved its worth in the close air support attack and SAR roles. With a remarkable weight-carrying capability, it had carried a 14,179-lb (6432-kg) useful load, including 10,689 lb (4849 kg) of ordnance on at least one occasion. The A-1 was ideal for missions requiring long endurance and a large ordnance mix. The skies of the North made the relatively slow 'Spad' vulnerable to the sophisticated defenses, however. The US and Vietnamese air forces, who had never routinely used the A-1 in heavily defended areas of the North, continued to have great success with the aircraft. But in the Navy, whose faster jets often had to orbit to allow the slower 'Spads' to catch up and which lacked the dedicated fixed-wing combat SAR mission, the A-1 was retired to the more modern technology of the Grumman A-6 Intruder and the Vought A-7 Corsair II.

Throughout the spring and summer of 1968, Navy attack aircraft were kept busy with missions in Laos, I Corps, and the panhandle area of North Vietnam. With the elimination of the daily bombardment of Hanoi and Haiphong, many of the defenses were moved to the urban and supply storage areas of the panhandle. The distance aircrew had to fly over enemy terrain was now much shorter, and although the pilots might see heavy resistance in the urban areas, there was very little on the way into or out from the targets. Flying in the panhandle, the aircrews could take some comfort in the knowledge that, if hit, it was only a short distance to the water of the Gulf and a safe ejection.

From the time of the president's speech in March, limiting the bombing of the North through October 1968, the United States had gradually moved politically further from the original objectives than when US forces were first introduced into South Vietnam. Endless one-sided concessions were made in attempts to woo the Communists to the negotiating table. Now the talk was merely of seeking an 'honorable peace'. On 1 November, President Johnson decided to cease all bombing of North Vietnam. The bombing halt went into effect at 21.00 Saigon time. The last Navy missions were flown earlier that day from *Constellation*.

The Tragedy of USS *Enterprise*

Earlier in the year, on 14 January 1968, history had repeated itself. While starting aircraft for a launch aboard *Enterprise* during workup exercises off Hawaii, a Zuni rocket under the wing of a VF-96 McDonnell Douglas F-4J was ignited by a jet starting unit. The explosion and resulting fire quickly spread to the tightly-packed group of ordnance-laden CVW-9 aircraft on the fantail. Three hours later, the fire was brought under control and *Enterprise* headed for Pearl Harbor and repairs. Twenty-eight men had lost their lives in the inferno and 15 aircraft had been destroyed. Damage esti-

Below: Crews stand down from the rigors of combat. Missions continued in South Vietnam and Laos, even when there were halts in bombing of North Vietnam. Reconnaissance missions were still flown over the North during these periods.

Above: Smoke and fire erupts from Enterprise's flight deck off Oahu on 14 January 1969. CVW-9 aircraft were fully loaded with fuel and ordnance when a Zuni missile was accidently fired into the pack resulting in 28 deaths and more than $50 million damage to the ship.

Above right: A VA-146 A-7 Corsair and VF-96 F-4 Phantom are silhouetted by explosion on the fantail of Enterprise (CVAN-65). The fire erupted during work-up exercises off Hawaii on 14 January 1969.

Below: Introduction of the A-6A Intruder to the fleet brought with it an added capability. The A-6 could carry a much bigger payload at high speeds and could deliver ordnance with greater accuracy than previous attack aircraft.

mates exceeded $50 million. Repairs were completed in early March and the carrier continued on its deployment to South East Asia. Although *Enterprise*'s steel flight deck had been severely damaged, the carrier could have resumed flight operations within a few hours of the initial explosion.

In 1968, public demonstrations in the US against American involvement in Vietnam had grown to major proportions and had become headline news. American television viewers were shown news programs of violent public reaction to Americans serving in this long war, interspersed with clips of American troops dying in battle. The people of the United States indicated that they wanted a solution to the Vietnam problem. By an overwhelming margin the Republican party was voted into power. Richard Nixon became president in 1969. The primary strategy put forth by the new administration was called 'Vietnamization', a plan designed to

give the South Vietnamese sufficient modern arms and training to take care of themselves.

The next two years brought little change in the war on either side. No startling developments occurred on either the military or negotiating fronts. The North Vietnamese had begun to meet with American negotiators in Paris but nothing of any substance was discussed.

For the Navy pilots, the war continued but was now concentrated on slowing the flow of matériel and supplies down the Ho Chi Minh Trail in Laos. The Ho Chi Minh Trail was not just one road, or 'trail'. The supply route exited North Vietnam through the mountainous passes into Laos, on hundreds of dirt roads intertwined through the jungle floor. South through the eastern and central portions of the country, these paths led to Communist sanctuaries in south eastern Laos and Cambodia as well as unsecured jungle areas of western South Vietnam.

During the day the traffic was light. The Communists had learned it was safer to move at night. Unhampered by ground opposition, supplies were moved by any means available: truck, bicycle, even by water buffalo and on foot. Toward sunrise

Left: VA-55 A-4F uses its 'buddy store' to refuel a VFP-63 RF-8G. Aerial refuelling was used to extend endurance and allow aircraft to launch with increased loads of ordnance.

vehicles were hidden in the dense jungle foliage and these truck parks, as they were known, became prime targets. Under forward air control (FAC), Navy pilots worked in co-ordination with the Air Force in pinpointing and attacking the flow. With the wide dispersal of supplies and natural cover of the high triple canopy jungle, slowing the flow at this point was all but impossible.

American carriers in the Tonkin Gulf launched routine missions against the trail day and night. The pass areas into Laos (Ban Karai, Mugia, Ban Raving) were regularly interdicted, but were just as regularly repaired and the traffic only temporarily slowed or stopped. If it was any consolation to the pilots who flew these missions, the defenses were not generally heavy, at least nothing like those encountered in the North. But the losses continued. Although regularly targeted missions ceased in October 1968, escorted photo reconnaissance missions continued over the panhandle area of North Vietnam. The current rules allowed action only if the photo plane was fired upon and the term 'protective reaction' strike was coined for the mission. Frustration was an obvious outgrowth of this restriction, when pilots had to wait for the

defenses to pick their most opportune moment to unleash their anti-aircraft weapons (which was inevitable) before they were allowed to 'react' and strike back. This real-life 'Russian roulette' led to occasional loose interpretation of the rules. This only further fueled the one-sided unwarranted mistrust of the military at home.

One of the brighter moments of the war for the carrier aviators came early in the morning of 21 November 1970. In the midnight darkness of the Gulf, aircrews manned aircraft aboard *Oriskany*, *Hancock* and *Ranger* for what was probably the most unique mission of the war. CVW-19, -21 and -2 launched the Navy's largest night sortie mission in support of the Son Tay Prison raid. Rear Admiral James D. 'Jig Dog' Ramage, ComCarDiv 7 and Officer in Tactical Command (OTC) of the Navy aircraft, ordered his air wings against Haiphong as a diversionary tactic to draw North Vietnamese attention and, hopefully, radars, to the east away from the prison camp 23 miles (37 km) west of Hanoi.

Confusion reigned as the enemy tried to sort out the strange events, principally massive flights of Navy aircraft over the Haiphong area, yet not

Attack Carrier Air Wing Nine photo-recce with escort. This 1972 photograph shows a VF-92 F-4J Phantom escorting an RVAH-11 RA-5C Vigilante on a practice mission over the island of Oahu during *Constellation*'s ORE en route to the combat zone.

A thirsty 'Black Knights' F-4B Phantom gets a drink from a VAH-4 KA-3B Skywarrior. Both squadrons flew from the deck of *Kitty Hawk* in 1968.

AIM-7 Sparrow and AIM-9 Sidewinder air-to-air missiles form the
armament of this VF-142 'Ghost Riders' McDonnell Douglas F-4B
Phantom II. Despite experimenting with a number of different
tactical camouflage schemes during the early years of the
Vietnam conflict, the Navy did not adopt any of these, choosing to
remain with the basically grey and white finish for the entire war,
and this provided an excellent canvas for many highly attractive
colour schemes. These particular markings were worn by VF-142
during its combat cruise aboard USS *Constellation* (CVA 64) as
part of Carrier Air Wing Fourteen (CVW-14) during 1968-69.

VF-142

USS CONSTELLATION

2244

VF-142

CONSTELLATION

2244

VF-142

NAVY

NK

Keith Fretwell

attacking. (The bombing halt was still in effect and the aviators were allowed only 'protective reaction' if fired upon.)

Although no POWs were rescued, all having been moved from the camp shortly before the raid, the raid itself and the Navy's mission were unqualified successes. Admiral John J. Hyland, CinCPac, lauded the Naval Aviators for an 'exceptional achievement', but the greatest result of the mission was the improved treatment received by the POWs from their captors. The mission had convinced Hanoi that the American POWs were important to their countrymen and that the US was willing to do whatever necessary to secure their freedom.

By the spring of 1972, it became apparent that the North Vietnamese were intending to launch a major new offensive. Twelve of the North's 13 main-force divisions were deployed outside North Vietnam by February 1972. Two divisions were massed in Laos by the northern portion of South Vietnam near military Region I, with an additional division north of the DMZ. Numerous surface-to-air missile sites had been set up in the region as well as large artillery capable of hitting targets in South Vietnam. In addition to the four operational airfields already in the panhandle, two new fields capable of handling MiGs were constructed.

One of these new fields was Quang Lang, a short dirt strip built on the jungle floor near mountains in the north western portion of the panhandle. The North Vietnamese moved MiG-21s down from Hanoi, Thanh Hoa and Bai Lhuong and operated them out of the Quang Lang field near the Laotian border. This deployment of MiG forces was an attempt to intercept US 'Arc Light' missions (flown by Boeing B-52s) in their tactical bombing runs over central Laos.

The fighters take on the MiGs

In late 1971, photo reconnaissance caught ground crews pushing a MiG-21 into a cave at Quang Lang and the decision was made for another intelligence run. Under the rules of engagement in force, if a photo reconnaissance aircraft was fired upon, only airborne aircraft available at the time could be used to defend the unarmed photo aircraft.

This mission, called 'Bluetree' by the planners, was scheduled for early January 1972, but the unco-operative weather postponed the effort. Aircrew briefed the mission and manned their aircraft nearly every day for a three-week period before the weather finally lifted enough for the mission to go. During that time the mission was alternately given to *Constellation* then to *Coral Sea* then back again to *Constellation*.

Finally, on 19 January, the overcast monsoon weather cleared just enough for the mission to go. *Constellation*'s CVW-9 launched for the long-delayed mission. The planned route called for the strike group to approach Quang Lang through the 'back door': the group was to cross northern South Vietnam near Hue, into Laos, then cross over the airfield. On previous reconnaissance of the field, over three weeks past, Quang Lang was unde-fended, but the Communists had ample time to change all that. Immediately, the North American RA-5C Vigilante came under intense ground fire. The escorting A-7s and A-6s a short distance behind lost little opportunity to roll in on their bombing runs against the airfield and its defenses. The sky was filled with 37-mm and 57-mm flak from the anti-aircraft fire. SAMs streaked airborne and pilots pulled their aircraft hard into the missiles to break their track. The VF-96 crew of Lieutenant Randy Cunningham and his RIO Lieutenant (JG) Willie Driscoll, along with other 'Fighting Falcons' F-4Js, had been assigned as MiGCap for the mission. Positioning their Phantoms 5 miles (8 km) north of the airfield in an attempt to intercept attacking MiGs from the north, they had inad-vertently positioned their planes over two active SAM sites.

Now caught in the battle to defeat the upcoming SAMs, Cunningham maneuvered his Phantom near its limits to counter the first missile. Glancing over his shoulder he caught sight of another missile as it streaked past his wingman, missing him by no more than 100 ft (30 m). But luck was with the wingman, since, for some unknown reason, the SAM did not detonate.

Defeating the first SAM, Cunningham reversed his aircraft only to spot another missile closing in fast. He put a counter move on the missile, only to have it continue tracking toward his Phantom. At the last moment, he broke hard into it as it continued harmlessly outside the radius of turn.

Now with the Phantom's nose straight down at 15,000 ft (4570 m) and his airspeed slowed from the

Left: An instant from launch: a VF-92 F-4J Phantom applies full burner as the pilot tenses himself for the catapult to release and punch his aircraft skywards. Carrier aircraft are designed to absorb this punishment (and the equally vicious landing) several thousand times during their expected service lives.

US Navy – PH3 R.A. Meadows

Right: Lieutenant (JG) Willie Driscoll (RIO, left) and Lieutenant Randy Cunningham (pilot, right) joke with fellow members of VF-96 after their mission of 19 January 1972. In the centre background is Lieutenant Jerry Sullivan, who flew in the wingman's aircraft during the mission.

attention fully back on the lead MiG, Cunningham pulled his aircraft's nose toward the fighter. But evidently the pilot had lost sight of the Phantom and now reversed his flight path directly in front of the F-4. Cunningham fired his second Sidewinder, which streaked off the rail and tracked straight to the MiG. Exploding in a yellow flash, the missile severed the MiG's tail section and the aircraft pitched violently, tumbling to the ground. The crew turned their Phantom toward the second MiG, but soon realized it had made good its escape, its pilot having no stomach for a fight. The Phantom crew had used much of their fuel on the first MiG and now turned back toward Laos for the long journey back to the boat. This encounter was the first MiG kill in 18 months and the first of five for Cunningham and Driscoll, which would make them the first aces of the Vietnam War.

defensive maneuvering, Cunningham spotted what at first appeared to be two A-7s in formation heading north east low over the jungle treetops. He then realized that both aircraft were in afterburner, and A-7s do not use afterburners! Reversing his aircraft back toward the departing aircraft, he accurately identified the planes as two shiny silver MiG-21s trying to escape from Quang Lang.

Lighting full burner and accelerating the F-4 through 690 mph (1110 km/h), the Phantom crew closed on the fleeing MiGs, which were no more than 500 ft (150 m) above the trees on the valley floor. Driscoll locked-up the lead aircraft with the radar and called for his pilot to shoot a Sparrow. But remembering previous Sparrow failures during training firings, Cunningham selected a Sidewinder, got a good launch tone and squeezed the trigger. Almost simultaneously with missile launch, the MiG broke hard into the attacking Phantom causing the missile to lose its track. The F-4 crew maneuvered their aircraft in a re-attack against the now hard-turning MiG driver, reversing momentarily to catch sight of the second MiG as it disappeared to the north east. Now, with his

31
Tet and a New Year

On 30 March 1972, with poor weather to aid in the element of surprise, the North Vietnamese launched a massive offensive in all four corps areas of South Vietnam. An infantry division and two regiments of tanks, accompanied by motorized artillery and anti-aircraft guns, were pushed south through the DMZ. In mid-April President Nixon directed a one-time strike of Hanoi and Haiphong. This was intended to inflict damage on military installations and POL in an effort to show the US was willing to use the strategic bombing of its Boeing B-52 force if necessary. Through this and numerous political warnings, the US indicated that North Vietnam would be running grave risks if it continued to push its offensive. The forces of South Vietnam, now without the vast US troop support, were still able to blunt the attacks effectively.

Addressing the nation on 8 May, President Nixon announced that 'Five weeks ago, on Easter week-

US Navy

Right: USS *Midway* (CVA 41) during operations in South East Asia in 1972. Aircraft from her air group were to play an important role in the mining of the major harbors in North Vietnam.

end, the Communist armies of North Vietnam launched a massive invasion of South Vietnam – an invasion that was made possible by tanks, artillery and other advanced offensive weapons supplied to Hanoi by the Soviet Union and other Communist nations.' The president went on to state that the bloodshed would worsen if the United States simply left Vietnam, and that '. . . I therefore concluded that Hanoi must be denied the weapons and supplies it needs to continue the aggression . . . All entrances to North Vietnamese ports will be mined to prevent access to these ports and North Vietnamese naval operations from these ports. United States' forces have been directed to take appropriate measures within the internal and claimed territorial waters of North Vietnam to interdict the delivery of supplies. Rail and all other communications will be cut off to the maximum extent possible. Air and naval strikes against military targets in North Vietnam will continue.'

Although air strikes against military targets in North Vietnam had resumed following the Easter invasion of South Vietnam, this was the first US pronouncement that the harbors and ports would be mined, a plan for which had been in existence since the early 1960s. For years, mining had been strongly recommended by the military commanders as a means of causing profound logistical difficulties in North Vietnam. Authorization from Washington had consistently been denied.

At the same time as the president's speech, halfway around the world Grumman A-6s and Vought A-7s from the carriers *Coral Sea*, *Constellation* and *Midway* were sowing minefields in the major harbors of the North: Haiphong, Hon Gai, Cam Pha and Thanh Hoa in the northern sectors and Vinh, Quang Khe and Dong Hoi in the panhandle. Aircrews encountered extremely heavy AAA and SAM defenses as they made their low-level drops. By the end of May, however, no shipping traffic was entering or leaving North Vietnamese ports. The long-sought result had been achieved.

With many of the restrictive rules of engagement now lifted, as well as the addition of more lucrative military targets, carrier strikes were flown against the North day and night.

US Navy

Aircrew met heavy defenses on these initial strikes, the heaviest near Haiphong and Hanoi. MiG activity also intensified, but continued to be both unpredictable and sporadic. The Navy accounted for one MiG in March and four more through 9 May, including the second kill for Cunningham and Driscoll. The USS *Chicago* (CG 11) launched a Talos missile the night of 8 May, downing a MiG attempting to intercept A-6s during the mining of Haiphong Harbor.

Air battles over Haiphong

Then, on 10 May 1972, came the biggest single fighter encounter of the war. *Coral Sea* and *Constellation* had been flying Alpha strikes daily into North Vietnam. With the large numbers of aircraft necessary to fly these co-ordinated strikes, the normal operating day consisted of three strikes. These were usually flown in succession and normally against different targets.

The morning strike of 10 May was to the POL storage areas north of Haiphong. VF-96 and sister squadron VF-92 in *Constellation* were assigned as

Above: An A-6A Intruder loaded with Mk 82s awaits launch on board *Constellation* in 1972. This VA-165 'Boomers' aircraft flew numerous day and night missions over North Vietnam.

Commander David P. Erickson

Left: 'Showtime 100' buddy bombs with two other VF-96 Phantoms. 'Showtime 100' is credited with three MiG-17 kills on 10 May 1972. The aircraft was downed by a Soviet SA-2 surface-to-air missile near Haiphong on the same mission.

Above: Toting AIM-9 Sidewinder air-to-air missiles, an F-8J Crusader of VF-211 'Checkmates' winds up to full power moments before launch from USS *Hancock* (CVA 19) at the start of a MiG-CAP mission over North Vietnam during the Linebacker I campaign of May 1972.

MiGCap for the strike with responsibility to position their aircraft between the strike group and any MiGs attempting to intercept. The strike proceeded as planned with the two VF-92 McDonnell Douglas Phantoms sweeping the area north west of the target. As the last of the strike aircraft cleared the target area, the 'Silver Kings' Phantoms accelerated and continued to the north west. Now swooping in low over Kep airfield north west of Hanoi, the VF-92 fighters caught two MiGs climbing out just after take-off. The heavily laden MiG-21s took a salvo of Sidewinders from the two Phantoms. One MiG, initially escaping destruction as a Sidewinder skimmed harmlessly over his wing, caught the full force of the next missile, exploded in mid-air and tumbled in flames to the ground. The second MiG

jettisoned his external fuel tank and turned sharply into the attacking aircraft. However, the Phantoms had too much speed advantage and headed for the safety of the Gulf. Lieutenant Curt Dosé and Lieutenant Commander Jim McDevitt were credited with the kill.

The second mission of 10 May was to the railyards and facilities at Hai Duong, an important rail switching point half-way between the two cities of Hanoi and Haiphong. For this mission, 11 fighters (seven of them from VH-96) were given escort duties. Because of the major importance of the switching facility, ground defenses were expected to be fierce. Several of the F-4s were given the assignment of flak suppression. The Phantoms could thus escort and provide protection for the strike group until approaching the target area, then their faster speed allowed them to accelerate out in front of the formation and be the first on the target. With an ordnance load of four Rockeye cluster bombs, the Phantoms were used to silence the AAA and SAMs for the precision bombing of the following A-7s and A-6s.

Cunningham and Driscoll, along with their wingmen Lieutenant Brian Grant and RIO Lieutenant Jerry Sullivan, were given the flak suppression mission.

All was unusually quiet as the strike group approached the target from the south. The cockpit radar warning devices, which were usually lit up like Christmas trees, gave only an occasional blip of a searching radar.

On each side of the strike formation, the A-7 'Iron Hand' aircraft nav-launched their anti-radar Shrike missiles at the predicted highest threat SAM sites. The flak suppression Phantoms acce-

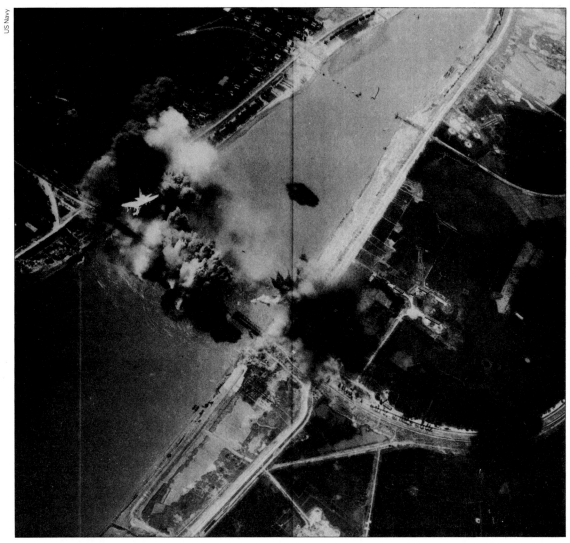

Right: An A-7E pilot pulls off target near Hai Duong, North Vietnam. This railroad highway bridge spans the Red River half way between Hanoi and the port city of Hiphong. This VA-195 Corsair II was from *Kitty Hawk*.

lerated over the target and began their bomb runs.

The puffs of 37-mm and 57-mm AAA could be seen forming over the target area as Hai Duong's defenses came alive. The tenseness was felt as pilots called in and off target, now obscured by smoke and bomb explosions. Aircraft jinked hard out of their bomb runs, snaking through the barrage of flak and SAMs shooting skyward toward the attacking planes.

Through the background of radio chatter came the calls from 'Red Crown' (the radar destroyer in the Gulf) that MiGs were airborne approaching the strike group. Climbing back to altitude after unleashing his bomb load, Cunningham was the first to spot the incoming MiGs. He called to his wingman, 'MiG-17! MiG-17! Brian, he's on my tail ... I'm dragging him, get 'im baby!' Going into afterburner and baiting the enemy pilot, Cunningham hoped to lure the MiG into an easy kill for his wingman. But only interested in a hit and run, the camouflaged MiG slashed across the Phantom's tail firing his belly cannons. He then dumped his nose, lit afterburner and accelerated toward the ground. Now seeing his wingman tied up with another MiG-17, Cunningham reversed his jet, pulling the Phantom's nose to the MiG and fired his first Sidewinder. The missile accelerated off the rail and tracked straight toward the fast-departing MiG, scoring a hit which caused the aircraft to disintegrate in a ball of fire.

It was a classic dogfight with aircraft everywhere. Confined to a small area directly over Hai Duong, A-7 and F-4 aircraft fought to break the gun-tracking solutions of MiG-17s and MiG-19s. Anti-aircraft fire filled the sky and SAMs came streaking up, indifferent to the presence of defending airplanes. Smoke trails from the burning remains of enemy planes arced across the sky and in the midst of this pandemonium, two dirty gray parachutes floated toward the ground.

Pitching back toward Hai Duong, Cunningham and Driscoll spotted a squadron F-4 in trouble, trailed by two MiG-17s and a sleek MiG-21. But they, too, had a MiG-17 beginning to close in on them. Using the Phantom's speed advantage, Cunningham maneuvered his aircraft to the outside of his squadron mate, getting a clear shot at one of the pressing MiG-17s, yet keeping his own attacker just out of range. Again the Sidewinder met its mark as it entered the MiG's tailpipe, followed by an orange fireball, then the enemy

pilot's ejection.

With four MiG-21s diving in from above, discretion became the better part of valor, and it was time to leave. Turning hard into the MiG-21s, Cunningham and Driscoll started their Phantom to the south to make their exit.

As the nose of their aircraft came steady and Cunningham shifted from the four MiG-21s now opening in the opposite direction behind him to the forward windscreen, he spotted another airplane low on the nose closing toward him. As it got closer he could identify it as yet another MiG-17. Moving his Phantom to pass the MiG close aboard as he had done so many times during training, he almost forgot about the lethality of the MiG's 23-mm and 37-mm cannon. The MiG's nose lit up as the enemy pilot chanced a head-on gun shot. Pulling quickly up into a vertical climb, the Phantom crew looked back only to be astounded that the MiG had done the same maneuver, a maneuver expected only of the most experienced and aggressive MiG pilot.

Canopy to canopy, the two aircraft spiraled straight up. As they slowed, the Phantom peaked out above the MiG at the top of the loop. Unshaken, the MiG pilot pulled the MiG-17's nose to the Phantom for a short gunshot before accelerating again toward the ground.

Cunningham used the quick acceleration of his F-4 to gain speed and distance. Then, as the MiG began to catch up, he would pull back vertical into a twisting, rolling scissors with the enemy pilot.

After several of these maneuvers, with advantage shifting from MiG to F-4 and back again to MiG, it was obvious that the MiG-17 driver was no easy bait. Up again in the vertical climb, this time Cunningham did the unexpected and retarded both throttles to idle and put out the speed brakes as he stomped full rudder to force the Phantom to the Mig's belly side.

The MiG, now just on the edge of slow-speed control, pitched back toward the ground and attempted to escape straight down. But the Phantom, now in perfect firing position, launched its third Sidewinder. The missile came off the airplane and went straight to the MiG. There was a little flash and for a moment, the F-4 crew thought the missile had missed. Suddenly, a big flash of flame and black smoke erupted from the stricken fighter. The MiG flew straight into the ground carrying its pilot with it.

Left: A VF-96 'Fighting Falcons' F-4J Phantom approaches *Constellation* in this 1973 photograph. Nose fuselage markings show the squadrons's eight MiG kills and that VF-96 was a two-time winner of the Rear Admiral Joseph C. Clifton Trophy given annually to the top US Navy fighter squadron.

Commander David P. Erickson

With only one Sidewinder left, and now vastly outnumbered as the other F-4s made their egress, Cunningham and Driscoll headed for the Gulf. Approaching the coastline near Nam Dinh they heard the SAM call on their radios but were too late in spotting the missile as it detonated just beyond their aircraft. At first it appeared as if the plane was undamaged, but soon the hydraulic gages began to fluctuate erratically. Slowly losing control of the Phantom, Cunningham forced the stick forward and, using a combination of manual rudder and afterburner, rolled the damaged plane toward the coast. Flames trailed the planes as the F-4 reached the coastline. The remaining controls burned through and the aircraft pitched over into a spin. The crew ejected safely and was rescued from the Gulf by Marine Boeing Vertol CH-46 helicopters from the *Okinawa* (LPH 3).

The Cunningham/Driscoll team was returned to a hero's welcome on board *Constellation*. They celebrated their third, fourth and fifth MiG kills, making them the first aces of the war. For their valor, Cunningham and Driscoll were awarded the Navy Cross. Other squadron mates had reason for celebration also, as in addition to the three kills of the new aces, two other VF-96 crews accounted for three additional MiGs during the Hai Duong engagement.

32
Rumors of Peace

The war in the North raged on through the summer months of 1972, but pilots reported a steady decrease of opposition. In July a force of six American aircraft-carriers were present in the Tonkin Gulf: the *Kitty Hawk, America, Hancock, Midway, Saratoga* and *Oriskany*, each engaging the enemy on a daily basis. No shipping entered or left the ports of North Vietnam, both the north west and north east rail lines into China were a shambles, and the flow of supplies had slowed to a trickle.

In Paris, the peace talks between Le Duc Tho, the hard-liner North Vietnamese negotiator and his American counterpart, Henry Kissinger, now began in earnest after months of stagnation. By October, it looked as if the peace talks in Paris would produce a ceasefire quickly and President Nixon called for cessation of the bombing of the

North to the 29th parallel. But the Communists, mistakenly perceiving a weakness in American resolve, again went about the tasks of rebuilding. With the pressures of the bombing gone, they again refused to negotiate a peace to end the conflict. The peace which had seemed so close now seemed so far away. On 13 December 1972, the North Vietnamese delegation in Paris arrogantly walked out of the negotiations.

With little choice left to persuade the Communists to negotiate in earnest, President Nixon called for the strategic might to once and for all resolve this conflict. On the night of 18 December, waves of USAF Boeing B-52s and General Dynamics F-111s struck the major complexes in Haiphong and Hanoi during Operation 'Linebacker II'. Co-ordinated with the strategic bombing, Navy Grumman A-6 and EA-6 aircraft flew special missions both in support of the bombing and on individual missions.

'Linebacker II' bombing missions continued day and night for 11 days. The bombing had produced the desired results. After the Communists had eagerly expressed a desire to resolve the issues in Paris, 'Linebacker II' missions were stopped on 29 December.

On 3 January 1973, all bombing ceased above the 20th parallel and several days later, negotiations to end all hostilities began seriously in Paris. Finally, on 23 January, with the United States and North Vietnam reaching mutual agreement, a ceasefire was announced. Provisions in the ceasefire agreement called for the US to clear the harbors of North Vietnam of the mines which had so effectively slowed resupply. Special US Sikorsky CH-53A Sea Stallions, flown by the Navy's HM-12 minesweeping squadron, started the sweeping operation 24 February. Joined by Marine CH-53As from HMH-463, Operation 'Endsweep' was completed by the end of July.

As part of the ceasefire agreement, the first American POWs were flown out of Hanoi on 12 February. The real heroes of the war were these American fighting men who, throughout the long conflict, had endured the political restrictions, the frustrations, the uncertainty of endless years of imprisonment and torture at the hands of the Communist regime in North Vietnam. The words of Captain Jeremiah Denton, USN, the first POW off the plane at Clark AFB, said it all: 'We are honored to have had the opportunity to serve our country under difficult circumstances. We are profoundly

Below: KA-3B, KA-6D, A-4, A-6 and A-7 aircraft were all used as tankers during the war. Only the KA-3B and KA-6D were specifically designed for the tanker mission. A-4, A-6 and A-7s were fitted with 'buddy stores' for tanker missions. Here a VA-155 A-7B refuels a VF-194 F-8J.

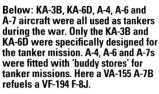

US Navy

Vietnam

Left: A VF-2 F-14A Tomcat taxies toward *Enterprise*'s catapult on 13 March 1975, while on the first deployment of the F-14 fighter. VF-1 and VF-2 Tomcats flew Combat Air Patrol missions over South Vietnam during the evacuation of Saigon in April.

Right: USS *Enterprise* (CVAN-65) replenishes from *Hassayampa* (AO-145) underway in the South China Sea during her 1973 cruise with CVW-14. In 1975 her aircraft would fly cover for the Saigon evacuation.

grateful to our Commander in Chief and to our nation for this day. God bless America.'

For the United States the war had been both long and costly. On 23 January 1973, the ceasefire agreement was officially signed. Although the frustrations for these airmen had been extreme, the professionalism never ceased. Including Air Force aircraft, nearly 3,700 planes were downed in Indochina during the 10-year war. The vast majority of these fell to AAA, the heaviest concentration of anti-aircraft artillery in the history of mankind. Nearly 85 percent of the losses were attributed directly to this vast firepower. Against the MiGs, Navy pilots fared better. Although it must be remembered that the North Vietnamese generally used the slower MiG-17 against the slower Navy attack aircraft to save the MiG-21 for the faster Air Force F-105s and F-4s to the west, carrier aviators downed 58 enemy aircraft for loss of 15 Navy aircraft of all types to both NVAF and Chinese Communist MiGs. In fighter-versus-fighter, nine Navy aircraft fell victim to enemy fighters, yet accounted for 54 MiGs, an exchange ratio of 6:1.

With the return of the POWs came the stories not only of the long years endured in prison, but also of isolation, inhumane treatment and torture. The accounts which followed once again revealed the valor of these men. Americans recognized that valor, for the very peace agreements had hinged upon the return of all US POWs. In all, 651 POWs were returned to their homeland, but many more American POWs and MIAs remain unaccounted for to this day.

US ground forces, which had reached a high of over one-half million troops at its peak, were all withdrawn from South Vietnam. American air missions into Laos and Cambodia, not addressed by the Paris agreements, ceased in August 1973. The inevitable Communist move was not long in coming. Cambodia, occupied by thousands of North Vietnamese and Viet Cong, fell. With Cambodia taken, the Communists turned to the major urban areas and airfields in South Vietnam. For the first time, the South Vietnamese army and air force was faced with operating without the vast military support of the United States. For a short time, they were able to hold out, but again, the inevitable happened. On 12 April 1975, the American Embassy was ordered evacuated. *Midway* and *Enterprise*, on their first cruise flying the newly acquired Grumman F-14A Tomcat, provided air cover for the evacuation of Saigon as the Communists swept southward toward the city.

Hancock, *Midway* and *Coral Sea* became mobile bases as US Marine and US Air Force helicopters shuttled Americans and South Vietnamese civ-

ilians to the ships. In the end, nearly 8,000 South Vietnamese refugees and American civilians were airlifted to the American fleet off shore. Thousands were left behind to become victims of the Communists. On 30 April 1975, Saigon fell to the invaders and South Vietnam came under Communist control.

Below: Map of North Vietnam showing the major airfields and railways, as well as the zones used by US aircraft. The two bridges, Paul Doumer and Thanh Hoa, which gave the attack aircraft a particularly hard time, are also shown.

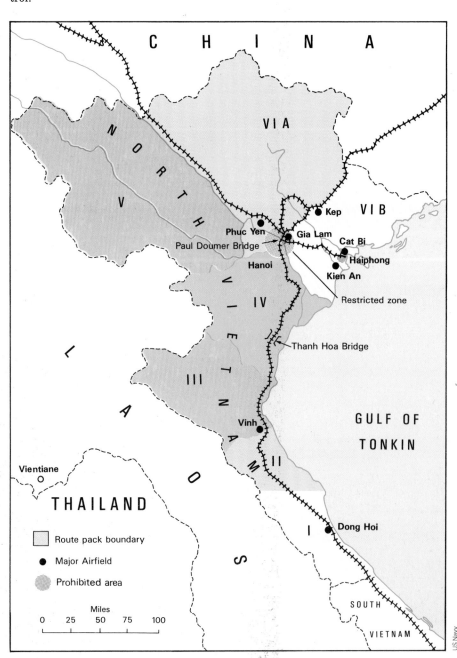

The Fleet Replacement Training Squadron for the F/A-18, VFA-125, was at Yuma in January 1982 for the first weapons training deployment of the Hornet. VFA-125 was the US Navy's first Hornet squadron.

Contemporary Situations and Plans

The war in South-East Asia was over, but the trauma remained. The armed forces suffered in the backlash of anti-war sentiment and political impotence. The debacle of the Iran rescue mission seemed to epitomize this dark period. But new political leadership gave way to increased budgets and a new spirit. The decline was arrested and new operational capability in Naval Aviation emerged.

Now the challenge is that of technology. Engineering advances in ship and aircraft design, the utilization of exotic materials and the domination of computers demand fundamental changes in the development, production, maintenance and operation of new equipment. The service is confident that it will once again fully meet that challenge and maintain its reputation as the finest fighting force in the world.

33
South East Asia and After

On 27 January 1973 the ceasefire ending the Vietnam War, the longest war in United States history, became effective. During the 12 years of the conflict, combat action cost Naval Aviation the lives of many pilots and aircrewmen killed or missing. A total of 538 fixed-wing aircraft and 13 helicopters of the US Navy were shot down by enemy fire. Marine Aviation losses were proportionately heavy in men and aircraft.

Thousands of bombing sorties were flown by carrier attack as well as fighter squadrons. The key jet attack aircraft employed were the Grumman A-6 Intruder and the Vought A-7 Corsair, but during the early years of the war the prop-driven Douglas A-1 Skyraider reigned supreme. An attack squadron pilot, Commander Denny Weichman, commanding officer of VA-153 in the USS *Oriskany*, ended the war credited with 625 combat missions, the highest number recorded for any naval aviator. Weichman flew his final mission on the day of the ceasefire in an A-7A Corsair II.

In accordance with the terms of the ceasefire agreement, the North Vietnamese and the Viet Cong commenced the release of US POWs on 12 February 1973. The last Americans released left Hanoi by 29 March. Two key elements in the agreement ending hostilities were commitments: by the North Vietnamese and Viet Cong to release all prisoners of war within 60 days and by the United States to clear North Vietnamese waters of all US-laid mines. As for the first agreement, controversy exists to this day over the Vietnamese return of all POWs. Without doubt, there has never been given a full accounting of all American POWs and MIAs. Action on the latter agreement commenced immediately with the establishment of Task Force 78 (TF-78) on the day the ceasefire went into effect. TF-78's mission was to carry out the minesweeping operations, codenamed 'Endsweep'. The task force included surface minesweeping elements plus the Air Mobile Mine Counter-Measure Command made up of helicopter squadrons HM-12, HMH-463 and HMM-165 and surface ships. On 6 February, surface craft began sweeping in the Haiphong harbor approaches to provide a safe

US Navy

anchorage for the ships of the task force, which included the USS *New Orleans* (LPH 11), *Inchon* (LPH 12) and *Tripoli* (LPH 10). The first aerial sweep sortie of the operation was flown in the Haiphong channel on 27 February by Commander Jerry Hatcher of HM-12 in a Sikorsky CH-53A Sea Stallion. On that day, TF-78 'Endsweep' operations were abruptly cancelled and the entire force moved out to sea. This action was in protest against the North Vietnamese failure to continue to free the American POWs, the first group of whom had been released on 12 February. On the following day, 28 February, Hanoi agreed to resume the release of the prisoners and on 4 March the sweep operations were resumed, continuing uninterrupted until 27 July. On that date the area was declared safe, TF-78 was deactivated and Operation 'Endsweep' was terminated.

As far as can be determined, this action was the first aerial minesweeping operations ever conducted involving live mines. Support for the operation had been provided by aircraft from the *Enterprise*, *Oriskany*, *Ranger* and *Coral Sea* on station in the Gulf of Tonkin.

Although the ceasefire was in effect for Vietnam, Naval Aviation continued to be involved in combat operations in Indochina. In January, 1973, the

Above: Lieutenant Commander Everett Alvarez, Jr. upon his return to the United States following 8½ years of captivity in North Vietnam. Alvarez was shot down as a lieutenant (JG) on 5 August 1964, while flying a VA-144 A-4C from *Constellation*.

Below: *Hancock* (CVA 19) arrives in Subic Bay on 3 May 1975 with Vietnamese refugees rescued from Saigon in Operation 'Frequent Wind' on 29 April.

US Navy—JO5N C. Moore

HMH-462 CH-53A Sea Stallions bring Americans rescued from Phnom Penh aboard *Okinawa* on 12 April 1975. Cambodian President Sankhm Khoy and American Ambassador John Gunther Dean were among those rescued by the US Marines.

Laotian government had requested support by the United States in its battle against Communist-supported guerrillas and invading North Vietnamese forces. Following the signing of the Vietnam ceasefire, the Gulf of Tonkin Yankee Station for the carriers was moved to a position off the northern coast of South Vietnam and operations continued. Combat sorties by air wings from the *Ranger*, *Enterprise*, *Constellation* and *Oriskany* reached a level as high as 380 per day. All combat operations were finally terminated 15 August, after more than six months of intensive bombing and close air support missions.

However, Naval Aviation was still not through with Indochina. Through 1974 and into 1975, the fighting in Laos and Cambodia continued, with the Communist forces gradually overcoming the resistance of the incumbent governments. In March, fighting broke out again in the wide area of South Vietnam as North Vietnamese forces overran much of the central highland provinces. Hordes of refugees fled to the south and the US recognized that evacuation of the remaining American citizens in the country would be necessary. *Hancock*, with a deckload of helicopters, was ordered to sail for the area late in March. Meanwhile, tens of thousands of South Vietnamese refugees crowded into the coastal areas seeking any means of transportation to supposedly safe areas farther south. In one day, 30 March, freighters and landing craft brought an estimated 30,000 people fleeing from Da Nang to Cam Ranh Bay.

Operation 'Eagle Pull', on 12 April 1975, flown by HMH-462 CH-53A Sea Stallions, evacuated 287 people including US Ambassador John Gunther Dean and Cambodian President Sankhm Khoy from Phnom Penh to *Okinawa* (LPH 3). The final action of the operation was retrieval of 31st Marine Amphibious Unit elements which had held a perimeter during the evacuation by HMH-463 helos from *Hancock*. By late April, more than 40 US Navy ships were on station off the Vietnam coast, standing by to aid in the evacuation of Americans from the threatened Saigon area. On 29 April, Operation 'Frequent Wind' was launched by USMC helicopters from the carriers offshore and, in just three

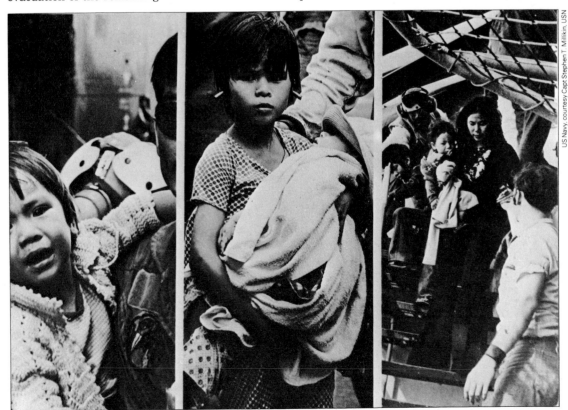

Vietnamese refugees are brought aboard *Okinawa* (LPH 3) in April 1975 by CH-53A Sea Stallions of HMH-462. Some 900 Americans and Vietnamese were evacuated from Saigon in three hours by US Marine helos.

hours, some 900 Americans were airlifted from Saigon to *Midway*, *Coral Sea*, *Hancock*, *Enterprise* and *Okinawa*. Cover for the operation was provided by fighters from the carrier air wings.

On 24 January 1979, Lieutenant Colonel Herbert Fix, USMC, was presented with the Harmon International Aviation Trophy. Colonel Fix was the commander of the USMC helicopters during 'Eagle Pull' and 'Frequent Wind'. The citation for the award noted that the missions were carried out 'without casualties among the aircrews of 16 rotary-wing aircraft although the operations took place under combat conditions involving anti-aircraft fire, machine gun and small arms fire, and in part at night with few navigational aids'.

Involvement in the Middle East

Meanwhile, on the other side of the world, an uneasy truce in the Middle East was broken when Israel and Egyptian planes clashed over the Gulf of Suez on 15 February 1973. Tensions continued to increase during the year, culminating in Egyptian and Syrian attacks on Israeli positions on 6 October. The crisis situation deepened when, on 17 October, the Arab oil-producing states announced a reduction in oil shipments to the US and other nations supporting Israel. On 21 October, a total embargo on oil shipments was announced. A US and Soviet effort to negotiate a truce succeeded and, on 27 October, Egypt and Israel agreed to a ceasefire.

As tensions had mounted during the year, *Kennedy* (CVA 67) and *Forrestal* (CVA 59), already in the Mediterranean, were alerted in May for possible contingency operations. With the outbreak of hostilities on 6 October, the *Independence* (CV 62), *Roosevelt* (CVA 42) and *Guadalcanal* (LPH 7) were put on full alert and *Kennedy*, on her way back to the US was ordered back to Gibraltar. Between 19 and 24 October, some 50 McDonnell Douglas A-4 Skyhawks were flown from the United States to reinforce the Israelis, staging through the Azores. The *Roosevelt*, standing by near Sicily, *Kennedy* off Gibraltar, and *Independence* near Crete, were also utilized for fuel stops. On 29 October, *Hancock* and her battle group were ordered to the Indian Ocean,

with tension mounting as a result of the Arab oil embargo.

Peace talks between the Arabs and the Israelis continued into 1974 and the US agreed to participate in a multi-national effort to clear the Suez Canal of unexploded ordnance so it could be reopened to ship traffic. On 22 April, Sikorsky RH-53D Sea Stallions of NAS Norfolk-based HM-12, began Operation 'Nimbus Star' flights in the Suez Canal. This was the first operational employment of the minesweeping version of the Sea Stallion, developed as a result of the Vietnam 'Endsweep' experience. Logistical support for HM-12 operations was provided by Lockheed C-130F Hercules transports from the Rota, Spain detachment of Navy transport squadron VR-24. Sweeping was completed and the canal was formally opened on

Contemporary Situations and Plans

5 June 1975. Sweep operations continued in the approaches to the canal until 23 July. Thus was completed the second phase of an entirely new role for Naval Aviation.

In 1979, tension in the Middle East heightened dramatically with Iran as the focal point. Ousting of the Shah, on 16 January, precipitated an internal situation which daily became more chaotic. On 14 February, two Marines at the US Embassy were injured when an armed Iranian mob shot its way into the Embassy compound. As had become routine in such situations, the 6th Fleet carriers in the Mediterranean were alerted to a contingency standby status and remained on alert for most of the year. The Iranian situation climaxed on 4 November with the seizure of the US Embassy in Tehran and more than 60 Americans taken hostage by armed Moslem terrorists. Although some 13 of the hostages were released during the following month, it was apparent that no early resolution of the situation was likely. *Kitty Hawk* (CVA 63) and her battle group were ordered to join *Midway* in a show of force, bringing the total number of US ships in the area to 21. In December, a 6th Fleet battle group headed by *Nimitz* (CVN 68) was ordered to relieve *Kitty Hawk* and her group. The *Nimitz* arrived in the Arabian Sea 22 January 1980 after an 18-day, 11,500-mile (18500-km) dash from the Mediterranean via the Cape of Good Hope. And, on 5 February *Coral Sea* relieved *Midway*, which had been on station since the hostage crisis began on 4 November. New records were established by the carriers during the year from time on station and days at sea. On 24 March 1980, after *Nimitz*'s 100th consecutive day at sea, a General Order of the Navy was relaxed by the Secretary of the Navy and two cans of beer were made available to each of *Nimitz*'s crewmembers. Alcohol had been banished from Navy ships since 1914 (1899 for enlisted men). Current Navy policy now allows issuance of beer to

crews after 45 consecutive days at sea. Between November 1979 and July 1980, six of the flat tops had spent 529 days on station in the Indian Ocean/Arabian Sea standing by for contingency operations.

At dusk on the evening of 24 April 1980, eight RH-53Ds on loan from HM-16 and flown by special joint-service crews, lifted from the deck of *Nimitz* in the Arabian Sea on a mission to rescue the American hostages being held by the Iranian terrorists. A joint-service commando team was embarked in the helicopters. A flight of six USAF C-130s carrying fuel and special equipment had previously launched from Egyptian bases to rendezvous with the Navy helos at a desert site some 200 miles (320 km) from Tehran. Ahead of the helos was a 600-mile (965-km) low-altitude night flight over hostile and completely unfamiliar terrain.

The mission, which had been carefully planned and rehearsed for 5½ months, was beset by problems almost immediately. Approximately two hours into the flight, one of the RH-53s was forced

Above: HM-16 RH-53D Sea Stallions from *Nimitz* (CVN 68)-based group assembled for the Iranian hostage rescue mission in April 1980 in flight over the Indian Ocean.

Below: Camouflaged Sikorsky RH-53Ds of HM-16 on loan to a special joint-rescue force, at rest aboard USS *Nimitz* on 24 April 1980. Four days later, eight of these Sea Stallions made a vain attempt to rescue hostages being held in the US Embassy in Tehran.

Above: 'CAG Bird' A-7E from VA-97 assigned to *Coral Sea*'s air group commander with special markings identifying aircraft of the support force for the Iranian hostage rescue team. The VA-27 A-7E in background prepares for catapult launch.

aircraft were destroyed in the ensuing conflagration, which caused the death of eight crewmembers and injury to five of the rescue force. Several other helos were damaged by resultant explosions.

Following this disaster the helos were abandoned and all remaining personnel were loaded aboard the other C-130s, which then returned safely to their base without further incident.

Standby air support for the rescue mission in the event it was intercepted, or the rescue force attacked, was to have been provided by *Nimitz*'s CVW-8 and CVW-14 in *Coral Sea*. To assure recognition, the fighter and attack aircraft were painted with special colored identification stripes on their starboard wings, reminiscent of the invasion stripes carried by Allied planes over the Normandy landings of World War II.

On 22 December 1980 *Dwight D. Eisenhower* (CVN 69), which had relieved *Nimitz* on 29 April, and her escorts *South Carolina* (CGN 37) and *Virginia* (CGN 38) returned to Norfolk after a 251-day deployment, the longest for any Navy ship since World War II. During the period *Eisenhower* had been under way at sea for 152 continuous days.

Carriers and the Gulf of Sidra

In 1972 the US Navy began reclassification of its attack carriers. With integration of the ASW forces into the CVWs, the carriers became CV and CVN as they were converted to handle the ASW mission. *Saratoga* was the first carrier classified CV since 1952. By 30 June 1975, all active CVAs were redesignated.

Another historical event occurred in January 1977 when, for the first time, both deployed US fleets were operating all-nuclear-powered battle groups. The 6th Fleet group in the Mediterranean, headed by *Nimitz* (CVN 68), included *California* (CGN 36) and *South Carolina*. The 7th Fleet group in the Pacific included *Enterprise* (CVN 65), *Long Beach* (CGN 9) and *Truxtun* (CGN 35).

In an international arena over the Gulf of Sidra off the coast of Libya, naval air power once again demonstrated to the world the capability of its aircrew and aircraft. On 19 August 1981, climaxing

down by mechanical failure. The crew was picked up by another of the helos and the mission continued toward the rendezvous. One hour later the formation encountered two unexpected dust storms common to the desert area. One helo was forced to return to *Nimitz* at that time. Finally reaching the rendezvous (Desert One) 50-58 minutes behind schedule, the remaining six helos landed to refuel. At this point, a third Sea Stallion was declared mechanically unfit to continue the mission. Criteria for successful completion of the mission required a minimum of six helos, and with the loss of the third helo the mission was aborted.

While being repositioned for refuelling from the C-130s, one RH-53 collided with a Hercules. Both

Right: A US Marine F-4N of VMFA-323 aboard *Coral Sea* (CV 43) receives special identification markings applied to the aircraft standing-by to support the Iranian hostage rescue mission.

In an international arena over the Gulf of Sidra off the coast of Libya, naval air power once again demonstrated to the world the capability of its aircrew and aircraft. On 19 August 1981, climaxing years of pilot and RIO training and design development of the Grumman F-14A Tomcat, two crews from Fighter Squadron 41 (VF-41), the 'Black Aces', countered an unprovoked attack by two Libyan air force Sukhoi Su-22 'Fitters' by shooting down both attackers. The action, over in less than one minute, developed when the two F-14s, flown by VF-41 commanding officer Commander Henry 'Hank' Kleemann and his RIO Lieutenant David Venlet, with wingman Lieutenant Larry Musczynski and RIO Lieutenant (JG) Jim Anderson, were vectored to intercept the 'Fitters' heading toward the *Nimitz*'s battle group. The Tomcats were on a CAP at 20,000 ft (6095 m) when the initial contact was made. As the F-14s turned to intercept the Su-22s the crews assumed that, as usual, a non-shooting engagement might develop and maybe an opportunity to photograph the 'Fitters'. Instead, as the two flights closed in a head-on approach, the lead Libyan plane fired an 'Atoll' heat-seeking missile which missed Musczynski's F-14, low and behind. Kleemann, tracking the Libyan wingman, observed the missile firing and announced by radio that he would fire a Sidewinder at his target in return. As Musczynski pulled into the six-o'clock position behind the lead 'Fitter' he also fired a Sidewinder. Both missiles from the F-14s found their marks and the two Sukhois went down, with one open parachute observed by Tomcat crews. This was the first air combat victory for the Grumman F-14 and the first Su-22 shot down by American aviators.

During a postflight interview, the 'Black Aces' crews emphasized the immense value of their constant training in air combat maneuvering. They were also confident that any crew in their air wing could have done what they did. When asked 'Just how good were the Libyans?', the answer was a forthright 'Not as good as we were.'

Naval Aviation began operations in 1982 with 13 active fleet carriers, adding a 14th, *Carl Vinson* (CVN 70), when she was commissioned on 13 March. Of these 14 ships, 10 were deployed at some time during the year with the others in major overhauls or rework programs. *Midway*, home-ported in Yokosuka, Japan since 1973, is forward deployed and not included in this figure. There were 12 active carrier air wings to support the battle groups (as task groups were redesignated). Additional aircraft assets are provided when needed from Marine squadrons.

Robert L. Lawson

34
Ship-based Aircraft Development

During the decade following the Vietnam War, Naval Aviation continued operating most of the same aircraft that had served so effectively in South East Asia. There were some retirements of well-known models and some new ones were introduced. The aircraft inventory had declined in numbers during the final years of the war, a 1968 operating total of more than 7,100 dropping to 5,590 by the end of 1973 and to 4,931 by 1976. The rate of decline shallowed then and had stabilized at about 4,436 by 1980 and continued at approximately that level through 1983. Within these totals, the number of aircraft in the several type categories declined at a similar rate. Fighters (VF), totalling 886 in 1968 were at 602 by 1980, then increased modestly to 643 in 1983. Attack (VA) aircraft numbers dropped from a 1968 total of 1,539 to 974 in 1982, then increased to an estimated 1,055 by 1983. Other fixed-wing types followed similar patterns of decline until the early 1980s when the trend was reversed.

Fighter assets at the beginning of the 1970s were the McDonnell Douglas F-4 Phantom and Vought F-8 Crusader. The workhorse Phantom continued in production for the Navy until 1971, with later Navy updates incorporating changes dictated by fleet service. Major models in Navy and Marine Corps use progressed from the F-4B and F-4J to the F-4N update of the F-4B and F-4S update of the F-4J. The Phantom actually was built in 14 models

Above: At Fallon in January 1981 on weapons training deployment, a VA-35 KA-6D tanker refuels a VF-41 F-14A while a second Tomcat waits its turn. Fast Eagle 107 and 102 were the two F-14s involved in the Libyan Su-22 shoot down later that year.

Right: A tranquil backdrop contrasts the continuing activity aboard an aircraft carrier as the crew of an F-4 climb to their cockpits to prepare for an evening mission. Now in the twilight of its operational career with the US Navy, the F-4 has undergone many modifications to update its capabilities.

Below: Grumman F-14A Tomcat from VF-41, the 'Black Aces' of CVW-1, aboard *Nimitz*. This squadron scored the double victory over attacking Libyan Su-22s over the Gulf of Sidra on 19 August 1981.

Lieutenant Commander Peter Clayton

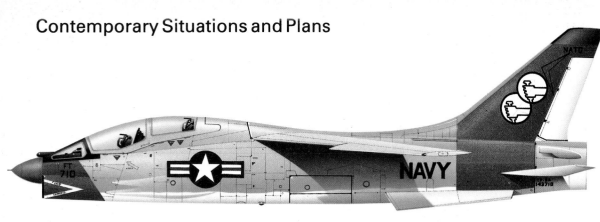

during the 20 years it was in production by McDonnell Douglas. The 5,000th Phantom, delivered on 24 May 1978, was decorated with the flags of the 10 nations which have flown it. It had also become the US Air Force's first-line fighter of the 1960s and early 1970s. The Marine Corps also has one squadron of RF-4B photo-reconnaissance Phantoms. As 1984 began, only two fleet squadrons still operated the Phantom: VF-151 and -161 with CVW-5 in *Midway* flying the F-4S. VF-21 and -154 with CVW-14 in *Coral Sea* flew the last regular Phantom deployment in 1983. returning with their F-4Ns to NAS Miramar on 11 September.

The Vought F-8 Crusader also enjoyed a long-lived production and operational life, going through F-8H, J, K and L modifications during the 1970s. When replaced in the fleet, many F-8s were transferred to the Naval Reserve for the remainder of their service life. Crusaders were phased out of the fleet in 1976 with VF-191 and VF-194 in *Oriskany* flying the F-8J on its final deployment. The F-8 was a star Naval Aviation performer in Vietnam, flying as a day and all-weather fighter, attack aircraft and as the RF-8G for photo-reconnaissance. With its four 20-mm guns and Sidewinder missiles, the Crusader fighter enjoyed the highest kill ratio of any US aircraft flying in Vietnam, earning it the

Robert L. Lawson

title of 'MiG Master'. The photo-reconnaissance RF-8G continued in fleet service until 1982 when VFP-63, its final operator, was disestablished. The aircraft were handed-over to Naval Reserve squadrons VFP-206 and -306, based at NAF Washington, DC which still operated them until September 1984. On 30 September VFP-306 was decommissioned. These two squadrons represented the Navy's only directional tactical reconnaissance units of the time.

Above: Illustrating two very different current color schemes are a VF-171 Det Key West McDonnell Douglas F-4N and A-4E en route to an air combat maneuvers (ACM) training area.

Below: The pilot of a Chance Vought RF-8G Crusader awaits instructions from a flight deck director before the start of another mission.

US Navy

Left: General Dynamics Grumman F-111B during carrier suitability trials aboard *Coral Sea* (CVA 43) on 23 July 1968. An ill-conceived joint USAF/USN use aircraft, the F-111B was discarded as unsuitable for the US Navy and led to the development of the F-14A Tomcat.

Finding a new state-of-the-art fighter for the fleet in the 1960s as a replacement for the F-4 and the F-8 proved to be a monumental task. It was one that stretched over more than 10 years before the Grumman-proposed F-14 was accepted. The first effort was the infamous TFX (Tactical Fighter Experimental) concept (a common fighter for the Air Force and the Navy) forced on the US Navy in the mid-1960s during Robert S. McNamara's tenure as Secretary of Defense. Developed as the USAF F-111A by program prime contractor General Dynamics, the Navy version, F-111B, was to have been modified and produced by Grumman as a subcontractor. Grumman built seven F-111Bs, five with R&D funds and two on the production contract. An extensive flight test program, beginning with a first flight of the no. 1 prototype on 18 May 1965, soon revealed totally unacceptable weight, performance and deck-handling characteristics. There were also major problems with the experimental Pratt & Whitney TF-30 turbofan engine with afterburner. The one positive result of the entire unfortunate experience was the Phoenix missile and AWG-9 weapon system, which was a spectacular success and ultimately incorporated in the F-14A. The F-111B program was cancelled by the Department of Defense 10 July 1968 after Congress refused to authorize production funds.

A major factor cited by the Congressional Armed Services Committees in support of the decision to stop work on the F-111B, was the information that several proposals had been announced for aircraft using the same engines and missiles, but unencumbered by the commonality requirements of the F-111B. One of these proposals was the Grumman design for a variable geometry (VG) multi-mission fighter which would incorporate the company's

unchallenged expertise in the design of naval aircraft and its recent experience with the F-111B. A preliminary Grumman proposal for the new lightweight airframe utilizing the TF-30 engine and avionics was submitted to the Navy in October 1967 as the VFX. The Navy studied the proposal carefully and was overwhelmed by the multi-mission performance predicted for the aircraft. Following cancellation of the F-111B, a Navy Request for Proposals (RFP) went out to the aerospace industry for the VFX fighter. Basic requirements included a two-man crew in tandem cockpits, two TF-30-P-412 engines, a weapon-control system with the capabilities of the AWG-9/Phoenix system and provisions for the Phoenix, Sidewinder and Sparrow missiles plus an M61A gun. Responses were received from North American-Rockwell, Ling Temco Vought, Grumman, McDonnell Douglas, and General Dynamics. Grumman and McDonnell were selected for a run-off final effort, and on 3 February 1969 the Navy and Grumman signed a contract for the development and production of the F-14A.

Enter the Tomcat

The F-14 made its first flight 21 December 1970, less than two years after the contract for its development had been signed. In spite of the loss of the first airplane in an accident caused by a hydraulic failure on 30 December, the flight test program progressed on schedule. Initial carrier suitability trials were completed successfully in June 1972 on board *Forrestal*. Flight tests to prove the integration of the Phoenix with the F-14 were completed later in the year. On 14 October 1972, VF-1 and VF-2, the first two squadrons slated for Tomcats, were commissioned at NAS Miramar. The F-14

Left: An early recipient of the F-14A was Fighting 14, which took its aircraft aboard *John F. Kennedy*. The colorful markings are typical of the 1970s.

US Navy – Graves/Gilpin

Above: This night view of *Ranger* (CV 61) demonstrates the capability of TARPS-equipped F-14s. This photo by a TARPS F-14A from VF-2 was made on 17 February 1982 off the southern California coast.

Below: During ACEVAL/AIMVAL, a joint USAF/US Navy weapons and fighter aircraft evaluation project in 1978, an experimental camouflage scheme developed by aviation artist Keith Ferris was also evaluated on VX-4 F-14s.

training squadron, VF-124, received its first production Tomcat on 8 October and began final preparations for the training it would provide for pilots, NFOs and maintenance personnel for fleet F-14 squadrons. On 17 September 1974, VF-1 and -2 embarked in USS *Enterprise* for the first deployment of the F-14A.

By early 1983, Grumman had completed and delivered 446 Tomcats to the Navy. (Another 80 were built for the Iranian air force, of which 79 were delivered.) The F-14s have been continually updated to correct problems disclosed by early opera-

tional experience and to enhance the Tomcat's capabilities. A 1980 change was the incorporation of provisions for TARPS (Tactical Air Reconnaissance Pod System), a centerline-mounted fuselage pod equipped with three cameras for photo-reconnaissance missions, which does not detract from the F-14's fighter capabilities. VF-84 made a successful first deployment to the Mediterranean with TARPS-equipped F-14s in late 1981 and VF-211, in *Constellation*, deployed to the Western Pacific with the pods early in 1982. In 1983 Tomcats began to be equipped with TCS (Television Camera Set), a variable lens

US Navy

One of the latest production examples of the Grumman F-14A Tomcat, shown in the insignia of VF-143 'Pukin' Dogs', part of CVW-7 aboard USS *Dwight D. Eisenhower* (CVN 69). The aircraft is carrying the standard maximum weapons load of four AIM-54A Phoenix, two AIM-7F Sparrow and two AIM-9L Sidewinder air-to-air missiles, a mix that permits it to counter threats across virtually the entire air-defense spectrum. In addition to the missiles, the F-14A is equipped with an integral Vulcan M61 20-mm cannon for close-in air combat.

television camera mounted under the forward fuselage which provides the crew a means of positive visual identification of targets far beyond normal range.

Updating the attack element

In the post-Vietnam War carrier air wings, the VA community included several types of attack aircraft. One of the best-liked and most capable was the McDonnell Douglas A-4 Skyhawk. During the period, it served in variants from A-4C to A-4M, filling the light attack needs of the Navy and Marine air wings. The A-4 series established a record by being in continuous production by Douglas for 26 years. The last Skyhawk, BuNo. 160264, was an A-4M delivered to VMA-331 in impressive ceremonies on 27 February 1979. It was the 2,960th A-4 built.

Supplementing the A-4 in the light attack role was the Vought A-7 Corsair II, with A-7A, B, C, E, and a two-seat trainer version, the TA-7C, in service. A long-standing need for the latter trainer version was filled in the late 1970s with the first aircraft delivered 31 January 1977. The TA-7Cs, converted from existing A-7Bs and Cs, have a primary mission of training replacement pilots for the fleet light attack squadrons.

Navy and Marine Corps requirements for medium attack assets are effectively filled by Grumman A-6 Intruders, undoubtedly the world's most capable attack aircraft. Variants of this plane in service during the 1970s and 1980s include the A-6A, B, C, and E. Deliveries of a new A-6E model, incorporating the TRAM (Target Recognition and Attack Multisensor) system began in late 1979. TRAM provides an ultra-sophisticated weapon control and attack recording system incorporating a laser target-designator/range-finder plus an infrared sensor. It is mounted in a turret under the nose radome forward of the nosewheel. Sensor information is displayed on a TV-like screen for the B/N's use during search and attack. TRAM's target-sensing capabilities are so sensitive that it can differentiate between full and empty fuel storage

Above: In late 1983 VA-46 A-7Es were at Fallon for CVW-1 weapons training. Color and markings of their Corsair IIs is the latest version of the low-visibility schemes in current use on fleet tactical aircraft.

Above left: Wearing the highly decorative tartan insignia of the 'Clansmen' of Light Attack Squadron VA-46, this A-7B Corsair II prepares to launch from USS *John F. Kennedy* (CV 67) during the course of a deployment with the 6th Fleet in the Mediterranean Sea.

Below: Air combat maneuver training (ACM) for Pacific Fleet fighter pilots is provided by adversary squadrons based at NAS Miramar. This VF-114 crew and their VC-13 TA-4J opponent maneuver for position in 1981.

Right: One of the first squadrons to receive the far more sophisticated A-6E variant of the Grumman Intruder was VA-65 at Oceana, Virginia.

Below: NAF El Centro-based VA-174 utilizes the A-7E and TA-7C for fleet pilot weapons delivery training. Here a 'Hellrazors' TA-7C drops Mk 82 bombs on a desert target in 1980.

Robert L. Lawson Collection

Above right: A VA-35 A-6E TRAM Intruder at Fallon in 1981 carries a full load of Mk 82 bombs during pre-deployment work-up.

Below: An A-6E Intruder bombardier-navigator's view of the drogue basket during the course of inflight refuelling from a KA-6D Intruder.

tanks in a target area. In 1981, the A-6E's already impressive weapons-delivery capability was augmented by the installation of launch and control equipment for the airborne version of the Harpoon anti-ship missile. Derivatives of the Intruder produced in small numbers for special missions included the A-6B and C. The KA-6D inflight-refuelling tanker, one of the most essential aircraft in the carrier air wings, continues in production with modification/rework of early A-6As, A-6Es and KA-6Ds.

The photo-reconnaissance requirements of the battle groups were satisfied by the Vought RF-8G until the Crusader was withdrawn from the fleet in 1982. The reconnaissance role was then assumed by TARPS-equipped F-14s. When required Marine photo-reconnaissance squadron VMFP-3 augments *Midway*'s CVW-5 with RF-4Bs. The North American Rockwell A3J-1 (A-5A) Vigilante was designed to be the Navy's strategic bomber until the mission was abandoned in favor of submarine-launched ballistic missiles in the early 1960s. This action left the Vigilante a plane without a mission until the decision was made to change the heavy attack

US Navy

Left: An RA-5C from RVAH-7 during its final deployment. The Vigilante, left without a mission after the abolition of the Navy's strategic attak role in 1962, was converted to the reconnaissance mission where it demonstrated outstanding capabilities during 15 years of service as a versatile photo-reconnaissance aircraft.

squadron's role from bombing to reconnaissance and to modify the aircraft for the new task. The RA-5C version had sophisticated reconnaissance systems and served well, deploying with carrier air wings to the Mediterranean and Southeast Asia from 1964 until 1979. During 1979 the RVAH squadrons and their functional wing were disestablished and, on 20 November, the last active RA-5C was ferried to storage. The RA-5C was highly regarded by its crews and commanders for its performance as a reconnaissance platform during its fleet service. By coincidence, Heavy Attack Squadron Seven (VAH-7) was both the first to deploy with A3J-1 in *Enterprise* in 1962 and the last, in *Ranger*, with the RA-5C in 1979.

Electronic warfare (EW) aircraft aboard the carriers, though few in number, perform a vital function for both the ship and the air wing. Grumman's E-1B Tracer, originally developed from the S2F ASW airplane as the WF-2 (and hence affectionately forever known as 'Willy Fudd') served until 1973. Its replacement, the E-2 Hawkeye, also from Grumman provides awesome capability to the fleet for early warning of attack threats and control of fighters for battle group defense. The Hawkeye has evolved from E-2A (W2F-1 until 1962) and E-2B to the E-2C model, with several periodic systems updates. The E-2A joined the fleet with VAW-11 in 1964. Its initial performance was disappointing, however. The version was modified, primarily to improve computer and avionics reliability, rejoining the fleet in 1970 as the E-2B. The E-2C, with overland tracking capability, was a quantum leap over the E-2B. It was accepted for service in April 1977 and made its first deployment with VAW-123 that September in *Saratoga*. Fleet EW assets, never very large, have fluctuated from a high of 136 in 1972 to a 1981 low of 90 with an estimated 112 in 1983.

The Douglas A-3 Skywarrior, an aircraft that can truly be called venerable, celebrated the 30th anniversary of its first flight 28 October 1982. It continues in its role as the fleet's multi-mission jack-of-all-trades airplane. It flies electronic

Right: A flight deck director signals the pilot to align his Rockwell RA-5C Vigilante on the catapult aboard USS *Ranger* (CVA 61). The highly streamlined design of the Vigilante helped it attain impressive speeds for such a large aircraft.

Below: Responsibility for airborne early warning is entrusted to the Grumman Hawkeye, represented here by an E-2C of VAW-125. Shown during recovery aboard USS *John F. Kennedy* (CV 67), this variant has now almost entirely replaced the older E-2B model.

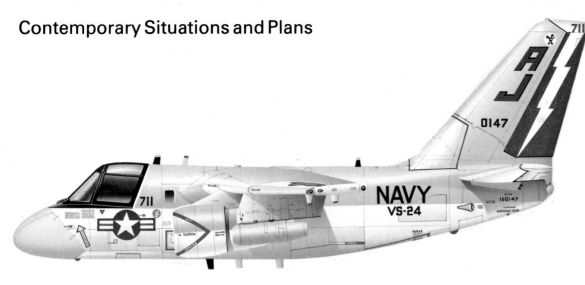

Left: At the time of writing, six Atlantic Fleet anti-submarine warfare squadrons are equipped with the Lockheed S-3A Viking, these being represented here by an aircraft from VS-24 which normally deploys aboard USS *Nimitz* (CVN 68) as part of CVW-8.

Below left: Naval Reserve Douglas KA-3B Skywarrior from VAK-308 refuels a VC-12 McDonnell Douglas TA-4J Skyhawk over Puerto Rico in April 1982.

countermeasures missions, electronic reconnaissance, and tanker missions in versions designated EA-, KA-, EKA- and ERA-3B. Scheduled for phase-out in the mid-1970s, the A-3 has outlasted the planners and is currently slated for extension of its service life well into the 1990s. The Skywarrior program may well end up with a service life of 50 years, well beyond the wildest imagination of its designers. In 1984 the A-3 was fleet operational with VQ-1 and -2 and used in an EW training role with VAQ-33 and -34. Two Reserve squadrons, VAK-208 and -308, operate KA-3B tankers.

Another facet of EW operations is electronic countermeasures, and this has and continues to be the responsibility of Grumman's EA-6A Intruder and EA-6B Prowler derivatives of the A-6 series. Limited Navy VAQ assets in the past have been augmented by the deployment of Marine squadron VMAQ-2 detachments with the carrier air wings. Updates of the Prowler's on-board systems have provided a continually improved and highly effective asset to the air wings. The EA-6B continues in production by Grumman with six aircraft per year planned through 1987, sufficient to provide a Navy VAQ squadron for each of the carrier air wings. The

Above: The prominent fuselage bulges and ventral fairing identify this Skywarrior as an EKA-3B.

Below: A Grumman EA-6B Prowler operated by VAQ-132. Derived from the highly successful A-6 Intruder, the four-seat EA-6B is the US Navy's first aircraft specifically built for tactical electronic warfare.

Right; After serving as a planeguard and general purpose helicopter for several years, most surviving examples of the Kaman Seasprite were modified to SH-2F configuration to fulfil the Mk 2 LAMPS requirement. This particular example is from HSL-33 at North Island.

Right: One of the most successful anti-submarine warfare aircraft yet conceived, the Grumman S-2 Tracker no longer serves with the US Navy. This S-2E – with the MAD boom extended – was from VS-31, which was stationed at Quonset Point, Rhode Island, until 1973.

Below: After operating the Grumman S-2 Tracker for many years, the 'Top Cats' of VS-31 re-equipped with the Lockheed S-3A Viking in the early 1970s and now form part of Carrier Air Wing Seven (CVW-7) aboard USS *Dwight D. Eisenhower* (CVN 69).

EA-6A serves with VAQ-33 as well as Navy and Marine Reserve squadrons in 1984.

Progress in ASW

Sea-based anti-submarine warfare is the mission of the carrier-based VS and HS squadrons as well as the LAMPS (Light Airborne Multipurpose System) helicopters operating from the battle group escort ships. The VS squadrons had been equipped with the Grumman S-2 Tracker for more than 20 years when the last S-2G was retired from the fleet (VS-37) in August 1976. The S-2s were replaced by the Lockheed S-3A Viking beginning in February 1974. First deployment of the Viking was with VS-21 in *Kennedy* and CVW-1 in 1975. During the late 1970s, a readiness improvement program for the by-then out-of-production Viking was initiated. This successful effort upgraded S-3A capability and led to the S-3B, with significant improvements, including provision for launching Harpoon anti-ship missiles. The carrier-based Viking incorporates the same ASW capabilities as its much larger land-based counterpart, the P-3 Orion.

US Navy

Featuring the distinctive multi-colored rudder stripes which indicate a 'CAG-bird' (Air Wing Commander's aircraft), this Lockheed S-3A Viking was assigned to Anti-Submarine Warfare Squadron VS-21 during 1975-6, when this unit undertook the first operational seagoing deployment of the Viking aboard USS *John F. Kennedy* (CV 67) with the 6th Fleet in the Mediterranean Sea. Since that time, the S-3A has become an integral part of carrierborne forces, and is to be the subject of a forthcoming updating effort which will result in the appearance of the more sophisticated and capable S-3B model. Noteworthy features are the numerous blade antennae and the wingtip ESM fittings.

Following the successful evaluation of a prototype conversion, a handful of early production Vikings have been modified for carrier offshore delivery (COD) duty as the US-3A. The initial conversion is portrayed here in the colours of VS-33.

Right: CH-46 Sea Knights shoulder the Navy's vertical on board delivery requirements for the battle groups at sea. HC-3 CH-46D is on replenishment mission for USS *Constellation* (CVA 64) in the South China Sea in September, 1974.

Below left: In a 1976 photo, a LAMPS Mk I SH-2F Seasprite from San Diego-based HSL-33 carries a Mk 66 training torpedo.

Robert L. Lawson Collection

ASW defense tasks are shared by the S-3s with the current LAMPS Kaman SH-2F and Sikorsky SH-60B helicopters beginning fleet introduction in 1984. Operating from battle group escort ships, the LAMPS squadrons complement the Sikorsky SH-3H HS squadrons aboard the carriers. A shortage of Seasprites led to the reopening of the Kaman production line in 1983 to build an updated SH-2F. These aircraft, referred to as LAMPS Mk I, are based on the smaller frigates. Sikorsky's Seahawk SH-60B, the LAMPS Mk III aircraft, operates from larger escorts and screen ships, providing ASW defense at the outer limits of the battle group formation plus over-the-horizon surveillance and attack-planning information. ASW assets in the fleet have remained relatively constant in number for the past 10 years for both fixed and rotary-wing aircraft.

Logistic support for the fleet at sea is the mission of the carrier on board delivery (COD) aircraft, the Grumman C-1A Trader and C-2A Greyhound. Additional support is provided by three US-3As, a modification of early S-3A Vikings. For many years each carrier was permanently assigned a C-1A Trader to expedite the movement of personnel and critical matériel between the ship and shore bases or, occasionally, to other carriers at sea. In 1983 the reciprocating engined C-1s were transferred to the shore-based VRC squadrons with the exception of one assigned to *Midway*.

The carrier-based, all-weather Sikorsky SH-3H Sea King is operated by fleet HS squadrons and is the key element in close-in ASW protection for the carrier battle group. The first US helicopter specifically designed for the ASW mission, it has been in fleet service since the early 1960s.

Below: Grumman C-2A Greyhounds deliver cargo and personnel to carriers at sea. Thirty-nine new C-2s are on order with deliveries to begin in 1985. Here a VRC-50 C-2A lands aboard *Constellation* (CVA-64) in South China Sea in September 1974.

Robert L. Lawson Collection

Left: Operated as a general-purpose transport by the Naval Weapons Center at China Lake, California, this C-117D originally served as the prototype for this version of the ubiquitous Skytrain and was eventually followed by 100 similar conversions.

Left: The Lockheed P2V-7 (SP-2H) still served in small numbers with Naval Reserve squadrons long after the front-line squadrons had re-equipped with the more capable (and younger) P-3 Orion.

35
Shore-based Aircraft Development

Naval Aviation's primary shore-based assets are the patrol squadrons (VP), dedicated to maritime patrol and ASW defense. Some 200 Lockheed P-3 Orions equip 24 operational patrol squadrons; another 40 P-3s serve in two replacement training squadrons. Thirteen Naval Reserve squadrons fly an additional 130 Orions.

The P-3's predecessor, the Lockheed P-2 Neptune (P2V series) served Naval Aviation well as the shore-based ASW aircraft from 1947 until the Orions began relieving them in 1962. The P-2s continued to serve in the Naval Reserve squadrons and a few were utilized in special assignments such as drone launching platforms or control ships. The last of the P-2s, an EP-2H, was retired in 1980 from VC-8.

Five of the fleet patrol squadrons are equipped in 1984 with the P-3B, while the others have the more capable P-3C with improved sensors and computers. A dramatically improved P-3C Update II model has been replacing the older Orions since production deliveries began in mid-1977. The P-3's offensive capability was enhanced in 1977 when it was approved for use of the Harpoon anti-ship missile. This gives the P-3 the option of launching at ranges of up to 60 miles (97 km), well beyond the range of AA guns or missiles.

Below: A P-3C Orion of VP-19 on an ASW training mission off the coast of central California 18 September 1977. Lockheed Orions are the US Navy's sole land-based ASW aircraft and are operated by both Regular and Reserve squadrons.

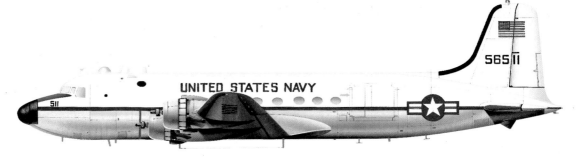

The backbone of Navy airlift squadrons for some time in the late 1940s and early 1950s, the Douglas R5D continued to serve as a general-purpose transport aircraft until the early 1970s. This particular example is a VC-540 used for staff transport tasks.

Right: Following a long career with the US Navy, the last deployment of the Constellation occurred when this aircraft, the last in service, flew to Puerto Rico on exercises. It is an EC-121 of VAQ-33.

A Douglas C-9B Skytrain II operated by Naval Air Reserve Squadron 55 (VR-55) with USS Enterprise in the background. The C-9B will become the Reserve's sole heavy-lift transport by the end of 1985.

Shore-based fleet EW squadrons (VQ) flew the Lockheed EC-121 Constellation, EC-130 Hercules and EP-3 Orion, and the Douglas EA-3B Sky-warrior during the 1973-83 era. Like many post-World War II naval aircraft, the Constellation enjoyed a long service life in a variety of roles. It first flew for the Navy in 1945 as the passenger/cargo transport R7O (later R7V). Later, with its cavernous fuselage filled with exotic electronic equipment and radomes above and below, it flew the radar early warning barrier patrols over the Atlantic and Pacific. In its last role as an electronic reconnaissance plane with VQ-1 and -2, it searched for and recorded electronic transmissions of all kinds. VAQ-33 retired the last NC-121K 'Connie' on 25 June 1982. The EC-130 continues to fly the EW mission, its long-range and heavy-lift capability suiting it well for the role. Some of the VQ squadron EC-130s are equipped to provide communications service to deployed submarines and are referred to as TACAMO planes (for 'take charge and move out!').

The post-Vietnam decade brought retirement from the Navy's transport squadrons (VR) of aircraft of legendary reputation and the acquisition of replacements with vastly increased capabilities. The last of the Douglas C-117D (R4D-8) aircraft, final version of the world's most famous transport airplane, the Douglas DC-3, was ferried to storage 12 July 1976. The Lockheed C-130 Hercules turboprop heavy-lift transport and McDonnell Douglas C-9B Skytrain II, military version of the commercial DC-9 jet transport, assumed the tasks assigned to the C-117 in the past. Preceding the old Skytrain into retirement was the four-engine Douglas C-54 Skymaster (R5D) which was taken out of service 2 April 1974 after more than 30 years of naval service. Six Douglas C-118B Liftmaster (R6D-2) continue in service with Naval Reserve VR squadrons, but are being replaced with C-9Bs in 1985.

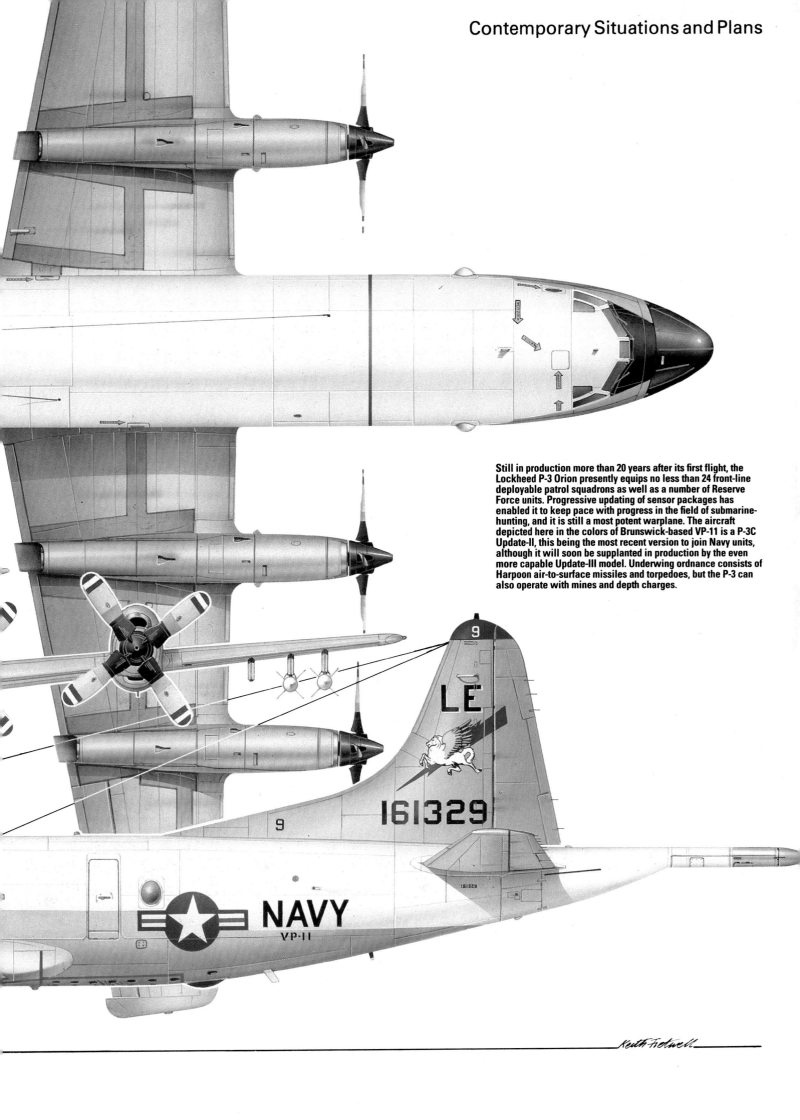

Still in production more than 20 years after its first flight, the Lockheed P-3 Orion presently equips no less than 24 front-line deployable patrol squadrons as well as a number of Reserve Force units. Progressive updating of sensor packages has enabled it to keep pace with progress in the field of submarine-hunting, and it is still a most potent warplane. The aircraft depicted here in the colors of Brunswick-based VP-11 is a P-3C Update-II, this being the most recent version to join Navy units, although it will soon be supplanted in production by the even more capable Update-III model. Underwing ordnance consists of Harpoon air-to-surface missiles and torpedoes, but the P-3 can also operate with mines and depth charges.

Left: Training Wing Four (TraWing 4) squadrons VT-28 and VT-30, based at NAS Corpus Christi, Texas, provide multi-engine night, instrument and cross-country training for US Navy and US Marine student pilots. The squadrons fly Beech T-44A Pegasus aircraft, maintained by Beech Aerospace Services personnel on contract.

Fleet Logistic Support Squadron Twenty-Four (VR-24) and Mine Counter Measures Squadron Twelve (HM-12) pioneered in the use of heavy-lift helicopters for fleet logistic replenishment in the Mediterranean, beginning in 1975. HM-12 maintained a part-time detachment at NAF Sigonella, Sicily with Sikorsky CH-53Ds after completing Operation 'Nimbus Star'. In 1978 it established a full-time detachment at Sigonella. The three-engine CH-53E Super Stallion joined the squadron in 1983, providing an unprecedented heavy-lift capability. In May 1983 the HM-12 detachment at Sigonella was redesignated Helicopter Combat Support Squadron Four (HC-4), nicknamed 'The VOD Squad', for Vertical On-board Delivery.

Utility transports

Supplementing the Navy VR squadrons are utility transports assigned to the naval air stations. The Grumman US-2, another derivative of the S-2 Tracker, was the usual airplane in this assignment until replacement began in the mid-1970s by the Beech UC-12B Super King Air, a turboprop passenger and light cargo transport.

The VRC squadrons are a vital link between the carriers at sea and the fleet support stations ashore,

transporting high priority/low bulk cargo and personnel and, perhaps most important, mail. VRC-30 at Norfolk, VRC-40 at San Diego and VRC-50 in the Philippines plus VR-24 in the Mediterranean provide these carrier on board delivery (COD) services. They utilize the aging Grumman C-1A Trader (in service since 1955), Grumman turboprop C-2A Greyhounds and Lockheed US-3A Vikings. In addition to COD operations, the VRC squadrons fly the jet Rockwell CT-39 Saberliner, turboprop UC-12B and C-130 Hercules. The non-carrier planes provide the capability for rapid-response cargo and personnel airlift between US fleet bases.

The last of the obsolescent fleet service-type aircraft in use as trainers in the training command were phased out in the 1970s. The Grumman TF-9J Cougar, a derivative of the F9F-8 fighter, flew its last training mission on 4 February 1974 when student pilots from Training Squadron Four landed aboard *Kennedy* for their carrier qualification landings. Another Grumman plane, the TS-2A, was replaced as a multi-engine pilot trainer by the Beech T-44A Pegasus in April 1977. Future fleet jet pilots currently receive their advanced training and carrier landing qualifications in the Rockwell T-2C Buckeye and McDonnell Douglas TA-4J, the latter

Right: US Navy and US Marine students pilots make their first qualification carrier landings aboard *Lexington* (AVT 16). VT-26 North American T-2C Buckeyes fly over the 'Lady Lex' off Corpus Christi on 14 July 1982.

Below: The versatile Grumman Tracker was used in a variety of roles during its US Navy career, including service with VC squadrons as target tugs for fleet gunnery practice. This VC-3 US-2C wears standard utility/composite squadron colours.

derived from the A-4 Skyhawk. Another veteran trainer, the 30-year old North American T-28 Trojan, is being phased out and replaced as the primary intermediate trainer by the Beech turboprop T-34C Turbo Mentor, which also replaced its T-34B progenitor.

Helicopter training continues as a Navy function in spite of repeated attempts to consolidate it with US Army rotary-wing training. The Navy's argument for continuing its own training is the unique character of many Navy and Marine rotary-wing operations. Navy helo training at NAS Whiting Field, Florida utilizes the Bell TH-1 Huey and TH-57A Sea Ranger. A later model, the TH-57C, is currently being introduced.

Aviation Ships and LAMPS

Major ships involved with the operation of naval aircraft are the carriers and the amphibious ships from which combat-troop landing operations are conducted. Carriers were reclassified in the mid-1970s to CV and CVN, replacing the earlier CVA and CVAN designators. The new system better describes the multi-mission character of the ships as they acquire the ASW role along with the VS and HS squadrons upon the abandonment of the CVS carrier concept.

Five carriers were decommissioned during the decade: *Shangri La* (CVS 38), *Ticonderoga* (CVS 14), *Intrepid* (CVS 11) and *Oriskany* (CV 34) of the 'Essex' class in 1971, 1973, 1974 and 1976 respectively, and *Franklin D. Roosevelt* (CV 42) of the 'Midway' class in 1977. These veterans were replaced by the three ships of the nuclear-powered 'Nimitz' class, *Nimitz* (CVN 68) in 1975, *Dwight D. Eisenhower* (CVN 69) in 1977 and *Carl Vinson* (CVN 70) in 1982. These are the world's largest

warships. They have an overall length of 1,092 ft (332.8 m), are 134 ft (40.8 m) at the beam and have a 93,400-ton combat load displacement. They carry a crew of approximately 6,000 men with their 90-aircraft air wings embarked. Fleet carriers at the end of the Vietnam War totalled 14, dropped to 13 in 1976 and returned to 14 in 1982. At least one carrier on each coast is usually out of service in overhaul at any one time. The training carrier at Pensacola, *Lexington* (ATV 16) is not included in these totals. Since 1980, one CV every 2½ years has undergone an extensive modernization and in-depth repair program called SLEP (Service Life Extension Program). SLEP is designed to add a minimum 15 years service life to these ships.

A new class of amphibious ship with significant aviation capabilities has joined the fleet, beginning with the lead ship *Tarawa* (LHA 1) in 1976. Sisters followed as *Saipan* (LHA 2) in 1977, *Belleau Wood* (LHA 3) in 1978, *Nassau* (LHA 4) in 1979, and *Peleliu* (LHA 5) in 1980. These are large diversely capable amphibious assault ships. At 820 ft (249.9 m) in overall length, displacing 39,000 tons, they can carry 1,800 troops, 250 vehicles and approximately 25 helicopters, including Boeing Vertol CH-46 Sikorsky CH-53 and Bell AH-1 models. The ships can also carry and operate McDonnell Douglas/British Aerospace AV-8 Harriers for air defense and close air support of the landed troops.

Although not, in the strictest sense, aviation ships, the carrier battle group escort destroyers and frigates, on which the LAMPS helicopters are

Above: The ubiquitous Lockheed C-130 Hercules has made its mark on US Naval Aviation, particularly in VX-6's support of the 'Deep Freeze' operations in the Antarctic. Ski-equipped undercarriage and a highly-visible color scheme are two of the features adopted for operations in this region, as illustrated by this LC-130R.

Above left: The task of testing missile armament is largely entrusted to the Pacific Missile Test Center at Point Mugu, California, this agency being descended from the Naval Missile Center, one of whose DT-28B Trojan drone controllers is seen near Point Mugu.

Below: Increasing emphasis is being placed on nuclear-powered aircraft-carriers in the modern US Navy, illustrated here by USS *Dwight D. Eisenhower* (CVN 69) and USS *Nimitz* (CVN 68) in the background. The Nimitz carrier group can steam at sustained speeds in excess of 30 kts for unlimited periods to anywhere in the world at short notice.

Typical of the fairly large number of Bell UH-1N Iroquois helicopters which presently serve with the US Navy, this example is assigned to the Base Flight at Agana, being employed on local rescue tasks and for routine liaison and communications duty.

Above: Fleet Replacement Training Squadron HSL-41 accepted the first production Sikorsky SH-60B Sea Hawk in late 1980. The SH-60B is the LAMPS Mk III ASW defense aircraft, based on the screen ships of the carrier battle group.

Far right: A welcome sight to a downed aviator during the Vietnam War was the Sikorsky HH-3A, the primary rescue aircraft, operated by HC-7's 'Big Muthas'. Today combat SAR squadron is HC-9, which inherited HC-7's helicopters.

Right: The *Midway* (CV 41) under way in the Pacific with CVW-5 on board. Ship and air wing have been forward deployed at Yokosuka, Japan since late 1973, the first such overseas basing of a fleet carrier and her aircraft since World War II.

based, are another facet of naval air power at sea. The original LAMPS Mk I system dates from the early 1970s when the Kaman UH-2 utility helo was modified to the SH-2D ASW configuration and based aboard the smaller surface force combatants. The system was updated in 1973 with the SH-2F and present planning continues LAMPS Mk I in service aboard 'Brooke', 'Knox' and 'Garcia' class FFs and FFGs. In addition to ASW defense using its onboard MAD, radar and sonobuoys, the SH-2F provides via datalink over-the-horizon targeting information for Harpoon launches and area surveillance.

LAMPS Mk I complements the newer Mk III system with the Sikorsky SH-60B Seahawk, which cannot operate from the smaller ships. The Mk III system, including the recovery assist, secure and traverse gear (RAST) aboard the ships, was tested in sea trials aboard *McInerney* (FFG-8) in May 1981. The first SH-60Bs began delivery to Replacement Training Squadron HSL-41 in 1983 at NAS North Island. LAMPS aircraft are operated by single-helicopter detachments of the HSL squadrons homeported at the major fleet support bases.

In the area of combat search and rescue, Naval Aviation has made no significant progress since Vietnam. HC-7, the Navy's only combat SAR squadron, was decommissioned 30 June 1975 with its assets eventually transferred to newly-formed Reserve squadron HC-9 at North Island. In 1984, HC-9, flying nine Sikorsky HH-3As, remains the only combat SAR unit in the Navy with no definite plan or program for the future. A long-range possibility for a replacement aircraft is the JVX, which would not be available until the mid-1990s. Combat SAR personnel would prefer a more immediately available version of the Sikorsky H-60, at least as an interim solution.

Naval Aviation organization changes

During the 1973-83 decade, changes to the organization of Naval Aviation forces were few in number, but nonetheless significant. In the Atlantic Fleet (AirLant), an internal reorganization to the functional wing concept was completed 1

April 1973 with the establishment of Air Antisubmarine Wing One (AASW-1) and Helicopter Antisubmarine Wing One (HASW-1).

The Pacific Fleet (AirPac) set a precedent when, for the first time, a carrier and her air wing were homeported overseas. *Midway* (CV 41) and CVW-5 were ordered to Yokosuka, Japan on 5 October 1973. The move, with obvious economic considerations, was also undertaken to improve ship and air wing crew morale by reducing separation from dependents. Strategically, the move is important in that it facilitates the deployment of carriers to the Western Pacific.

Another 1973 event with long-term implications was the reorganization of the Naval Reserve Forces, ordered by the Secretary of the Navy on 1 January. Aviation and surface forces were consolidated under a Chief of Naval Reserve, headquartered in New Orleans, Louisiana. The new organization followed the 1970 establishment of two Reserve

The epitome of US naval aviation air power in its shipborne element is illustrated by USS *John F. Kennedy* with a major part of her air group arrayed on her flight deck. The four steam catapults used for aircraft launching from the bow and waist positions are clearly visible.

Carrier Air Wings (CVWR), 12 VP squadrons and three VR squadrons. The air wing staffs are located on each coast with the assigned squadrons stationed at 10 Navy or Naval Reserve air stations throughout the US. Additionally, there is one Marine Reserve Air Wing.

The Naval Air Training Command (CNATRA) was also reorganized to a functional wing concept. Beginning in mid-1972, the Advanced Training Command (CNAVANTRA) at NAS Corpus Christi, Texas, was decommissioned. More than 84,000 Naval Aviators were trained by CNAVANTRA during the 30 years of its existence at Corpus Christi. The Basic Training Command (CNABATRA) at NAS Pensacola was also decommissioned, the two commands being replaced by eight training wings to implement a 'single base' concept in which a student, on completion of primary flight training, is assigned to one base and one program (jet, prop, or helo) for the remainder of his training.

The Chief of Naval Air Training and his headquarters staff moved from Pensacola to Corpus Christi as a part of this restructuring of the command.

The end of an era came at NAS Key West, Florida 28 September 1979, when RVAH-7, last of the former heavy attack squadrons, was disestablished. The CREW-1 wing and its nine squadrons completed disestablishment by 7 January 1980.

In a major move to improve the administration and operational control of some AirLant helicopter squadrons, Helicopter Tactical Wing One was established at Norfolk on 1 October 1982. The wing is responsible for squadrons HC-6 and -16, as well as HM-12, -14 and -16, constituting the heavy-lift and mine-countermeasures assets of the fleet.

Naval Aviation's commissioned manpower remained at essentially constant levels for the 10-year period after 1973 at about 9,500 officers, including pilots, NFOs and ground personnel. Enlisted personnel decreased from a 1973 high of 59,000 to about 57,000 in 1980, reflecting a continuing problem with the retention of personnel. Enlisted numbers include aircrewmen and all non-flying personnel. In the early 1980s, enlisted retention began improving remarkably.

Personnel

Significant 'people' events during the decade were many, with increased introduction of women into the service probably receiving the most attention both within and outside the Navy. The first woman ordered to flight training reported in

January 1973. On 22 February 1974, the first woman Naval Aviator, Lieutenant (JG) Barbara Ann Allen received her wings and commission at Corpus Christi. Later assigned duty in the Training Command as an instructor and married, Lieutenant Commander Rainey, tragically, was killed in a training accident 13 July 1982 at Whiting Field. She thus also became the first woman Naval Aviator to die in an aircraft accident.

On a happier note, VRC-40's Lieutenant Donna Spruill was the first woman to qualify for carrier landings in a fixed-wing aircraft when she completed CarQuals in a Grumman C-1A aboard *Independence* on 20 June 1979.

Increased emphasis by the Navy in the area of minority recruiting also came in the 1970s. Ensign Brenda E. Robinson was the first black woman to become a Naval Aviator. Her mother pinned on her wings at Corpus Christi on 6 June 1980. Ensign Robinson was the 59th woman to enter Navy flight training and the 42nd to earn her wings. Her first duty assignment was to VRC-40 at Norfolk to fly the C-1A.

The last of the 3,700 men who served as enlisted pilots, the NAPs (Naval Aviation Pilots) with the Navy, Marine Corps and Coast Guard retired during the 1973-83 decade. On 30 April 1973, MGSGT Patrick J. O'Neil, USMC, retired after more than 30 years continuous service. The last Navy NAP, Master Chief Robert K. Jones, retired 31 January 1981, after 38 years of service.

Although the NAP era ended with Master Chief Jones' retirement, another opportunity for Navy enlisted personnel to fly came with the Flying

Above: Lieutenant Commander Barbara Rainey, née Allen was the US Navy's first woman Naval Aviator, and is seen at the controls of a T-39 Sabreliner in 1977. Rainey lost her life in a training accident on 13 July 1982, to become the US Navy's first woman Naval Aviator to die in an aircraft accident.

Right: Navy Fighter Weapons School (Topgun), the post-graduate ACM training squadron at NAS Miramar, flew the Northrop F-5E as aggressor aircraft for ACM training in 1982.

Left: One of the most recent additions to the range of tasks performed by helicopter is that of minesweeping. Mine Countermeasures Squadron HM-12 pioneered many of the techniques involved with the CH-53D and RH-53D during the 1970s and has since been joined by two more squadrons.

Limited Duty Officer program initiated in 1980. The first 35 candidates were selected and reported to Pensacola for training in April 1981. These student pilots, on completion of flight training, are designated Naval Aviator and commissioned Ensign. Most of the graduates are ordered to duty as instructors in the Training Command. The first two men to complete the training, ASW Aircrewman First Class Michael A. Gray and Chief Yeoman Douglas L. McGowan, Jr, received their wings and commissions on 28 January 1982 at Corpus Christi. The first woman to complete the FLDO training was Air Controller First Class Jannine Weiss, who received her wings and commission on 30 July 1982. The FLDO naval aviators are restricted to duty within the training command or in non-operational flying billets in carriers or at naval air stations and staffs.

36
Naval Air Power's Contribution to the Future

When asked in a recent interview what he thought naval air power could contribute to the future, Vice Admiral Robert F. 'Dutch' Schoultz, Deputy Chief of Naval Operations for Air Warfare, had this to say: 'For the remainder of this century, through the year 2000, Naval Aviation will be the predominant force available to the United States. It will influence foreign affairs by its presence – by its outstanding capability to provide just the level of force required – anywhere in the world where there is a crisis situation and where there are international waters.'

In an earlier interview, quoted in *Naval Aviation News* (March/April 1983), Admiral Schoultz had stated his goals for Naval Aviation: 'Our short-range goal is to be ready to fight and win in today's world with today's weapons. Our long-range goal is to improve our capability, to be flexible enough to change, and to ensure our personnel will improve their skills as we receive equipment with greater capabilities.'

As it has in the past, the Navy will in the future continue to support research and development in aircraft design, seeking to maximize multi-mission capability in its aircraft. Many projects are undertaken as pure research into the technology involved, with no identifiable direct relationship to establish Navy requirements for a specific capability. Such projects develop technology which, in the past, has led to new aircraft design concepts and, ultimately, to new-design fleet aircraft in operation. Two examples of this approach in action are the continuing development of the Sikorsky XH-59A and the Bell XV-15 which resulted in the Bell-Boeing Vertol JVX. Both these programs are joint-service supported research into vertical take-off and landing (VTOL) aircraft with multi-mission potential. The XH-59A is a helicopter with counter-rotating rigid rotors designed to develop and demonstrate the advancing blade concept (ABC) which derives lift from the advancing side of each rotor disc. In addition to the potential for 345 mph (555 km/h) speeds at altitude, the concept offers improved maneuverability, reduced noise levels and increased hover capability. Currently funded jointly by the Navy and the Army, the ABC program has also received funding from NASA and the USAF.

The Bell-Boeing Vertol JVX is a tilt-rotor design, the concept of which is flying as the XV-15 in another joint-service/NASA development program. Results of early testing, which include operations on board the *Tripoli* in August 1982, were so promising that a Preliminary Design Phase development contract was awarded to Bell-Boeing Vertol on 26 April 1983. This award could lead to a major production program and operational aircraft for all of the services by the early 1990s. Missions considered for this vehicle include electronic warfare (EW), combat search and rescue (SAR), fleet logistic support, amphibious landing operations and intra/inter theater deployment.

Organizational studies
US carrier-based aviation has continued to operate in essentially the same organizational structure which had evolved during World War II and through the following years to the 1960s. The addition of the Lockheed S-3 to the air wings for ASW defense in the 1970s and the termination of

In August 1982, the JVX Development Program research aircraft, the XV-15, demonstrated its carrier suitability aboard *Tripoli* (LPH-10).

Robert L. Lawson Collection

Lieutenant Glenn Mickle

Above: VF-114 'Ardvark's' XO, Commander Pat Kilkenny, and his RIO, Lieutenant Jim Shay, launch an AIM-54A Phoenix missile at a target drone during a training mission over the Pacific Missile Range in April 1984.

the RA-5C operations were the major aircraft changes in the composition of the carrier air wings of the period. The imminent availability of the McDonnell Douglas F/A-18A has prompted studies of the organizational structure of the wings. For example, *John F. Kennedy* and CVW-3 in late 1983 began experimental operations with two A-6 squadrons and no A-7s, as a test of future wing composition possibilities to maximize carrier battle group striking power.

The commissioning of three new nuclear carriers by the early 1990s will require additional air wings, bringing the total to 15, comprising 14 active duty and one wing of Naval Reserve squadrons. Through the late 1980s, present planning is for USMC F/A-18 squadrons to deploy with the carrier air wings, augmenting Navy fighter and attack assets during the build-up of the Navy F/A-18 inventory. Marine squadrons VMFA-314 and -323 have been nominated to deploy with *Coral Sea*'s new Carrier Air Wing Thirteen in 1985 for the first implementation of this plan. The three active Marine Corps air wings (plus the Marine Reserve wing) will maintain current organizational structure except for these temporary commitments.

The first-line fighter in the fleet through the end

of the century will be the Grumman F-14 Tomcat. This versatile airplane and its primary weapon, the Phoenix missile, will have updates incorporated to improve an already mind-boggling capability in the fleet air-defense role. Production will continue, with 24 additional Tomcats funded in the 1984 budget, and an eventual planned total of more than 800 to be delivered by the late 1990s, including 300 F-14Ds with upgraded engines.

Improved versions of both the AIM-7M Sparrow and the AIM-9M Sidewinder will be available for the F-14 in the future, and an advanced medium-range air-to-air missile (AMRAAM) to replace Sparrow has been developed and is being tested. The only current weapon not scheduled for an update is the M61A-1 Vulcan 20-mm gun.

Looking into the future, Naval Air Systems Command has begun study and planning for a distant replacement for the F-14 Tomcat under the VFMX requirement and some preliminary reviews have been completed. The proposed aircraft is described currently as a multi-mission follow-on to both the F-14 and the A-6. But a near-future go-ahead on such a project with adequate funding for the development effort would still be unlikely to produce any hardware earlier than the mid to late

Commander David P. Erickson

Unique photograph of a VF-51 F-14A Tomcat. Wing sweep is programmable from 20° for slow speed flight to 68° for high speeds. Here the wings are at 68° which allows the aircraft to reach speeds up to Mach 2.5.

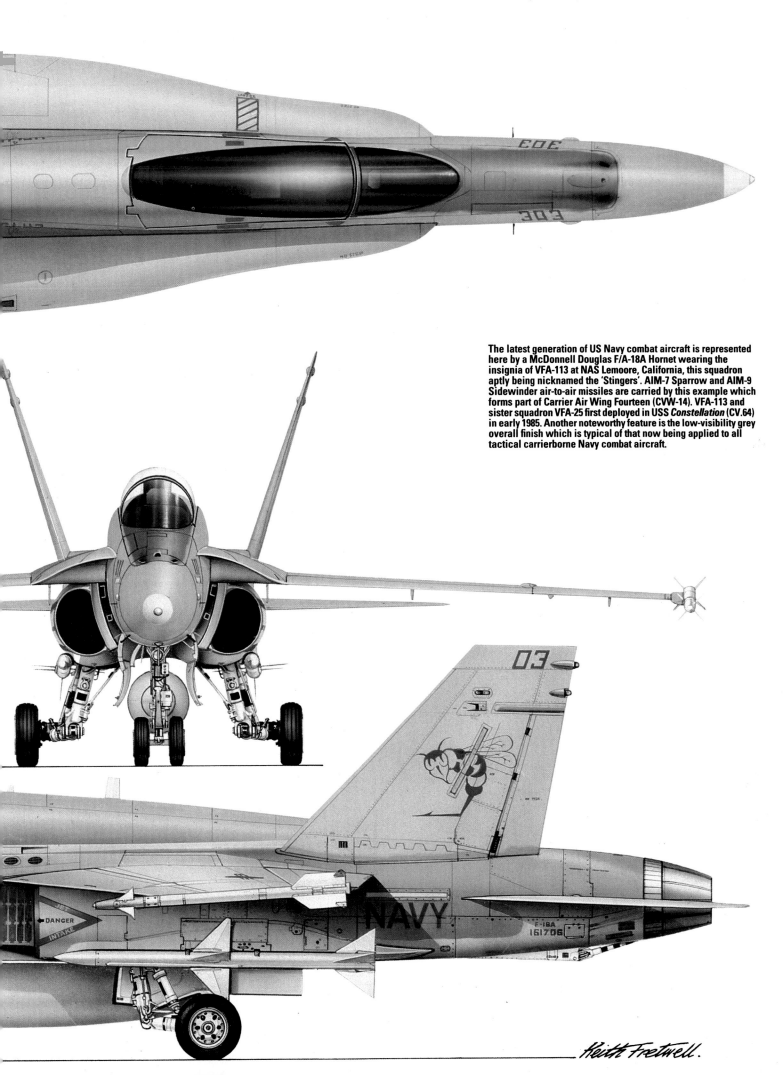

The latest generation of US Navy combat aircraft is represented here by a McDonnell Douglas F/A-18A Hornet wearing the insignia of VFA-113 at NAS Lemoore, California, this squadron aptly being nicknamed the 'Stingers'. AIM-7 Sparrow and AIM-9 Sidewinder air-to-air missiles are carried by this example which forms part of Carrier Air Wing Fourteen (CVW-14). VFA-113 and sister squadron VFA-25 first deployed in USS Constellation (CV.64) in early 1985. Another noteworthy feature is the low-visibility grey overall finish which is typical of that now being applied to all tactical carrierborne Navy combat aircraft.

Keith Fretwell.

Contemporary Situations and Plans

1990s and no operational aircraft until early into the next century.

The controversial multi-mission McDonnell Douglas F/A-18 joined the fleet with the Replacement Training Squadron VFA-125 at NAS Lemoore, Calif. The first operational commands were Marine Fighter Attack Squadrons VMFA-314,-323 and -531 at MCAS El Toro, Calif. The first Navy tactical squadron to get the F/A-18 was VFA-113 'Stingers' at Lemoore in 1983. with VFA-25 'The Fist of the Fleet' following close behind. Navy Hornet VA squadrons are redesignated as VFA (Strike Fighter) squadrons upon transition to the new aircraft. In its fighter role the Hornet will provide fleet air defense as back-up for the F-14 and fighter escort for strikes in carrier operations. With the Marines, the F/A-18 will be responsible for close air support and strike escort as a fighter. Marine Hornet squadrons deployed with carrier wings will fly both fighter and attack missions.

Hornets flying attack missions can deliver as much as 18,000 lb (8165 kg) of assorted ordnance on an assigned target, then fight their way clear of the target area. Both Navy and Marine employment of the F/A-18 will capitalize on the plane's load-carrying ability and on the precision delivery of ordnance made possible by the capability of the onboard sensors and controls at the pilot's fingertips.

There can be little doubt that the F/A-18 will be a major asset to naval air power in both its roles for the remainder of this century and well into the next. The airplane is in full production and is joining fleet squadrons in increasing numbers. Reports on its performance, reliability, maintainability and safety leave little to be desired. Pilots like to fly it and apparently do so at every opportunity. Aircraft availability in the Marine squadrons has been so high that operating fund allowances have been too-quickly expended at times by enthusiastic pilots, forcing commanders to restrict flight operations!

For the Navy the Grumman A-6, in its primary role, will provide the major strike force to the battle group commander for the forseeable future. The

well-proven Intruder will, however, serve in an important secondary role as the air wing's inflight-refuelling tanker. As the KA-6D, or with a 'buddy' store on board, the A-6 can provide fuel to any of the aircraft equipped for probe and drogue refuelling. The 'buddy' store capability provides an essential service as effectively as would a dedicated tanker but, on short notice, the A-6 can have the tanker store unloaded and return to its primary attack role. The KA-6D has no attack capability. All Navy tactical aircraft are equipped for aerial refuelling.

The proven A-6 airframe, continuing in production, provides the Navy with an economical medium attack aircraft, readily modified and updated, with multi-mission capability. The Navy has no plans at the present time for an A-6 replacement and foresees the Intruder as a major asset to the carrier air wings through the remainder of this century.

An A-6F version of the basic A-6, re-engined and extensively modified for STOL capability, is a planned item in the 1986 Navy budget. Although a firm need for this aircraft has not yet been established, the Navy is interested in the technology involved and its possible application to projected future requirements for a STOL attack aircraft to operate from smaller ships.

Above: Near Guantanamo, Cuba (Gitmo), a VA-35 A-6E with 'buddy' store in-flight refuelling tank tops-off a KA-6D in a reversal of usual roles.

Below: VFA-113, the 'Stingers', first US Navy tactical squadron to fly the McDonnell Douglas F/A-18A Hornet, made its initial weapons and ACM training deployment to MCAS Yuma, Arizona, in late 1983.

Right: A 'Black Ravens' EA-6B from VAQ-135 at Fallon for predeployment training at Fallon in October 1983. Prowlers enhance combat survival for strike aircraft with their multitudinous electronic capabilities.

In the future, each of the planned carrier air wings will include an EA-6B squadron as electronic warfare assumes an increasingly important role in the battle group mission. Grumman's EA-6B Prowler, undoubtedly the world's premier EW aircraft, will be the primary ECM platform and current planning is for 15 squadrons equipped with the Prowler. At present there are 10 squadrons serving the 12 active carriers, with the additional squadrons to be activated during alternate years in the future.

Developing the eyes of the Fleet

The EA-6B is dramatically improved in capability over its predecessor EA-6A. Planned future modifications promise to continue to increase the airplane's performance in its primary role. An update program, implemented in stages, has been completed through ICAP-I and ICAP-II (Improved Capability) and ADCAP (Advanced Capability) will be incorporated in the near future. ADCAP will provide for computer software changes, and by the 1990s the Prowler will have on board capability for reprogramming transmitters to cover the entire EW spectrum.

The Grumman E-2C Hawkeye will continue to fill the AEW role with planned updates enhancing its already impressive warning and control capabili-

ties. The E-2C squadrons currently deploy with the carrier air wings and will continue to do so in the future.

Production of the E-2C continues, with a planned buy of six aircraft per year through 1987. Long-range planning for an E-2C replacement includes consideration of a version of the tilt-rotor JVX aircraft. If successful, such an AEW asset could be moved from the carriers to cruiser or destroyer decks, an advantage to both ship types by relieving the carrier of handling of the AEW aircraft during deck recycles and enhancing early warning capabilities of the other ships.

Defense of the battle group against the threat of submarine attack will continue to be entrusted to the air wing Lockheed S-3 Vikings and aged Sikorsky SH-3H Sea Kings along with the LAMPS Mk III Sikorsky SH-60B Seahawks based aboard battle group destroyers and frigates. The updated S-3B, with improved sensors/avionics and Harpoon missile-launch capability will be a major multi-mission asset to the battle group through the end of the century.

In spite of some high-level opposition, budget plans for 1986 and 1987 include funds for the SH-60F as a replacement for the carrier-based SH-3H. The advanced version of the Seahawk would follow the SH-60B in production and would be equipped

Right: E-2C ARPS displays distinctive VAW-123 'Screwtops' markings during CVW-1 weapons training at Fallon in late 1983. Over-land detection capability of the Hawkeye was greatly increased with the E-2C.

Carrierborne air power in action:
three F-14 Tomcats, three A-6
Intruders, eight A-7 Corsair IIs and an
EA-6 Prowler take part in an exercise
at NAS Fallon. Note three aircraft in
old-style paint schemes.

with AQS-13F dipping sonar for close-in protection of the battle group against submarines that penetrate the carriers' ASW screen.

LAMPS is another major ship-based element of Naval Aviation ASW assets. Operating from the larger battle group screen DDs and FFs, the LAMPS Mk III SH-60B Seahawk is well-equipped for its mission with the ALQ-142 electronic surveillance system, the ASD-81 magnetic anomaly detection gear (MAD), and other avionics including datalink for real-time co-ordination of threat information. LAMPS Mk III assets, currently below battle group requirements, will reach required levels in the late 1980s and early 1990s.

The interim LAMPS helicopter, suitable for operations from the smaller surface craft, is the Kaman SH-2F Seasprite, a modification of a 25-year-old utility design. Initially deployed in 1972 as the SH-2D, the helicopter was extensively remodified and will continue in fleet use to the end of the century, filling a complementary role to the larger SH-60. In 1983, an order was placed with Kaman for 18 SH-2Fs, the first production models of this version.

The planned and budgeted fleet build-up now underway includes three new carriers, the USS *Theodore Roosevelt* (CVN 71), *George Washington* (CVN 72) and *Abraham Lincoln* (CVN 73), all nuclear-powered. *Roosevelt* is scheduled to be commissioned by 1987 and the others in the early 1990s. These ships, plus the carriers and air-capable amphibious ships now in commission, will constitute the Naval Aviation ship forces operating through the remainder of this century. Another ship type which may figure in the future of naval air power in this century is one now under study as the LDDX. However, even if the program is approved, it is unlikely that the ship would be completed until the late 1990s. The design being considered proposes a convertible ship with an LHA-type hull and a flight deck which could provide a limited-effort strike force carrier for contingency and 'show the flag' type operations. The study considers a temporarily installed ski-jump ramp for STOL and conventional aircraft launching for certain operations.

Studies have also been undertaken of the design for a smaller conventional carrier (CVV) to be equipped with V/STOL aircraft, but no firm plans for such a ship have resulted and there is no funding at present to continue the studies. This study included consideration of a launch ramp in lieu of catapults for conventional aircraft. However, recent leadership of Naval Aviation has shown little, if any, enthusiasm for smaller carriers.

A concept born in the early 1970s, Arapaho is, quite possibly, the most cost-effective means ever conceived for taking air power to sea. In simplest terms, it consists of the temporary placement of militarized cargo containers aboard a merchant container ship to provide a base for seaborne aircraft operations during a national emergency. Naval Reserve helicopter squadrons, air and ground crew personnel, shelter for the crews, command and control equipment and personnel, and fuel tank modules complete the Arapaho kit. Tests have demonstrated that the kit can be installed aboard a ship at any container port in a matter of hours, with the ship then ready to go to sea with a limited capability for ASW or other missions. The Navy-developed kit provides a 100×40 ft (30.5×12.2 m) hangar and a 200×64 ft (60.1×19.5 m) flight deck which can be placed on almost any commercial container ship. Tests, including day and night flight operations by various helicopters, were conducted successfully in Chesapeake Bay during October 1982.

The aircraft-carrier based at Pensacola will continue to be an essential element of naval air training. The *Lexington*, currently assigned the training task, is scheduled to remain at Pensacola until 1992, when she is slated to be relieved by *Coral Sea*. Some improvement to NAS Pensacola's harbor facilities will be required to accommodate the larger ship, but should pose no significant problem. *Coral Sea* will bring added capability to the assignment. She will have facilities and equipment to support the F/A-18 incorporated during a 1984 overhaul and modification. Naval Reserve and Marine Corps Reserve squadrons which could provide an air wing for *Coral Sea* will be F/A-18-equipped by the time the ship is scheduled to arrive at Pensacola, which is conveniently located as a base for contingency operations in the Caribbean and Central America should such a need arise.

The Orion marches on

Naval air power's major asset in future shore-based operations will be the Lockheed P-3C Orion, with a continuing program updating its already extensive multi-mission capabilities. Planned improvements to the onboard sensors and avionics suite will assure the Orion's continued status as the Western world's premier shore-based ASW aircraft for the remainder of this century.

No replacement for the P-3C is currently being considered, though alternative aircraft for its mission have been studied by the Naval Air Systems Command for several years. These include

Below: Anti-submarine patrol is one of the major elements of US Navy endeavor, with no less than 26 front-line squadrons, all equipped with versions of the Lockheed P-3 Orion. Normal squadron complement is nine aircraft, these deploying on a routine basis to overseas bases for periods of up to six months at a time.

US Navy

Right: 'Miss Piggy', a VRC-50 US-3A based at Diego Garcia in late 1981, provided COD support to the carriers operating on Gonzo Station in the Indian Ocean. In six years of COD missions, 'Miss Piggy' delivered the astounding total of some 2.5 million lb (1.134 million kg) of mail and cargo to the deployed carriers, accumulating more than 9,000 flight hours and nearly 1,000 carrier landings during the period.

derivatives of commercial turbofan airliners and candidate proposals to meet the requirements specified by the Navy VPX program. Cost factors during the austere defense budgets under the Carter administration were a major consideration and forced the decision to continue P-3 production and update program. Orion's Harpoon missile launch capability will also be upgraded, significantly enhancing the P-3's offensive role.

Future fleet logistic support will be provided by the McDonnell Douglas C-9B Skytrain II, the Beechcraft UC-12B Super King Air and the Sikorsky CH-53E Super Stallion heavy-lift helicopter. COD support will depend on the recently modernized Grumman C-2A Greyhound. The first of 39 new aircraft are scheduled to join the fleet in 1985. A special mission Lockheed US-3A version of the Viking is operated by VRC-50. Three of these aircraft provide long-range logistic support when special equipment or personnel are required in an emergency situation in deployed forces. They have proven extremely valuable to battle groups operating in the Indian Ocean. Additional S-3As could be modified to the COD configuration in the future but there are no plans for such a program or for production of a COD Viking.

A dark-horse entry in the multi-mission HXM program studies for a new transport helicopter could well be the Bell-Boeing Vertol JVX if the current development program is successful and budget support is continued.

There has been speculation and discussion regarding the use of shore-based tankers and early warning aircraft to augment carrier-based assets in a future contingency operation, but this grass-roots proposal is not looked on favorably at higher command levels. There are complex command and control considerations regarding support by elements not reporting directly to the on-scene commander, and these require further study. There is no doubt, however, that the commander on the scene in a emergency situation would utilize all available assets to augment his forces.

The Navy has studied the use of modified aircraft, especially a stretched version of the Boeing 707, as a shore-based tanker, but there are no plans for procurement of such an aircraft at present.

A unique new airplane for Naval Aviation will be the communications relay E-6A. A Boeing derivative of the Model 707 commercial airliner and the USAF AWACS E-3A, the E-6 is under study to provide world-wide secure communications to the

Fleet-support EW missions are flown by shore-based Lockheed Hercules EC-130Qs of the VQ squadrons. This TACAMO EC-130 assigned to VQ-4, based at NAS Patuxent River in 1980, provides long-range communications for the Navy's Fleet ballistic missile submarines.

Trident missile submarine fleet. The E-6A is scheduled to join the fleet in the late 1980s, with a planned service life of more than 30 years. The E-6A will initially supplement and eventually replace the Lockheed EC-130 TACAMO aircraft currently flown by VQ squadrons.

Naval Aviation training will experience major changes during the 1980s and 1990s; the most significant being the implementation of a new program for students in the jet pipeline. This new (and first) Navy Undergraduate Flight Training System (VTXTS) is a fully integrated program consisting of simulators, computers, academics, a training management system and the British Aerospace/McDonnell Douglas T-45A Hawk aircraft. The Hawk has been in service with the Royal Air Force since 1976. The tandem-cockpit T-45A will be produced by McDonnell Douglas in the US with deliveries to the Naval Air Training Command scheduled to begin in early 1988.

Another new trainer will be the Cessna T-47A Citation II, scheduled to be delivered in 1984 to Pensacola-based Training Wing Six for NFO inflight training. Coincidental with the introduction of the T-47A will be the full implementation of a training services contract with Cessna Aircraft Co. and other associated civilian firms to provide aircraft, flight crews, maintenance, logistic support and simulators as well as instructors for ground radar training. The old T-39D-based NFO training system will be phased out as transition to the new system commences on 1 August 1984. Plans call for replacement of all T-39D aircraft by the T-47As by May 1985.

The North American T-28B Trojan, mainstay of Naval Aviation training for some 20 years, began phasing out of the program in the late 1970s, with the last of the Trojans to be retired by early 1984. Replacement for the T-28 is the Beechcraft T-34C Turbo Mentor for primary and intermediate flight training. The T-34C is a major improvement over the venerable propeller-driven Trojan. Reduced noise levels, air-conditioned cockpits, increased performance and significantly reduced operating costs are some of the 'Charlie's' advantages. Students in the maritime pipeline will complete primary and intermediate flight training in the Turbo Mentor, then go to Training Wing Four at Corpus Christi, Texas for advanced multi-engine flying in the Beechcraft T-44A Pegasus.

Rotary-wing student pilot training will also be significantly upgraded. Deliveries of the Bell TH-47C Ranger advanced instrument trainer commenced early in 1983. This advanced version of the TH-57A will eventually replace the TH-1 Huey at HT-18. The Navy's TH-57A was the first turbine-powered helicopter to be utilized by any service in the primary training role.

The future of Naval Aviation has never been brighter. New technological advances provide unlimited horizons for the Naval Aviator of years to come. With the establishment of the Naval Space Command on 1 October 1983 under astronaut Captain Richard Truly, USN, a carrier aviator, a whole new realm of possibility has now been opened.

Right: The US Navy's Flight Demonstration Squadron, the 'Blue Angels', began flying A-4F 'Super Fox' Skyhawks with P408 engines in 1974. Here the 'Blue Angels' demonstrate their precision flying.

Bottom left: Beech T-34C Turbo Mentors are utilized for primary and intermediate flight training in TraCom squadrons VT-2, VT-3, and VT-6 at NAS Whiting Field, Florida. This unusually marked TraWing 5 Turbo Mentor was photographed at NAS Moffett Field, California, in May 1980.

Below: An HT-8 TH-57A over Santa Rosa island near Pensacola. Bell JetRangers were the first jet primary trainers for any US service. Late-model TH-57Cs are currently entering the Training Command.

INDEX

Note: Page numbers in **bold type** refer to illustrations

A

A-1: see Curtiss
A-1 Skyraider: see Douglas
A-1H: see Douglas
A-2: see Curtiss
A2F-1: see Grumman
A-3: see Douglas
A-3B: see Douglas
A3D: see Douglas
A3D-1: see Douglas
A3J-1: see North American
A-4: see Douglas
A-4C: see Douglas
A4D: see Douglas
A4D-1: see Douglas
A4D-2: see Douglas
A-4E: see Douglas
A-4F: see Douglas
A-4M: see Douglas
A-6: see Grumman
A-6A: see Grumman
A-6C TRIM: see Grumman
A-6E: see Grumman
A-6E TRAM: see Grumman
A-6F: see Grumman
A6M: see Mitsubishi
A-7: see Vought
A-7A: see Vought
A-7B: see Vought
A-7E: see Vought
A-20: see Douglas
AB-2: see Curtiss
AB-3: see Curtiss
AD: see Douglas
AD-1: see Douglas
AD-2: see Douglas
AD-3: see Douglas
AD-4: see Douglas
AD-5: see Douglas
AD-5W: see Douglas
AF-2S/2W: see Grumman
AGM-4 Shrike anti-radar missile 165, 182, 197
AH-1: see Bell
AH-1: see McDonnell
AH-3: see Curtiss
AH-10: see Burgess-Dunne
AH-12: see Curtiss
AIM-7 Sparrow air-to-air missile 135, 168, 172, 192, 195, 214, 217, 241
AIM-9 Sidewinder air-to-air missile 130, 135, 148, 172, 183, 186, 192, 195, 197, 198, 199, 210, 214, 217, 241
AIM-54 Phoenix air-to-air missile 214, 217, 241
AJ-1: see North American
AJ-2: see North American
AM-1: see Martin
AMRAAM missile 241
AMS-N-2 Bat 83
AP-2H: see Lockheed
ATC (Air Transport Command), USAAF amalgamation 107
AU-1: see Vought
AV-8: see British Aerospace/McDonnell Douglas
AV-8A: see British Aerospace/McDonnell Douglas
AV-8B: see British Aerospace/McDonnell Douglas
AV-8C: see British Aerospace/McDonnell Douglas
AWACS: see Boeing E-3A
AX3D-1: see Douglas
Adsid acoustic sensor 174
Advanced Training Command 238
Aeromarine Model 39-B **11**, **16**
Aichi D3A 64
Airacomet: see Bell YP-59A
Air Antisubmarine Wing One 235
Airborne Early Warning Wing, Pacific 148
Aircraft Squadrons, Battle Fleet 18, 20
Air Group 2 88, 123
Air Group 5 110
Air Group 15 89, 100, 101
Air Group 20 96
Air Group 30 93
Air Group 41 100
Air Group 53 100
Air Group 82 119
Air Group 89 143
Air Group 91 100
Air Mobile Mine Counter-Measure Command 204
Air Transport Command (ATC), USAAF amalgamation 107
Allen, Lt (JG) Barbara Ann 238
Allied codenames:
'Betty' 63
'Judy' 88
'Kate' 64, 67
'Val' 64, 67
Alpha strikes 164, 196
Alvarez, Lt (JG) Everett 156, **204**
Amen, Commander W.T. 112
Anderson, Lt (JG) Jim 210
Anti-Submarine Development Detachment 51
Antoinette monoplane **11**
Armstrong, Neil A. 149
Army-Navy Technical Board, established 14
'Atoll' air-to-air missile 210
Attack Carrier Air Wing 5 186
Attack Carrier Air Wing 11 169
Attack Carrier Air Wing 14 171
Attack Carrier Air Wing 15 160
Aurand, Commander Evan 'Pete' 112, 119
Avenger: see Grumman/General Motors RBM
Avenger: see Grumman TBF and TBF-1
Avenger: see Grumman/General Motors TBM, TBM-1 and TBM-3
Aviation Volunteer Specialist 75

B

B-1: see Wright
B5N: see Nakajima
B-24: see Consolidated
B-25: see North American
B-36: see Convair
B-52: see Boeing
BF2C-1: see Curtiss
BFC-2: see Curtiss
BG-1: see Great Lakes
BM-1/2: see Martin
BT-1: see Northrop
BTC: see Curtiss
BTD-1: see Douglas
BTK: see Kaiser-Fleetwings
Banshee: see McDonnell F2H, F2H-1, F2H-2, F2H-3 and F2H-4
Basic Training Command 238
Bat, USN's first stand-off missile 83
battles
Coral Sea 64-70 passim, 100
Eastern Solomons 65-70 passim
Java Sea 62
Leyte Gulf 96
Midway 61-70 passim
Philippine Sea, first 89
Philippine Sea, second 97, 143
Santa Cruz 65-70 passim
Batson, Lt J.D. 168
Baxter, Lt (JG) D.F. 84
Baxter, RM1/C Robert P. 84
Bearcat: see Grumman F8F, F8F-1, F8F-2
Beech airplanes
T-34C Turbo Mentor 234, 250, **250**
T-44A Pegasus 232, **232**, 250
UC-12B Super King Air 232, 249
Bell airplanes
AH-1 234
TH-1 234, 250
TH-47C Ranger 250
TH-57A/C Sea Ranger 234, **250**
UH-1B 174, **174**, **175**
UH-1N Iroquois **235**
XV-15 240, **240**
YP-59A Airacomet 118, **118**
Bellanca XSOE-1 25
Bell/Boeing Vertol JVX 235, 240, 245, 249
Bellinger, Commander Dick 171, **171**
Bellinger, Lt (JG) P.N.L. 12, 36
Bennett, Floyd 55
Benson, Rear Adm. W.S. 21
Berlin Airlift 108
Billingsley, Ensign W. 11
Blackburn Swift 22
'Black Cat' squadrons 77, 78
Blue Angels Flight Demonstration Squadron **109**, 132, **251**
Boeing airplanes
B-52 194, 195, 199
E-3A AWACS 249
E-6A 249, 250
F2B-1 **18**
F2B1-1 27
F3B 27, 71
F4B **71**
F4B-4 27, **28**, **29**
FB-1 26
NKC-135A **249**
XF8B-1 **124**
Model 707 249
Boeing-Stearman airplanes
N2S 72, **72**
N2S-5 **73**
Boeing Vertol CH-46 Sea Knight 199, **227**, 234
Bogan, Jerry 88
Bolt, Maj. John 112
Booth, Lt Cdr T. 42
Bordelon, Lt Guy P. 112
Brehm, Commander H. Paul H. 116
Brewster airplanes
F2A-1 Buffalo 27, 31
F2A-2 Buffalo **30**
F2A-3 Buffalo 36, 62
SB2A-4 **75**
Briggs, Pilot Off. 40
Bringle, Commander W.F. 46
British Aerospace/McDonnell Douglas airplanes
AV-8 Harrier 234, 251
AV-8A, AV-8B and AV-8C Harrier 251
T-45A Hawk 250
TAV-8B Harrier 251
Bronco: see North American OV-10
Brown, Ensign E.W. 112, 113
Brown, Ensign Jesse L. 116
Brown, Lt (JG) George 93
BuAer: see Bureau of Aeronautics
Buckeye: see North American/Rockwell T-2C
Buffalo: see Brewster F2A-1, F2A-2 and F2A-3
Bullpup air-to-surface missile 133, 183
BuOrd: see Bureau of Ordnance
Bureau of Aeronautics 18, 26, 32, 105, 107, 149
Bureau of Ordnance 64, 149
Bureau of Weapons 149
Burgess-Dunne airplanes
AH-10 12
biplane 12
Burns, Lt (JG) J.A. 84
BuWeps: see Bureau of Weapons

C

C-1: see Curtiss
C-1A: see Grumman
C-2A: see Grumman
C-9B: see McDonnell Douglas
C-54: see Douglas
C-117: see Douglas
C-118B: see Douglas
C-130: see Lockheed
C-130F: see Lockheed
CH-46: see Boeing Vertol
CH-53: see Sikorsky
CH-53A: see Sikorsky
CH-53D: see Sikorsky
CH-53E: see Sikorsky
CS-1: see Curtiss
CT-1: see Curtiss
CT-29: see Rockwell
CVG air groups
2 113, 122, 123
3 110, 113
4 110, 114, 117, 122
5 110, 112, 119
6 110
7 114
9 114
11 110, 111, 119
12 114
13 135
14 114
15 114
17 110
19 113
82 119
101 114
Cairn, Lt. (JG) J.W. 180
Caldwell, Commander Turner 100
Camel: see Sopwith
Carrier Aircraft Service Detachments 75
Carrier Airborne Early Warning Squadrons, establishment 107
Carrier Aircraft Service Unit 75
Carrier Qualification Training Unit 74
Catalina: see Consolidated PBY, PBY-1, PBY-3, PBY-4, PBY-5 and PBY-5A
catapult launch, first from warship 12
Cessna T-47A Citation II 250
Chamberlain, Lt (JG) W.F. 49
Chambers, Capt. W.I. 10
Chevalier, Lt (JG) Guy de C. 16
Churchill, Prime Minister W.S. 42
Citation II: see Cessna T-47A
Clark, 'Jocko' 88
Clarke, Commander C.E. 107
Clarke, Lt John M. 86
'Cold War' 108, 150
Combat SAR 179
Condor: see Focke-Wulf Fw 200
Consolidated airplanes
B-24 Liberator 50, 82
P2Y-1 33, **33**, 34, 35, 40
P2Y-2 33, **40**
P2Y-3 33
PB2Y Coronado 34, 35, **35**, 78
PB2Y-3 Coronado 36, 78, **78**
PB2Y-5 Coronado **79**
PB4Y-1 Liberator 50, **50**, **51**, 52, 53, 73, **82**, 83, **83**
PB4Y-2 Privateer 50, 73, 83, **83**, 114, 145, **145**
PBY Catalina 35, 36, 40, **40**, 50, **50**, 51, 52, 56, 60, **61**, 73, 76, **77**, 78, **78**, 79, 82
PBY-1 Catalina 33, **33**, 34
PBY-3 Catalina 36
PBY-4 Catalina 34, 36
PBY-5 Catalina 34, 36, **40**, 41
PBY-5A Catalina 34, 36, **50**, **52**, **77**
XP3Y-1 33
XPB2Y-1 **34**
XPBY-1 34
XPBY-5A 34
XPY-1 33
Constellation: see Lockheed EC-121
Constitution: see Lockheed R60-1
Convair airplanes
B-36 108, 109
F2Y-1 Sea Dart **127**
P4Y-2S 145
R3Y-2 Tradewind **130**
RB-36H **108**
XFY-1 'Pogo' **125-126**
XP5Y-1 130
Coolidge, President Calvin 20
Coral Sea, battle of the 64, 66, 67, 70, 100
Coronado: see Consolidated PB2Y-2, PB2Y-3 and PB2Y-5
Corsair: see Vought AU-1
Corsair: see Vought F4U, F4U-1, F4U-4 and F4U-5
Corsair: see Vought O2U-1 O2U-2 and O3U-1
Corsair II: see Vought A-7, A-7A, A-7B, A-7E and TA-7C
Cougar: see Grumman F9F-6, F9F-8 and TF-9J
Crusader: see Vought F-8, F-8A, F-8D, F-8E, F-8H, F-8J, RF-8, RF-8A, RF-8G and TF-8A
Crusader: see Vought F8U, F8U-1
Cuban missile crisis 150
Cuckoo: see Sopwith
Cunningham, Lt Randy 194, **195**, 196-199
Curtiss, Glenn H. 10, 11, 35
Curtiss airplanes
A-1 **10**, 11
A-2 11
AB-2 **12**
AB-3 12, **12**
AH-3 12
AH-12 **8**
BF2C-1 27, **30**
BFC-2 27
BTC 122
C-1 11
CS-1 22
CT-1 22
F-5L **15**, 16, 31, 32, **33**
F6C-1 26
F6C-3 **27**
F8C-4 Helldiver 27
F11C-2 27
H-4 13
H-12 13, **13**, 14, 16, 33
H-16 **13**, 16, 33
HS-1 14, **14**, 16
HS-2 **13**, 16, 22
JN 13
Model H 13
N-9 12, **12**, 14
NC flying-boats **13**
O2C 25
OC 25
P-40 Warhawk 42, 43, **43**, 60
R-2 13
R-6 14, **21**, 22, 24
SB2C Helldiver 86, **88**, 93, **93**, 96, 154
SB2C-1 Helldiver 36, 64, **76**, 86, **86**
SB2C-3 Helldiver **98-99**
SB2C-4 Helldiver 98, **100**
SB2C-5 Helldiver 119, 122, 123
SBC-3 21, 23
SBC-4 36, **36**
SC-1 Seahawk 85, **85**, 143, **143**
SOC Seagull 25, **25**, 26, 36, **42**, 84
SOC-1 Seagull 84
SOC-3 Seagull **84**
TS-1 26, 31
XBT2C-1 **124**
XF14C-2 **124**
XF15C-1 **124**
Cutlass: see Vought F7U, F7U-1, F7U-2 and F7U-3

D

D3A: see Aichi
D-558-1 Skystreak: see Douglas
D-558-2 Skyrocket: see Douglas
DC-4: see Douglas
DT-2: see Douglas
DT-28B Trojan: see North American
Dauntless: see Douglas SBD, SBD-1, SBD-2, SBD-3 and SBD-5
Davidson, Lt Cdr. Jim 118
Davies, Commander Tom 128
Davis N-1 22
Davison, 'Dave' 88
D-Day, Normandy landings 52, 53
Dean, Ambassador John Gunther 206
Demon: see McDonnell F3H
Denfeld, Adm. Louis E. 109, 110
Denton, Capt. Jeremiah 199
De Soto Patrol 155, 156
Destroyer: see Douglas BTD-1
Devastator: see Douglas TBD-1
Dewey, Adm. George 10
Dixie Station 160, 169
Doenitz, Adm. Karl 48-51
Doremus, Lt Cdr R.B. 168
Dosé, Commander Bob 140
Dosé, Lt Curt 194, 197
Douglas airplanes
A-1 Skyraider 79, **150**, **156**, 164, 180, 186, 188, 204
A-1H Skyraider **117**, **157**, **158-159**, **164**
A-3 Skywarrior 220, 222
A-3B Skywarrior **160**
A-3D Skywarrior 129, **140**
A3D-1 Skywarrior 128, **129**
A4 Skyhawk 164, 165, 169, **169**, 171, 172, 179, 180, 181, **181**, 182, **186**, 207, 218
A-4C Skyhawk **150**, 156, **156**, **160**, 164, 171, 172, 181, 204
A4D Skyhawk 129
A4D-1 Skyhawk 129, **129**
A4D-2 Skyhawk 130
A-4E Skyhawk **212**
A-4F Skyhawk 129, **162-163**, **190**, **251**
A-4M Skyhawk 129
A-20 77
AD Skyraider 112, 115, **115**, 119, 122, 123, **140**, 145, 155
AD-1 Skyraider **123**
AD-2 Skyraider **116**
AD-3 Skyraider 112
AD-4 Skyraider **112**, 115, **117**, **123**
AD-5 Skyraider 112
AD-5W Skyraider 142, **176**
AX3D-1 129
BTD-1 Destroyer **123**
C-54 55, 229
C-117 **228**, 229
C-118B Liftmaster **148**, 229
D-558-1 Skystreak **127**
D-558-2 Skyrocket **127**
DC-4 144
DT-2 **21**, 22
EA-1 Skyraider 123, **161**
EA-3 Skywarrior 173
EA-3B Skywarrior 178, 228
EKA-3B Skywarrior 129, **222**
F3D-1 Skyknight 132, **132**
F3D-2 Skyknight **112**, 132
F4D-1 Skyray 132, **132**, 133
F4D-2 Skyray 133
F5D-1 Skylancer 133
F6D-1 Missileer 133
F-10B Skyknight 132
JD-1 144, **144**
KA-3B Skywarrior **191**, 199, 222, **222**
RA-3B Skywarrior **171**, **173**
PD-1 32, **32**
R5D Skymaster 56, 108, 229, **229**
R5D-3 Skymaster **108**
R6D-2 Liftmaster **148**
SBD Dauntless 23, 24, 36, **42**, 43, 46, 47, 51, 62, **63**, 64, **64**, **66**, **67**, 84, 86, **92**, 93, **97**, 154
SBD-1 Dauntless 24, **24**
SBD-2 Dauntless **61**
SBD-3 Dauntless 42, **42**, **43**, **63**, **67**, **96**
SBD-5 Dauntless **38**, **89**
TB2D 122
TBD Devastator 23, **23**, 36, 62, **63**, 64, **65**, 66
TF-10B Skyknight 132
XA2D Skyshark **124**
XA4D-1 129
XBT2D-1 123
XF4D-1 132
XP3D-1 33
XSB2D-1 123
XTB2D-1 **124**
Dragonfly: see Sikorsky HO3S-1
Drane, Lt Cdr W.M. 48
Driscoll, Lt (JG) Willie 194, **195**, 196-199
Duck: see Grumman J2F and JF-2
'Dumbo' missions 77, 78
Duncan, Commander George C. 145

E

E-1B Tracer: see Grumman
E-2 Hawkeye: see Grumman
E-2A Hawkeye: see Grumman
E-2B Hawkeye: see Grumman
E-2C Hawkeye: see Grumman
E-3A AWACS: see Boeing
E-6A: see Boeing
EA-1 Skyraider: see Douglas
EA-3 Skywarrior: see Douglas
EA-3B Skywarrior: see Douglas
EA-6A Intruder: see Grumman
EA-6B Prowler: see Grumman
EC-121 Constellation: see Lockheed
EC-130 Hercules: see Lockheed
ECV-130 Hercules: see Lockheed
EKA-3B Skywarrior: see Douglas
EP-3 Orion: see Lockheed
EP-3B Orion: see Lockheed
Earl, Lt (JG) D.R. 182
Earnest, Ensign Bert 66
Eastern Solomons, battle of the 65-67, 70
Eisenhower, President Dwight D. 144
Elder, Commander R.M. 'Bob' 112, 119
Ellyson, Lt T.G. 'Spuds' 10, 11, **11**, 12
Ely, Eugene 10, 11
'Empire Express, The' 79
Escadrille Lafayette 43
Estocin, Lt Cdr Michael J. 165

F

F.2: see Felixstowe
F2A-1 Buffalo: see Brewster
F2A-2 Buffalo: see Brewster
F2A-3 Buffalo: see Brewster
F2B-1: see Boeing
F2B1-1: see Boeing
F2F-1: see Grumman
F2H Banshee: see McDonnell
F2H-1 Banshee: see McDonnell
F2H-2 Banshee: see McDonnell
F2H-3 Banshee: see McDonnell
F2H-4 Banshee: see McDonnell
F2Y-1 Sea Dart: see Convair
F3B: see Boeing
F3D-1 Skyknight: see Douglas
F3D-2 Skyknight: see Douglas
F3F-1: see Grumman
F3F-3: see Grumman
F3H Demon: see McDonnell
F-4 Phantom II: see McDonnell Douglas
F-4A Phantom II: see McDonnell Douglas
F4B: see Boeing
F-4B Phantom II: see McDonnell Douglas
F4B-4: see Boeing
F4D-1 Skyray: see Douglas
F4D-2 Skyray: see Douglas
F4F Wildcat: see Grumman
F4F-3 Wildcat: see Grumman
F4F-4 Wildcat: see Grumman
F-4G Phantom II: see McDonnell Douglas
F4H-1 Phantom II: see McDonnell Douglas
F-4J Phantom II: see McDonnell Douglas
F-4N Phantom: see McDonnell Douglas
F-4S Phantom II: see McDonnell Douglas
F4U Corsair: see Vought
F4U-1 Corsair: see Vought
F4U-4 Corsair: see Vought
F4U-5 Corsair: see Vought
F5D-1 Skylancer: see Douglas
F-5E Tiger II: see Northrop
F-5L: see Curtiss
F6C-1: see Curtiss
F6C-3: see Curtiss
F6D-1 Missileer: see Douglas
F6F Hellcat: see Grumman
F6F-3 Hellcat: see Grumman
F6F-5 Hellcat: see Grumman
F6U Pirate: see Vought
F7F Tigercat: see Grumman
F7F-2 Tigercat: see Grumman
F7U Cutlass: see Vought
F7U-1 Cutlass: see Vought
F7U-2 Cutlass: see Vought
F7U-3 Cutlass: see Vought
F-8 Crusader: see Vought
F-8A Crusader: see Vought
F8C-4 Helldiver: see Curtiss
F-8D Crusader: see Vought
F-8E Crusader: see Vought
F8F Bearcat: see Grumman
F8F-1 Bearcat: see Grumman
F8F-2 Bearcat: see Grumman
F-8H Crusader: see Vought
F-8J Crusader: see Vought
F8U Crusader: see Vought
F8U-1 Crusader: see Vought
F8U-1T Crusader: see Vought
F9F-2 Panther: see Grumman
F9F-3 Panther: see Grumman
F9F-5 Panther: see Grumman
F9F-6 Cougar: see Grumman
F9F-8 Cougar: see Grumman
F9F-9 Cougar: see Grumman
F-10B Skynight: see Douglas
F-11A Tiger: see Grumman
F11C-2: see Curtiss
F11F-1 Tiger: see Grumman
F-14A Tomcat: see Grumman
F-86 Sabre: see North American
F-105: see Republic
F-111: see General Dynamics
F-111B: see General Dynamics
F/A-18A Hornet: see McDonnell Douglas
FAC (forward air control) 157, 174, 190
FASRON (Fleet Air Service Squadrons) 110
FB-1: see Boeing
FF-1: see see Grumman
FH-1 Phantom: see McDonnell
FJ-1 Fury: see North American
FJ-2 Fury: see North American
FJ-3 Fury: see North American
FJ-4 Fury: see North American
FM Wildcat: see Grumman/General Motors
FM-1 Wildcat: see Grumman/General Motors
FM-2 Wildcat: see Grumman/General Motors
FR-1 Fireball: see Ryan
FT-1: see Fokker
FU-1: see Vought
Fw 200 Condor: see Focke-Wulf
Fast Carrier Task Force 88, 143
Felixstowe F.2 14
Felt, Adm. Harry D. 155
Fido homing torpedo 48

Fighter Director officers 65, 76
Fireball: see Ryan FR-1 and XFR-1
Fiske, Rear Adm. B.A. 21
'Fitter': see Sukhoi Su-22
Fix, Lt Col. Herbert 207
Flatley Jr., Lt Cdr Jim 85
Fleet Air Service Squadrons (FASRON) 110
Fleet Airships Atlantic 56
Fleet Airships Wing 4 56
Fleet Air Wing
  6 114
  7 52
  10 83, 123, 181
  15 51, 52
  16 50, 51
  17 51, 77
Fleet Logistics Air Wings 148
Fletcher, Rear Adm. Frank J. 67, 70
Flying Limited Duty Officer Program 238, 239
Focke-Wulf Fw 200 Condor 51, 52
Fokker FT-1 22
Forrestal, James V 106
Forward Air Control (FAC) 157, 174, 190
Franke Jr, Lt. F.A.W. 134
Fruin, Lt J.K. 'Pappy' 144
Fuchida, Commander Mitsuo 70
Furtek, Lt (JG) A.J. 144
Fury: see North American FJ-1, FJ-2, FJ-3, FJ-4 and XFJ-1

G

G4M: see Mitsubishi
GMGRU-1 (Guided Missile Group One) 133, 148
GMGRU-2 (Guided Missile Group Two) 148
GMU-90 (Guided Missile Unit 90) 115
Gallery, Capt. D.V. 49
Genda, Commander Minoru 70
General Dynamics airplanes
  F-111 199
  F-111B 214, **214**
Glenn, Lt Col. John H. 149
Gordon, Lt Nathan 77, 78
Graf Zeppelin 32, 56
Grant, Lt Brian 197
Gray, Aircrewman First Class Michael A 240
Great Lakes airplanes
  BG-1 20, 23
  TG-1 23
  TG-2 **22**, 23
Greyhound: see Grumman C-2A
Griffin, Lt V.C. 18
Grumman airplanes
  A2F-1 **130**
  A-6 Intruder 165, 168, 172, 188, 194, 196, 197, 199, 204, 218, 219, 222, 241, 244
  A-6A Intruder **130**, **165**, **169**, **183**, **184-185**, **189**, 218
  A-6C TRIM 176
  A-6E Intruder **196**, **219**, **244**
  A-6E TRAM 176, 218, **219**
  A-6F Intruder 244
  AF-2S/2W Guardian 142, **142**
  C-1A Trader 226, 232, 238
  C-2A Greyhound 226, **226**, 232, 249
  E-1B Tracer 142 **150**, **155**, **181**, 220
  E-2 Hawkeye 220
  E-2A Hawkeye **164**
  E-2B Hawkeye 220
  E-2C Hawkeye 220, **220**, 245, **245**
  EA-6A Intruder 222, 245
  EA-6B Prowler 222, **222**, 245, **245**
  F2F-1 27, **27**
  F3F-1 20, **20**
  F3F-3 27
  F4F Wildcat 41, 42, **42**, 43, 44, 46-49, 63, 66, **66**, 67, 79, 86
  F4F-3 Wildcat **30**, 31, 33, 36, **36**, **41**, 62, **62**, **63**
  F4F-4 Wildcat **30**, 31, 36, 41, 42, **42**, **44-45**, **46**, 47, **47**, **48**
  F6F Hellcat 44, **85**, 86, **88**, 89, 92, **92**, 96, **101**, 154
  F6F-3 Hellcat 46, 86, **86**, **87**, 88, **100**
  F6F-5 Hellcat 46, **46**, 47, 86, **90-91**, **105**, **109**, **115**, 119, 122
  F7F Tigercat 105
  F7F-2 Tigercat **105**
  F8F Bearcat 155
  F8F-1 Bearcat **107**, 119, **120-121**
  F8F-2 Bearcat 122
  F9F-2 Panther 112, **112**, **113**, **114**, 115, 119
  F9F-3 Panther 112, **112**, 113
  F9F-5 Panther **108**, **117**, **123**, 130
  F9F-6 Cougar **102**, **123**, 130
  F9F-8 Cougar **128**, 130, **131**, 148
  F9F-9 Cougar 132
  F-11A Tiger **132**
  F11F-1 Tiger 132, **132**
  F-14A Tomcat 124, 134, 200, **200**, 210, **210**, 214, **214**, 215, **215**, **216-217**, 219, 241, **241**, 244
  FF-1 27
  J2F Duck 54
  J4F Widgeon 54, **54**
  JF-2 Duck **53**
  KA-6D Intruder 199, **210**, 219, 222, 244, **244**
  S-2 Tracker 176, 223
  S-2E Tracker **177**, **223**
  S2F Tracker 142, 220
  S2F-1 Tracker **136**
  SF-1 **27**
  TBF Avenger 36, 46, 47, **47**, 48, **66**, 86
  TBF-1 Avenger 42, **47**, 48, 64, 66, **68-69**, **70**
  TBN-3E 141
  TBN-3W 141
  TF-9J Cougar 130, 232
  TS-2A 232
  US-2 Tracker 232, **232**
  XF6F-1 30
  XF9F-2 118
  XF10F-1 Jaguar **124**
Grumman/General Motors airplanes
  FM Wildcat 86
  FM-1 Wildcat **93**
  FM-2 Wildcat 47, 93
  TBM Avenger 47-49, 64, 85, 86, 93
  TBM-1 Avenger **97**
  TBM-3 Avenger **106**, 111, **116**, 119, **119**, 122, 123
Guardian: see Grumman AF-2S/2W
Guided Missile Group One (GMGRU-1) 134, 148
Guided Missile Group Two (GMGRU-2) 148
Guided Missile Unit 90 (GMU-90) 115
'Guideline' surface-to-air missile 181
Gulf of Tonkin Resolution 154, 156

H

H-4: see Curtiss
H-12: see Curtiss
H-16: see Curtiss
HD-1: see Curtiss
He 111: see Heinkel
HH-2C Seasprite: see Kaman
HH-3A: see Sikorsky
HNS-1 Hoverfly: see Sikorsky
HO3S-1 Dragonfly: see Sikorsky
HO4S: see Sikorsky
HS-1: see Curtiss
HS-2: see Curtiss
HU-2B: see Kaman
HSS-1 Seabat: see Sikorsky
HUS-1: see Sikorsky
HXM program 249
Haiphong, attack on **181**
Halsey, Vice Adm. William F. 70, 88, 96, 100
Hanriot HD-1 26, **26**
Harding, President Warren G. 18
Harpoon: see Lockheed PV-2
Harpoon anti-ship missile 228, 245, 249
Harrier: see British Aerospace/McDonnell Douglas AV-8, AV-8A, AV-8B, AV-8C and TAV-8B
Hart, Adm. T.C. 60
Hatcher, Commander Jerry 204
Hawk: see British Aerospace/McDonnell Douglas T-45A
Hawkeye: see Grumman E-2, E-2A, E-2B and E-2C
Hawkins, Lt Cdr Sam 181, 182
Hayward, Capt. John T. 'Chick' 128
Heinemann, Ed 123, 129
Heinkel He 111 47
Helicopter Antisubmarine Wing One 235
Helicopter Tactical Wing One 238
Hellcat: see Grumman F6F, F6F-3 and F6F-5
Helldiver: see Curtiss F8C-4
Helldiver: see Curtiss SB2C, SB2C-1, SB2C-3, SB2C-4 and SB2C-5
Hendershott, Lt (JG) R.W. 84
Hercules: see Lockheed C-130, C-130F, EC-130 and LC-130R
Hickman, ARM2/C Arthur 84
Hoover, President Herbert 20
Hornet: see McDonnell Douglas F/A-18A
Hoskins, Rear Adm. John M. 'Peg Leg' 110
Hoverfly: see Sikorsky HNS-1
Hudner, Lt (JG) Thomas J. 116
Hudson: see Lockheed PBO-1
Hughes, Charles E. 18
Hwachon Dam, attack on 115, **115**
Hyland, Adm. John J. 194

I

Il-10: see Ilyushin
Ilyushin Il-10 112
Ingalls, David 26
Intruder: see Grumman A2F-1
Intruder: see Grumman A-6, A-6A, A-6E, A-6F, EA-6A and KA-6D
Iroquois: see Bell UH-1N

J

J2F Duck: see Grumman
J4F Widgeon: see Grumman
JD-1: see Douglas
JF-2 Duck: see Grumman
JM-1 Marauder: see Martin
JN: see Curtiss
Ju 87: see Junkers
Ju 88: see Junkers
JVX: see Bell/Boeing Vertol
Jackson, Commander H.J. 136
Jaguar: see Grumman XF10F-1
Java Sea, battle of the 62
jet blast deflectors 139
Johnson, Louis A 109, 111
Johnson, President Lyndon B. 156, 160, 186, 188
Joint Task Group One 105
Jones, Master Chief Robert K. 238
Junkers airplanes
  Ju 87 64
  Ju 88 52

K

KA-3B Skywarrior: see Douglas
KA-6D Intruder: see Grumman
Kaiser-Fleetwings BTK 122
Kaman airplanes
  HH-2C Seasprite 179, **180**
  HU-2B 179
  SH-2D Seasprite 235
  SH-2F Seasprite **223**, 226, **226**, 235, 238
  UH-2 180, 235
Kamikaze operations 86, 97, 100
Kennedy Jr, Lt Joseph P. 52
Kennedy, President John F. 150
Kepford, Lt C 'Ike' 95
Khe Sanh, seige of 183
Khoy, President Sankhm 296
Kilkeny, Commander Pat 241
King, Adm. Ernest J. 40, 88
Kingfisher: see Vought OS2U, OS2U-1 and OS2U-2
Kimmel, Adm. H.E. 35
Kinkaid, Rear Adm. Thomas C. 67
Kissinger, Henry 199
Kleenmann, Commander Henry 'Hank' 210
Kleisch, Lt A. 55
Koelsch, Lt (JG) John M 116
Korean People's Republic, established 110
Korth, Fred 141
Krushchev, Premier Nikita 150
Kurita, Vice Adm. 96

L

La-7: see Lavochkin
LABS (low altitude bombing system) 129, 130, 133
LAMPS (light airborne multipurpose system) 223, 226, 234, 235, 245, 246
LC-130R: see Lockheed Hercules
Laddon, I.M. 33
Langley, Professor S.P. 10
Lassen, Lt (JG) Clyde E. 180, 181
Lavochkin La-7 145
Lawler, Lt Cdr Joe 96
Lend-Lease Act 34
Lerwick: see Saro
Leslie, Lt Cdr Maxwell F. 70
Lewis & Vought VE-7 **17**
Leyte Gulf, battle of 96
Liberator: see Consolidated B-24 and PB4Y-1
Liberty, US Standard Aircraft Engine 14
Liftmaster: see Douglas C-118B and R6D-2
Lockheed airplanes
  AP-2H Neptune **174**
  C-130 Hercules 208, 209, 229, 232
  C-130F Hercules 207
  EC-121 Constellation 148, 173, 228, **229**
  EC-130 Hercules 228, 229, 250, **250**
  ECV-130 Hercules 130, 229
  EP-3 Orion 228
  EP-3B Orion **173**
  LC-130R Hercules **234**
  NC-121K 228
  OP-2E Neptune **174**
  P-2 Neptune 172, 174, 176, 228
  P2V-3 Neptune 114, 128, **128**, 145
  P2V-5 Neptune 145, **145**
  P2V-7 Neptune **228**
  P-3 Orion 172, 173, 178, 223, 228, **248**, 249
  P-3B Orion 146
  P-3C Orion **228**, **230-231**, 248
  PBO-1 Hudson 34, **34**, 36
  PV-1 Ventura 53, **74**, **77**, 79, **79**, 80, **82**
  PV-2 Harpoon 79, **80-81**, 82
  PV-3 Ventura **49**, 51, 52, 73
  R60-1 Constitution **108**
  S-3A/B Viking **222**, 223, **223**, **224-225**, 226, 240, 245
  SP-2H Neptune **146-147**, **177**, **228**
  TV-2D **148**
  US-3A Viking **226**, 232, 249, **249**
  WV-2 Warning Star **148**
  XFV-1 **127**
Loening OL-2 24, **24**
Los Angeles (ZR-3) 32
Louis, Joe 52

M

MATS (Military Air Transport Service) 108, 148, 149
  formation 107
MDAP (Mutual Defense Assistance Program) 155
Me 210: see Messerschmitt
MiG-15: see Mikoyan-Gurevich
MiG-17: see Mikoyan
MiG-19: see Mikoyan
MiG-21: see Mikoyan
MO-1: see Martin
MT-1: see Martin
MacArthur, Gen. Douglas 96
Marauder: see Martin JM-1
Mariner: see Martin PBM, PBM-1, PBM-2, PBM-3 and PBM-5
Marlin: see Martin P-5 and SP-5B
Marr, Commander H.L. 170, **170**, 171
Marshall, Gen. George C. 111
Martin airplanes
  AM-1 Mauler 122, **122**, 123, **123**
  BM-1/2 23
  JM-1 Marauder **97**
  MO-1 24
  MT-1 **21**
  P3M-1 33
  P3M-2 33
  P4M-1 Mercator 145, **145**
  P-5 Marlin 172, 173
  P6M-2 Seamaster **127**
  PBM Mariner 41, 50, **51**, 73, 78
  PBM-1 Mariner 34, 36, **41**
  PBM-2 Mariner 34
  PBM-3 Mariner 36, **51**, **53**, 79, **79**
  PBM-5 Mariner 114, **114**, 145
  SC-1 22
  SC-2 22
  SP-5B Marlin **172**, **173**
  T3M-1 **18**, **19**, 22
  T3M-2 22, **22**
  T4M 22, 23
  TM-1 22
  XBTM-1 122
  XP6M-1 127
  XPB2M-1 34
  XPBM-1 34
  YP6M-1 127
Martin, Commander William I. 100
Matthews, Francis P. 109
Mauler: see Martin AM-1
McCain, Vice Adm. John S. 88
McCampbell, Commander David 89, 97, **101**
McClusky, Lt Cdr Wade 70
McDevitt, Lt Cdr Jim 194, 197
McDonnell airplanes
  F2H Banshee **116**, 132
  F2H-1 Banshee 118, **118**, 119, 144
  F2H-2 Banshee **117**, 132, **132**
  F2H-3 Banshee 132
  F2H-4 Banshee 132
  F3H Demon **133**, 135, **135**, **136**, **140**
  FH-1 Phantom 118, **118**, 122
  XF3H-1 134
  XFD-1 118
  XFH-1 **135**
McDonnell Douglas airplanes
  AH-1 Phantom II 135
  C-9B Skytrain II 229, **229**, 249, **249**
  F-4 Phantom II 168, 172, 178, **178**, 179, **189**, 194, 195, **196**, 196-200, 210, **211**, 214
  F-4A Phantom II 135
  F-4B Phantom II 135, **152**, 168, **172**, **179**, **191**, **192-193**, 210
  F-4G Phantom II **170**
  F4H-1 Phantom II 134, 136, **136**
  F-4J Phantom II 135, 188, **190**, **194**, **197**, 210
  F-4N Phantom II **209**, 210, 212, **212**
  F-4S Phantom II 210, 212
  F/A-18A Hornet 130, **201-202**, 241, **242-243**, 244, **244**, 248
  RF-4B Phantom II 212, 219
  RF-4C Phantom II 135
  TA-4J Skyhawk **218**, **222**, 232
McGowan Jr, Chief Yeoman Douglas L. 240
McKeever, Ensign W 46
McNamara, Robert S 141, 214
Medal of Honor 63, 78, 82, 116, 165
  first to Naval Aviation 63
Mercator: see Martin P4M-1
Messerschmitt Me 210 52
Metcalf, Victor A 10
Meyers, Commander L.R. 'Moose' 186
Midway, battle of 61, 62, 64, 65, 67, 70
Mikoyan-Gurevich MiG-15 112, 113, 145
Mikoyan airplanes
  MiG-17 158, 168, 170, 171, 172, 196, 198, 200
  MiG-19 198
  MiG-21 170, 171, 182, 194, 195, 197, 198, 200
Military Air Transport Service (MATS) 108, 148, 149
  formation 107
Millikin Lt Steve 180
Mills, Commodore G.H. 56
Missileer: see Douglas F6D-1
Mitchell: see North American B-25 and PBJ
Mitchell, Gen. W.M. 18
Mitscher Adm. Marc A. 88, 92, 93, 96
Mitsubishi airplanes
  A6M Zero 60, 62, 64, 66, 84, 86, 100
  G4M 63
Model 39-B: see Aeromarine
Model 75: see Stearman
Model 707: see Boeing
Model H: see Curtiss
Moffett, Rear Adm. W.A. 18, 32
Moranville, Lt K.E. 'Ken' 155
Morse code 73
Musczynski, Lt Larry 210
Mustang: see North American P-51
Mustin, Lt Cdr H.C. 12
Mutual Defense Assistance Program (MDAP) 155

N

N-1: see Davis
N2S: see Boeing-Stearman
N2S-5: see Boeing-Stearman
N3N: see Naval Aircraft Factory
N-9: see Curtiss
NAGPAW (North American general-purpose attack weapon) 129
NATO (North Atlantic Treaty Organization) 106
NATS (Naval Air Transport Service), amalgamation 107, 108
NC: see Navy/Curtiss
NC-121K: see Lockheed
NKC-135A: see Boeing
Nagumo, Vice-Adm. Chuichi 65, 70
Nakajima B5N 64
National Military Establishment, formation 108
National Security Act 1947 108
Naval Air Transport Service (NATS) amalgamation 107, 108
Naval Aircraft Factory 13, 33
Naval Aircraft Factory airplanes
  N3N **71**, 72, **72**
  PN-7 31, **31**
  PN-8 30
  PN-9 31, 32, **32**
  PN-12 32
  PT-1 22, 23
  PT-2 22
  SON 36
Navy/Curtiss NC **14**, 15, 32
Neal, AM3 George M. 116
Neptune: see Lockheed AP-2H, OP-2E, P-2, P2V-2, P2V-3, P2V-5, P2V-7 and SP-2H
Neutrality Patrol 23, 24, 40, 41, 50
Nieuport 28 26
Night Air Group 90 100
Nimitz Adm. Chester 70
Nixon, President Richard M. 185, 195, 199
North American airplanes
  A3J-1 Vigilante 129, 133, 219
  AJ-1 Savage 128
  AJ-2 Savage, 128, **128**, **129**, 144
  B-25 Mitchell 77, 79, 88
  DT-28B Trojan **234**
  F-86 Sabre 112, 133
  FJ-1 Fury 112, 119, **119**, 134
  FJ-2 Fury 133
  FJ-3 Fury 133, **133**, 148, **148**
  FJ-4 Fury 133, **133**, **140**
  OV-10 Bronco 173, **173**, **174**
  P-51 Mustang 78
  PBJ Mitchell 73, **88**
  RA-5C Vigilante 130, **130**, **170**, 173, 194, **212**, 220, **220**, **221**, 240
  SNJ Texan 72, **74**, **75**
  SNJ-4 Texan **73**
  T-28 Trojan 234, 250
  T-39 Sabreliner 238
  T-39D 250
  XAJ-1 128
  XFJ-1 Fury 118
  YA3J-1 130
North American general-purpose attack weapon (NAGPAW) 129
North American/Rockwell T-2C Buckeye 232, **233**
North Atlantic Treaty Organization (NATO) 106
Northrop airplanes
  BT-1 **23**
  F-5E Tiger II **239**
  XBT-2 24

O

O2C: see Curtiss
O2U-1 Corsair: see Vought
O2U-2 Corsair: see Vought
O3U-1 Corsair: see Vought
OC: see Curtiss
OL-2: see Loening
OP-2E Neptune: see Lockheed
OS2U Kingfisher: see Vought
OS2U-1 Kingfisher: see Vought
OS2U-2 Kingfisher: see Vought
OV-10 Bronco: see North American
O'Hare, Lt Edward H. 'Butch' 62, 63
O'Neil, MGSGT Patrick J. 238
operation
  Anvil/Dragoon 45, 56
  Bluetree 194
  Crossroads 105, 106
  Deep Freeze 234
  Eagle Pull 205
  Endsweep 199, 204, 206, 207
  Flaming Dart One 160
  Frequent Wind 201, 204, 205, 207
  Game Warden 174
  Iron Hand 165
  Leader 38, 46
  Linebacker I 197
  Linebacker II 199
  Luzon 173
  Market Time 173
  Motel 173
  Nimbus Star 207, 232
  Overlord 53
  Rolling Thunder 164, 169
  Rolling Thunder 9 178,
  Rolling Thunder 50 169
  Sea Orbit 150
  Shufly 154
  Torch 42, 44, 46, 51
  Vittles 108
Orion: see Lockheed EP-3, EP-3B, P-3, P-3B and P-3C
Ozawa, Vice-Adm. 96, 97

P

P-2 Neptune: see Lockheed
P2V-2 Neptune: see Lockheed
P2V-3 Neptune: see Lockheed
P2V-5 Neptune: see Lockheed
P2V-7 Neptune: see Lockheed
P2Y-1: see Consolidated
P2Y-2: see Consolidated
P2Y-3: see Consolidated
P-3 Orion: see Lockheed
P-3B Orion: see Lockheed
P-3C Orion: see Lockheed
P3M-1: see Martin
P3M-2: see Martin
P4M-1 Mercator: see Martin
P4Y-2S: see Convair
P-5 Marlin: see Martin
P6M-2 Seamaster: see Martin
P-40 Warhawk: see Curtiss
P-47 Thunderbolt: see Republic
P-51 Mustang: see North American
PB2Y-2 Coronado: see Consolidated
PB2Y-3 Coronado: see Consolidated
PB2Y-5 Coronado: see Consolidated
PB4Y-1 Liberator: see Consolidated
PB4Y-2 Privateer: see Consolidated
PBJ Mitchell: see North American
PBM Mariner: see Martin
PBM-1 Mariner: see Martin
PBM-2 Mariner: see Martin
PBM-3 Mariner: see Martin
PBM-5 Mariner: see Martin
PBO-1 Hudson: see Lockheed
PBY Catalina: see Consolidated
PBY-1 Catalina: see Consolidated
PBY-3 Catalina: see Consolidated
PBY-4 Catalina: see Consolidated
PBY-5 Catalina: see Consolidated
PBY-5A Catalina: see Consolidated
PD-1: see Douglas
PN-7: see Naval Aircraft Factory
PN-8: see Naval Aircraft Factory
PN-9: see Naval Aircraft Factory
PN-12: see Naval Aircraft Factory
PT-1: see Naval Aircraft Factory
PT-2: see Naval Aircraft Factory
PV-1 Ventura: see Lockheed
PV-2 Harpoon: see Lockheed
PV-3 Ventura: see Lockheed
Pacific Task Fleet 143
Page, Commander L.C. 168
Panther: see Grumman F9F-2, F9F-3, F9F-5 and XF9F-2
Parachute Experimental Unit 144
Pearl Harbor, attack on 60, **60**, 62
Pegasus: see Beech T-44A
Phantom: see McDonnell FH-1
Phantom II: see McDonnell Douglas AH-1, F-4, F-4A, F-4B, F-4G, F4H-1, F-4J, F-4N, F-4S, RF-4B and RF-4C
Philippine Sea
  First battle of 89
  Second battle of 97, 143
Phillips, Commander Bill 158
Phoenix AWG-9 missile 214, 217, 241
Pilot Training Program 72
Pirate: see Vought F6U-1 and XF6U-1

Plog, Lt (JG) Leonard H. 112, 113
'Pogo': see Convair XFY-1
Porte, Lt J.C. 13
Privateer: see Consolidated PB4Y-2
Project 'Aphrodite' 52, 53
Project 'TRIM' 174
Prowler: see Grumman EA-6B
Pup: see Sopwith
Pyle, Ernie 71

R

R-2: see Curtiss
R3Y-2 Tradewind: see Convair
R-4: see Sikorsky
R5D Skymaster: see Douglas
R5D-3 Skymaster: see Douglas
R-6: see Curtiss
R6D-2 Liftmaster: see Douglas
R-34 airship 32
R-38 (ZR-2) airship 32
R60-1 Constitution: see Lockheed
RA-3B Skywarrior: see Douglas
RA-5C Vigilante: see North American
RAF No. 209 Squadron 40
RAST (recovery assist secure and traverse) gear 235
RB-36H: see Convair
RF-4B Phantom II: see McDonnell Douglas
RF-4C Phantom II: see McDonnell Douglas
RF-8 Crusader: see Vought
RF-8A Crusader: see Vought
RF-8G Crusader: see Vought
RH-53D Sea Stallion: see Sikorsky
RIO (Radar Intercept Officer) 135
Radar Intercept Officer (RIO) 135
Radford, Adm. Arthur W. 108
Radford, 'Raddy' 88
Rainey, Lt Cdr Barbara 238, **238**
Ramage, James D. 'Jig Dog' 92, 120
Ranger: see Bell TH-57C
redesignations
  aircraft 1946 107
  air groups 1946 107
  air groups 1948 108
  squadrons 1946 107
  squadrons 1948 108
Reeves, Lt M.C. 84
Reeves, Rear Adm. J.M. 20
Regulus missile 148, **148**
Replacement Air Groups, established 149
Republic airplanes
  P-47 Thunderbolt 77, 78
  F-105 Thunderchief 200
Republic of Korea, formation 110
Reserve Carrier Air Wings 235
Rice, Capt. L.K. 110
Rlner, Lt Jim **70**
Roberts, Lt H. 48
Robinson, Ensign Brenda E. 238
Rockeye cluster bomb 197
Rockwell CT-39 Sabreliner 232
Rodgers, Lt J. 11, 32
Roosevelt, President Franklin D. 20, 34, 40, 53
Roosevelt, President Theodore 10
Ryan airplanes
  FR-1 Fireball 119, **119**, 122
  XFR-1 Fireball 118

S

S-2 Tracker: see Grumman
S-2E Tracker: see Grumman
S2F Tracker: see Grumman
S2F-1 Tracker: see Grumman
S-3A/3B Viking: see Lockheed
SB2A-4: see Brewster
SB2C Helldiver: see Curtiss
SB2C-1 Helldiver: see Curtiss
SB2C-3 Helldiver: see Curtiss
SB2C-4 Helldiver: see Curtiss
SB2C-5 Helldiver: see Curtiss
SB2U-1 Vindicator: see Vought
SB2U-2 Vindicator: see Vought
SBC-3: see Curtiss
SBC-4: see Curtiss
SBD Dauntless: see Douglas
SBD-1 Dauntless: see Douglas
SBD-2 Dauntless: see Douglas
SBD-3 Dauntless: see Douglas
SBD-5 Dauntless: see Douglas
SBU-1: see Vought
SC-1: see Martin
SC-1 Seahawk: see Curtiss
SC-2: see Martin
SF-1: see Grumman
SH-2D Seasprite: see Kaman
SH-2F Seasprite: see Kaman
SH-3A Sea King: see Sikorsky
SH-3H Sea King: see Sikorsky
SH-60B Seahawk: see Sikorsky
SH-60F: see Sikorsky
SLEP (service life extension program) 234
SNJ Texan: see North American
SNJ-4 Texan: see North American
SOC Seagull: see Curtiss
SOC-1 Seagull: see Curtiss
SOC-3 Seagull: see Curtiss
SON: see Naval Aircraft Factory
SP-2H Neptune: see Lockheed
SP-5B Marlin: see Martin
ST-1: see Stout
Su-22 'Fitter': see Sukhoi
Sabre: see North American F-86
Sabreliner: see North American T-39
Sabreliner: see Rockwell CT-39
Santa Cruz, battle of 65, 67, 70
Saro Lerwick 34
Savage: see North American AJ-1 and AJ-2
Schoultz, Vice Adm. Robert F. 'Dutch' 240
Seabat: see Sikorsky HSS-1
Sea Dart: see Convair F2Y-1
Seagull: see Curtiss SOC, SOC-1 and SOC-3
Seahawk: see Curtiss SC-1
Seahawk: see Sikorsky SH-60B
Sea King: see Sikorsky SH-3A and SH-3H
Sea Knight: see Boeing Vertol CH-46
Seamaster: see Martin P6M-2
Sea Ranger: see Bell TH-57A/C
Sears, Commander Harry 82
Seasprite: see Kaman HH-2C and SH-2F
Sea Stallion: see Sikorsky CH-53A and RH-53D
Seventh Task Fleet 143
Shay, Lt J. 241
Shenandoah (ZR-1) 32
Shepard, Commander Alan B. 149
Sherman, Adm. Forrest P. 110, 111, 136
ships (for US Navy see under USS)
  Akagi 70
  Argus 17, 22
  Arromanches 154
  Béarn 154
  Bismarck 34, 40
  Dixmude 154
  Furious 16, 17
  Hermes 62
  Hiryu 70
  Hiyo 93
  Hood 40
  Jean Bart 43, 46
  Jupiter 17
  Kaga 70
  LaFayette 154
  Musashi 96
  Shoho 66, 70, 74
  Shokaku 21
  Soryu 70
  Triumph 110, 111
  Yarmouth 16
  Zuikaku 21, 97
Short Seaplanes 16, 22
Short Sunderland 34, 114
Shrike, AGM-45 anti-radar missile 165, 182, 197
Sidewinder, AIM-9 air-to-air missile: 130, 133, 148, 172, 183, 186, 192, 195, 197-199, 210, 214, 217, 241
Sikorsky airplanes
  CH-53 Sea Stallion 234
  CH-53A Sea Stallion 199, 204, 205, **205**
  CH-53D Sea Stallion **206**, 232
  CH-53E Sea Stallion 232, 249
  HH-3A Sea King 235, **235**
  HNS-1 Hoverfly 54, **54**, 55, **55**, 143
  HO3S-1 Dragonfly 112, 116, 141, **141**, 143
  HO4S 142, **142**
  HSS-1 Seabat 142, **142**
  HUS-1 149
  R-4 54
  RH-53D Sea Stallion **206**, 207, **207**, 208, **208**, 209, **238**
  SH-3A Sea King 142, 179, 180, **180**, 181
  SH-3H Sea King 226, **226**, 245
  SH-60B Seahawk 226, 235, **235**, 245, 248
  SH-60F 245
  XH-59A 240
  XPBS-1 34
  XR-4 54
Sims, Adm W.S. 14
Skyhawk: see McDonnell Douglas A-4, A-4C, A4D, A4D-1, A4D-2, A-4E, A-4F, A-4M and TA-4J
Skylancer: see Douglas F5D-1
Skymaster: see Douglas R5D and R5D-3
Skyknight: see Douglas F3D-1, F3D-2, F-10B and TF-10B
Skyraider: see Douglas A-1, A-1H, AD, AD-1, AD-2, AD-3, AD-4, AD-5, AD-5W and EA-1
Skyray: see Douglas F4D-1
Skyrocket: see Douglas D-588-2
Skyshark: see Douglas XA2D
Skystreak: see Douglas D-558-1
Skytrain II: see McDonnell Douglas C-9B
Skywarrior: see Douglas A-3, A-3B, A3D, A3D-1, EA-3B, EKA-3B, KA-3B and RA-3B
Smith, Ensign L.B. 34, 40
Smith, Lt J.C. 168
Sopwith airplanes
  Camel 17, 26
  Cuckoo 22
  Pup 16
Southeast Asia Treaty Organization (SEATO) 150
Spanish-American war 10
Sparrow AIM-7 missile 134, 135, 168, 172, 192, 195, 214, 217, 241
Spikebuoy acoustic sensor 174
Spitfire: see Supermarine
Sprage, Rear Adm. Clifton 96
Sprague, Rear Adm. Thomas L. 143
Spruance, Rear Adm. Raymond A. 67, 70, 88
Spruill, Lt. Donna 238
Stearman Model 75 73
Storm, CHMAC C.E. **144**
Stout ST-1 22
Stroop, Rear Adm. P.D. 149
Struble, Vice Adm. Arthur D. 110
submarines
  I-52 49
  UB-32 14
  U-76 52
  U-118 **49**
  U-134 56
  U-166 54
  U-487 48
  U-505 49
  U-569 48
  U-805 **55**
  U-1229 49
Suerstedt, Lt Cdr H. 'Hank' 115, 155
Sukhoi Su-22 'Fitter' 210
Sullivan, Commodore E.J. 56
Sullivan, John L. 109
Sullivan, Lt Jerry **195**, 197
Sunderland: see Short
Super King Air: see Beech UC-12B
Supermarine Spitfire 41, **41**, 42, 53
Support Force Atlantic Fleet 40
Swartz, Lt Cdr Ted 'T.R.' 172
Swift: see Blackburn
Swift Boat **175**

T

T-2C Buckeye: see Norrh American Rockwell
T3M-1: see Martin
T3M-2: see Martin
T4M: see Martin
T-28 Trojan: see North American
T-34C Turbo Mentor: see Beech
T-39 Sabreliner: see North American
T-39D: see North American
T-44A Pegasus: see Beech
T-45A Hawk: see British Aerospace/McDonnell Douglas
T-47A Citation II: see Cessna
TA-4J Skyhawk: see McDonnell Douglas
TA-7C Corsair II: see Vought
TARPS (Tactical Air Reconnaissance Pod System) 215, 219
TAV-8B Harrier: see British Aerospace/McDonnell Douglas
TB2D: see Douglas
TBD-1 Devastator: see Douglas
TBF Avenger: see Grumman
TBF-1 Avenger: see Grumman
TBM Avenger: see Grumman/General Motors
TBM-1 Avenger: see Grumman/General Motors
TBM-3 Avenger: see Grumman/General Motors
TBN-3E: see Grumman
TBN-3W: see Grumman
TCS (Television Camera Set) 215
TF-8A Crusader: see Vought
TF-9J Cougar: see Grumman
TF-10B Skyknight: see Douglas
TFX (Tactical Fighter Experimental) 214
TG-1: see Great Lakes
TG-2: see Great Lakes
TH-1: see Bell
TH-47C Ranger: see Bell
TH-57A/C Sea Ranger: see Bell
TM-1: see Martin
TRAM A-6E: see Grumman
TRIM (Trails and Roads Interdiction Multisensor) 174
TS-1: see Curtiss
TS-2A: see Grumman
TV-2D: see Lockheed
Tactical Air Reconnaissance Pod System (TARPS) 215, 219
Tactical Fighter Experimental (TFX) 214
'Taffy Two' 96
'Taffy Three' 96, 97
Task Force
  38/58, 88, 89, 92, 93, 96
  72 143
  77 110, 114, 143, 148, 150, 157, 164
  78 204
  95 111
Task Group 70 144
Television Camera Set (TCS) 215
Test Pilot Training Division 144
Texan: see North American SNJ and SNJ-4
Thach, Lt Cdr John S. 'Jimmy' **62**, 63, 111
Than Hao bridge **178**
Thunderbolt: see Republic P-47
Tiger: see Grumman F-11A and F11F-1
Tiger II: see Northrop F-5E
Tigercat: see Grumman F7F and F7F-2
Tomcat: see Grumman F-14A
Towers, Lt J.H. 11, 12, 13, 35
Tracer: see Grumman E-1B
Tracker: see Grumman S-2, S-2E, S-2F, S2F-1 and US-2
Trader: see Grumman C-1A
Tradewind: see Convair R3Y2
Trails and Roads Interdiction Multisensor (TRIM) 174
Tripp, Lt Dick **87**
Trojan: see North American DT-28B and T-28
Truly, Capt. Richard 250
Truman, President Harry S. 108-111
Turbo Mentor: see Beech T-34C
Two-Ocean Navy Act 35
Type 39-B: see Aeromarine

U

UC-12B: see Beech Super King Air
UH-1B: see Bell
UH-1N: see Bell Iroquois
UH-2: see Kaman
UO-1: see Vought
US-2 Tracker: see Grumman
US-3A Viking: see Lockheed
US Air Force, established as independent force 108
US Coast Guard 53, 54, 55
US Coast Guard
  Air-sea Rescue Service 56
  Patrol Bombing Squadron 6 54
US Marine Corps
  Air Group 11 36
  Air Group 21 36
  Reserve Wing 238
  Squadrons
    HMH-462 205
    HMH-463, 199, 204, 205
    HMM-165 204
    VMA-231 251
    VMA-324 144
    VMA-542 251
    VMAQ-2 222
    VMCJ-2 150
    VMF-115 132
    VMF-211 36
    VMF-214 111
    VMF-221 36
    VMF-323 111
    VMFA-312 112
    VMFA-314 241, 244
    VMFA-323 209, 241, 244
    VMFA-531 244
    VMFN-513 112
    VMFP-3 219
    VMJ-3 108
    VMO-151 36
    VMSB-131 36
    VMSB-132 36
    VMSB-231 36
    VMSB-232 36
    VO-7M 24
US Naval
  Academy 63
  Air Advanced Training 106
  Air Basic Training 106
  Air Operational Training Command 105
  Air Reserve 122
  Air Reserve Training 106
  Air System Command 149, 248
  Air Test Center 144, 174
  Air Training and Operating Procedures Standardization Program 149
  Air Training Command 71, 72, 75, 105, 238, 250
  Air Transport Service (NATS) amalgamation 107, 108
  Aviation Pilots 74, 75, 238
  Intermediate Training Command 106
  Reserve Air Base New York 36
  Reserve Forces 235
  Space Command 250
  Test Pilot School 144
  Weapons Center 228
US Navy
  Air Group
    2 82, 123
    5 110
    15 89, 100, 101
    20 96
    30 93
    41 100
    53 100
    82 119
    89 143
    91 100
  airships/ blimps
    ZPG-3W **150**
    ZPK 55, **56**, **57**
    ZPK-74 56
    ZPK-109 56
    ZPK-123 56
    ZPK-130 56
    ZPL 55
    ZPM 55
    ZR-1 *Shenandoah* 32
    ZR-2 *R-38* 32
    ZR-3 *Los Angeles* 32
    ZRS-4 *USS Akron* 32
    ZRS-5 *USS Macon* 32
  Air Task Group 1 115
  Air task Group 2 115
  Fighter Weapons School 238
  Fleet Air Wing
    6 114
    7 52
    10 83, 123, 181
    15 51, 52
    16 50, 51
    17 51, 77
  Guided Missile Unit 90 115, **115**
  Helicopter Squadron
    HA(L)-3 174
    HC-3 227
    HC-4 232
    HC-6 238
    HC-7 180, 235
    HC-9 235
    HM-12 199, 204, 207, 232, 238
    HM-14 238
    HM-16 208, 238
    HMR(L)-262 149
    HS-1 143
    HS-2 180
    HS-3 142
    HS-4 142
    HS-5 142
    HS-6 179
    HSL-33 223, 226
    HSL-41 226
    HT-8 250
    HT-18 250
    HU-1 116, 141, 143
    HU-2 143
  Joint Task Group One 105
  Patrol Wing
    1 34, 36
    2 34, 36
    3 34, 36, 50
    4 34, 36
    5 34, 36, 50
    7 34, 36, 50
    8 36
    10 36, 60, 61
  Reserve Air Group 102, 113, 114
  Reserve Squadron
    VA-702 116
    VF-781 113
    VF-791 116
    VFP-206 212
    VFP-306 212
  Squadron
    RVAH-7 220, 238
    RVAH-11 170, 190
    VA-15 180, 181
    VA-17A 122
    VA-19A 123
    VA-20A 123
    VA-25 123, 156, 186
    VA-27 183, 209
    VA-34 181
    VA-35 184, 210, 219, 244
    VA-42 130
    VA-45 117
    VA-46 148, 218
    VA-52 158, 180
    VA-54 123
    VA-55 129, 171, 190
    VA-64 150
    VA-65 123, 150, 219
    VA-66 134, 150
    VA-72 129
    VA-75 165, 168
    VA-76 150
    VA-84 122
    VA-85 122, 168, 169
    VA-97 183, 209
    VA-126 133
    VA-144 204
    VA-146 171, 182, 189
    VA-147 182, 183
    VA-153 160, 164, 204
    VA-155 199
    VA-156 132
    VA-164 129
    VA-165 196
    VA-174 122, 219
    VA-192 180
    VA-195 112, 115, 197
    VA-196 183
    VA-212 129, 162
    VA-216 133
    VAH-1 129, 130, 160
    VAH-3 130
    VAH-4 191
    VAH-6 129
    VAH-7 128, 130, 220
    VAH-21 174
    VAK-208 222
    VAK-308 222
    VAL-4 173, 174
    VAP-61 171, 173
    VAP-62 128
    VAQ-33 123, 128, 186, 222, 223, 228
    VAQ-34 222
    VAQ-132 222
    VAQ-135 245
    VAW-11 155
    VAW-12 150, 176
    VAW-13 160
    VAW-33 123
    VAW-123 220, 245
    VAW-125 220
    VB-1B 27
    VB-2 36, 62
    VB-3, 23, 36
    VB-4, 38, 46
    VB-5 36, 63, 92
    VB-5B 31
    VB-6 23, 36, 62
    VB-8 36, 67, 70
    VB-10 92, 97
    VB-17 86
    VB-20 93
    VB-87 100
    VB-106 82
    VB-110 52
    VB-135 79
    VB-142 80
    VC-1 47
    VC-3 112, 132, 133, 134, 232
    VC-4 111-113, 122, 132
    VC-5 128
    VC-6 128, 144
    VC-8 228
    VC-9 48, 49
    VC-11 48
    VC-12 222
    VC-13 48, 218
    VC-29 47
    VC-35 115
    VC-54Q 229
    VC-58 49
    VC-61 114
    VC-69 49
    VC(N)-1 105
    VC(N)-2 105
    VCP-61 128
    VCS-15 143
    VD-1 82
    VD-2 82
    VD-3 82
    VD-4 82
    VD-5 82
    VF-1 26, 200, 214, 215
    VF-1B 27
    VF-2 20, 26, 27, 31, 36, 62, 200, 214, 215
    VF-2B 26, 27
    VF-3 36, 62
    VF-4 20, 41, 42, 44, 46, 100
    VF-5 36, 41, 63
    VF-5A 112, 119
    VF-5B 27, 31
    VF-6 36, 62
    VF-6B 29
    VF-8 36
    VF-9 42, 48
    VF-11 117, 132, 134
    VF-14 132
    VF-15A 107
    VF-16 86, 89
    VF-16A 107
    VF-17 86, 88, 95, 96
    VF-17A 118, 122
    VF-20 96
    VF-21 132, 168, 212
    VF-22 117
    VF-24 102, 123
    VF-26 43
    VF-27 91
    VF-30 93
    VF-31 113, 122
    VF-32 102, 130, 134
    VF-41 36, 119, 210
    VF-42 36, 63
    VF-51 112, 113, 122, 152, 241
    VF-52 122
    VF-53 166
    VF-54 115
    VF-61 134
    VF-62 117, 132
    VF-64 123
    VF-66 118
    VF-71 36, 114, 122
    VF-72 36, 41, 107
    VF-74 46, 135
    VF-81 130
    VF-84 215
    VF-92 115, 190, 192, 197
    VF-96 188, 189, 194-199
    VF-111 112, 122, 152, 157
    VF-112 122
    VF-114 170, 172, 218, 241
    VF-121 135

VF-123 130
VF-124 137, 215
VF-131 135
VF-142 133, 192
VF-143 217
VF-151 182, 212
VF-154 212
VF-161 135, 212
VF-162 171
VF-171 118, 122, 144, 212
VF-172 122
VF-173 133
VF-191 115, 134
VF-193 113
VF-194 115, 135, 199
VF-211 170, 183, 197
VFA-25 243, 244
VFA-113 243, 244
VFA-125 202, 244
VF(AW)-3 132, 133
VF(N)-75, 88
VFP-62 150
VFP-63 134, 160, 165, 190, 212
VFP-206 134, 212
VFP-306 134, 212
VGF-28 44
VO-1B 24
VO-2 143
VO-4B 25
VO-67 174
VOF-1 46, 47
VP-1 145, 146, 176, 177
VP-3F 33, 34
VP-6 114, 145
VP-6F 34
VP-7 32
VP-9 145
VP-10 33
VP-10F 33, 35
VP-11 36, 231
VP-12 36, 77
VP-13 35, 36
VP-14 35, 36
VP-19 145
VP-21 34, 36
VP-22 36, 145
VP-23 36
VP-24 36
VP-26 145
VP-28 114, 145
VP-31 36
VP-32 36
VP-40 172, 173
VP-41 36
VP-42 36
VP-43 36
VP-44 36, 40
VP-46 114, 145
VP-47 114
VP-51 36
VP-52 36, 40, 78
VP-54 77
VP-55 78
VP-63 52
VP-71 36
VP-72 36
VP-73 36, 41, 50
VP-74 36, 41
VP-81 36, 77
VP-82 34, 36
VP-83 36
VP-91 36
VP-101 36, 60
VP-102 36, 60
VP-103 52
VP-105 52
VP-110 51
VP-731 145
VPB-101 82
VPB-102 82
VPB-104 82
VPB-109 83
VPB-118 83
VPP-1 83
VPP-2 83
VQ-1 145, 173, 178, 222, 228
VQ-2 222, 228
VQ-4 250
VR-1 229
VR-3 108
VR-21 148
VR-23 116
VR-24 207, 232
VR-30 229
VR-55 229
VR-56 229
VRC-30 232
VRC-40 232, 238

VRC-50 226, 232, 249
VS-1 31
VS-1D5 51
VS-2 36, 62
VS-3 36
VS-3B 27
VS-5 21, 36, 61, 63
VS-5D4 25
VS-6 36, 64
VS-7 84
VS-8 36
VS-20 142
VS-21 111, 223, 225
VS-24 142, 222
VS-27 123
VS-31 223
VS-32 119
VS-33 226
VS-38 138
VS-41 36, 43, 173
VS-42 23, 36, 42
VS-51 89
VS-64 96
VS-71 36
VS-72 36
VSF-3 181
VT-1B 22
VT-2 22, 36, 62, 97, 250
VT-3 36, 62, 250
VT-4 46
VT-5 36, 63
VT-6 23, 36, 65, 250
VT-8 36, 66, 70
VT-9 22
VT-19 97
VT-24 93
VT-26 132, 232
VT-28 232
VT-30 93, 232
VT-44 97
VU-1 97
VU-4 105
WW-1 106, 107
WW-2 106, 107
WW-11 148
VX-1 106
VX-3 118, 140, 143
VX-4 135, 215
VX-6 234
ZP-1 149
ZP-3 149
ZP-21 56
Undergraduate Flight Training System (VTXTS) 250
USS Abraham Lincoln 248
Akron (ZRS-4) airship 32
Albermarle 40
Altamaha 48
America 141, 184, 199
Antietam 105, 109, 111, 114, 137, 142, 143
Arkansas 22
Badoeng Strait 106, 110, 111, 142, 149
Bairoko 111
Bataan 110-112
Belleau Wood 93, 234
Bennington 127, 140
Birmingham 10, 10, 12
Block Island 48, 93
Bogue 47-49
Bon Homme Richard 100, 104, 114, 140, 148, 172, 183, 186
Boxer 105, 109, 110, 112, 113, 115, 117, 119, 142-144
Brook 226
Bunker Hill 86, 88, 96, 100, 104, 142
Cabot 85, 110, 142, 143, 149
California 24, 209
Card 47, 48
Carl Vinson 210, 234
Charger 86
Chenango 43, 43
Chicago 196
Childs 60
Columbia 85
Constellation 135, 141, 156, 170, 183, 188, 190, 192, 194-199, 204, 205, 226, 227, 243
Coral Sea 104, 110, 128, 136, 136, 140, 152, 160, 161, 164, 165, 182, 194, 196, 200, 204, 207-209, 209, 212, 214, 241, 248
Core 48
Cowpens 58, 92
Curntuck 173
Dwight D. Eisenhower 209, 217, 223, 234, 234
Enterprise 20, 21, 23, 35, 62, 63, 65-67, 67, 70, 71, 84, 86, 92, 93, 97, 100, 104, 106, 130, 141, 141, 142, 150, 169, 170, 184, 188, 189, 189, 200, 201, 204, 205, 207, 209, 215, 220, 229
Essex 85, 88, 89, 100, 104, 114, 116, 144, 148, 150, 176

Forrestal 133, 141, 141, 179, 207, 214
Franklin D. Roosevelt 104, 106, 110, 118, 128, 136, 140, 207, 234, 251
Gambier Bay 96
George Washington 248
Goldsborough 41
Guadalcanal 49, 76, 207
Guam 85
Hancock 129, 138, 137, 140, 160, 162, 164, 166, 170, 178, 183, 190, 197, 199, 200, 204, 204, 205, 207
Hornet 21, 63, 65-67, 70, 71, 97, 133, 155, 170
Huntington 24
Inchon 204
Independence 88, 100, 106, 141, 150, 165, 168, 207, 238
Intrepid 137, 140, 142, 143, 164, 171, 176, 178, 181, 183, 234
Iwo Jima 104
John F. Kennedy 128, 141, 207, 214, 218, 223, 225, 232, 236-237, 241
Jouett 181
Kasaan Bay 46
Kearsage 109, 110, 114, 122, 148, 179
Kitty Hawk 141, 164, 168-170, 172, 191, 195, 199, 208
Lake Champlain 105, 112-114, 117, 137, 142, 142, 149
Langley 16, 17, 18, 20, 26, 31, 60, 63, 97, 154
Lexington 17, 19, 20-23, 26, 27, 31, 35, 62, 63, 66, 70, 86, 89, 92, 93, 97, 104, 129, 134, 138, 140, 232, 234, 248
Leyte 107, 109-111, 113, 116, 138
Long Beach 209
Long Island 35
Macon (ZRS-5) airship 32
Maddox 150, 155
Mahan 180
Maryland 24
McInerney 235
Midway 104, 110, 136-140, 148, 150, 154, 164, 168, 195, 196, 199, 200, 207, 208, 210, 212, 219, 226, 235, 235
Mindoro 110
Mississippi 11, 12, 26, 37
Missouri 104, 106
Monterey 89, 93
Nassau 234, 251
New Orleans 204
Nimitz 207, 208-210, 222, 234, 234
Northampton 84, 85
North Carolina 12, 12, 24
Okinawa 199, 205, 207
Oriskany 104, 113, 114, 136, 140, 160, 171, 182, 183, 190, 199, 204, 205, 212, 234
Palau 110
Peleliu 234
Pennsylvania 10, 11
Philippine Sea 109-112, 142, 144
Preble 180
Princeton 91, 97, 104, 109, 112, 113, 115, 116, 141, 142
Randolph 119, 148
Ranger 18, 20, 21, 23, 27, 31, 35, 38, 40-43, 46, 63, 104, 106, 141, 157, 160, 171, 182, 190, 204, 205, 215, 220, 221
Rendova 111
Reprisal 104
Saipan 109, 110, 118, 122, 136, 144, 144, 149, 234
Salerno Bay 119
Sangamon 42, 43
San Jacinto 84, 85
Santa Fe 84, 85
Santee 42, 43, 47, 47, 48
Saratoga 17, 18, 20-23, 26, 27, 29, 35, 62, 70, 88, 100, 104, 106, 129, 141, 149, 199, 220
Shangri-La 140, 142, 234
Sicily 106, 110-112, 142
Solomons 48
South Carolina 209
St Lô 97
Suwanee 42, 44, 46
Tangier 79
Tarawa 104, 107, 109, 142, 144, 234
Texas 26
Thetis Bay 149
Theodore Roosevelt 248
Ticonderoga 100, 104, 123, 135, 137, 140, 142, 155, 156, 158, 165, 169, 176, 180, 183, 234
Topeka 143
Tripoli 204, 240
Truxtun 209
Tulagi 46
Turner Joy 156
United States 109, 128, 136
Valley Forge 109, 110, 110, 111-113, 142
Virginia 209
Wasp 20, 21, 36, 40, 41, 63, 70, 92, 144, 148
West Virginia 12, 25

William B. Preston 70
Wolverine 75
Wright 109, 110, 136, 138
Yorktown 20, 21, 23, 35, 41, 61-63, 66, 70, 70, 85-88, 92, 102, 104, 136, 148

V

V-1 missile site 53
V-1 program 71, 72
V-5 program 71, 72
V-173: see Vought
VE-7: see Lewis & Vought
VE-7: see Vought
VE-7H: see Vought
VE-7SF: see Vought
VFMX requirement 241
VFX fighter 214
VJ-Day 104, 118
VOS units 53, 84, 85
VPX program 249
VTXTS (Navy Undergraduate Flight Training System) 250
Vampatella, Lt (JG) Phil 170, 170, 171
Vanguard booster 149
Van Voorhis, Lt Cdr Bruce 82
Vejtasa, Lt Stanley 'Swede' 67
Venlet. Lt David 210
Ventura: see Lockheed PV-1 and PV-3
Verdin, Lt Cdr James B. 132
Vigilante: see North American A3J-1 and RA-5C
Viking: see Lockheed S-3A/B and US-3A
Vindicator: see Vought SB2U-1 and SB2U-2
Vought airplanes
  A-7 Corsair II 162, 182, 188, 189, 194-198, 204, 218, 241
  A-7A Corsair II 182, 204, 218
  A-7B Corsair II 198, 218
  A-7E Corsair II 156, 183, 197, 209, 218, 218, 219
  AU-1 Corsair 134, 144, 144
  F4U Corsair 86, 88, 134
  F4U-1 Corsair 30, 36, 46, 76, 86, 94-95, 96
  F4U-4 Corsair 111, 111, 113, 116, 116, 119, 119, 122
  F4U-5 Corsair 111, 112, 122
  F6U-1 Pirate 119, 133
  F7U Cutlass 133, 134
  F7U-1 Cutlass 133, 134
  F7U-2 Cutlass 133, 134
  F7U-3 Cutlass 133, 134, 134, 137
  F-8 Crusader 155, 155, 168, 170, 171, 182, 193, 210, 212, 214
  F-8A Crusader 134, 134
  F-8D Crusader 157
  F-8E Crusader 166-167
  F-8H Crusader 186
  F-8J Crusader 134, 197, 199
  F8U Crusader 134, 135, 140
  F8U-1 Crusader 134, 134, 154
  F8U-1T Crusader 212
  FU-1 26, 27
  O2U-1 Corsair 24, 25, 36
  O2U-2 Corsair 24, 25
  O3U-1 Corsair 25
  OS2U Kingfisher 51, 54, 84, 84, 85
  OS2U-1 Kingfisher 25, 37
  OS2U-2 Kingfisher 25, 36
  RF-8 Crusader 134, 154, 160, 165, 173
  RF-8A Crusader 150, 154, 156, 181
  RF-8G Crusader 190, 212, 212, 213, 219
  SB2U-1 Vindicator 23 23, 36
  SB2U-2 Vindicator 20, 36, 42
  SBU-1 20, 23, 23, 71
  TA-7C Corsair II 218, 219
  TF-8A Crusader 212
  UO-1 24, 26
  VE-7 24, 26
  VE-7H 24
  VE-7SF 17, 18, 26, 26
  XC-142A 127
  XF4U-1 30
  XF5U-1 124
  XF6U-1 Pirate 118, 118
  XF7U-1 133
  XF8U-1 134
  XF8U-1T 212
  XF8U-3 135, 134
Vraicu, Lt Alexander 89, 93

W

WV-2 Warning Star: see Lockheed
Walleye glide bomb 183

Wanamaker, Rodman 13
Warhawk: see Curtiss P-40
Warning Star: see Lockheed WV-2
War Training Service 72
Washington Conference on limitation of armaments 18
Washington Treaty 20, 21, 62
Weakley, Lt (JG) Michael 164
Weichman, Commander Denny 204
Weiss, Air Controller First Class J. 240
Wheatley, Commander J.P. 128
Widgeon: see Grumman J4F
Wildcat: see Grumman F4F, F4F-3 and F4F-4
Wildcat: see Grumman/General Motors FM, FM-1 and FM-2
Wilkins, Capt. James V. 116
Willey, Lt B. 53
Wilson, President T. Woodrow 18
Wrenn, Ensign George 67
Wright B-1 11
Wright biplane 10
Wright brothers 11

X

XA2D Skyshark: see Douglas
XA4D-1: see Douglas
XAJ-1: see North American
XBT-2: see Northrop
XBT2C-1: see Curtiss
XBT2D-1: see Douglas
XBTM-1: see Martin
XC-142A: see Vought
XF3H-1: see McDonnell
XF4D-1: see Douglas
XF4U-1: see Vought
XF5U-1: see Vought
XF6F-1: see Grumman
XF6U-1 Pirate: see Vought
XF7U-1: see Vought
XF8B-1: see Boeing
XF8U-1: see Vought
XF8U-1T: see Vought
XF8U-3: see Vought
XF9F-2 Panther: see Grumman
XF10F-1 Jaguar: see Grumman
XF14C-2: see Curtiss
XF15C-1: see Curtiss
XFD-1: see McDonnell
XFH-1: see McDonnell
XFJ-1 Fury: see North American
XFR-1 Fireball: see Ryan
XFV-1: see Lockheed
XFY-1 'Pogo': see Convair
XH-59A: see Sikorsky
XP3D-1: see Douglas
XP3Y-1: see Consolidated
XP5Y-1: see Convair
XP6M-1: see Martin
XPB2M-1: see Martin
XPB2Y-1: see Consolidated
XPBM-1: see Martin
XPBS-1: see Sikorsky
XPBY-1: see Consolidated
XPBY-5A: see Consolidated
XPY-1: see Consolidated
XR-4: see Sikorsky
XSB2D-1: see Douglas
XSOE-1: see Bellanca
XTB2D-1: see Douglas
XTB2F: see Grumman
XV-15: see Bell

Y

YA3J-1: see North American
YP6M,-1: see Martin
YP-59A Airacomet: see Bell
Yak-9: see Yakovlev
Yakovlev Yak-9 112, 113
Yankee Station 160, 169, 179, 181, 182, 296
Yarnell, Rear Adm. H. 20

Z

Zeppelin, first destroyed by ship-based aircraft 16
Zero: see Mitsubishi A6M

Squadron/Unit Designations

VA(AW) All-Weather Attack
VA Attack
VA(AW) Night Special Mission; All Weather
VAH Heavy Attack
VAHM Mining
VAK Aerial Refueling
VAL Light Attack
VAN Night Attack
VAP Photographic
VAQ Tactical Electronic Warfare
VAW Carrier Airborne Early Warning
VB Bombing (WWII)
VBF Fighter Bomber (WWII)
VC Composite (WWII); Composite Photo (c. Korea); post-1965 Fleet Composite
VCN Night Composite
VCP Composite Photographic
VD Photographic (WWII)
VE Evacuation (WWII)
VF(AW) All-Weather Fighter; Special Mission
VF Fighter
VFN Night Fighter (WWII)
VH Rescue (WWII)
VFP Light Photographic
VGE Escort Fighter (WWII)
VGS Escort Scouting (WWII)
VJ Utility (WWII)
VK Special Task Group
VO Observation (WWII)
VOC Composite Observation (WWII)
VOS Scout Observation
VP Patrol
VPB Patrol Bombing (WWII)
VPM Patrol Mining
VPP Patrol Photographic
VPW Patrol Meteorological, later Patrol Warning
VQ Fleet Air Reconnaissance
VR Transport (WWII); Fleet Tactical Support; Fleet Logistics Support
VRC Fleet Logistics Support Carrier Onboard Delivery
VRF Transport Ferry (WWII); Aircraft Ferry Squadron
VRJ Transport Utility (WWII), also VRU
VRS Transport Service
VS Scouting (WWII); Antisubmarine Warfare
VSF Antisubmarine Fighter
VT Torpedo (WWII); Training
VTN Night Torpedo (WWII)
VU Utility (post-WWII-1965)
VW Early Warning (land-based)
VX Experimental/Development (WWII); Test and Evaluation
VXE Antarctic Development
VXN Oceanographic Development
RVAH Reconnaissance Heavy Attack

Helicopter Squadrons

HAL Light Attack
HC Combat Support
HM Mine Countermeasures
HS Antisubmarine
HSL Antisubmarine Light
HT Training
HU Utility

Blimp Squadrons

ZJ Utility
ZP Blimp Squadron (WWII); later Patrol
ZW Barrier

Miscellaneous

CASU Carrier Aircraft Service Unit (WWII).
CQTU Carrier Qualification Training Unit (WWII)
FASRON Fleet Air Service Squadron
FAW Fleet Air Wing
SOSU Scout Observation Service Unit

Ship Designations (selected)

ACV Auxiliary Aircraft Carrier; original designation for CVEs
AKV Aircraft Ferry Carrier; also Cargo Transport
AVG Aircraft Escort Vessel; second designation for CVEs
AVT Auxiliary Aircraft Transport
BB Battleship
CA Cruiser
CGN Guided Missile Cruiser Nuclear*

CL Light Cruiser
CV Aircraft Carrier
CVA Attack Carrier (originally 'Heavy', CVA-58 only)
CVB Large Carrier (popularly 'battle')
CVE Escort Carrier
CVHA Helicopter Assault Carrier
CVHE Helicopter Escort Carrier
CVL Small Carrier (popularly 'light')
CVN Aircraft Carrier Nuclear*
CVS Antisubmarine Warfare Support Carrier
CVT Training Carrier
CVU Utility Carrier
DD Destroyer
DE Destroyer Escort
FF Frigate
LHA Amphibious Assault Ship (General Purpose)
LPH Amphibious Assault Ship (Helicopter)

* Designations containing 'N' are nuclear powered ships; 'G' have guided missile capability

Glossary

ACM Air Combat Maneuvering
AEW Airborne Early Warning
Alpha Strike A major strike effort designed to deliver firepower with minimum exposure of aircraft to hostile fire
Angels Altitude of an aircraft in thousands of feet (eg 'Angels Three-Five' = 35,000 ft)
ASP Antisubmarine Patrol
ASW Antisubmarine Warfare
Bandit Enemy aircraft
BARCAP Barrier Combat Air Patrol: CAP between battle group and threat
B/N Bombardier/Navigator; NFO in the A-6
Bogie Unidentified aircraft
Bolter Carrier landing where tailhook fails to engage an arresting wire, causing aircraft to go around
Buster Full military power
CAG Carrier Air Group; old term for CVW. Commonly used to refer to the Commander of the Carrier Air Wing
CarQuals Carrier Qualification Landings
Cat Catapult
CATCC Carrier Air Traffic Control Center
CCA Carrier Controlled Approach; instrument approach comparable to a GCA, except it is conducted aboard ship
CIC Combat Information Center
CNATRA Chief of Naval Air Training
CNO Chief of Naval Operations
CO/XO Commanding Officer/Executive Officer
CQ Carrier Qualification (also CarQual)
CUT Mandatory signal from LSO telling pilot to cut his power and land
CVG Designation for Carrier Air Group (1948-63)
CVW Carrier Air Wing (after 20 December 1963)
DME Distance Measuring Equipment; also used interchangeably with distance
EW Electronic Warfare
FCLP/FMLP Field Carrier/Mirror Landing Practice; shorebased practice for carrier landings
FDO Fighter Director Officer
FORCAP Force Combat Air Patrol, CAP over battle groups
FRS Fleet Replacement Squadron. Current term for RAG
Gate Maximum power
GCA Ground Controlled Approach; a type of instrument approach where a radar controller on the ground talks a pilot down to landing
GCI Ground Control Intercept
GTMO or GITMO Guantanamo Bay, Cuba
HAC Helicopter Aircraft Commander
HIFR Helicopter Inflight Refueling; usually accomplished while in a hover over an aviation facility ship
HUK Hunter-Killer, ASW team
ICS Intercockpit Communication System
IFF Identification, Friend or Foe; an electronic device in the aircraft used by air traffic controllers to identify aircraft. Different codes can be assigned to the aircraft
ILS Instrument Landing System
IO Indian Ocean
Ironhand SAM suppression mission
JP-4/5 Types of jet fuel
KIAS Knots Indicated Airspeed

LAMPS Light Airborne Multiple Purpose System: helicopters launched from small deck, destroyer-type ships
Loose Deuce A two-section flight of aircraft separated for mutual support
LSE Landing Signal Enlisted; the enlisted man who assists helicopters in landing aboard carriers and their helo-suitable locations
LSO Landing Signal Officer; the man stationed on the 'platform' at the aft end of a carrier who assists fixed-wing pilots in carrier landings. Also known as paddles
LTA Lighter Than Air
MAD Magnetic Anomaly Detector. Originally Magnetic Airborne Detection
MiGCAP MiG Combat Air Patrol
NAAS Naval Auxiliary Air Station
NAF Naval Air Facility
NARTU Naval Air Reserve Training Unit
NAS Naval Air Station
NATOPS Naval Air Training and Operating Procedures Standardization; a system for ensuring standardization of procedures for many different naval aircraft and activities. Every naval aircraft has a NATOPS manual which explains the aircraft systems and operating procedures
NATS Naval Air Transport Service
NavAirLant/Pac Naval Air Force Atlantic/ Pacific
NavCad Naval Aviation Cadet
NFO Naval Flight Officer; non-pilot officer crewmember
NORDO No Radio; aircraft that is unable to communicate due to radio failure
NOTS Naval Ordnance Test Station
NRAB Naval Reserve Air Base (pre-World War II)
OFT Operational Flight Trainer; flight simulator
OLF Outlying Field
OOD/SDO Officer of the Deck/Squadron Duty Officer; the officer who is responsible for handling the daily routine of the squadron/ship/base
OpNavInst Written instructions coming from the Chief of Naval Operations
ORE Operational Readiness Evaluation; formerly ORI (Inspection)
PAR Precision Approach Radar; type of radar used in GCA approaches. Also used interchangeably with GCA to identify type of approach
PIC Pilot in Command
PLAT Pilot Landing Assistance Television; video tape camera that films all carrier landings and launches for later critique
RAG/CRAW Replacement Air Group/Carrier Replacement Air Wing; the old and new terminology for the units that train aviators in the Fleet aircraft they have been assigned to prior to their assignment to Fleet Squadrons
RAT/EPP Ram Air Turbine/Emergency Power Package; backup power systems that are driven by ram air
RIO Radar Intercept Officer; NFO in the F-4 and F-14
RON Remain Overnight
SAR Search and Rescue
Splash Enemy aircraft destroyed
TACAN Tactical Air Navigation; a piece of electronic equipment used as the primary method of air navigation for tactical jet aircraft
TARCAP Target Combat Air Patrol. Fighter cover over target for strike group
TRAM Target Recognition Attack Multisensor
Trap Arrested landing
UHF Ultra High Frequency; sometimes used interchangeably to refer to the radio in tactical jet aircraft
VA/VF/VP Designations for different type squadrons; V refers to fixed wing; H refers to rotary wing. A is attack; F is fighter; P is patrol; T is training
Vector GCI heading to fighter for bogie interception
VERTREP Vertical Replenishment; underway restocking of a ship via helicopters shuttling from a supply ship
VFR/IFR Visual Flight Rule/Instrument Flight Rules
VMC/IMC Visual/Instrument Meteorological Conditions
VORTAC Very high frequency Omnidirectional Range combined with a TACAN facility; two types of navigational aids
Waveoff Mandatory signal from LSO to pilot not to land. The act of aborting a carrier approach after turning final.